Library of
Davidson College

SUCCESSION TO HIGH OFFICE
IN BOTSWANA

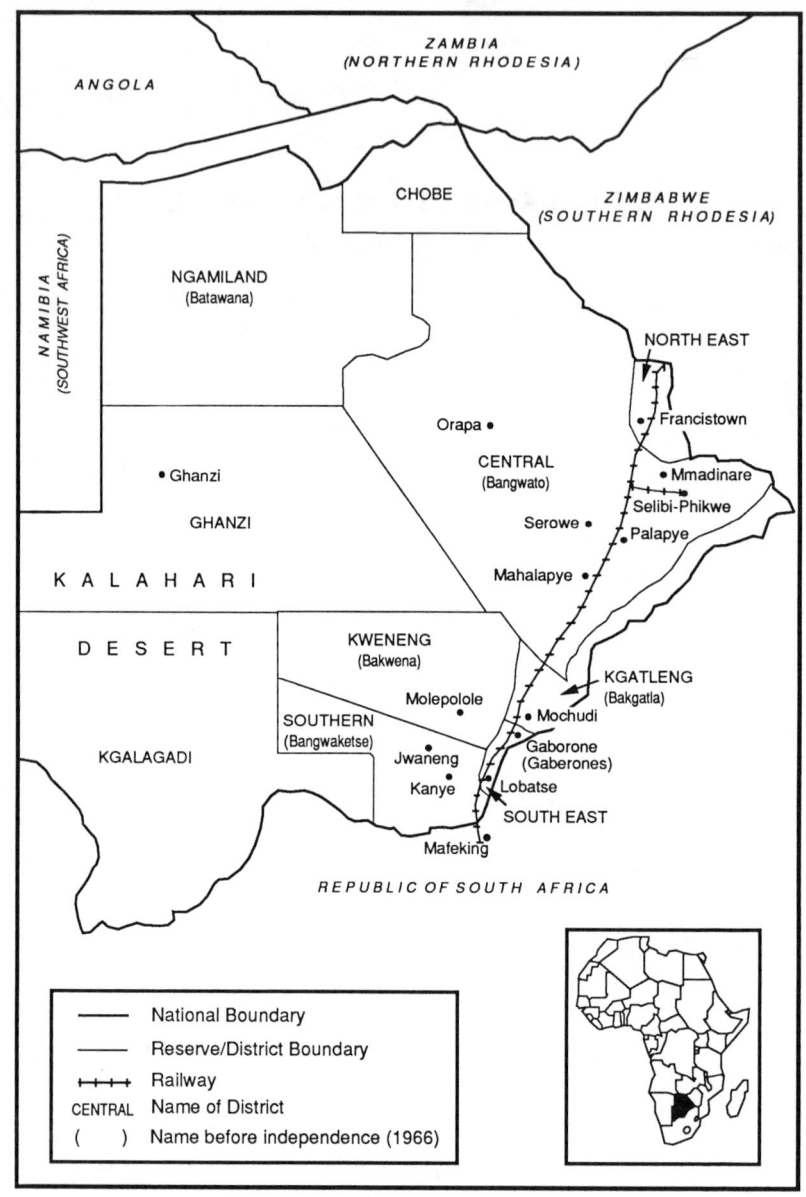

Location Map of the Republic of Botswana (Bechuanaland Protectorate). The boundaries of Batawana, Bangwato, and Bangwaketse reserves varied somewhat from the present district boundaries.

SUCCESSION TO HIGH OFFICE IN BOTSWANA

Three Case Studies

edited by

JACK PARSON

with contributions by

Michael Crowder
Jack Parson
Neil Parsons

Ohio University Center for International Studies
Monographs in International Studies

Africa Series Number 54
Athens, Ohio 1990

© Copyright 1990 by
Jack Parson, Neil Parsons, and
the Estate of Michael Crowder

Printed in the United States of America
All rights reserved

The books in the Center for International Studies Monograph
Series are printed on acid-free paper

**Library of Congress Cataloging-in-Publication
Data**

Succession to high office in Botswana : three case studies /
  edited by Jack Parson ; with contributions by Michael
  Crowder, Jack Parson and Neil Parsons
    p.   cm. – (Monographs in international studies.
  Africa series; no. 54)
    ISBN 0-89680-157-8
    1. Heads of State–Botswana–Succession. 2.
Legitimacy of governments–Botswana 3. Botswana-
–Politics and Government.
    I. Parson, Jack. II. Crowder, Michael, 1934- . III.
Parsons, Neil. IV. Series.
JQ2760.A61S83 1990
321.8'04'096883–dc20   90-30851
                                          CIP

CONTENTS

PREFACE ix

Chapter   page

1. Legitimacy and Faction: Tswana
   Constitutionalism and Political Change 1
   Michael Crowder, Jack Parson, and Neil Parsons

2. The Succession Crisis Over the Illness
   and Death of Kgosi Sekgoma II of the
   Bangwato, 1925 33
   Michael Crowder

3. Seretse Khama and the Bangwato
   Succession Crisis, 1948-1953 73
   Neil Parsons

4. Succession, Legitimacy, and Political
   Change in Botswana, 1956-1987 97
   Jack Parson

Appendices 143

A. Letter from Sekgoma Khama to J.
   Ellenberger, Resident Commissioner,
   requesting the banishment of Phethu
   Mphoeng from Sekgoma's country, received
   on 18 January 1924 145

Appendices

B. Petition to the Resident Commissioner from Phethu Mphoeng and Others complaining about Sekgoma Khama's rule, 21 January 1924 149

C. Minutes of a meeting held at the Kgotla, Serowe, at 8 a.m. on Thursday, 29 October 1925 to discuss whether Chief Sekgoma should be treated by a European doctor or a traditional doctor 153

D. Minutes of a meeting held at the Resident Magistrate's office, Serowe, at 10 a.m. on the 19th December 1925 to discuss the future of the tribal Advisory Council formed after Sekgoma's death but prior to the assumption of power by the Regent, Tshekedi Khama 161

E. List of Members on the Bamangwato Council, 1925. Attachment to the Letter from the Resident Commissioner to the High Commissioner, 21 November 1925 165

F. Letter from the Resident Magistrate, Serowe, informing the Government Secretary, Mafeking, of the Resident Magistrate's view in favor of retaining the Bamangwato Advisory Council, 21 December 1925 167

G. 'Rex Versus S. and O. Ratshosa': Evidence given by the Regent Tshekedi Khama on 22 and 23 June 1926 in the trial of Simon and Obeditse Ratshosa for the attempted murder of Tshekedi Khama 169

Appendices

H. Reports on the proceedings of the three kgotlas held during the period from November 1948 to June 1949 to discuss Seretse Khama's marriage to Ruth Williams 195

I. The British Government Secretary of State for Commonwealth Relations' Memorandum to the Cabinet titled the "Bechuanaland Protectorate: Succession to Chieftainship of the Bamangwato Tribe" on the subject of whether to establish a judicial enquiry, C.P.(49) 155, 19th July 1949 311

J. Report of the Judicial Enquiry Re Seretse Khama, of the Bamangwato Tribe, "The Harragin Report," 1 December 1949, finding that Seretse Khama should not be recognized as Chief of the Bamangwato Tribe 317

K. The British Government Secretary of State for Commonwealth Relations' Memorandum to the Cabinet recommending that Seretse Khama not be recognized as Chief of the Bamangwato, and Cabinet conclusions C.P.(50) 13, 26 January 1950 351

L. Reports of meetings between the external "Observers" and various public gatherings during August 1951 on the question of the return of Tshekedi Khama to the Bamangwato Reserve 365

Appendices

M. Reports of "Observers" on the attitude of the Bamangwato Tribe to the return of Tshekedi Khama to the Bamangwato Reserve (1951) 385

N. Notes on a meeting between the Resident Commissioner and the Chiefs at Lobatsi on the 23rd of June 1962 during which the Chiefs expressed their concerns about the role of chieftaincy in the process of constitutional development 407

O. Notes on a meeting between the Resident Commissioner and the Chiefs at Lobatsi on the 28th August 1962 at which the Resident Commissioner addressed the concerns of the Chiefs about their role in constitutional and political party development 415

P. Notes on a meeting between Her Majesty's High Commissioner and the Chiefs at Lobatsi on the 14th April 1964 to discuss constitutional and political developments related to the role of Chiefs 429

PREFACE

The origin of this volume was a panel presented by the authors during the 1985 African Studies Association annual meeting in New Orleans, Louisiana. Suzanne Miers and Gifford Doxsee of Ohio University (with one other person) constituted the entire audience. They encouraged us to consider publishing the papers in the international monograph series published by the Center for International Studies at Ohio University. We decided to do so together with much of the original documentary base for the case studies. Published as appendices, most of the documents are being made available for the first time outside their respective archives.

The events chronicled in the case studies take place in the major periods of Botswana's twentieth century history—colonial, nationalist, and post-colonial. Each also touches directly or indirectly on the life and times of Seretse Khama, first president of the Republic of Botswana. These periods and the events presented are linked through a concern with the concepts of legitimacy, succession, and political change in modern Botswana.

The case studies derive from each author's larger research work in progress done in Botswana during 1984 and 1985. Michael Crowder was finishing his very productive tenure as Professor of History and Head of the Department of History at the University of Botswana. He was also undertaking a prodigous research project on the life and times of Tshekedi Khama, regent for Seretse Khama of the Bangwato during the latter's minority. In the course of research on Tshekedi's life Michael explored several tangential incidents which were not necessarily central to Tshekedi's story but each of which were illuminating in the context of imperial history in the Bechuanaland Protectorate. One such incident was the so-called "flogging" of Phinehas McIntosh in the Serowe kgotla in 1933. Michael's narrative about the flogging has since been published by the Yale University Press as *The Flogging of Phinehas McIntosh: A Tale of Colonial Folly and Injustice, Bechuanaland 1933* (1988). A second incident encompassed the events upon the illness, death, and succession occasioned by the passing of Sekgoma II, father of the then child and heir to the Bangwato throne, Seretse Khama. It is this incident during the earlier period of colonial rule in Bechuanaland (1925) which forms the material for Michael's case study in this book.

In 1984-1985 Neil Parsons was continuing his research on the history of Botswana. One aspect of that work was a collaborative effort to produce a biography of Seretse Khama. The portion of that biography for which Neil had primary drafting responsibility involved the "middle" period of Seretse Khama's life up to the time when he became president of the republic. A formative personal and political event of this era was Seretse Khama's marriage in 1948 and the ensuing eight year period of political controversy and exile. That episode forms the basis for the case study of the late colonial and early nationalist period in the book.

I returned to Botswana in 1984 and 1985 on a Fulbright research grant to participate in a research project on the 1984 Botswana general elections. My participation in that project followed on research on the political economy of contemporary Botswana I had done during my appointment to the faculty of the University of Botswana from 1973 to 1978. One of my interests was in trying to explain the foundations for the apparently stable multi-party liberal democratic electoral system. The case study of the late colonial and early post-colonial periods is a result of some of that work.

Michael Crowder died, tragically, during the final stages of manuscript preparation in the fall of 1988. His death was a personal loss for me and his other many friends in Africa, Europe, North America, and around the world. It is especially important to me and to Neil that Michael's contribution here, one of his last, should be published and made widely available. He will be missed, not least because of what he might have produced. He will also be remembered for the rich legacy of his writing which is an important and lasting contribution to world scholarship.

I would like to acknowledge the assistance of Lynda Worstall for work done on the manuscript in the final stages and to thank Suzanne Miers for her encouragement and James Cobban for his effort in seeing the project through. We would also like to acknowledge with thanks the assistance of the staff of the Botswana National Archives and in particular extend special thanks to Mr. Gilbert N. Mpolokeng whose knowledge of the archives and assistance in finding documents know few limits. While acknowledging this assistance we also remain mindful that responsibility for the interpretations put forward remains with the authors.

Jack Parson

Chapter 1

LEGITIMACY AND FACTION: TSWANA CONSTITUTIONALISM AND POLITICAL CHANGE

Michael Crowder, Jack Parson, and Neil Parsons

This book is about the process through which the mantle of leadership passes from one leader to another in the life of political generations. It focuses on three connected instances of succession to high office in Botswana over the course of more than half a century: the 1925 factional struggles on the illness and death of Sekgoma, Chief of the Bangwato; the political crisis which followed upon the 1948 marriage of Sekgoma's son Seretse Khama to an English woman; and the succession of Quett Masire to the presidency of the Republic of Botswana upon the death of Seretse Khama, the first president who held office from the day of independence, 30 September 1966, until his death on 13 July 1980.

Our interest in these case studies has to do only incidentally with the purely technical process of leadership selection. It has much more to do with developing an understanding of the legitimacy for the institutions of political leadership in the history of the Botswana polity. Through these case studies we are able to explore the conditions under which political institutions and those who head them are able to claim the allegiance and loyalty of the populations they rule, and as a result of that allegiance the extent to which those populations follow the behavioral patterns dictated by those institutions and leaders. Extending our purview back to 1925 from the present day, we can cover a critical aspect in the political evolution of the political system in Botswana in greater time depth than is possible in most African countries.

The successions in 1925, 1948, and 1980 span the colonial, nationalist, and post-colonial periods. Each of these cases yields insights, if in a limited way, into the ability of local ("tribal"), colonial, and post-colonial governments to rule. This is because every succession is in a sense a fundamental challenge to the legitimacy of a system. The moment of succession is a critical event in the maintenance and change of any political system. It tests the extent to which a population accepts the right of rulers to rule, and therefore the extent to which automatic obedience directly follows. Thus the cases not only span the key periods of twentieth century Botswana history but are hinged around a key feature of the maintenance and change of political systems in general—the smooth succession of individuals in positions of authority.

For the sociologist Max Weber, legitimate authority derived from one of three "ideal" types: traditional, charismatic, or legal-rational. Each type was based on the acceptance of one or another organizing principle: time-honored descent in the case of traditional authority, a magnetizing or mesmerizing personality in the case of charismatic authority, or acceptance of a set of rules in the case of legal-rational authority. The persistence of popular obedience to any person in authority stemmed from adherence to one or another organizing principle. So long as that principle prevailed, so too did the authority of the rulers over the ruled.

Instances of succession in Botswana politics involve most directly the principles of traditional and legal-rational authority, as our case studies will show. These cases examine the extent to which the transition from colonial to post-colonial periods involved the introduction of legal-rational legitimacy in the dominant political institutions, and the extent to which such legal-rational authority has since become dominant and routine. At the same time there are questions about the extent to which the persistence of traditionally legitimate tribal chiefs in the post-colonial period is a reflection of certain forceful individual personalities among them, is merely tolerated by those who maintain authority through the legal-rational mechanism, or is important for the maintenance of legal-rational legitimacy itself.

Traditional legitimacy–based on male primogeniture–was a key principle of succession in precolonial Botswana. It was strengthened rather than weakened as a form of resistance to colonial over-rule. While the British colonial government attempted to assert its paramount legal authority, ultimately based upon its command of armed force, the acceptance of that authority continued to depend upon its cooption of traditional rulers in the system of colonial (indirect) rule. The resulting tension between the two systems provided a particular texture to the colonial period. Recalcitrant chiefs in colonial Botswana could not be removed easily to suit colonial officers of the day. Candidates for chief favored by the colonial administration could not be installed at will. As a result, chiefly non-compliance or a lack of enthusiasm could undermine colonial policy to a degree rare elsewhere in colonial Africa.

When it finally came in the late 1950s and early 1960s, decolonization directly confronted the traditional order. Representative (liberal democratic) national and local governments were the only types seriously considered in the constitutional build-up to independence which took place on 30 September 1966. A national assembly composed of single member districts of roughly equal population size and a universal adult franchise electing those members emerged as the rules for selection to hold national legislative office. Legislative selection of the chief executive was the method for reaching the highest office. Acceptance of these rules became the basis for the assertion of legitimate authority at the national level, and for the elected local councils in the districts paralleling the tribal hierarchy led by the chief. While Botswana's history since independence has not been primarily about the confrontation between competing principles of legitimacy, that confrontation has persisted since independence.[1]

---

[1] In contrast to John Wiseman who argued that it was precisely the conflict between chiefs and the new national government which formed the post-colonial political pattern. See John Wiseman, "The Organization

Through the study of that one aspect there is much to be learned about political legitimacy.

A focus on legitimacy in the context of succession to office puts into some relief other important factors in a historical, political analysis of Botswana. The rules of succession (whether traditional or legal-rational) are the institutional context within which many political events and controversies are played out. The emergence and activities of factions based on personality, social, or class distinctions operate within that context; and these factions reflect the underlying structure of political society, which determines in the end the answer to the whole question of the legitimacy of the constitution of the formal political system itself.

Constitutions, unwritten and written either traditional or legal-rational, contain rules creating institutions, processes, and political roles. Popular acquiescence to the actions of political institutions, participation in their processes, and voluntary obedience to the authority of those who have political roles, define the legitimacy of the constitutional order. Legitimacy, therefore, is constantly being tested and reaffirmed through the course of day-to-day "normal" politics. People constantly monitor the actions of political institutions, their own participation in political processes, and their responses to assertions of state authority. The resulting evaluation creates the degree of popular acceptance of the authority asserted through institutional actions and political processes.

Once established, legitimate authority is not eternal. Legitimacy may be called into question. Calling into question the underlying constitutional order of things requires persuading a population that fundamental change, in detail unknowable, is required, and that the rules need to be rewritten. This is not easy and can rarely be accomplished without reference to more than one particular instance of the wrongful use of authority. It must

---

of Political Conflict in Botswana: 1966-73" (Ph.D. Thesis, University of Manchester, 1976).

be the result of an accumulation of experience over a period of time.

The experience which accumulates is the foundation for acquiescence or rejection. It is the "stuff" of normal politics created primarily in political factional struggles. Political factions are composed of individuals who share a common interest, ideology, or relationship to other individuals. The basis for such factions are social, economic, and political characteristics as well as ideas and relationships. Economic interest is the most enduring building block. Factions also tend to be complex collective entities in which a number of characteristics are closely interrelated. They have in common the desire to realize a recognized and beneficial collective result and the necessity at least to influence if not to control the institutions and power of the state.

Succession as a process and as politics, therefore, takes place within the wider context of political society. While our concern is to carefully follow through with a focus on legitimacy and legitimate succession, the discussion of legitimacy which follows in this introduction and in the case studies must be fixed firmly in that context. We begin with an overview of the evolution of the Khama royal dynasty within the Bangwato polity, the primary stage for the drama of two of our case studies. The discussion is then widened to include succession and legitimacy in the Tswana polities under colonialism. The final section of this introduction describes the process creating an independent national state based on principles of legal-rational authority and succession.

Faction and Succession in the Ngwato State

The two case studies concerned with the Khama dynasty and the Ngwato state highlight the persistence of traditional ideology in 1925 and the emergence of modern political ideology after 1948. To understand the origins of the Khama royal dynasty we have to turn back to the beginnings of the Ngwato state in the late eighteenth century, when it was a small chiefdom of recent immigrants from the south settled in the Shoshong Hills. The chiefdom weathered the storm of early nineteenth century wars, known as the *difaqane*. It expanded its territory and subjected neighboring peoples to its rule. Like other Tswana states, the Ngwato state was constituted in such a way that it could absorb culturally diverse subject peoples. Foreign chiefdoms were incorporated as wards in the capital town or as outlying villages. Their chiefs became headmen paying tribute to the *kgosi* (supreme chief or king). Foreigners without chiefs were incorporated into existing wards as families paying tribute to the ward headman. Some such people, hunters and herders from the semi-arid Kalahari, were attached to royal wards as servants or serfs without civil rights. Other adult male foreigners had the obligation to be members of age-regiments, and the right to attend and even speak at large assemblies. These regiments and assemblies brought people together to discuss matters of national importance and to provide the manpower for hunting, war, and labor in the royal service. The Ngwato state thereby promoted Ngwato nationality among a population which otherwise maintained a diversity of local customs and Tswana dialects or non-Tswana languages.

The Ngwato chiefdom achieved its sovereignty as a kingdom over east-central Botswana in 1850, when it drove the rival Kaa chiefdom from the Shoshong hills. This was under the rule of Sekgoma I (c. 1835-1875). However, Bangwato historians trace the royal lineage back to Mathiba (died c. 1795) as kgosi, and the constitution of royal authority to the short rule of Kgari (1817-1828). Kgari is credited both with being a conqueror, as the "hammer" of the Batswapong subject people who gave him tribute in iron goods, and with being a constitutional reformer in grouping the numerous wards under a few non-royal *batlhanka* (servant or vassal) superior headmen. Like barons with direct allegiance to a feudal king, keeping royal dukes in check and lesser lords and knights under their direct control, these batlhanka headmen became a key group of powerful loyal commoners in maintaining royal sovereignty and succession in the Ngwato state. But Kgari's ambitions of conquest were to prove his undoing. In 1827-1828, Kgari marched north to within the present borders of Zimbabwe to conquer the Rozvi kingdom of the Bakalanga. His army was ambushed and defeated in a mountain pass. Kgari was killed and his people were scattered until Kgari's son Sekgoma I brought the Bangwato together again in the 1840s.

Sekgoma I achieved personal legitimacy through having re-constituted and expanded the Ngwato state. But he suffered from the achilles heel of there being a missing heir to his father in terms of traditional legitimacy–the primogeniture of the eldest son of the senior wife of a kgosi. This missing heir was Macheng who had been born to Kgari's senior widow after Kgari's death. (It had been the *seantlo* duty of Kgari's brother to raise such seed with the widow on his dead brother's behalf: as in the Levirate custom of the Bible, the issue traditionally was accepted as the legitimate child of Kgari and heir to the royal line.) Macheng, younger but senior to Sekgoma, however, had been captured during the difaqane wars by Amandebele people who, unlike Kgari, had successfully conquered the Rozvi kingdom in the area that is now south-west Zimbabwe. Macheng was impressed into the Ndebele army as a common soldier, and might have been forgotten had it not been for the dynastic machinations of another Tswana king, Sechele.

Sechele, king of the Bakwena, lived around present-day Molepolole to the south of the Bangwato. He was the most powerful Tswana monarch of the mid-nineteenth century. An early convert to Christianity, he profited from the Cape-Kalahari ivory trade and defied Boer expansionism by offering refuge and protection to Tswana refugees from the Transvaal. He also tried to extend his political authority over and derive economic benefit from the Bangwato kings, exploiting the traditional precedence of the Kwena dynasty over its Ngwato scion. Over the course of two decades, Sechele skillfully played on the dynastic insecurity and internal factions of the Bangwato.

In 1858 Sechele produced Macheng as if from nowhere, by using British Christian missionary influence on the Amandebele to release him, and had him presented at the Ngwato court. *Dikgosana* (royal headmen) and batlhanka headmen proved receptive to the long lost heir of Kgari. There followed a temporary dual monarchy as Sekgoma ruled jointly with Macheng for some months. Subsequently Sekgoma retired to exile in high dudgeon. However, Macheng proved to be a king in the absolutist stamp of his former Amandebele masters. He employed and sheltered behind Amandebele bodyguards and consumed the cattle of dikgosana and batlhanka headmen as state property vested in the royal person, rather than as *mafisa* ("feudal") cattle held in trust by the royals and headmen. After four years in exile and with the support of Sechele and the Bangwato notables, Sekgoma seized back the monarchy from Macheng. But Sekgoma's second rule only lasted eight years before he in turn was removed in a *coup d'etat* by Macheng in 1866. Sekgoma's eldest son, Khama III, removed Macheng in 1872. Khama III abdicated in his father's favor in 1873, giving Sekgoma a third period of rule. But Khama III once more seized power in 1875 and then ruled until 1923.

Khama III quickly established himself in power. He exiled his discredited father, Sekgoma I, together with the next in line to the throne, his brother Kgamane. But he recruited the allegiance and collaboration of the next two brothers in line, Seretse and Kebailele, and of other key dikgosana. More important he recruited the allegiance of batlhanka headmen by giving them "ownership" of the contentious royal cattle, managing his own herds under household servants as a form of personal property. Khama himself had married the daughter of a *motlhanka* headman, the mother of his heir Sekgoma II, in monogamous Christian marriage and was to that extent the creature of batlhanka interests.

Khama established Christianity as the state religion–though not as strictly prohibitive of "heathen" customs as in 1872-73, which had led to his previous downfall. The state church and school were staffed by British and Batswana missionaries of the London Missionary Society. Albeit a state church, it was run on congregational principles which allowed it to become a political forum, like the kgotla, for the educated elite. This elite was drawn predominantly from the dikgosana "class," although education was also a passage to power and marriage for individuals from "lower" classes.

In addition to the missionaries Khama established a close relationship with British traders by treating them as if they constituted a "ward" of his town, with its own customs and traditions but under the presidency of Khama in its ward kgotla. (The most persistent issue of contention was enforcement of Khama's anti-liquor laws.) The control of trade and firearms permitted the state to expand territorially, both over Kalahari hunting lands and over *bafaladi* (foreigners and immigrants) such as the Bakalanga on the frontiers of the Ndebele state.

The Ngwato state under Khama thereby superceded the Kwena state under Sechele. British colonial rule when it came—symbolically in 1885 and effectively after 1891—built itself upon the legitimacy and stature of the Ngwato state as the biggest, richest, and friendliest polity in central-southern Africa. Through the London Missionary Society, and a deputation to London by Khama and others in 1895 to protest at Rhodesian attempts to take over the Bechuanaland Protectorate, Khama developed sources of political support deep within the metropolitan establishment of the British Empire. Such actions stood his state and the Bechuanaland Protectorate as a whole in good stead in resisting incorporation into either Southern Rhodesia or the Union of South Africa.[2]

The Khama dynasty therefore was established by both expanding and transforming the bases of its political legitimacy. However, even as old threats abated, new factors emerged of political struggle and coalescence of factions around individuals. Sekgoma I died and Kgamane was reconciled to Khama. The "class warfare" of dikgosana and batlhanka moved into interpenetration of interests. But ecclesiastical intrigues burst into the rebellion and breakaway of Khama's brothers Mphoeng and Raditladi. Jealousy of increased commoner power (in the form of Ratshosa, Khama's Secretary) and of the loss of royal prerogative to newly-enfranchised bafaladi headmen, as well as delayed reaction to the loss of cattle wealth to batlhanka headmen, resulted in the breakaway of Khama's own son Sekgoma II. All of these people

---

[2] See Anthony Sillery, *The Bechuanaland Protectorate* (Cape Town: Oxford University Press, 1952); Jackson Mutero Chirenje, *Chief Kgama and His Times* (London: Rex Collings, 1978); Quentin Neil Parsons, "Khama III, the Bamangwato and the British, 1895-1923" (Ph.D. Thesis, University of Edinburgh, 1973).

(Sekgoma, Raditladi, Mphoeng and Kgamane) were to be reconciled with Khama before the end of his rule. Their names, usually as the surnames of their descendants–together with the names of Ratshosa, Kebailele and Seretse–featured in the factional politics surrounding the Ngwato succession crises of 1925 and 1948-1953.

Legitimacy and Succession in the Tswana Polities Under Colonialism

Beyond the Bangwato polity, pre-colonial Tswana polities generally contained within them a strong sense of constitutionalism regarding political succession, policy making, and the implementation of policy. The constitution was undemocratic in the liberal-democratic sense of today. Legitimate succession to high office depended on birth. Large segments of the population were excluded by birth from both any part in succession as well as normal politics. There seems to have been a relatively deep attachment to the maintenance of clear rules of succession. Adherence to these rules structured the ordinary, day-to-day course of politics. One may speculate that the successful transition of power from the first president of Botswana to his legitimate constitutional successor in 1980–a transition in detail quite alien to the traditional pattern–owes something to this attachment to clear rules.

In the pre-colonial Tswana states the rule for succession to the kingship was clear: it was determined by male primogeniture. The kgosi was succeeded by the eldest son of the senior wife, or if he had no son by his immediate younger brother. This reflected the pattern of succession to more junior offices such as that of headman, and the pattern of inheritance within each family.[3]

Most of the Tswana kings converted to monogamous Christianity before the end of the nineteenth century. Before such conversion male primogeniture was complicated by polygyny. The

---

[3]I. Schapera, *A Handbook of Tswana Law and Custom* (London: Frank Cass & Co., 1970), pp. 53-57. First published in 1938.

successor was the first born son of the wife recognized by the *morafe* (pl. *merafe*, the nation, usually rendered as the "tribe" by the colonial administration) as the *mohumagadi* or queen. She might in fact be the second or third woman married by the kgosi but in genealogical terms her "house" was the first house of her husband because of the prestige of her own paternal genealogy. Succession crises could arise as a result of disputes as to which wife had been properly recognized as the mohumagadi. Some rulers tried to advance the claims of a son by a more favored "junior" wife. Once rulers adopted Christianity as the state religion—as did Khama III in 1875—this major source of dispute was eliminated because these rulers became monogamous. Thus in 1925 and later in 1932 the claims to the Ngwato throne made by Gasetshware, son of Sekgoma II by Mary, the sister of his second wife, Serero, were rejected on the grounds that he was illegitimate in Christian as well as in traditional terms. Mary had not married Sekgoma either in a Christian or in a traditional ceremony. Gasetshware's claim was rejected even in traditional terms on the grounds that though a barren wife could bring in a sister to bear children on her husband's behalf, as a seantlo, Mary had not been recognized in this capacity and therefore was no more than a concubine whose sons could never succeed.[4]

After the adoption of Christianity there was as little doubt as to the reigning monarch's successor as there was with the European monarchies that practised male primogeniture: *Kgosi ke kgosi ka a tsetswe:* (A chief is chief because he is born to it).[5] Even in pre-Christian times, when the polygny practiced by the Tswana rulers could lead to claims and counter-claims as to the legitimate successor, the power struggle took place within the royal family. There were no instances of a commoner attempting to

---

[4]Theophilus Mooko, "The Role of Royal Women in Bangwato Politics Under the Regency of Tshekedi Khama, 1926-1949" (University of Botswana, History Department Dissertation in partial fulfillment of the requirements for the B.A. Degree, 1985), p. 12.

[5]Schapera, *A Handbook of Tswana Law and Custom*, p. 53.

usurp the chieftainship,⁶ or of the son of a chief's sister or daughter claiming the throne.⁷

Though the Tswana speaking peoples do not form an overwhelming majority in the modern Republic of Botswana, the majority of its population lived in one or other of the eight merafe that were enclosed within its border by 1900.⁸ Thus most of the people of non-Tswana origin shared in the political culture of their rulers as well as spoke their language. In Gamangwato, for instance, Bangwato proper formed only some 10 percent of the inhabitants of the morafe, yet in 1948 an overwhelming majority of the total population gave their support to Seretse Khama, the legitimate heir to the *bogosi* (kingship), against his uncle, Tshekedi Khama, who had acted as Seretse's regent for the previous twenty-two years. This sense of legitimacy, then, was not exclusive to the core Tswana ruling groups of the morafe but also to the bafaladi, the immigrants, subjugated peoples, and refugees who in some instances constituted a substantial majority of the state. Against this interpretation is the assertion of the anthropologist John Comaroff based on his case study of the Barolong-boo-Tshidi that achievement rather than ascription was the determining factor in access to high office in the Tswana states and that legitimacy was negotiable.⁹ The Barolong-boo-Tshidi and their kgosi lived around

---

⁶Caroline Fraser Seeley, "The Reaction of the Batswana to the Practice of Western Medicine" (M.Phil. Thesis, University of London, 1973), p. 33 and Thomas Tlou, "*Melao Yaga* Khama: Transformation in the Nineteenth Century Ngwato State" (M.A. Thesis, University of Wisconsin-Madison, 1968), p. 3.

⁷Schapera, *A Handbook of Tswana Law and Custom*, p. 54.

⁸Bangwato, Bakgatla, Bakwena, Bangwaketse, Batawana, Balete, Batlokwa, and Barolong (the Barolong chief resided in Mafeking where most of his people were to be found).

⁹John L. Comaroff, "Rules and Rulers: Political Processes in a Tswana Chiefdom," in *Man, Journal of the Royal Anthropological Institute* 13/1 (1978): 1-20.

Mafeking in a Tswana state that was incorporated into the Union of South Africa, though some Barolong were enclosed within the Bechuanaland Protectorate.

From his study of the Tshidi, Comaroff concludes that 80 percent of all cases of succession to the chieftainship represent anomalies from the stated norm of male primogeniture and that in "such circumstances, the jural determinist assumption simply cannot be entertained: stated prescriptions do *not*, in general, decide who is to succeed."[10] Comaroff, however, is arguing from a special case: the succession disputes until 1919 that began with the death of the non-Christian Kgosi Montshiwa in 1896. Thus, Comaroff outlines the rules of succession only as they obtained in a pre-Christian polity. This is irrelevant to most of the Tswana states in the late nineteenth and early twentieth centuries since the majority of their rulers had by then become Christian, notably four of the five principal merafe of the Bechuanaland Protectorate. One of the main sources of potential dispute—who was the mohumagadi or principal wife—ceased to be of relevance once the Tswana rulers had become monogamous. So too did another source of potential dispute, the provision whereby if a chief died without an heir a close surviving agnate could cohabit with his widow in order to bear sons on his behalf. When Tebogo, third wife and in 1925 widow of Sekgoma II, became pregnant eighteen months after her husband's death, Tshekedi went to great pains as a devout Christian to deny that he was the father and had thereby taken advantage of this traditional custom. Nor again did the provision whereby a barren wife could bring in a substitute or seantlo to bear children on her behalf continue to operate as the case of Gasetshware demonstrates. Both these provisions had been used to back claims in the 1896-1919 succession disputes among the Barolong-boo-Tshidi.

Comaroff accepts that the model for succession was primogeniture whereby the males of the royal family are ranked in order of their genealogical proximity to the incumbent ruler. He

---

[10]Comaroff, "Rules and Rulers," p. 2.

goes on to assert, however, that in fact legitimacy is negotiable and the "degree to which his performance is considered to be satisfactory is thought to determine the extent of the office-holder's legitimacy, expressed in the willingness of the public to execute his decisions."[11] Comaroff accepts that power is not allocated by popular consent alone and chiefs do not watch impassively as their regimes are evaluated. Nevertheless he suggests that his model of negotiation "represents a medium through which debate over the chiefly performance and legitimacy may proceed."[12] In the 1930s, if not in the 1960s when Comaroff did his fieldwork, the Barolong-boo-Tshidi, seemed much more sure of the principle by which they acceded to office. Under cross examination in 1936, Richard Lekoko, who was acting for Lotlamoreng Montshioa, chief of the Barolong-boo-Tshidi, was asked how he came to act for the chief when he was absent from his capital, Mafeking. He answered without hesitation: "By birth."

> Question: Are you next in right of birth to the Chief, after his own sons, who are minors?
> Answer: Yes, that is so.
> Question: With regard to the people who preside over these junior kgotlas, are they appointed over these junior kgotlas?
> Answer: They hold their positions by right of birth.[13]

---

[11]Comaroff, "Rules and Rulers," p. 7.

[12]Comaroff, "Rules and Rulers," p. 7.

[13]"Tshekedi and Bathoen v. High Commissioner, 1936." We believe the transcript of the case is contained in the District Commissioner, Lobatse, papers in the Botswana National Archives and we are grateful to Jeff Ramsay for that information. Michael Crowder elsewhere cites the case from BNA S447/7, S422/4, and S422/5 as well as *High Commission Territories Law Reports: Decisions of the High Courts and Special Courts of Basutoland, the Bechuanaland Protectorate, and Swaziland, 1926-1953*, edited by Sir Harold William, CMG (Maseru, 1955). See "Tshekedi Khama and Another v. the High Commissioner,"

What seems clear from Comaroff's analysis of the Barolong-boo-Tshidi case is that because his arguments are based on the disputes over the succession to the super-polygamous and long-reigning Montshiwa (ruled 1849-1896), focusing on whether his barren mohumagadi had taken a seantlo and whether she was indeed mohumagadi, and whether his deceased son's "house" had been entered to raise seed on his behalf, there was as a consequence plenty of room for argument as to who was the rightful heir. Powerful factions consequently were able to form around putative candidates for office. From these disputes as to who were the rightful heirs to Montshiwa and his successors up to the accession in 1919 of Lotlamoreng (1919-1954), Comaroff argues that succession depended as much on the strength of one's factional support and perceived abilities as on a pre-emptive right by virtue of genealogical proximity. What Comaroff seems to fail to underline is that even if the rules were manipulated by rival factions their success depended on asserting that their particular candidate had pre-emptive genealogical precedence and that claims to office were restricted to the immediate royal family. Thus even in the case of the Barolong-boo-Tshidi, ascription, putative or otherwise, took precedence over achievement as the criterion for access to office.

The danger of generalizing from the case of the Barolong-boo-Tshidi about Tswana attitudes to succession and legitimacy without considering other Tswana states becomes clear when one looks at problems related to succession that arose, for instance in the Kwena and Kgatla states in the Bechuanaland Protectorate, as well as the two case studies from the Ngwato state in this book. From a study of these it becomes clear that adherence to the stated norms of succession were strictly adhered to and widely accepted. The only way to overcome them was for the next in line of succession or his supporters to drive the incumbent into exile or kill him–techniques familiar elsewhere in the world where primogeniture was the basis for succession. Assassination was

---

p. 31.

indeed used, unsuccessfully, during the colonial period in the Ngwaketse state when in 1916 Moyapitso assassinated his elder brother, Seepapitso III. Instead of succeeding Seepapitso, however, Moyapitso was hanged by the British for his pains. Tshekedi Khama of the Ngwato state was quite clear that the mechanisms for dealing with unpopular rulers in pre-colonial Botswana were little different from what obtained in other states which practiced similar rules of succession to high office. When cross examined in 1936 on the matter he was asked "If there was no provision under statute law for deposing chiefs how would you under native custom depose them?" Tshekedi answered: "In our days it meant civil war if there was a dispute, if the tribe was not satisfied with the Chief it would mean civil war, or it could be an assassination."[14]

A further point that has to be borne in mind when considering rules of succession in the Tswana states of Botswana is that for the most part the states were of recent dynastic origin, with the Ngwato and Tawana dynasties only becoming effectively independent toward the end of the eighteenth century. Significantly the eponymous founder of the Ngwato state was a junior brother of the ruler of the Kwena state. Similarly the eponymous founder of the Tawana state was a brother of the rightful heir to the Ngwato leopard skin. One way of circumventing the "iron law" of primogeniture was for a junior brother to establish his own kingdom, with his followers voting for him with their feet. Furthermore the Tswana states of Botswana only became recognizable as such in the second half of the nineteenth century, after they had weathered the difaqane wars and were able to take advantage of the economic opportunities presented by the penetration of Cape traders on their way to the north, the

---

[14]"Tshekedi and Bathoen v. High Commissioner, 1936." In the contemporary era there was an alleged plot to assassinate Kgosi Monare Gaborone of Batlokwa in February 1988, an allegation leaked to the press by the royal uncles because they feared for the chief's life. It was reportedly the second such plot and involved a split in the village over the chieftaincy. *Botswana Daily News*, 10 February 1988, p. 1.

development of which coincided with the conversion of the rulers to Christianity.

As far as demonstrating popular concern for legitimacy among the Tswana, the deposition of Sebele II of the Bakwena by the British in 1931 is most instructive. In 1918 Sebele had succeeded his father, Sechele II, as ruler of the senior Tswana morafe in the Bechuanaland Protectorate. The British were sufficiently disturbed by his ways—he was known to his people as *kgomo ya tlhaba* or "wild ox"—that he was never confirmed in office by them.[15] His behavior evoked opposition from some of his royal uncles and councillors and exasperated the British. In 1928 some of his uncles drew up a petition asking for his removal and this petition was to provide the interventionist resident commissioner of the Bechuanaland Protectorate, Charles Rey, with the opportunity he sought to make an example of one of the Tswana chiefs who collectively he thought a thoroughly bad lot. They "practically do as they like—punish, fine, tax and generally play hell."[16] Sebele he considered the worst of them, and added that everyone—missionary and trader included—was "in agreement as to the deplorable condition of things and the necessity for drastic action in regard to the Chieftainship."[17] Rey based the case for Sebele II's deposition not on incompetence and lack of cooperation alone but also on the assumption that his people wanted his

---

[15]Except where otherwise indicated by references, the following account of Sebele's deposition and the imposition of Kgari Sechele by the British is based on Titus Mnyamana-ka-Mbuya, "Legitimacy and Succession in Tswana States: The Case of Bakwena, 1930-63" (University of Botswana, History Department dissertation in partial fulfillment of the requirements for the B.A. Degree, 1984).

[16]Sir Charles Rey, *Monarch of All I Survey, Bechuanaland Diaries 1929-37*, edited by Neil Parsons and Michael Crowder (London: James Currey, 1988), entry for Sunday 20 October to Sunday 17 November, 1929, p. 4.

[17]Botswana National Archives (BNA), S176/6, Resident Commissioner's Report, November 1930.

removal. As it turned out, to avoid popular demonstrations and possible violence in response to their action, the British had to depose him clandestinely. Instead of deposing him before his people after an enquiry, they summoned him on a pretext to Mafeking, the protectorate headquarters which anomalously were situated within the Union of South Africa, and sent him into exile to Ghanzi in the western Kalahari.

Publicly the British continued the pretence that he had been deposed by popular demand, and reiterated this forcefully to other chiefs at a meeting with the high commissioner in Cape Town. Of the many contentious issues raised by Tshekedi and his fellow chiefs was the fact that the administration had deposed a ruler without even so much as an enquiry and imposed a successor without consulting the people.[18] The successor, Kgari Sechele, had in no way been accepted by the people, and was only third in line of succession to his brother Sebele. It seems the administration did not even consider the device of appointing Kgari as regent or acting chief which might have been acceptable to the people but insisted instead on installing him with the leopard skin of office. In private they had to admit that Kgari Sechele was little but an administrative chief who was not recognized by his people. Indeed Kgari, a young man at school in South Africa, was entirely the choice of the administration and the few royal uncles who had connived at Sebele II's removal. The majority of the people continued to recognize Sebele II as their rightful ruler. Thus in 1935 the administration wrote in their annual report for the Kweneng that "the fact that Chief Kgari is not a chief in his own right, but was placed in the Chair through Government influence, is undoubtedly one of the main reasons why he has so readily accepted" the new native administration proclamations which other chiefs had so bitterly opposed. "He is not popular with his Tribe. . . . It is surprising that although it is an accepted fact that the deposed Chief Sebele was a waster and totally unsuitable, he

---

[18]BNA, DCS 16/19, Interview between the High Commissioner and Tshekedi Khama, Bathoen II etc., Cape Town 23-24 February, 1934.

still enjoys the support of the Tribe."[19] It was not really until the death of Sebele II in 1939 that Kgari Sechele began to gain some legitimacy in the eyes of his people. Even though Sebele had fathered a son in exile there was doubt about the child's claims to the chieftaincy. Kgari Sechele had gained some authority in the tribe, strengthened after he led their contingent to the Middle East during the Second World War. But the continued opposition to him by the Bakwena while Sebele II was alive was based not so much on resentment of his ways but because they did not regard him as their "rightful Chief."

It might be argued that the continued support for Sebele II resulted not from the people's concern with legitimacy but from a perception that he was an opponent of the colonial regime. He was much more popular with his people than the colonial authorities thought. Furthermore the reaction of the Bakwena was very similar to that of the Bakgatla whose Chief Molefi was deposed for a variety of administrative sins including harsh treatment of his own people. Nevertheless the Bakgatla did not accept his replacement, Mmusi. As Rey's successor as resident commissioner, Charles Arden-Clarke, informed the high commissioner in May 1939: "As in the case of the Bakwena and their banished Chief [Sebele II], so in the minds and hearts of the great majority of the Bakgatla, Molefi is still regarded as Chief and will be so regarded until his death."[20] This was confirmed a year later by the district commissioner at Gaborone.[21] Similarly in 1933 when Tshekedi, the regent of the Bangwato, was suspended by the British, they could find no other royal to take over. Even though the royal family was riven with faction, there was agreement that

---

[19]BNA, S144/14 Annual Reports for 1935: Kweneng.

[20]BNA, S 335/5 Resident Commissioner to High Commissioner May 1, 1939.

[21]BNA, District Commissioner, Gaberones, 1940. We are unable to trace a full reference.

Tshekedi had been the rightful one to take over as regent being next in line of succession to Seretse.[22]

The British in West Africa rarely had difficulty in finding a candidate in elective or competitive monarchies to replace the monarch they had deposed. The new monarch would have a body of support from the section of the ruling lineage or house he represented: thereby the British had merely hastened its turn for access to the fruits of office. It was only when the British flagrantly violated the rules and imposed a successor without title to office that trouble ensued. Thus in Bussa in Northern Nigeria their deposition of the Emir, Kitoro Gani, in 1915 and his replacement by an administrator of slave origin provoked revolt. They were eventually forced to restore him in 1925 in order to be able to administer the emirate. After his second deposition in 1935 he was replaced by a brother, who in the event of his death would have had the right to succeed; this change was accepted by the people.[23]

One could cite further examples. Thomas Tlou for instance has examined a number of cases in the Tawana state where there have been disputes over, and administrative interference in, the succession. He concludes that even though there were attempts at violating the basic law of succession by primogeniture for the same reasons outlined above, the fundamental tenet of the people was *kgosi ke kgosi ka a tsetswe*: they could not accept a "made chief."[24]

---

[22]See Michael Crowder, *The Flogging of Phinehas McIntosh: A Tale of Colonial Folly and Injustice, Bechuanaland 1933* (New Haven and London: Yale University Press, 1988).

[23]Michael Crowder, *Revolt in Bussa: A Study of British "Native Administration" in Nigerian Borgu, 1902-1935* (London: Faber & Faber, 1973).

[24]Thomas Tlou, "The Nature of Batswana States: Towards a Theory of Batswana Traditional Government—The Batawana Case," in *Botswana Notes and Records* 6 (1974): 66-67.

The concept of legitimacy in the Tswana states, then, was very strong and focussed on the law of primogeniture. The people as well as the royal family knew who the successor to the reigning monarch would be as soon as he was born, and had in mind a clear set of rules determining access to the leopard skin. In the period 1885 to 1966 these rules were broken not by the people themselves but by the British rulers, who were subsequently forced to admit that the chiefs they placed on the throne contrary to the rule of primogeniture–however close in line of succession that might be–were unrecognized by the people even when they were manifestly more competent and less abusive of the interests of their subjects than the legitimate rulers they replaced. What is clear is that in no case in the period after Comaroff begins his study did a chief in the Bechuanaland Protectorate accede to power who was not the one who would rightfully have done so by the rule of primogeniture, except where he was imposed by the British. Such chiefs were not recognized as legitimate rulers by the people but as agents of the British. The British, in fact, were trying to do just what Comaroff argues the Tswana, or at least the Barolong-boo-Tshidi, did, that is to manipulate succession rules to ensure that a "competent" member of the royal house succeeded to the throne. In British eyes the Bakwena perversely refused to give their support to a ruler whom they considered more competent than the one deposed by the colonial administration. The Barolong-boo-Tshidi case seems to be eccentric to, rather than typical of, the Tswana states over the past hundred years. The law of succession was not negotiable: it could only be broken by force, by assassination or civil war ending in exile for the incumbent, or by the intervention of the colonial state. We can conclude therefore, that in Tswana states in Botswana, whether traditional or modern, there was a strong sense of legitimacy and an acceptance of given rules for succession to high office. The principle of succession and legitimacy was changed quite fundamentally, however, in the nationalist period beginning in 1948 and ending in 1966. The changed principles at the national level underlay important aspects of political practice in the post-colonial period.

Michael Crowder, Jack Parson, Neil Parsons

Legitimacy and Succession in the Post-Colonial Polity

The creation of a sovereign Botswana nation in 1966 was premised on a legal-rational set of constitutional rules. The constitution of the Republic of Botswana defined political institutions, processes, and powers. The acceptance of the constitution, drafted by British Colonial Office officials in consultation with political party and chiefs' representatives, resulted in the exercise of constitutional authority by the new national government. In the constitution the rules for succession to the highest office, that of president of the Republic of Botswana were fixed; but the rules contradicted the succession rules of the precolonial and colonial Tswana states outlined above. Generally, the president was elected by a majority of the elected members of the Botswana national assembly. In practice the leader of the majority party became president. These principles and rules more or less defined the day-to-day functioning of national government institutions after 1966.

The constitution was premised on the principle of representative parliamentary government. Authority to make and enforce laws, policies, and budgets was placed in the hands of the national assembly, a body composed of individuals elected from single member districts of roughly equal populations. In 1984 there were thirty-four such constituencies an increase from thirty-one at the time of the first election in 1965. To become a candidate for election to the assembly, an individual had to be a citizen of Botswana, at least twenty-one years of age, a registered voter, and, until 1989 when Setswana became a language of debate, sufficiently fluent in English "to take an active part in the proceedings of the Assembly."[25]

---

[25]The legal documents relevant to the institutions of national and local government and elections are the *Constitution of Botswana*; the *Electoral Act*, CAP 02:07, Laws of Botswana; the *Local Government (District Councils) Act*, CAP 40:01, Laws of Botswana; and the *Local Councils (Conduct of Elections) Regulations*. All are printed by the Government Printer, Gaborone.

Local government institutions were created under the authority of the national assembly. (In 1989 there were nine district councils, four town councils, and one city council.) As nearly as possible the district council boundaries coincided with the boundaries of the preexisting tribal territories. The councils existed under statutory law and were composed of elected, ex-officio, and nominated members. For electoral purposes the members of the councils were chosen from polling districts, constituencies of roughly equal population size taking into account geographical features and accessibility. Candidacy required age and citizenship qualifications similar to those for the national assembly.

The highest office, that of the president of the republic, was governed by a set of legal-rational rules.[26] An election for president took place whenever the office was vacant or when parliament was dissolved. Normally parliament was subject to a maximum life of five years. When an election was called each candidate for an assembly seat at the time of nomination declared his/her support for a candidate for president.[27] Candidates for president had to show evidence of support by at least one thousand registered voters and declare their willingness to be supported by parliamentary candidates. If after the general election a presidential candidate was supported by a majority of members elected to the national assembly, then that person was declared elected and assumed office on that day. The president subsequently appointed a vice president, from among members of the national assembly, who acted in the absence of the president or assumed the higher office upon the death or resignation of the president.

---

[26]See in particular Section 32 of the *Constitution of Botswana*.

[27]The qualifications for becoming a candidate for and holding the office of president are straightforward: the candidate must be a citizen born in Botswana or be a citizen who is a child of a father born in Botswana, have attained the age of thirty years, and be qualified to be an elected member of the National Assembly.

Succession to the presidency was covered in Section 35 of the constitution. If the office became vacant, then the national assembly had to meet by the seventh day after such vacancy. Candidates for president had to be nominated by ten or more members of the national assembly prior to the assembly's sitting. The speaker of the national assembly then conducted a secret ballot of members entitled to vote.[28] If a candidate was supported by more than one half of the electorate then that person was declared elected and took office on the same day. If no candidate received a majority, then a further two ballots were taken at additional sittings of the assembly. Fourth and fifth ballots, again at separate sittings, could be taken if "in the opinion of the Speaker the holding of further ballots [was] likely to result in the election of a President."[29] If in the end no candidate received a majority of the votes, then parliament automatically stood dissolved and a new general election had to be held.

The ability of a president to exercise the considerable powers of his/her office depended upon his/her having achieved office according to these rules. Whether elected as a result of a general election or succeeding through the provisions covering a vacancy in the office, presidential authority was legitimated by observance of these constitutional provisions. Public officers, members of the assembly, and the general public had a legal obligation to obey directives from the president if his/her election conformed to constitutional rules. If this obedience also coincided with an acceptance of the constitutional rules themselves, then a system of legal-rational authority was expressed.

This system of legitimate authority directly contradicted the traditional system observed in the precolonial and, for the most part, colonial periods. The principles upon which each system was founded were mutually exclusive. The conflict of laws between

---

[28]Which excludes the Speaker and the Attorney General but includes presumably the four specially elected members making a total electorate of 36.

[29]*Constitution of Botswana*, Section 35 (5)(f).

national and "tribal" principles was in a sense a carry-over of the conflict between colonial and "tribal" laws. But the new national state had a degree of constitutional legitimacy, derived from internal sources, which was inherently greater than that of the colonial regime. The latter was essentially an arbitrary imposition from external sources of legitimacy never internalized inside the territory.

The introduction of the republican constitution at independence raised the question of acceptance of the new authority system by both the population at-large and office holders—traditional and elected. The competing bases for popular loyalties raised questions about the ability of the national government to command the automatic obedience and support of the population. In the short run this issue was clouded because Seretse Khama was not only the first president but simultaneously was a traditionally legitimate chief. The succession question, kept open until 1980, was whether a "commoner" constitutionally succeeding to the office of president could command the obedience of the population or would he de facto have to rely on the chiefs or coercion for the command of that obedience?

Once constitutional change in the direction of an independent Botswana nation became the policy of the colonial government, events moved rapidly. There was never any serious doubt that the new national government would be one based on elective office-holders organized through political parties. It was also clear that the authority of the new national government would be superior to tribal authority. The only questions concerned the place of traditional chiefs in the new dispensation and the length of time they would survive.

There were several reasons why the debate on constitutional issues took this form rather than one of directly incorporating traditional authorities into the new order. Unlike Swaziland or Basutoland, the other two High Commission Territories, colonial Bechuanaland did not have an even nominal paramount ruler in its territory. Indeed a large portion of Bechuanaland was state land where there was no semblance of indigenous traditional authority. None of the chiefs could therefore claim authority over another, and through that claim an even informal, let alone traditional, legitimate paramount position.

Furthermore, none of the Batswana tribes in their tribal territories were so disproportionately important that significant concessions to them had to be made. Unlike Uganda, where creating a Uganda nation required significant concessions to the *kabaka* (king) of Buganda, none of the traditional authorities in Bechuanaland held the key to a successful transition to national independence. One might also contrast the weakness of traditional claims to national authority in Bechuanaland with the strength of those claims by the Asante in the Gold Coast (Ghana) or the position of traditional rulers in Northern Nigeria.

While the creation of a non-traditional national government in Bechuanaland was very likely, its particular form and implementation were still problematic and subject to dispute.[30] Colonial authorities and sections of the "new men" beginning to engage in political party activity recognized that from their perspective the chiefs still wielded considerable influence and were still the legitimate authority for large numbers, perhaps a majority, of the population. The active opposition of chiefs to the new dispensation needed to be avoided. If possible, their acquiescence or more desirably their active support was sought.

Certain of the chiefs, including Chief Bathoen II, were skeptical about the constitutional changes, recognizing that inevitably their own influence and ability to control the people would be eroded. Their reaction was almost by definition a defensive one. Constitutional changes toward the introduction of self-government and national political party politics, initiated in 1959 and begun seriously in late 1960, had by 1962 become part of a process leading to independence. The chiefs were by then cast in the role of dragging their feet. At a meeting between the

---

[30]A useful description of this era, particularly the discussion of the role of chiefs and the place of local in comparison to national government is contained in Louis Picard, *The Politics of Development in Botswana: A Model for Success?* (Boulder: Lynne Rienner Publishers, 1987), particularly pp. 46-69 and pp. 177-201.

resident commissioner (the most senior British colonial officer in the territory reporting directly to the high commissioner) and the chiefs in June, 1962, for example, Chief Mokgosi complained that "In his opinion the parties wanted to spoil the chieftainship and he did not think that they had been formed for the welfare of the country."[31] He basically felt that the political parties had emerged because of a breakdown of the chieftaincy in the Ngwato reserve. Chief Mokgosi's solution "to the problem might be to reconstitute the government of the country on a federal basis with regional governments for the Northern Protectorate and Southern Protectorate; such an arrangement would facilitate more rapid changes in the North where this was desired but permit the Southern Tribes to proceed at a more leisurely pace in accordance with the wishes of their people."[32] Chief Bathoen II supported fully the suggestion of the establishment of regional governments for the North and South.[33] Chief Bathoen II had long felt that political parties emerging in the north (that is in the Bangwato state) were the result of Seretse Khama's marriage and the dispute over it. During the kgotla discussions of 1948 and 1949 Bathoen II told Seretse that "you have destroyed your chieftainship" and now in 1962 could only lead through parties, thus destroying the chieftaincy for others.[34]

Colonial authorities, on the other hand, made it clear that national government authority would be based on the elective principle; that this was to be a unitary, not federal, state; and that chiefs would have to come to terms with political parties and

---

[31] BNA, H.145/GP, Notes on a meeting between the Resident Commissioner and the Chiefs at Lobatse on 23 June 1962, p. 1 (see Appendix N).

[32] BNA, No.H.145/GP, p. 2.

[33] BNA, No.H.145/GP, p. 5.

[34] See kgotla speech by Chief Bathoen II in Appendix H, BNA, DCS 37/2.

politicians. In August of 1962 the resident commissioner, in a further meeting with the chiefs, counselled the chiefs that

> we must be realistic. We have started on the road of constitutional development and the Chiefs associated themselves with the decision to do so. Now we cannot stop and, as you know, the formation of parties always follows quickly after the first steps in constitutional development and indeed, it is only through parties that the later steps become possible. This is because parties are concerned with national, as opposed to tribal policies, and if the people of this country are to play an increasing part in the government of the country they must organise themselves on a national basis.[35]

The resident commissioner went on to say that "the only advice I can give you is that you must come to terms with them [the parties] and of course they must come to terms with you."[36] He argued that in the future "the Chiefs' right to rule will not depend on any divine rights. It will depend on the extent to which each one of them plays a part with their Councils and Executive Committees in fostering sound development and in resolving the conflicts between the conservative forces and the radical ones."[37] He concluded that he did not believe that "any of [them could] frustrate the forces of nationalism . . . [but] . . . should move with them."[38] Ensuing constitutional discussions and the final laying to rest of the issue of incorporating Bechuanaland into South Africa led Her Majesty's Commissioner for Bechuanaland, Basutoland,

---

[35]BNA, H.145/GP, Resident Commissioner's remarks to a meeting of the Chiefs, 28 August 1962, p. 4 (see Appendix O).

[36]BNA, H.145/GP, p.4.

[37]BNA, H.145/GP, p. 7.

[38]BNA, H.145/GP, p. 7.

and Swaziland in April 1964 to tell the chiefs that "it was now clear that the only acceptable future for Bechuanaland lay in the development of the Territory towards independence and economic viability."[39] He told the chiefs that a federal structure for the national state was impracticable and that a "unitary state was therefore essential."[40] That being the case the commissioner pointed out that "it followed from this that the Chiefs and Tribal Administrations would in future be recognised more as local government authorities than in the past."[41]

On the other hand, the official discussions about the details of the new constitution included the chiefs and an attempt to meet certain of their concerns. In the context of the inevitability of a new national government the chiefs and tribal authorities were left to decide how to handle the activities of political parties within their respective territories and jurisdictions. Chiefs retained the authority to authorize specific meeting places and times. The chiefs were initially given an important role in the new elected district councils as chairmen. In addition, the chiefs were to constitute the House of Chiefs. The House of Chiefs was a purely consultative chamber without any substantial authority to block or alter proposed legislation. Its purview included legislation about the status and powers of the chiefs and tribal administrations.[42] Thus at independence there persisted two sets of institutions reflecting two possible and potentially competitive bases for legitimate authority. One of these, the national government, was pre-eminent, but the traditional institutions could not be ignored.

---

[39]BNA, I/6/2986, H. 145 V, Notes on a meeting between Her Majesty's Commissioner and the Chiefs at Lobatse on 14 April 1964, p. 1. (see Appendix P).

[40]BNA, I/6/2986, H. 145 V, p. 2.

[41]BNA, I/6/2986, H. 145 V, p. 2.

[42]Additional detail on the House of Chiefs is available in J. H. Proctor, "The House of Chiefs and the Political Development of Botswana" *Journal of Modern African Studies* 6/1 (1968): 59-80.

The main details of the resulting tensions and relationships are presented in the case study of the post-colonial period. Broadly, the two systems of legitimacy co-existed although the national system appeared to have consolidated its formal superiority. The legal power of the traditional authorities declined in important respects. The establishment of district councils, and their role in the same geographical areas as tribal authorities, diminished the authority of chiefs in policy and service areas such as education. It was also increasingly unlikely that anyone would seriously suggest abolishing legal-rational selection of the national government's chief executive in favor of replacing that person with a senior traditional authority. However, the national government was no more successful than its colonial predecessor in authoritatively dealing with chiefs who used their traditional authority to protect and further, in their chiefly view, the welfare of their tribal citizens and clients. Kgosi Bathoen II Gaseitsiwe, while he was chief of the Bangwaketse, and Kgosi Linchwe II Kgafela of the Bakgatla are cases in point.

At the same time, the development of popular acceptance of the authority of the national government arguably grew. The holding of regular elections with substantial voter turnout, by American if not European standards, indicates just that. Most important, acceptance of legal-rational succession to the highest office, that of president of the republic, appears to have gained considerable ground. The constitutional succession to that office by Q.K.J. Masire in 1980, upon the death of Seretse Khama, and Masire's subsequent election in his own right following the 1984 general elections is evidence in support of that conclusion. This is all the more important given the fact that Masire, unlike Khama, has no claim to high office under any of the rules governing succession in traditional society.[43]

---

[43]Masire's traditional status is as brother of the head of a minor "alien" (Hurutshe or Kgalagadi-Hurutshe) ward among the Bangwaketse. This has put him at a theoretical disadvantage to the seniority of the Ngwaketse Kgosi, and also to the Hurutshe Kgosi in South Africa who happens also to be President of the "independent" South African

At both mass and elite levels, then, there appears to be in Botswana an acceptance of legal-rational authority at least in terms of national governance and in its local units; but the issue of competing systems of legitimacy remains on the agenda of the political process at the local level and is likely to remain there for some time to come. Even at the national level there have been lingering questions about the depth of Masire's support because of his lack of high ascriptive position. In the Mochudi kgotla, for example, soon after his accession to power, he was publicly referred to as Seretse Khama's motlhanka (traditional vassal). Conversely, speculation about the political ambitions of Ian Khama, Seretse's eldest son who was also chief of the Bangwato and major general and deputy commander of the Botswana Defence Force, has persisted precisely because of his traditional status.

"homeland" of Bophutatswana (Lucas Mangope). However the latter is in turn junior in precedence to a Hurutshe Kgosi in Botswana, who is a mere village headman within the Ngwaketse state.

Chapter 2

THE SUCCESSION CRISIS OVER THE ILLNESS AND DEATH OF KGOSI SEKGOMA II OF THE BANGWATO, 1925

Michael Crowder

Kgosi Sekgoma II of the Bangwato died on 14 November 1925. The crisis over his succession was not about who should succeed him: his elder legitimate son, Seretse, aged four. Nor was it about who should act as regent for the young chief during his minority. By the rules of primogeniture followed by the Tswana states the usual choice of regent was the next adult male in line of succession. This would be Tshekedi, Sekgoma's twenty year old half-brother, or, should he decide not to take up the regency and continue his studies at the South African Native College at Fort Hare, Gorewan Kgamane, Tshekedi's first cousin and next to him in line of succession. Rather, the crisis was about which of the two major factions in the royal family would have access to the fruits of office at the disposal of the incoming regent. This factional rivalry between the supporters of Phethu Mphoeng, cousin of Sekgoma II and Tshekedi, on the one hand, and the Ratshosas, who had married into the royal family over two generations, on the other, had roots in the late nineteenth century. It had intensified almost immediately after Sekgoma II's accession in 1923 and was not resolved in Phethu's favor until nearly six months after Sekgoma's death.

The dispute between Phethu and the Ratshosas was distinguished by the way in which the two factions lined up behind the two different health care delivery systems then available for the treatment of their ailing ruler: Western medicine and traditional medicine. The British administration of the Bechuanaland Protectorate, which had exercised overall authority in the Ngwato state since the acceptance of its rule in 1885 by Sekgoma's father, Khama III, did not directly support one faction or the other. It was, however, an interested party in that it was anxious to keep Sekgoma alive since Tshekedi would be a young and inexperienced regent, while his alternative in that post generally was acknowledged to be a weak and incompetent man. The natural prejudices of the British administration were strongly in favor of Sekgoma's treatment by Western medicine. Thus its representatives together with the resident missionary in Serowe indirectly backed the Ratshosa faction which favored the treatment of their kgosi by Western doctors. Conversely, Phethu and his supporters wanted him to be treated by traditional doctors. What makes this instance of factional rivalry so fascinating is that it did not represent a division between traditionalists and modernizers backing the appropriate health care system, but rather between two important segments of the royal family that had taken advantage equally of the cultural, political, and economic opportunities presented by the colonial situation.

Sekgoma and the Ratshosas

As the elder surviving son of Khama III, Sekgoma was his rightful successor. Until 1916 there was a possibility that he might not succeed because, after a series of bitter disputes with his father over matters both public and personal, he had been driven into exile at the turn of the century. As Neil Parsons put it, the root of the problem was the effort of "a son, well into his maturity, to assert his independence of thought and action from a masterful father."[1]

---

[1] Quentin Neil Parsons, "Khama III, The Bamangwato and the British With Special Reference to 1895-1923" (Ph.D. Thesis, Edinburgh University, 1973), p. 211.

The Illness and Death of Sekgoma II, 1925

Among the many matters of conflict between the two willful men was the rise to power of Ratshosa Motswetle. Himself of distant royal descent, Ratshosa married Sekgoma's imperious full sister, Bessie, who took advantage of her brother's estrangement from their father to seek the succession for herself and her children. For a while Khama entertained such a possibility and threatened Sekgoma with it, although there was no precedent either for the succession of a woman to the office of kgosi or of succession through the female line.[2] Nevertheless Ratshosa accumulated great power and wealth, succeeding Sekgoma as Khama's secretary. It was only in 1902 with the death of Bessie that Ratshosa and his three sons ceased to be a major dynastic threat; their position was further undermined in 1905 when Semane, Khama's fourth wife in a series of monogamous marriages that had ended as a result of death or divorce, gave birth to a son, Tshekedi. In 1907 Khama publicly disowned Sekgoma in favor of Tshekedi whom he also made legal heir to his fortune but not to the chieftaincy. Although Ratshosa remained in office as Khama's secretary, he began to offer support to Sekgoma's house, to which he belonged by marriage, against Tshekedi's house. By 1910 he had fallen out of favor with Khama who replaced him as secretary but he further cemented relations with Sekgoma's house that year when his second son, Simon, married Oratile, Sekgoma's eldest daughter.[3]

In 1916 the elderly Khama was kicked by a horse and had to undergo several operations. Sekgoma took the opportunity to effect a reconciliation with his father and took up residence in his *lolwapa* (household). It seemed clear that Sekgoma would now take his rightful place as heir to Khama, though the latter did not officially present him to the British administration as such until

---

[2]Parsons, "Khama III," p. 217. Khama's words were: "And to you Sekgoma I swear that you will never get the chieftaincy. . . . I must warn you I can deny you the chieftaincy and pass it on to the Ratshosas if I like."

[3]Parsons, "Khama III," p. 376.

1920 when Khama took him to see the resident commissioner of the Bechuanaland Protectorate, Sir John Macgregor, who immediately telegraphed the good news to his high commissioner, Prince Arthur of Connaught, who was also Governor-General of South Africa.[4] Macgregor, apparently aware of the attachment of the Tswana to the rule of primogeniture as far as succession was concerned, said that he had never doubted that Sekgoma would succeed.[5] For the British the reconciliation must have come as a relief since Tshekedi was still a schoolboy and Gorewan, the next in line of succession, was known to be a weak man. Ratshosa died shortly after the reconciliation but at the time was himself still out of favor with Khama. However, in 1919, Khama appointed Ratshosa's son, Johnnie, as his secretary while Simon, who was headmaster of the Serowe Public School, also helped him with state affairs. In 1921, Sekgoma's wife, Tebogo, daughter of Khama's most trusted brother, bore him his first legitimate son, Seretse, and two years later a second son. The succession now seemed doubly secure and the position of the Ratshosas entrenched with both the current Bangwato ruler and his heir. Tshekedi, once heir-apparent, had now become third in line of succession.

The rise to, and arrogant use of, power by the Ratshosas inevitably evoked the resentment of less favored branches of a royal family which, since Khama's father had been polygamous, was

---

[4]The British High Commissioner in South Africa was responsible for the administration of the so-called High Commission Territories—the Bechuanaland Protectorate, Basutoland, and Swaziland. Until 1931, the offices of governor-general and high commissioner were combined.

[5]Botswana National Archives, (BNA), S. 25/8, "Khama and Sekgoma: Resumption of Friendly Relations Between," Macgregor to High Commissioner, 18 August 1920: "I was never in any doubt about the succession, as that, in the last resort, is always decided by the people the bulk of whom would surely support the heir."

very extensive.⁶ Among those most resentful of the Ratshosas was Phethu Mphoeng, Khama's nephew. Although Phethu's father, Mphoeng, who was Khama's half-brother, had gone into exile in 1895 over a dispute about Khama's position as head of the church in Gamangwato, Phethu was reconciled with his uncle in 1903. In 1912 his father also was reconciled with Khama. Phethu cemented his relations with Khama by marrying his daughter, Milly. Khama then made him *mmoemela-kgosi* or governor over the important district of Mmadinare in 1904. The Ratshosas resented Phethu as a rival while he in turn, as Parsons puts it, "stood in dread of losing the assurance of patronage on Khama's death."⁷ This prospect was made the more fearsome in that Phethu was seen as a supporter of Khama's church, the London Missionary Society (LMS), which in a biography of their patron had not only injudiciously attacked the influence of the Ratshosas but described Sekgoma as "weak and easy-going."⁸

Sekgoma's Accession and the Downfall of Phethu

On Monday 19 February 1923 Khama III died and was succeeded without dispute by Sekgoma. Born in 1869, Sekgoma was fifty-four years old when he came to the Bangwato throne, apparently in reasonable health and son of a man who had lived well into his nineties. There was no reason at the time for either the British administration or the royal family to expect that there would be a further change in regime for some years to come. Indeed there was every reason to hope that Sekgoma would

---

⁶BNA, DCS 8/6, "Rex versus S. and O. Ratshosa," Trial before Capt. Robert O'Malley Reilly, 22 June 1926. Many of the witnesses alluded to the high-handed ways of the Ratshosas in the heyday of their power. Appendix G contains excerpts from the evidence given at the trial.

⁷Parsons,"Khama III," p. 425.

⁸John Charles Harris, *Khama, The Great African Chief* (London: Livingstone Press, 1922), p. 102.

continue the stable administration that had characterized the last fifteen years of Khama's reign. Not long after taking office, however, encouraged by the Ratshosas, Sekgoma fuelled a bitter dynastic feud by accusing his cousin, Phethu, of plotting to kill him. Phethu's close supporters were named as his younger brother, Oteng, and his cousins Lebang and Keletlokhile Raditladi, whose own father had gone into exile at the same time as Mphoeng in the dispute with Khama over the headship of the Church in Gamangwato. Like the Ratshosas, the Mphoengs and the Raditladis had prospered as a result of the penetration of the capitalist economy into the Bechuanaland Protectorate and owned extensive herds of cattle and a good deal of other private property. They had also taken advantage of the opportunities offered by the Western education they had been given.[9] Oteng, for instance, was a teacher in the local school at Mmadinare, and ran a prosperous creamery.[10]

Phethu Mphoeng was accused of threatening to kill Sekgoma either by assassination or through witchcraft and of trying to set himself up as an independent ruler.[11] Among his principal accusers were the Ratshosa brothers whom Phethu in turn accused of usurping his tax collecting functions and interfering with his administration of Mmadinare. In the enquiry that eventually led to the exile of the Mphoengs and their cousins, the Raditladis, the bitterness of both these families at the power of the Ratshosas surfaced time and time again. While the official who conducted

---

[9]Phethu and Oteng Mphoeng and Disang Raditladi had all been to Lovedale. G.T. Koagile, "The Biography of Phethu Mphoeng" (University of Botswana History Department dissertation in partial fulfillment of the requirements for the B.A. Degree), 1986.

[10]BNA, S. 3/6, "Phethu Mphoeng: Disturbances, 1923," O.D. Schreiner to H.J. Stanley, High Commissioner's Office, Cape Town, 7 February, 1926.

[11]See the transcript of the enquiry held by the Assistant Resident Commissioner from 20 December 1923 to 2 January 1924 in BNA, S. 3/6, "Phethu Mphoeng: Disturbances, 1923."

the enquiry felt that there was no evidence to support the accusation that Phethu and his alleged associates had indeed contemplated assassinating their chief, it was clear that Sekgoma himself was convinced that his life was in danger from Phethu, who, the administration believed, had much wider support and a more powerful following than was immediately evident from the enquiry at which few spoke on his behalf.[12] In every one's mind was the recent assassination in 1916 of the Bangwaketse ruler, Seepapitso, by his own brother: one way of ridding a Tswana state of an unpopular kgosi was assassination which would open up the succession to the next in line. But as far as the Bangwato ruler was concerned Phethu was not genealogically close. As Sekgoma himself stated: "There are none who can claim the chieftainship from me, they are of collateral branches and have no claim."[13] Much more to the point was Sekgoma's later remark that there cannot be two bulls in one *kraal* (cattle-holding pen), for it does seem that Phethu in Mmadinare was very much a law unto himself.[14] Concluding his indictment of his cousin, Sekgoma expressed surprise at Phethu as a Christian using witchcraft: "His wife is a Christian. I am surprised at my Sister. Where did she get the poisons? My Father, Khama, did not teach us these things."[15]

In an attempt to avoid exile, Phethu and his associates petitioned the British administration, and among other things accused the Ratshosas of monopolizing education in Serowe.[16]

---

[12]BNA, S. 3/6, Resident Commissioner to High Commissioner, 10 January 1924.

[13]BNA, S. 3/6, Evidence of Chief Sekgoma, 21 December 1923.

[14]BNA, S. 3/6, Evidence of 1 January 1924.

[15]BNA, S. 3/6, Statement of Sekgoma II in kgotla, 17 December 1923.

[16]BNA, S. 3/6, Petition to Resident Commissioner, 21 January 1924, reproduced as Appendix B.

Even the resident magistrate at Serowe felt that the Ratshosas were trying to get control of money matters and had been gaining power ever since the death of Khama and that this was resented by many headmen. In particular, Keletlokhile Raditladi, later to be ordained as a minister in the London Missionary Society, felt as a result of losing a case he had brought before Sekgoma against Simon Ratshosa, that "whenever they wanted to do anything they were baulked if it affected the Ratshosas–suggesting Chief Sekgoma always favoured the Ratshosas."[17] Phethu himself denied ever trying to dispute the chieftainship and time and again acknowledged that Sekgoma was his chief: "The talk of banishing us from the Country is not the Chief's words they are Simon Ratshosa's words."[18] Phethu also declared: "As for witchcraft I do not believe in it."[19] Nevertheless the Mphoeng and Raditladi brothers were banished reluctantly from the Bamangwato Reserve by the British high commissioner, who since the establishment of British rule alone could authorize such a punishment.

The Reconciliation Between Sekgoma and Mphoeng

Phethu and his companions in exile accepted their fate. Apart from a lame attempt to get O.D. Schreiner, the Cape Town lawyer and champion of African causes, to take up their case with the high commissioner soon after their banishment order was served, the administration seems to have had no trouble from them. But back in Serowe the political situation had developed in such a way as to favor Phethu's later attempts to seek his ruler's forgiveness. Sekgoma himself was beginning to chafe under the

---

[17]BNA, S. 3/6, Acting Resident Commissioner to High Commissioner, 26 November 1926.

[18]BNA, S. 3/6, Evidence of 31 December 1923. See also Appendix A, a letter from Sekgoma to the resident commissioner requesting Phethu's banishment.

[19]BNA, S. 3/6, Evidence of 1 January 1924.

excessive influence of the Ratshosas, in particular the two elder brothers Johnnie, his secretary, and Simon, his son-in-law, who was married to his only daughter, Oratile. Though Sekgoma had been sent by his father to Lovedale for education, he was not much interested in the paper-work side of administration and had left all this to Johnnie Ratshosa, who kept all the chief's papers and dealt with all his correspondence. It seems Simon also had access to his father-in-law's papers. The growing rift between Sekgoma and the Ratshosas only came into the open when Phethu sought, in Sekgoma's words, "to come and give in."[20]

Phethu met Simon Ratshosa in Francistown, just outside the Bamangwato Reserve, where he told him of his desire to make his peace with the chief. Simon asked Phethu why he did not go to Serowe anyway, for there was nobody to stop him since "there is no Chief in Serowe."[21] On learning this Sekgoma informed the resident magistrate that he could not use Johnnie Ratshosa to interpret for him when he came to see the magistrate about Phethu's request to return to Serowe "because John, Simon and Obeditse are one thing." He therefore wanted to take a "fresh man" with him to Mafeking when he went to the protectorate headquarters to see the resident commissioner about the matter. He also said he was quite restless about the fact that against his wish all his correspondence was kept at Ratshosa's house. Sekgoma had learnt of Simon's treachery only a few days before he wrote this letter when he was at Palapye Road to meet the Prince of Wales. Phethu had approached him and formally asked forgiveness, which Sekgoma did not refuse but insisted that it had to be sought properly in Serowe in the presence of all the

---

[20]BNA, S. 3/7, "Simon Ratshosa: Question of Phethu and Others Returning to the Bamangwato Reserve," Sekgoma to Resident Magistrate, Serowe, 30 June 1925.

[21]BNA, S. 3/7, "Simon Ratshosa."

people.²² Of course Phethu's statement about his encounter with Simon may have been mere calumny against a member of the family whom he saw as responsible for his exile in the first place. If that is what it was, it certainly fell on fertile ground, for in a statement made on 4 July to the resident commissioner Sekgoma declared "I do forgive Phethu" and that the troubles arose through people at whose instance Phethu and his companions were banished.

> I do not wish the Administration to intervene at this stage. I only wish His Honour to know how things were and when trouble does begin it will be through the Ratchosas [sic]. When Phethu comes to apologise I will tell His Honour and tell him also the terms on which I have forgiven Phethu, which will be that he must not drink or brew beer and must come when I send for him. Simon Rathchosa is in the habit of reviling me to the people wherever he goes and wherever he writes to them from, but so far no trouble has arisen because I have taken no notice of his actions.²³

Sekgoma also complained that it had been reported that certain "native leaders," among them Simon Ratshosa, were to see the governor-general about the matter of incorporation into the Union and that he had not been "detailed by me to deal with such matters nor has he any right to do so."²⁴

Sekgoma concluded his remarkable attack on his son-in-law by asking the resident commissioner to take care lest messages purporting to come from him be in fact from Simon Ratshosa. In

---

²²BNA, S. 3/7, Statement of Sekgoma of 4 July 1925 recorded by Resident Magistrate.

²³BNA, S. 3/7, Statement of Sekgoma.

²⁴BNA, S. 3/7, Statement of Sekgoma.

The Illness and Death of Sekgoma II, 1925

future all letters to him should be delivered personally by the resident magistrate at Serowe and not through Johnnie Ratshosa or anyone else. Even so, he did not at this stage propose to call on Johnnie to return his private and official correspondence until he had built a new office. Phethu duly made submission to Sekgoma and the administration lifted the banishment order on the Mphoengs and Raditladis on the 24 July 1925 so that they were able once again to take part in the political life of the tribe.[25] The timing from their point of view could not have been better for the Bangwato state was about to be thrown into a three-month long crisis as a result of Sekgoma's increasingly serious ill-health.

The Illness of Sekgoma II

At about 1.00 p.m. on 30 July while he was looking at some horses at Parr's store in Serowe, Sekgoma II "suddenly got a peculiar staring look in his eyes" and walked away towards the B.T.A. Store "staggering like a drunken man."[26] Nevertheless he acknowledged the greeting of a passer-by. He then tripped over a log and collided with a pole. A white trader, Smith, helped him to his car where he had two seizures. The medical officer at Serowe, Dr. Drew, had been called and reached him shortly after the second seizure. He then became comatose and appeared to be unable to use his left arm and leg for about an hour. Then at 4.00 p.m. he was assisted to his house where he slept. At 8.30 p.m. just as Drew was coming into his room the chief had an epileptic fit. The following morning he seemed quite recovered except for a bad headache and informed Drew that he had had similar attacks at intervals of about a year though not every year. One of Sekgoma's attendants told the doctor that he had seen the

---

[25]BNA, 3/7, High Commissioner to Resident Magistrate, 24 July 1925, telegram: "Request that you will express to Chief Sekgoma my satisfaction at learning that these natives have been forgiven."

[26]BNA, S. 11/4, Minute by Dr. D. Drew, Medical Officer, Serowe, to Principal Medical Officer, Mafeking, 31 July 1925.

chief in two such attacks, one on the way up to Nata and one when he was out shooting near N'Kali.

Drew sent in a very detailed report to the principal medical officer at protectorate headquarters in Mafeking in "view of the importance of this ailment from an administrative point of view."[27] The principal medical officer, who had previously been an asylum officer, instructed Drew to keep Sekgoma under medical observation and suggested trying out a new drug—luminol—rather than the conventional bromide, which in old people sometimes caused a great deal of mental confusion. He also suggested that the chief be checked for kidney disease and cerebral syphilis—understandably since syphilis was a prevalent complaint in the protectorate at that time.[28]

Meanwhile the chief seemed to have recovered and went about his business, including a trip to one of his cattle posts some thirty miles from Serowe. There on Sunday 23 August he had three fits, at 2.00 a.m., 5.00 a.m., and 9.00 a.m. A message was sent to the administration, and Major Hannay, the acting resident magistrate, asked Dr. Drew to go and fetch him. Drew found Sekgoma in fairly good condition but complaining of difficulty in passing urine. The chief was brought to Serowe on Tuesday morning. In the evening the medical officer at Francistown arrived and the two doctors gave the chief a thorough examination. They both agreed that the epilepsy was not of the Jacksonian or partial variety but was grand mal. The two doctors were clearly up-to-

---

[27]BNA, S. 11/4, Minute by Dr. Drew.

[28]BNA, 3/7, Series of minutes exchanged between the Principal Medical Officer and Dr. Drew. The sister in charge of the Serowe Maternity Centre reported in the 1930s that congenital syphilis was so rampant that she seldom saw a healthy placenta at childbirth. See Andrew Chiponde Selemani Mushingeh, "A History of Disease and Medicine in Botswana" (Ph.D. Thesis, Cambridge University, 1984), p. 230. The account that follows is based on Drew's reports and the evidence of John Ratshosa at the trial of his brothers, BNA, DCS/6, p. 263.

date in their reading because in view of a recent article in *The Lancet* on modern techniques in treating epilepsy they ruled against using luminol and stuck to the more conventional bromide treatment. They sent his blood for a Wasserman test for syphilis, and concurred with the recommendation of some headmen—unfortunately unnamed—that he be sent down to the coast for a holiday, where he would be relieved of all administrative worries. These had become particularly burdensome during the Prince of Wales' visit. Since it also appeared that he had a urethral stricture, he could have an operation there. The principal medical officer concurred with these recommendations, in particular with regard to the operation for the stricture which apparently Sekgoma had had for many years and which if "unduly delayed the result may at any time prove disastrous," especially if the chief were out of reach of assistance, as of course he had been when he had had the fits at his cattle post.[29]

Sekgoma was finally persuaded to go to Cape Town for a rest. Gorewan Kgamane, Sekgoma's cousin, and fourth in line of succession, was appointed acting chief. Dr. Drew volunteered to accompany him as Sekgoma's own attendants "get into an absolute panic when there is anything wrong with the Chief."[30] Meanwhile as preparations for Sekgoma's departure were being made, his condition was causing increasing anxiety among his people. He became very excited whenever discussing tribal politics and was suffering from frequent amnesia, no doubt brought on in large part by the bromide treatment. Arrangements were made for him to stay at the Monastery Nursing Home at Seapoint but there was some consternation as to whether he would be accepted by the Reverend Mother since it was suspected that the cause of his stricture might be venereal in origin.

In the meantime Dr. Targett-Adams, the medical officer at Francistown, sent in a five page handwritten report outlining all

---

[29] BNA, DCS/6, Principal Medical Officer to Drew, 29 August 1925.

[30] BNA, DCS/6, Drew to Principal Medical Officer, 1 September 1925.

the possible causes of Sekgoma's condition over and above epilepsy.[31] Targett-Adams clearly saw himself as something of a psychologist of the African, for apart from attributing Sekgoma's condition to the worry and anxiety associated with the duties of chief, fears of witchcraft were thought to be a contributing stimulus to his epileptic fits. Furthermore, he suggested, there were in Serowe at least three factions pulling in contrary directions. The first comprised those "(like Sekgoma himself) who believe in (the folly) of bewitchment—a very real belief indeed in Natives." The second comprised Khama's widow, Semane, who was Sekgoma's immediate nurse and attendant who together with some of his relatives were very reasonable and immediately agreed to the treatment suggested by Targett-Adams and Drew. A third party favored getting a native doctor or doctors to see him. This course, Targett-Adams suggested, must be avoided at all costs since in his experience "it adds to the unfortunate patient's and friends' troubles" because traditional doctors were not only concerned with the physical treatment of a malady but also with "smelling out" the one who had bewitched the patient. "Sekgoma is now in mortal terror of these superstitions." It was therefore essential to get him to Cape Town as soon as possible. Targett-Adams' ultimate prognosis was gloomy in the extreme: "Bad, he will probably last some time, but gradually become and perhaps slowly a physical and mental wreck." In forwarding his comments on traditional doctors to the principal medical officer, Targett-Adams suggested that these were beliefs "from which we have not parted so very many years ago; & in Scotland even later than in England." There was little Western medical treatment could do at this time to control epileptic seizures.

---

[31]BNA, DCS/6, Targett-Adams to Principal Medical Officer, 30 August 1925.

Sekgoma in Cape Town

Sekgoma finally left by train for Cape Town on 9 September accompanied by Dr. Drew and Headman Mathiba, the Chief Hut Tax Collector. Before leaving, Drew wrote to the principal medical officer that he was not optimistic about Sekgoma's being able to take an active part in tribal matters in the future. The headmen and people took the attitude that their chief was in his hands, that what he considered best must be done. He felt that if he failed them he would lose their confidence. He regarded the loyalty of these "natives" to their chief in his illness as quite "pathetic and charming."[32]

Sekgoma proved a very difficult patient in Cape Town where he was admitted to the Victoria Hospital at Wynberg rather than the monastery. The doctors agreed that apart from the epilepsy, his major ailment was his urethral stricture on which it was advisable to operate as soon as he was fit enough. A negative Wasserman test confirmed Dr. Drew's earlier opinion that Sekgoma's condition was nothing to do with syphilis, which Robertson incorrectly said was the diagnosis of the British doctors.[33] However, even if they persuaded him to undergo the operation, would Sekgoma cooperate in the long after-treatment? He hated being in hospital, was homesick, and could not understand why so many different doctors were attending him. It

---

[32]BNA, DCS/6, Drew to Principal Medical Officer, 8 September 1925.

[33]BNA, DCS/6, Report of Dr. W.P. Mulligan of 18 September 1925: "Wasserman reaction: completely negative." Harold H. Robertson in "From Bechuanaland Protectorate to Republic of Botswana" (Ph.D. Thesis, Dalhousie University, 1979), states (using the same file) that the Principal Medical Officer diagnosed Sekgoma as having cerebral syphilis whereas in fact he merely suggested that it might be a possibility. See Robertson, pp. 40-41. Subsequent investigation indicates that Sekgoma II was suffering from diabetes, a hereditary tendency in the Khama family not yet understood by Western medicine in 1925.

seemed to him that "all the doctors in the country were gathered around him to bleed him of what money they can."[34] The administration tried their best to reassure him through a carefully worded letter from the resident commissioner and by visits from Sir Herbert Sloley, chief secretary at the high commission, who helped him with his financial affairs.

By the end of September, Drew was beginning to think that Sekgoma ought to return to Serowe. Sekgoma had accepted the idea of the operation but could not be made to understand the post-operative pain that would be involved and the extent of the after-care required. There was also the problem that the chief might succumb under anaesthetic and Sir Herbert Sloley considered that from a political point of view it would be most undesirable for the chief to die in Cape Town. Further, since his cooperation in after-care could not be guaranteed he might in the event receive no benefit from the operation. The best thing, Drew felt, would be for the chief to return to Serowe and let the illness take its course which, given his epilepsy and his stricture, effectively meant that he would die within six months.[35] The principal medical officer felt that his subordinate was being unduly pessimistic and that provided the chief agreed, he should be operated upon. The resident commissioner therefore instructed that the operation should go ahead, political and other consequences notwithstanding. However, soon after the resident commissioner had cabled these instructions to Drew, the specialist in Cape Town suggested that in view of Sekgoma's general disposition it would be best to dilate the stricture as much as possible in Cape Town and then send him back to Serowe for the full operation which would be performed there by Dr. Drew, provided the headmen accompanying Sekgoma agreed.

---

[34]BNA, S. 11/4, Drew to Principal Medical Officer, 21 September 1925.

[35]BNA, S. 11.4, Drew to Principal Medical Officer, 30 September 1925.

The Illness and Death of Sekgoma II, 1925

Matters were in fact settled not by the headmen, but by Sekgoma's daughter, Oratile, who had arrived in Cape Town with her husband Simon. She expressed the wish that the operation take place in Serowe and the two headmen agreed with her.[36] Slyly, the resident commissioner instructed Drew to make it clear to Oratile and the headmen that "they must accept responsibility for any unfavorable consequences of refusing the operation in Cape Town."[37] On 15 October Dr. Drew set off for Serowe by train accompanied by two male nurses supplied by the Union Defence Force. There was some concern in Serowe as to how they were to be accommodated since Drew had not made it clear whether they were European or Colored.[38] The former being the case, they were accommodated in the local hotel.

The Factions Gird Themselves

Just before leaving for Cape Town it seems that Oratile's husband, Simon, had sent a report to *The Johannesburg Star* about the deterioration in the situation at Serowe as a result of the absence of Sekgoma. Published on 8 October, it suggested that people in Serowe were taking advantage of the chief's illness: "Khama's country, the only portion of South Africa that knew complete prohibition, has reverted to the debauchery of beer-drinking." The report further talked of shameful and humiliating conditions which had arisen since Sekgoma's unfortunate illness.[39] The source of the accusation that Simon was the author of the despatch was Major Hannay and from confidential information he

---

[36]BNA, S. 11/4, Telegram from Government Secretary to Drew, 12 October 1925.

[37]BNA, S.11/4, Telegram.

[38]BNA, S. 11/4, Telegram from Government Secretary to Drew, Telegram 15 October 1925.

[39]*The Johannesburg Star,* 8 October 1925: "Beer Drinking in Khama's Land. Taking Advantage of Chief's Illness."

reported that the original article "was full of scurrilous abuse of Sekgoma and the acting Chief but was returned for amendment by the Press."[40] Simon was known to be the avowed enemy of the acting chief, Gorewan Kgamane.[41] Discussing the article with Gorewan, Major Hannay agreed that in future there would be no further official communication sent from his office to the acting chief by means of his official interpreter, Obeditse Ratshosa, younger brother of Johnnie and Simon, since Gorewan did not trust him.[42] On the 18th of October the chief and his attendants were met at Mafeking by the assistant government secretary. Although Sekgoma's face lit up on seeing him he gave "the impression. . . that he will never again be able to resume duty as Chief."[43] On Dr. Drew's advice, steps were also taken to remove all firearms from the Chief's house before his return.

In the words of the local missionary in Serowe, the Rev. R. Haydon Lewis, when Sekgoma returned to Mafeking he looked "much worse than he looked before he left for the Cape. This gave the Native doctors just what they wanted, and immediately the idea was spread about that whitemen were killing the Chief."[44] This visual evidence of the Western doctors' failure to do anything to improve their chief's condition was a major weapon in the hands of those who wanted him treated by the traditional doctors. And it is here that the response of the Batswana to the two

---

[40] BNA, S. 11/4, Hannay, Acting Magistrate Serowe to Government Secretary.

[41] BNA, S. 11/4, Hannay.

[42] BNA, S. 11/4, Hannay.

[43] BNA, S. 11/4, Government Secretary to High Commissioner. It is not clear from the letter whether in fact it was the resident commissioner rather than the government secretary who went to the station.

[44] Rev. R. Haydon Lewis, "The Death of Sekgome Khama [sic]," *The Congregationalist*, February, 1926, p. 7.

systems of medicine available for his treatment becomes crucial. The choice of one or the other was not automatic, since as Caroline Seeley makes clear "Tswana medical attitudes by tradition were eclectic, and whichever available method of treatment proved successful was accepted."[45]

Tswana medicine, Seeley points out, had four basic aspects: protective, curative, productive in the sense of ensuring rain or fertility, and destructive. The specifically curative aspect of Tswana medicine was practised by *dingaka tse dichochwa* who were not involved in ritual matters and had little status in Tswana society. The *dingaka tsedi dinaka* (the bone-throwers) on the other hand were men of high status and influence:

> Like that of the Chief the role of the bone thrower was multi-faceted, combining that of healer, protector, political adviser, priest, and sorcerer. All that constituted the Tswana universe came under his jurisdiction—the social, moral, and physical well-being of the individual, his family, his crops, cattle and immediate environment. His practice encompassed every aspect of life, including its destruction.[46]

Nothing that might affect the tribal welfare was attempted without the presence and consent of a dingaka tsedi dinaka, a status supplanted by the Christian missionaries in Tswana states in the second half of the nineteenth century. The missionaries, particularly those of the London Missionary Society who were active in Gamangwato, combined proselytization with the practice of Western medicine, which at that time, as Seeley points out, like Tswana herbalism was little more than a rudimentary therapeutic

---

[45]Caroline Fraser Seeley, "The Reaction of the Batswana to the Practice of Western Medicine" (M. Phil. Thesis, University of London, 1973). See also her article written under her married name, Caroline Dennis, "The role of *Dingaka tsa Setswana* from the 19th Century to the Present," *Botswana Notes and Records*, 10, n.d., pp. 53-66.

[46]Seeley, "The Reaction of the Batswana," p. 66.

system.[47] But the missionaries of the London Missionary Society also followed a policy of attaching themselves to the rulers of the Tswana states and in the complex political situation in Southern Africa of the time soon became their major political advisers. Once rulers converted to Christianity the missionary supplanted the traditional priest-doctors of the state in their role of ritual assistants. In Gamangwato, for instance, at Khama's installation instead of being ritually doctored by the priest doctor of the morafe, Hepburn of the LMS officiated at a Christian service which was held in the kgotla. Thereafter Khama began every meeting of the kgotla with prayers and encouraged his headmen to do so in theirs.[48] Khama thus abandoned his role as high priest of the tribe and refused to use the healing and ensorcelling powers of the dingaka. Instead of them he consulted his missionary.[49] If the traditional priest-doctors had lost their function at the national level to the missionary, at the local level they still continued to practice though in 1889 Khama announced that there would be no more divination or doctoring of cattle and lands or use of protective and productive medicine. But as Schapera points out little was in fact done to put this order into force except at court.[50]

For the majority of Bangwato, of course, access to the missionary in any of the capacities for which the dingaka were traditionally used was limited. Furthermore, as Seeley suggests, the Tswana saw the missionary as similar to their own traditional priest doctors: "The Christian context in which missionary medicine was administered corresponded closely to the traditional magico-

---

[47]Seeley, "The Reaction of the Batswana," p. 75

[48]Seeley, "The Reaction of the Batswana," p. 114.

[49]Seeley, "The Reaction of the Batswana," p. 114.

[50]Isaac Schapera, *Tribal Innovators: Tswana Chiefs and Social Change 1795-1940* (London: Athlone Press, 1970), cited in Seeley, "The Reaction of the Batswana," p. 131.

religious framework within which the *ngaka* functioned; in enacting his multiple role the missionary practised the four types of Tswana medicine. . . ."[51]

With the imposition of the protectorate, state and church were divorced as the resident magistrate became the official adviser of the chief and took precedence over the missionary in the kgotla which the latter nevertheless continued to attend. Similarly, medicine and religion were separated as the new colonial state took over responsibility for medical services in Gamangwato from the missionaries. These were very limited in nature, however, with only one doctor available for the whole of Gamangwato at the time of Sekgoma II's illness.[52] The majority of people had perforce to rely on their traditional doctors, for even the local missionary at that time was untrained as a doctor.

Despite the failure of the administration to provide medical services that could in any way cope with the needs of the Bangwato, they considered traditional medicine as a system that should be suppressed as quickly as possible, their attitude being summed up in their description of traditional doctors as witch-doctors. It was in this spirit that they introduced the Witchcraft Proclamation soon after Sekgoma's death and took no heed of the warning of Tshekedi, his successor, that as far as the Tswana were concerned, sorcery represented one of the main causes of sickness and misfortune and formed an important part of the traditional magico-religious belief system to which even those who had accepted Christianity, like Tshekedi himself, still subscribed.[53] As

---

[51]Schapera, *Tribal Innovators*, p. 117.

[52]There was only one government doctor stationed at Serowe. The LMS, unlike missionaries elsewhere in Africa, including other parts of Botswana, did not maintain even a dispensary at this time.

[53]Seeley, "The Reaction of the Batswana," p. 146. See also BNA, DCS 6/1 "Record of the Proceedings of an interview granted by his Excellency the High Commissioner to certain Bechuana Chiefs . . . 21st and 22nd November, 1927."

Seeley emphasizes, no matter how extensive the medical facilities provided by the Government, "they would be apposite to only one aspect of the complex whole which formed the Tswana concept of medicine."[54] The British had made available to Sekgoma the most advanced offerings of their system of medicine but in the eyes of the Bangwato those offerings had failed signally. For a people who were accustomed to trying alternative curative systems and who readily associated the cause of illness with sorcery, the time had come to use the skills of their own doctors. Indeed epilepsy, according to Andrew Mushingeh the Zambian scholar, was considered as a Tswana disease which could only be effectively dealt with by indigenous therapies. Traditionally it was ascribed to a pigeon in the victim's head which produced fits.[55] Against this background a delegation of headmen, led by Gorewan, called on the resident magistrate to discuss the future medical treatment of their chief with Dr. Drew. After hearing Dr. Drew's report of what happened at Cape Town, they informed the resident magistrate that in the opinion of the tribe the chief's "present physical condition and general weakness debarred him from undergoing an operation."[56] It was then that they dropped their bombshell—would the administration sanction calling in a Mongwato doctor to attend the chief?[57]

The acting magistrate said he would refer the matter to the resident commissioner but that they must realize that once a Mongwato doctor were called in, all government responsibility for their chief would end and Dr. Drew himself would have to withdraw from the case. Later that day the magistrate saw the

---

[54]Seeley, "The Reaction of the Batswana," pp. 141-42.

[55]Mushingeh, "A History of Disease," pp. 221 (note), 273, 300-1.

[56]BNA, S. 11/4, Hannay to Government Secretary, 20 October 1925.

[57]BNA, S. 11/4, Hannay to Government Secretary.

chief who, while he felt he had derived no benefit from his treatment in Cape Town, was perfectly satisfied with Dr. Drew.[58]

The magistrate thought it wise not to raise the controversial issue of treatment by a traditional doctor at that stage, while Gorewan, who had accompanied him on his visit to the chief, now "wished unreservedly to withdraw the suggestion he had made in conjunction with the other Headmen."[59] Major Hannay also reported that he had heard that Simon Ratshosa had "given it out to certain members of the tribe that to all intents and purposes the Chief is as good as dead."[60] Dr. Drew was increasingly convinced that Sekgoma was becoming permanently deranged. Factions were jockeying for control of him and if at any moment of temporary sanity family or tribal business was raised he became very excited. He told Drew that people were trying to make trouble between himself and his brother, Tshekedi.[61] Furthermore, there was a concerted attempt to put him in the hands of traditional doctors. Drew noted gloomily, "I hope they will not get an opportunity, because if they overdo things, I shall get the blame."[62]

On 28 October Drew finally concluded that the chief's mental derangement

> is permanent and that Sekgoma will never be able to take an active part in the affairs of the tribe. In the interests of the Chief, himself, and of the tribe, I would suggest that Sekgoma be relieved of the chieftaincy. At present Sekgoma is merely the centre for intrigues on

---

[58]BNA, S. 11/4, Hannay to Government Secretary.

[59]BNA, S. 11/4, Hannay to Government Secretary.

[60]BNA, S. 11/4, Hannay to Government Secretary.

[61]BNA, S. 11/4, Drew to Principal Medical Officer, Mafeking, 28 October 1925.

[62]BNA, S. 11/4, Drew to Principal Medical Officer, 22 October 1925.

the part of various factions, and it is not unlikely that some of them may try and do him harm while he is still nominally Chief, whereas if he becomes a private individual, these schemes will cease.[63]

He reported that this was also the view taken by Khama's widow, Semane. At the chief's request she had taken charge of his house. Furthermore, rumors were rife not only that the chief was being bewitched by his own people but that the European doctors were trying to kill him. He was also talking indiscreetly, letting out family secrets. To curb this unfortunate development was one of the aims of the headmen in sending him for treatment by a traditional doctor.

The resident commissioner agreed with Dr. Drew's recommendation and instructed the resident magistrate to suggest to Sekgoma, during a period of sanity, that it would be better from all points of view if he relinquished the chieftainship and led the life of a private individual. If it were too much for him to make such an announcement in kgotla, he should at least make it to his headmen and tell them whom he wished to take over as regent for his young son, Seretse. The resident commissioner also noted that in a lucid moment Sekgoma had told Major Hannay that if anything happened to him he would like Tshekedi, his half-brother, to act as regent. "I do not want to force him on the tribe," the resident commissioner concluded, "but I think it will be generally admitted by the headmen and people that in the circumstances he is the proper person to take charge of the tribe."[64] As it was, other pressures had been put on Sekgoma. His daughter, Oratile, no doubt urged on by her husband and anxious to keep power in her own house during her half-brother's minority, and following the earlier example of her aunt Bessie, had asked her father to

---

[63]BNA, S. 11/4, Separate Minute of 28 October 1925.

[64]BNA, S. 11/4, Resident Commissioner to Resident Magistrate, Serowe, 6 November 1925.

name her as his successor.⁶⁵ Sekgoma had refused. Similarly, Baboni, Sekgoma's sister, had pressed the claim of his illegitimate son, Gasetshware, who had been born to him by the sister of an earlier and barren wife.⁶⁶ Again Sekgoma had refused. So, in the event of his permanent incapacity, it looked certain that Tshekedi would have to take over as regent.

The Debate Over the Treatment of the Chief

The debate in the tribe as to whether Sekgoma should continue to be treated by the European doctors, who seemed to have had conspicuously little success, or whether he should be put into the hands of traditional doctors came out into the open on Thursday 29 October when a kgotla to discuss the issue was held by Gorewan at 8.00 in the morning. Some eight to nine hundred members of the tribe were present as well as Major Hannay, the acting resident magistrate, Rev. R.H. Lewis, the resident missionary of the London Missionary Society, Dr. Drew, and Mr. Germond, the young assistant to the magistrate.⁶⁷

A full transcript of the proceedings of this kgotla was made in English by the resident magistrate's office.⁶⁸ The magistrate opened the kgotla in a belligerent fashion, asking the assembly why, "if you have so much faith in your Native Doctors, did you

---

⁶⁵See Theophilus Mooko, "The Role of Royal Women in Bangwato Politics Under the Regency of Tshekedi Khama, 1926-1949" (University of Botswana History Department dissertation submitted in partial fulfillment of the requirements for the BA Degree,1985), p. 7.

⁶⁶Mooko, "The Role of Royal Women," pp. 12-13.

⁶⁷BNA, S. 11/4, Minutes of a Meeting held at the Kgotla, Serowe, at 8 a.m. on Thursday, 29th October, 1925. These minutes are reproduced as Appendix C. In Appendix C the document is cited as BNA, DCS 4/6. It has not been possible to determine which citation or whether both citations are accurate.

⁶⁸BNA, S. 11/4, Minutes (Appendix C).

send for the White Doctor?" although there had been a native doctor, Mathobe, present at the cattle post on the second occasion that Sekgoma suffered epileptic fits. "I admit," he continued, "that some Native Doctors have a good knowledge of various herbal remedies and are able with the help of these to cure wounds, colds, stomach troubles etc. But I know your Doctor is going to make use of the 'Bones' and in this I have no faith whatsoever and am strongly opposed to it." He repeated his earlier threat that once a native doctor entered the chief's house Dr. Drew and the European nursing orderlies would leave. "Also please understand," he warned them, "that if anything happens while under the treatment of the Witch Doctor, you and you alone, Bamangwato, will be to blame."

Gorewan, the acting chief, responded to the resident magistrate, trying to hedge his bets with both factions. Personally he had nothing against native doctors but he did not wish the chief to be treated exclusively by one. As far as the chief was concerned all doctors, white and black, were the same, "but if the Magistrate was not willing to have a Native doctor called he was quite willing to remain in the hands of Dr. Drew." Other speakers were less equivocal. Headman Baipedi wanted to know who had "spoilt matters" for he had been under the impression that at their earlier meeting with Major Hannay the latter had agreed to the chief being treated by a native doctor. The majority of headmen supported Baipedi.

Interestingly enough one of the first to declare himself against the treatment of Sekgoma by a native doctor was the senior member of the Raditladi clan, Headman Disang, who declared: "I have great faith in European doctors and very little in Native Doctors." In so stating he joined hands with his erstwhile family enemies, the three Ratshosa brothers. When the magistrate called on those in favor of Sekgoma being treated by traditional medicine to step back half a dozen, unfortunately unnamed, headmen stood with them and the acting chief.

What was clear was that the assembled tribe was not impressed by the results of the treatment so far given by the European doctor, nor by the fact that the chief's own daughter was against treatment by traditional methods and least of all, apparently, by the magistrate's call on the memory of the great Khama, who had "chased Native Doctors out of the country." As Johnnie Ratshosa bravely told the tribe:

> I do not know what has happened to us Bamangwatos. In Khama's time no Witch Doctors were allowed in the place but today not only are they allowed among us but they are allowed to practice. I have been brought up by Khama and know that he hated Native Doctors. As a boy when I fell ill he placed me in the hands of European Doctors.

To which Native Doctor Boiditswe replied as follows:

> Your words are false, for I Boiditswe, was once called by Khama to treat the Chief's children who were suffering from ear-ache–the Chief's wife can bear me out in this. What is more, I am firmly convinced that I am able to cure the Chief himself. I have treated similar cases before and have been successful.

Sekgoma himself seems to have been persuaded by the majority feeling in the tribe, for shortly after this kgotla he dismissed the European orderlies and paid off Dr. Drew. Undoubtedly the stand taken by the two senior Ratshosa brothers in kgotla against the treatment of Sekgoma by traditional doctors brought further odium on their small but powerful group.[69]

The Death of Sekgoma

Under the care of the traditional doctors, Sekgoma appeared to make a rapid and amazing recovery. Captain Neale, the

---

[69]See the evidence in the trial of Simon and Obeditse Ratshosa, BNA, DCS 8/6.

resident magistrate, accompanied by Major Hannay, visited him on 5 November and found him "sane and more or less normal." Only four days earlier Dr. Drew had recommended that he be certified insane. He was now attending kgotla and carrying on his usual occupations. In view of this, it was decided not to discuss with him the matter of his abdication.[70] He was even alert enough to query some of Dr. Drew's charges, in particular the fee of five pounds a day for accompanying him to Cape Town.[71] He was also writing to other correspondents about cattle.[72] Drew, however, was not as impressed by his apparent recovery as was the resident magistrate. He reported on 8 November that he considered Sekgoma's condition was worse than when he saw him three days before: he was walking very badly though he spoke quite rationally. Nevertheless, when questioned about the decision not to face Sekgoma with the decision to abdicate, Drew agreed that it should be deferred for the present, though he held to the opinion that the chief would be unfit to undertake the duties of his office.[73] From the point of view of the Bangwato their decision must have seemed an apposite one since Sekgoma did improve under the care of native doctors. Resident Commissioner Ellenberger attributed the sudden improvement to the fact that the "use of a native doctor to remove any spell which Sekgoma might think had been cast over him through witchcraft would naturally relieve his mind and this would produce a change for the better in his condition but it is very doubtful that such a change will be

---

[70]BNA, S. 11/4, Resident Magistrate, Serowe to Government Secretary, 10 November 1925, and, Drew to principal medical officer, 1 November 1925.

[71]BNA, S. 11/4, Sekgoma Khama to Resident Magistrate, 6 November 1925.

[72]Sekgoma Khama Papers, (SKP), (Pilikwe), Letter Book.

[73]SKP, Drew to principal medical officer, 8 November 1925 and 10 November 1925.

The Illness and Death of Sekgoma II, 1925

of permanent character."[74] Very soon, Ellenberger and Drew were to be proved correct in their prognostications.

After nearly two weeks of treatment by traditional doctors, on Friday 13 November Sekgoma sent for the Rev. Mr. Lewis who found him "prostrate and in the condition in which he was before his visit to the Cape."[75] Semane had continued to nurse him, though the traditional doctors, according to Lewis, had made her life a misery. Sekgoma asked the missionary for medicine, which he gave him, but after it had taken its effect the traditional doctor returned. Next afternoon Sekgoma, taking a serious turn for the worse, discharged his traditional practitioners and called for Lewis and Dr. Drew. They arrived to find him in a critical condition. His kidneys had ceased to function and he suffered a further series of epileptic fits. At 2.45 a.m. the next day, Sunday, the doctor was called for by some headmen. Drew asked them why they had not called their own doctor, but they did not reply. Nevertheless he went with them and found the chief in the midst of a fit. From then on until 11.40 a.m., one fit was to follow another in rapid succession until he died, having *in extremis* returned to the fold of Western beliefs and Western medical practice.[76] He was buried two days later next to his father.

Reactions to the Death of Sekgoma

Despite the fact that Sekgoma had effectively died at the hands of traditional doctors—though there was clearly little they

---

[74]SKP, Resident Commissioner to High Commissioner, 14 November 1925.

[75]Lewis, "The Death of Sekgoma Khama," p. 8. See also the report of his death in *The Argus*, 19 November 1925: "Dramatic Scene at Death Bed of Sekgoma."

[76]Lewis, "The Death of Sekgoma Khama," and report of Resident Commissioner to High Commissioner, 21 November 1925 in BNA, S. 11/4.

could have done to save him beyond achieving a miracle–the distraught Bangwato took out their grief and anger at their chief's death on those who had been most closely associated with his treatment by Western medicine and who had ministered to him in his last hours. They punched, shoved, and cursed Dr. Drew and Rev. Lewis whom they accused of killing their chief with medicine. Neither Drew nor Lewis was hurt, and Gorewan, who was threatened with his life, fled to the police camp. Semane, who had nursed Sekgoma to the end but apparently had the most to gain by his death, was accused of poisoning him and her house was attacked. She was threatened by a group of women, led by Khama's daughters Baboni and Mmakhama who were bitter that Semane had not permitted them to see their brother. She was saved by the Ratshosas with whom she was apparently on close terms. Like Semane, the Ratshosas, as proponents of Western medicine, were also objects of the mob's vengeance but saved themselves by firing rifle shots above the heads of their attackers. Worse violence was averted by a fortunate downpour of rain and Semane was able to take refuge in the mission with the Lewises.[77] Thereafter, the resident magistrate, Captain Neale, restored order. Meanwhile Resident Commissioner Ellenberger, alerted to the situation by telegram, took the next train up to Palapye Road to sort out the succession.

Despite the attacks on him, Dr. Drew had managed to do the necessary to preserve Sekgoma's body for burial early on the morning of Tuesday 17 November. On the afternoon of his burial, the resident commissioner accompanied the frightened Gorewan into the kgotla. He then asked the people whom they looked upon as their chief and they "unanimously declared that, by virtue of his birth and rank, Gorewan was the proper person to lead them until Khama's son Tshekedi could take over from him and until Sekgoma's son (a boy five years of age) could himself occupy

---

[77]Lewis, "The Death of Sekgoma Khama," pp. 8-9; *The Argus*, 20 November 1925: "New Order for the Bangwato? Council of Headmen in Place of Paramount Chief. Scene After Death of Sekgoma. Danger of Bloodshed and how it was Avoided."

the Chief's chair." Because he considered Gorewan a weak man, Ellenberger followed up Captain Neale's proposal that a council of the best men of the tribe be formed to assist him. This would be responsible to the government for the management of tribal affairs and the maintenance of peace and good order in the tribe "until Tshekedi could assume duty as Regent."[78] The thirteen members of the council included the two elder Ratshosa brothers, their enemy Phethu Mphoeng, and three other members of the royal family.[79]

Phethu's Revenge: The Rise of Tshekedi and the Downfall of the Ratshosas

Tshekedi was preparing for his matriculation examination at Fort Hare Native University College when he heard news of his half-brother's death. He made arrangements to see the resident commissioner on 14 December. He was informed officially that he would be expected to be regent for Seretse. Until his arrival, Gorewan was acting as chief and was being advised by a council whose composition was communicated to Tshekedi. Ellenberger also informed him that his mother wanted him to continue with his studies, and then to travel before he assumed his duties as chief.[80] This hardly conformed with the picture her royal enemies had drawn of Semane as one who was scheming to get her own son on the throne and had even gone so far as to poison Sekgoma to achieve this end. Tshekedi's own first inclinations were to return to complete his studies at Fort Hare. The resident commissioner assured him that when he eventually did decide to take over as

---

[78]BNA, S. 11/4, Resident Commissioner to High Commissioner, 21 November 1925.

[79]The full list of names is reproduced as Appendix E.

[80]BNA, S. 11/5, Resident Commissioner to Tshekedi Khama at Fort Hare, 24 November 1925.

regent, should he and the tribe wish to abolish the council there would be no objection on the part of the administration.[81]

The initial instinct of the Ratshosas was to try and ingratiate themselves with the young man who was likely to take over as their new ruler. With the intention of offering him the hand of friendship, they waited for him at the station at Palapye Road where passengers for Serowe usually alighted. But their opponents were more cunning and sent an escort to meet Tshekedi at Mafeking and bring him back to the capital by way of Mahalapye, the stop before Palapye Road, even though this would involve him in a considerably longer journey by car.[82]

Although the Ratshosas later argued that they wished the chief nothing but well, and indeed had not only joined with his mother, Semane, in insisting on Sekgoma being treated by Western medicine, but had also helped save her from attack by the Serowe mob, Tshekedi soon realized that with regard to the Ratshosas the majority of the tribe had "decided that they were not to be trusted."[83] Undoubtedly he was influenced in this by Phethu, who, as a royal cousin, had right of access to Tshekedi. The Ratshosas certainly saw Phethu as instrumental in all their troubles with their new regent, though Tshekedi denied that he had been in any way influenced in his attitude towards them by their enemy.[84] What does seem clear is that soon after his arrival Tshekedi began to see that if he were to exercise the same control over his subjects as his father, he would have to take over without delay. No doubt he already knew of his half-brother's fear of the power the Ratshosa family were gathering to themselves.

---

[81]BNA, DCS 4/1, "Tshekedi Khama," Resident Commissioner telegram to Resident Magistrate, 24 December 1925.

[82]Evidence of Simon Ratshosa, BNA, DCS 8/6, pp. 313-14.

[83]BNA, DCS 8/6, Evidence of Tshekedi, p. 71.

[84]BNA, DCS 8/6, pp. 58-60.

In Serowe, it became clear that the Ratshosas saw the temporary council set up to advise Gorewan as something that could be manipulated to their advantage during the regency of their young and inexperienced uncle, if only it could be made a permanent feature. Thus it was that *The Times*, no doubt inspired by Simon (who seems at a very early stage to have learnt the political uses to which the press could be put) carried an article that the council was inspired by incipient democrats seeking to curb the powers of chiefs.[85] This has led two scholars to believe that the council really was the inspiration of Simon Ratshosa rather than an administrative device—albeit one that the British would ideally have liked to keep—to assist the weak Gorewan, who had already behaved in a cowardly fashion at the first sign of difficulty, until Tshekedi took up office.[86]

On oath later, both Johnnie and Simon denied that the council had been any other than the resident commissioner's idea. Johnnie even said that he had suggested to the resident commissioner that "the Council should not be formed, but the people then said that it must be formed." He alleged that it was a calumny against the Ratshosas that their subsequent support of the council "was a trick to break down the Chief's power, and that he would not have the same power as his forefathers, and that power would be in the hands of the white men."[87] Simon himself asserted that even when he was elected to the council "[he] objected to be a member. [He] did not like to be among untruthful people."[88] But Simon later became reconciled to the

---

[85] *The Times*, 23 November 1925. See also *The Argus*, 20 November 1925 whose "special correspondent" asserts that the council was the idea of "democrats" within the tribe.

[86] Quentin Neil Parsons, "Shots for a Black Republic? Simon Ratshosa and Botswana Nationalism," in *African Affairs* 73/293 (1974): 449-59, and, Robertson, "From Bechuanaland Protectorate," pp. 41-42.

[87] BNA, DCS 8/6, Evidence of John Ratshosa, p. 266.

[88] BNA, DCS 8/6, Evidence of Simon Ratshosa, p. 313.

council and increased his unpopularity by supporting it in the first kgotla presided over by Tshekedi on 19 December. There the young regent found that "not only was the majority of the Tribe opposed to this council but all the Members save three were dissatisfied with it."[89] Accordingly Tshekedi, his predecessor, Gorewan, members of the council and some other headmen adjourned to the resident magistrate's office to inform him of their wish to disband it. Without trying to bully the delegation into retaining the council, the resident magistrate did stress what he considered were points in its favor. It was purely advisory in nature and only differed from the informal advisory council of the Bangwato chiefs in that its composition was known to and recognized by the government. Second, the new chief was "young and inexperienced and [was] therefore in need of such a Council from which he could obtain reliable advice."[90]

In the discussion that followed Simon Ratshosa was the only speaker who supported retention of the council. Simon Ratshosa declared his support for the council

> because it answers my every wish and desire, and also because I am convinced that if run on the right lines it would prove a great help in the government of our country . . . The council does not as some of you seem to think eliminate the Chief's power, but, in my opinion, strengthens it.[91]

The other speakers merely conceded that if the council had been established after the arrival of Tshekedi their attitude might have

---

[89]BNA, DCS 4/1, "Tshekedi Khama," Minutes of a Meeting held at the Resident Magistrate's Office, Serowe, at 10.00 a.m., 19 December 1925.

[90]BNA, DCS 4/1, "Tshekedi Khama."

[91]BNA, DCS 4/1, "Tshekedi Khama."

been different. Mathiba, the Chief Hut Tax Collector, asked them to remember why the council had been formed in the first place:

> in a hurry . . . under the pressure of the grave events which followed the death of the late Chief. At the time the idea was, and still is, that the Council was to protect and advise the Acting Chief Gorewan. Gorewan as we all know is a weak Chief and was in dire need of such a Council.[92]

Among the strongest critics of the council at the meeting was Phethu Mphoeng, who called for Tshekedi's opinion on the matter. Tshekedi was told by the magistrate "that it depends on you whether there shall be a Council or not." Though his own view was clear, Tshekedi asked for time to think the matter over. Meanwhile the Ratshosas had been isolated and Phethu, as leader of the other most powerful faction in the tribe, staked out his position as Tshekedi's chief supporter. Tshekedi in fact did not have to think over the matter of retaining the council. All its members with the exception of the two Ratshosa brothers resigned. Tshekedi cunningly informed the magistrate that he personally had nothing against the council but that he was merely following the wishes of the tribe.[93] Reporting the dissolution of the council, the resident magistrate regretted its demise. "There are many progressive natives in the Bamangwato Reserve, who, apart from the Ratshosas, wish the old style of autocratic rule to be definitely finished with. There seemed to be an excellent chance for a more progressive system to be tried upon the young Regent's accession."[94] The resident commissioner, who had believed

---

[92]BNA, DCS 4/1, "Tshekedi Khama."

[93]BNA, DCS 8/6, Resident Magistrate, Serowe, to Resident Commissioner, 21 December 1925. See Appendix F.

[94]BNA, DCS 8/6, Resident Magistrate, Serowe.

Tshekedi would indeed return to Fort Hare, was now requested to sanction his installation and the abolition of the council.

Tshekedi was duly installed in the presence of the resident commissioner on Tuesday 19 January with Phethu as one of the main speakers. This time Phethu did not make the mistake of falling foul of the chief he had just helped install. Instead he watched with satisfaction the downfall of those who had been responsible for his exile two years before. The Ratshosas accepted Tshekedi's accession without their influence with bad grace. Simon's attitude towards the chieftainship was one of open defiance which caused a good deal of ill-feeling among the tribe.[95] Tshekedi therefore set about disarming Johnnie, their principal source of power. He organized his removal as tribal secretary, even though Captain Neale believed he did not support his brother Simon in his attitude toward the young regent "but of course the family more or less pull together." This attitude of Simon gave Phethu the chance he had been waiting for and the latter came back with the fixed intention of getting his revenge if possible against the Ratshosa family.[96]

Phethu, whom Neale reported as having a great deal of influence with Tshekedi, did not have long to wait before he witnessed the total destruction of his opponents. Despite pleadings from the administration that Tshekedi keep Johnnie on as secretary or at least relieve him of office graciously, he dismissed him publicly and summarily. Meanwhile Simon's overtly antagonistic attitude was goaded on by his formidable and embittered wife, Oratile; she, along with Sekgoma's sisters, had declared that they would never recognize Tshekedi, who was merely their servant. Tshekedi countered Simon by provoking him into an open act of defiance. He summoned Simon and his brothers to a kgotla which was to take place while they were attending a wedding. They refused to come and were then

---

[95]BNA, DCS 4/1, Resident Magistrate to Government Secretary, 25 January 1926.

[96]BNA, DCS 4/1, Resident Magistrate to Government Secretary.

brought forcibly in and sentenced to a flogging by Tshekedi for their disrespect. Their protests that as "royals" and "sons of chiefs" they could not be so treated were to no avail. Johnnie was beaten, but Simon and Obeditse in fury escaped to their house and got guns with which they then tried to assassinate their chief. They failed in their attempt, paying for it, in accordance with tradition, with the complete destruction of their property, including that of Johnnie, by regiments led by Phethu. They only narrowly escaped with their lives by seeking sanctuary at the resident magistrate's compound. Simon and Obeditse were tried and sentenced to ten years' imprisonment.[97] Johnnie, Oratile, and Tshekedi's aunts were exiled and the Ratshosas ceased to be a force in Bangwato politics, which they had dominated for so long. Phethu was now in the ascendant.

Conclusion

The succession crisis that developed during the illness of Sekgoma II is instructive at several levels. In the first place, the series of enquiries that took place before and after the death of Sekgoma, involving the various protagonists in the dispute, enables us to trace the growth, alignment, and realignment of factions with rare precision even for the colonial period. In the second place, their rivalry focused on a crucial area of change in Bangwato society, where the new colonial world interfaced with the traditional Tswana world in the field of healing. And yet, though the dispute was in essence one that pitched tradition versus change, the protagonists did not divide conveniently into adherents of the Western way of life and those still attached to their precolonial, pre-Christian culture. Members of both factions had received Western education in South Africa. Indeed it was a complaint of

---

[97]See the account in my joint article with Suzanne Miers "The Politics of Slavery in Bechuanaland: Power Struggles and the Plight of the Basarwa in the Bamangwato Reserve, 1926-1940" in Suzanne Miers and Richard Roberts, (eds.), *The Ending of Slavery in Africa* (Madison: University of Wisconsin Press, 1988).

Phethu and his supporters that the Ratshosas were "a blockade in the way of education; that teachers were being turned out of schools without wrong being committed by them;" that the missionaries had "no means of progressing in education;" and that the tribe had "no voice in education." "But we want progress and education," they declared in their petition to the resident commissioner against their banishment.[98] Again, the alignment of the two groups cannot be seen in terms of support for or antagonism towards the Christian religion. The Ratshosas were perceived by the LMS as enemies while Phethu was seen as a supporter, yet over the question of Sekgoma's medical treatment, the Ratshosas found themselves on the side of the missionaries, while Phethu was in the opposite camp. Even so, in their petition, Phethu and his followers had spoken out roundly against traditional medical practitioners: "Whereas the power of the witchdoctors is growing a good deal now among the tribe, and our chief and tribe believe in them, and we have found that they are the cause of this trouble, we therefore humbly beg to ask the Government to enforce a law against them as in all civilized countries."[99]

The guiding motive for opposition to the continued treatment of Sekgoma by the European doctors seems to have been twofold: first, it was clear to all, after Sekgoma returned from Cape Town, that Western medicine had been conspicuously unsuccessful in improving his condition; second, this development became a convenient stick to beat the Ratshosas with, since they had staked so much on treating him with Western techniques. It was an opposition that was certainly likely to gain support from the tribe, which had little access to Western medicine, and which, despite Khama's outlawing of traditional doctors, continued to use them and believe in them. The Ratshosas had most to gain by keeping Sekgoma alive and no doubt Simon, a man of formidable intelli-

---

[98]BNA, S 3/6, Petition of Phethu Mphoeng and his Followers to the Resident Commissioner, dated 21 January 1924.

[99]BNA, S 3/6, Petition of Phethu Mphoeng.

The Illness and Death of Sekgoma II, 1925

gence, and his wife Oratile were aware of the implication of the prognoses as reported by the European doctors and realized that continued treatment by the latter was their only hope. Even Simon hedged his bets and hoped to curry the favor of the young regent-to-be. As it turned out, Phethu and his allies were able to win a considerable victory over their opponents when Sekgoma died since they were able to impute that it was the Ratshosas' tenacious support of continued Western treatment that had led to his death. We know that without the operation to relieve his stricture there was little hope of his surviving, and the fact that Oratile was so reluctant to authorize it is comprehensible in terms of the likelihood of her father succumbing on the operating table, quite apart from his own reluctance to undergo surgery.

We come finally to the two persons involved in the succession—Sekgoma and Tshekedi. It is clear that, unlike his father, Sekgoma had not the single-minded faith in the missionary dispensation. His instinct was to trust the Western doctors. Indeed even on his deathbed he was writing to his friend, Dr. S.M. Molema in Mafeking, to ask him why he no longer came to check his patients in the Serowe area.[100] Not long before he had sent his daughter Oratile for an examination by Dr. Targett-Adams in connection with her apparent barrenness.[101] But he also had respect for traditional medical practitioners. Even Khama's much better educated second son, Tshekedi, shared his half-brother's belief in the efficacy of traditional doctors, accusing his own first wife in 1937 of trying to bewitch and poison his mother and having her condemned as a witch.[102]

---

[100] SKP, Pilikwe, Letter book, Sekgoma to Dr. S.M. Molema, 9 November 1925. Sekgoma was still clearly optimistic about his recovery since he enclosed a check for £ 360 for the purchase of a motor car.

[101] SKP, Pilikwe, Miscellaneous, Dr. P. Targett-Adams to Sekgoma, 19 July 1925.

[102] BNA, Bamangwato Tribal Administration: "Statement by Tshekedi Khama before a meeting of the Banwato [sic] Tribe held at the Kgotla,

It is clear that the root of the Ratshosas' downfall did not necessarily result from a structural enmity between them and Tshekedi, since they were prepared to offer him the friendship they had given to his mother, Semane, provided that they retained their privileged position as chief advisers to the royal family. Nor did it necessarily result from the feud between them and Phethu, who was initially largely an unknown quantity as far as Tshekedi was concerned. Clearly what clinched the Ratshosas' eclipse was the fact that early on Tshekedi realized just how unpopular they were with the tribe and that if he were to rule successfully as regent with so little experience of his people he had better seek the support of those who commanded the respect of the majority of the tribe. The Ratshosas had alienated themselves from the bulk of the kgotla not only through their arrogant ways but by the gamble they had taken on Western medicine which had failed. Simon sealed their fate by his desperate bids to cut Tshekedi down to size once it became apparent that power was slipping from their hands. In all this, the European doctors were largely helpless actors, doing their best in a situation in which decisions were being made not to safeguard the interests of the patient in Western medical terms but to ensure victory for one faction over another.

Serowe, on the 10th May, 1937."

Chapter 3

SERETSE KHAMA AND THE BANGWATO SUCCESSION CRISIS, 1948-1953

Neil Parsons

Tuesday, 26 January 1937:
Tshekedi brought the future Chief, his nephew Seretse, to see me this morning. The lad has improved a good bit, and seems pleasant enough and well grown . . . There will be trouble when Seretse succeeds. Thank goodness I shan't be here then.[1]

Introduction

The unjust exile and barring of Seretse Khama from royal succession in Bechuanaland was one of the hottest African news stories of the early 1950s in the international press. It became a

---

[1]Sir Charles Rey, *Monarch of All I Survey: Bechuanaland Diaries, 1929-37*, edited by Neil Parsons and Michael Crowder (London: James Currey, 1988). This chapter draws on research primarily conducted in the Botswana National Archives, Gaborone, and the Public Record Office, London. The material will be further developed in a collaborative biography of Sir Seretse Khama (1921-1980) presently in preparation. The author wishes to gratefully acknowledge a grant from the Ford Foundation which enabled him to conduct research and initiate writing in 1984-85.

focal issue for anti-colonial movements. His only "crime" had been to marry the woman of his choice, a European, while he was heir to an important chiefdom. He was then barred from that chieftainship and exiled from his homeland indefinitely. The international press, and colonial students in Britain even more so, caught the whiff of white racist pressure on the British government. Worse still, in the eyes of establishment liberals, was the blatant violation of an individual's human right to live in his own country. Successive British governments, Labour and Conservative, smugly denied Seretse Khama (and later his uncle Tshekedi) any right of due process in explaining the reasons for his exile. The case of Seretse Khama became an important issue in British internal politics and nearly toppled the Labour government in a ground swell of popular support from both right and left which developed behind Seretse Khama and Tshekedi Khama.

Within the Bechuanaland Protectorate the Bangwato succession crisis was only partially resolved in 1953, and arguably has never been resolved fully within the Bangwato "tribal" state.[2] Its resolution was effected by the transformation of the "tribal" chieftainship into a presidential republic within the national state of Botswana. Seretse Khama became prime minister in 1965 and president of the republic in 1966. To unravel some of these paradoxes, we first must examine the narrative of the crisis.

---

[2]Despite the formal succession of Ian Seretse Khama as Kgosi Seretse in 1978, he has not become the substantive chief resident in Serowe. He has maintained his career as deputy commander of the Botswana Defence Force, leaving Mokgacha Mokgadi as Deputy Chief at Serowe until 1988, and subsequently, Sediegenge ("States") Kgamane (son of Setuhile Kaelo Kgamane). This position remains controversial, having been challenged both by his cousin Leapeetswe Khama and by President Masire in 1985-87. See "'States' to Lead Bangwato," *Mmegi wa Dikgang/The Reporter*, (Gaborone & Serowe) 5/11 (26-30 March 1988): 1,3 and previous articles in the same weekly newspaper.

Outline of Events 1948-1953

Seretse Khama married Ruth Williams in London on 29 September 1948 without prior consultation of his uncles back home–notably Tshekedi Khama, who had acted as regent since 1926 for his infant and later student nephew. Tshekedi ordered Seretse to fly home to explain himself. Tshekedi was to give Seretse an ultimatum either to divorce Ruth and become chief, or to keep Ruth and never become chief. Seretse duly appeared at Serowe, the Bangwato capital, for a kgotla (town forum) assembly of elders that lasted from 15 to 19 November 1948. Seretse was roundly condemned by all except a few "young bloods." But by the time of a second kgotla assembly on 28-29 December 1948 Seretse was beginning to gather support from uncles and others opposed to Tshekedi. Tshekedi's regency can be characterized as an enlightened despotism, progressive in appearance only in the liberal circles overseas where Tshekedi was greatly admired.

Seretse flew back to his wife in Britain, to return to Bechuanaland in June 1949. Meanwhile Tshekedi became obsessed by the matter, and alienated even greater numbers of his people. The third kgotla of 20-26 June 1949 proved to be a triumph for Seretse. Tshekedi received the support of the top forty headmen, but Seretse was acclaimed chief or king (*kgosi e kgolo*) by four thousand commoners and significant but disaffected headmen.[3]

Tshekedi and forty-two of his leading supporters announced their retreat into voluntary exile on 6 July, and all looked set for Seretse's "coronation." The cabinet of the Labour government in London then decided to appoint a judicial enquiry into the Bangwato succession question.[4] The enquiry, under Mr. Justice "Pops" Harragin, duly sat and gathered evidence in November and

---

[3]See Appendix H, the reports of the kgotlas on Seretse Khama's marriage, 1948-1949.

[4]See Appendix I, British government cabinet memorandum, 19 July 1949.

reported in secret to the British government in December 1949. The cabinet considered the Harragin Report and decided not to release it for publication. (It was not released until January 1981 under the Public Records Office thirty-year rule.[5])

In February 1950 Seretse Khama was summoned to London for consultations at the Commonwealth Relations Office.[6] He was given the option of abdicating voluntarily. When he refused, he was barred from the chieftainship and exiled from Bechuanaland for five years. This arbitrary act, condemned as "disreputable" by Winston Churchill, leader of the Conservative opposition, led to a public outcry. Seretse was allowed back to Bechuanaland in April-August 1950 to settle up his affairs and to collect his wife (who had been living at Serowe since August the previous year).

Seretse and Ruth Khama remained in exile in London from August 1950 until October 1956. Meanwhile–to make a right by two wrongs–Tshekedi Khama was also barred from the chieftainship, and his voluntary exile within Bechuanaland made compulsory. The Bangwato were left with a white chief in the form of the district commissioner who took over tribal responsibilities. Tshekedi added fuel to the fire of publicity by flying to London in March 1951 where he remained till July to lobby his friends in parliament against his exile. The Labour government obliged by sending out three neutral observers to assess Bangwato opinion in July-August 1951.[7] (Marguerite Bourke-White of *Life* magazine referred to them as the three Marx brothers, and others made similar fun of the incongruous trio.) The observers arrived in the wake of June demonstrations against Tshekedi's followers and

---

[5]See Appendix J, the report of a judicial enquiry into the designation of Seretse Khama as chief. The "Harragin Report" was published for the first time in *Botswana Notes and Records* 17 (1985).

[6]See Appendix K, British cabinet conclusions on the judicial enquiry on Seretse Khama.

[7]See Appendix L, the reports of the meetings with the "observers" on the question of Tshekedi Khama's return to the Bangwato reserve.

reported a flat refusal to have Tshekedi back into Bangwato country even as a commoner let alone as a chief.[8]

The Labour government in Britain fell in a snap election of October 1951 and was replaced by the Conservatives. The new government announced that Tshekedi could return home as a commoner. This announcement was followed by another in March 1952 that Seretse Khama's exile abroad was permanent. Bangwato delegates in London who had been sent to petition the return of Seretse were thereby rebuffed and humiliated. When the delegates arrived home in Serowe to report on their failure, the Bangwato rebelled against their white rulers. In a brief but bloody riot in the kgotla on a Sunday in June of 1952 three policemen were killed.

The British authorities then tried to engineer the popular election of Rasebolai Kgamane, third in line of succession after Seretse and Tshekedi Khama, as kgosi e kgolo. This failed, so Rasebolai was imposed as "Native Authority" in place of the district commissioner in May 1953 but could not be designated as full chief. At this juncture, events and opinions in Bangwato country began to quiet down. The question of Seretse Khama's exile surfaced less regularly in the British parliament. Tshekedi Khama turned to the agitation of "national" rather than tribal issues of Bechuanaland and its relationship with South Africa and/or the Central African Federation. The earlier private reconciliation between Seretse and Tshekedi now became public. In August-September 1956 Seretse Khama publicly abdicated the right to chieftainship of the Bangwato and was permitted to return home. He returned to Bechuanaland on 10 October 1956 to scenes of great public emotion. The Bangwato chieftainship,

---

[8]See Appendix M, the reports of the "observers." Previously published in *Botswana Notes and Records* 10 (1978): 137-48; See also M. Crowder, "Professor Macmillan on Safari: the British Government Observer Team and the Crisis over the Seretse Khama Marriage," in H. Macmillan and S. Marks, editors, *Africa and Empire: W.M. Macmillan, Historian and Social Critic* (London: Templesmith, 1989), pp. 254-78 and 322-28.

which had lapsed with the resignation of Tshekedi as regent in early 1950, was not to be revived until 1978 when it was taken in titular form by Seretse Khama's eldest son.

External Causes of the Crisis

Why was Seretse Khama barred from the Bangwato chieftainship and exiled abroad? As far as the British government would admit, the Harragin Enquiry was set up in response to Tshekedi's objections to the acclamation by the Bangwato masses of Seretse as kgosi. Harragin was commissioned to establish whether the June 1949 kgotla assembly was properly convened and constituted to take such a decision, and to establish whether Seretse Khama was "a fit and proper person to discharge the functions of Chief." Harragin's conclusions were an unequivocal affirmative to both questions, but he recommended that Seretse be barred from the chieftainship for completely different reasons.[9] The Harragin Report was therefore injudicious, and probably unjudicial, unable to be defended in a court of law, and therefore had to be suppressed by administrative fiat. As a Commonwealth Relations Office official put it, on one of the numerous files concerning the Bangwato succession crisis: "What we can and must do . . . is to ensure that the law is such that . . . the Courts will have to give the answer we desire."

The Harragin Enquiry was rigged but failed in its aims. As a result the British government's public reasons for barring and exiling Seretse Khama remained suspect in the extreme. Informed opinion knew that the government had given way to white settler pressure from the Union of South Africa and possibly from Southern Rhodesia. But the minister responsible, the overly ambitious new commonwealth secretary Patrick Gordon-Walker, told the House of Commons on 8 March 1950: "We have had no communication from the Government of the Union nor have we made any communication to them. There have been no

---

[9]See Appendix J.

representations and no consultation in this matter." This statement was an outright lie. Gordon-Walker had overstepped his brief by speaking so categorically and by making so unqualified a statement. It was a lie however, that both Labour and Conservative governments learned to live with, and which further compromised them towards the South African Government. Of course, purred D.F. Malan the South African prime minister, in the flurry of correspondence that followed Gordon-Walker's statement, the South African government would exercise "all possible discretion so as to avoid embarrassment to Gordon-Walker."

The truth is that the South African high commissioner in London had run to the Commonwealth Relations Office, on the instructions of Malan, four days after Seretse Khama was acclaimed kgosi in June 1949. (Bechuanaland's administration was supervised by the Commonwealth Office, rather than the Colonial Office, because of its proximity to the Union of South Africa and Southern Rhodesia). The high commissioner had told the commonwealth secretary, then Philip Noel-Baker, that his government earnestly requested that Seretse Khama should not be recognized as Bangwato chief. Noel-Baker referred to this interview as "semi-official or private representations" as no aide-memoir was left behind by the high commissioner. The high commissioner later expressed himself as being "extremely surprised that this impression had been left in Noel-Baker's mind." Malan confounded things further by claiming in public speeches of September and October 1949 that his government "had immediately dispatched a telegram *to the British government.*" In fact, his office had cabled its high commissioner in London.

When the matter first came to the British cabinet on 21 July 1949, Noel-Baker told his colleagues that there were two reasons for not recognizing Seretse as chief: the dubious constitutional validity of the kgotla that acclaimed him and "far-reaching and damaging effects on our relations with South Africa" which would lead to South Africa demanding to incorporate the Bechuanaland Protectorate into the Union. But the cabinet was persuaded by its voluble Colonial Secretary, Arthur Creech-Jones, who was responsible for British colonies north of the Zambezi, that the government should in no way openly admit concession to "pressure of European opinion in South Africa," as it would be widely criticized:

> the Government should vigorously rebut any suggestion that their attitude to this question was in any way determined by purely racial considerations. The principal objective of policy must be to safeguard the future well-being of the Bamangwato themselves, and there could be no doubt that . . . a white wife might have consequences gravely prejudicial to good government . . . a judicial enquiry would afford time for reflection.

The Harragin Report invited the British cabinet—as Prime Minister Clement Attlee pointed out—"to go contrary to the desires of the great majority of the Bamangwato Tribe, solely because of the attitude of the governments of South Africa and Southern Rhodesia." Attlee added: "It is as if we had been obliged to agree to Edward VIII's abdication so as not to annoy the Irish Free State and the U.S.A." This left the British government with only one tune to play in public: the suggestion by Harragin that recognition of Seretse Khama as chief "would undoubtedly cause disruption in the Bamangwato Tribe." This assertion was to be belied by the events of the next eighteen months: it was to be *non*-recognition which caused such disruption. But the Labour government played the tune for all it was worth. It also attempted to introduce other reasons for barring Seretse Khama: that Seretse had been personally irresponsible in contracting such a marriage; that an interregnum was needed to democratize the processes of chieftainship; and that black South Africans and West Africans opposed the marriage on principles of racial purity. All these justifications backfired; not only did Seretse prove to be eminently reasonable and responsible, but Bangwato democrats and black nationalists throughout Africa became vocal in their support for Seretse Khama.

Meanwhile, the Commonwealth Relations Office fed the Labour cabinet with alarmist notions of "possibly forcible action," including military invasion, by extremists in the Union and the great threat of the Union of South Africa declaring itself a republic and breaking away from the British Commonwealth of Nations. The result was that Seretse was exiled abroad as well as barred from office.

The new Conservative government of late 1951 came to power without the hostility of the British press, which had hounded the Labour government in every possible way including over the Seretse Khama affair. The Commonwealth Relations Office thought it had persuaded the new Conservative commonwealth secretary, Lord Ismay, to admit the facts about Seretse's exile, in order to make it permanent. Ismay decided to play down the charade of internal reasons for barring Seretse from office, and to play up the previously undisclosed external reasons for exiling Seretse. South Africa and Southern Rhodesia were to be reassured that their interests were paramount. Ismay told the cabinet on 19 November 1951, that to let Seretse return (even as a commoner) could result in "economic sanctions" by South Africa against the British colonies of Basutoland and Swaziland as well as Bechuanaland, and that Britain would probably lose the colonies to South Africa. This was because white South Africans were "very sensitive and emotional over racial purity." Ismay even coined the phrase of sacrificing one good man (Seretse) for the "future well-being and happiness" of one million people–in Basutoland, Bechuanaland, and Swaziland. But the conventional wisdom of the previous Labour cabinet prevailed. The Conservative government backed down from admitting in public the importance of "European opinion" in South Africa, by deleting the relevant paragraph from the March 1952 announcement of Seretse Khama's permanent banishment. Nevertheless Ismay managed to slip in his pet phrase about one for a million edgeways into debate in the House of Lords.

That Britain was really kowtowing to the white racist government of South Africa has always been suspected by commentators on the Seretse Khama affair. Since 1981, with all but three files open (and those closed till 2003), it can be confirmed in the British public records.[10] Those records go further to reveal an even deeper level of explanation for British government actions, which was concealed by the Commonwealth Relations Office from everyone in the Labour cabinet except the commonwealth secretary and the prime minister. (Attlee, as a former commonwealth secretary, kept close tabs on the Commonwealth Relations Office.) This level of explanation was concealed also from Prime Minister Malan and his National party cabinet in South Africa. It was essentially a conspiracy of interests between the Commonwealth Relations Office and the pro-British opposition led by General Jan Smuts in the South African parliament, mediated by Evelyn Baring the British high commissioner in South Africa and D.D. Forsyth the secretary for external affairs (and personal secretary to the prime minister) of the South African government.

Baring, a British aristocrat from a Dutch banking family, was profoundly sympathetic to white settlers in Africa, as he was also later to show as governor of Kenya. He struck up a close relationship with Smuts between Baring's arrival in 1944 and Smuts' removal as prime minister in 1948. Forsyth had been Smuts' personal secretary and secretary for external affairs since 1941. Malan retained Forsyth in those positions in 1948 when the National party replaced the United party in power. Malan probably knew he had a British/opposition "mole" or "deep throat" by his side, but found Forsyth valuable enough to keep.[11]

Following the June 1949 acclamation of Seretse as kgosi, the executive committee of the Dutch Reformed Church general

---

[10]Files to be opened in the year 2003 are D.O. 35/4130; 4143; & 4150.

[11]In 1954, when he retired, D.F. Malan was presented by the staff of the Department of External Affairs with a desk-lamp, with a flexible head that could face in any direction. Malan told the retirement party that he would name the lamp "D.D. Forsyth" (personal reminiscence of Patrick van Rensburg, Gaborone, 20 Jan. 1985).

assembly in South Africa made forceful representations to Malan as prime minister. Malan consulted his own cabinet and then Forsyth, who cabled the South African high commissioner in London on 30 June to make urgent representations to the commonwealth secretary. On 7 July Forsyth went from Cape Town to Pretoria to persuade Baring not to recognize Seretse as kgosi. By his own admission, Baring was already being pressured by an underling in his office named Cairns, "a reputably rich young South African" who was the cause of "a lot of the trouble" according to the then resident commissioner of Bechuanaland. Baring was impressed to see Forsyth, a man naturally cautious and not alarmist, waxing so emotional. Forsyth told Baring that the recognition of Seretse would provoke such a public outcry among whites that the National party would be strengthened over the United party, and the republican extremists under J.G. Strydom would overthrow Malan within the National party. As Baring put it to his superiors in London: "this incident on the edge of the Kalahari might lead to the complete secession of South Africa from the Commonwealth."

Baring was interviewed to similar effect in Pretoria by an envoy of Malan, General Ras Beyers, who flew to London to lobby the Commonwealth Relations Office directly. Baring then received two private letters, dated 7 and 8 July, from Godfrey Huggins the prime minister of Southern Rhodesia, couched in more urbane terms against the recognition of Seretse Khama as chief. "I am being bombarded to interfere," reported Huggins. Huggins had less than two months earlier made public statements advising "the good citizen" to discourage in every way intermarriage of black and white. "It's a very poor show," Huggins told the press,"disastrous lack of pride in the Bamangwato . . . dreadful."

The receipt of Baring's views led to a fluster of racist sentiment in the Commonwealth Relations Office. Percival Liesching, its civil service head, lapped up General Beyers' words that white settlement in Africa "depended, in view of the numerical inferiority and defenselessness of the white population, upon the principle that the native mind regarded the white woman as inviolable." Liesching remained "doctrinally correct" in finding the color bar repugnant, but baulked stereotypically at the thought of his own son or daughter marrying "one of the negro race." Gordon-Walker, then assistant commonwealth secretary to Noel-Baker, nailed his racist colors to the mast in a hand-written minute of 15 July with the extraordinarily naive suggestion that all African chiefs should be barred by law from having white wives.

Baring stressed the Smuts connection in steeling the Commonwealth Relations Office to exile Seretse Khama in March 1950. Prefacing his remarks with a bit of scare-mongering about the National party government sending troops into Bechuanaland if necessary, Baring revealed a conversation which he had had that morning with Smuts–"he spoke very seriously to me." The South African government would call a snap general election if Seretse was allowed back, and would wipe out the United party in the election on the twin issues of incorporating the High Commission Territories (Basutoland, Bechuanaland, and Swaziland) and seceding from the Commonwealth as a republic. The point was underlined again in June 1951 by Strauss, Smuts' successor as leader of the United party. Any hint of allowing Seretse back home from exile would drive whites into the arms of the Nationalists who would therefore win the general elections scheduled to be held by 1953.

The British establishment regarded Smuts up to his death in 1950 as the natural leader of South Africa, and the United party as its natural government. The establishment regarded Malan and the Nazi-sympathizing Nationalists, who had stormed in after the 1948 elections, as a temporary aberration which would pass. But the United party failed to regain power in 1953, perhaps because National party *apartheid* was not so very different from United party "liberal" segregationism. As was pointed out within the Commonwealth Relations Office, fundamentally white South Africans were at one on the "color question." Seretse Khama was allowed back home from exile in 1956 when all hope of a United party revival had been dissipated.

Internal Effects of the Crisis

Tshekedi Khama precipitated the Bangwato succession crisis in 1949 by refusing to accept the legality of the kgotla acclamation and calling for a judicial enquiry. But the succession crisis was exacerbated and perpetuated by external factors—ultimately white settler sentiment in neighboring countries. The crisis developed and continued despite the reconciliation between Tshekedi and Seretse which began tentatively in 1950-1951 and was fulfilled in 1956. Meanwhile, the British placed their nominee, Rasebolai Kgamane, as Native (soon renamed "African") Authority in 1953. (When Seretse and Tshekedi returned to Bangwato politics after 1956, it was to be as vice-chairman and secretary respectively of the tribal council, under Rasebolai as chairman.) But if the Bangwato succession crisis was externally induced, it none the less had real internal effects. As crises tend to do, it took the lid off internal struggles and social developments among the Bangwato.

The succession crisis had already opened up a threefold division of the Bangwato men in kgotla by January 1949, between what Anthony Sillery the then resident commissioner called die-hards or whole-hoggers supporting Tshekedi, moderates who would eventually accept Ruth Khama, and a third party of "bright young things" who welcomed the marriage. The die-hards are easy to categorize as the forty-two prominent followers of Tshekedi Khama, who retreated with him into exile at Rametsana. They are therefore remembered as "Bo-Rametsana." Most prominent among them was Rasebolai Kgamane. The moderates are a much less coherent group, including the majority of Bangwato men who took no active role in politics beyond attendance of kgotla assemblies.

The "third party" took three more years to emerge as a political force in January-February 1952. It distinguished itself as the friend of Seretse with democratic nationalist ideas, and distanced itself from the moderate Bangwato leaders who had filled the power vacuum after the withdrawal of Tshekedi and Bo-Rametsana. The senior figures of the third party were L.D. Raditladi and K.T. Motsete. Raditladi, who ran the Francistown African Employees Union and founded the short-lived

Bamangwato National Congress in June 1952, went on to found the Bechuanaland Protectorate Federal party in 1958. Motsete, proud possessor of three London University degrees and a founder member of the Nyasaland African Congress (1944), went on to co-found and lead the Bechuanaland People's party in 1960. The core of the "third" party in 1952 was seven young men who backed a petition for democratic local government, staffed by educated people. Two of the seven—Lenyeletse Seretse and Mout Nwako—were to rise to high office within Seretse Khama's Democratic party (founded in 1962). One of the seven, Kenneth Koma, was even then thought to be a communist by Tshekedi. After receiving an education in Britain, Czechoslovakia, and the Soviet Union, Koma returned to Bechuanaland where he founded the Botswana National Front in 1965.[12]

The third party of Bangwato tribal politics in 1952 encapsulated many of the leading figures of Botswana national politics—liberal, populist, democrat, and socialist—during the subsequent three decades. Not that 1952 was the beginning of ideological foment in Bangwato country: two decades earlier a visiting journalist had noted unexpected interest among intelligent people in "tribal development" passing from monarchy to aristocracy, from aristocracy to bourgeoisie, and from bourgeoisie to proletariat.

A third party also appeared in British colonial administrative ranks in early 1952. The administrative cadre of the Bechuanaland Protectorate had previously been recruited almost entirely within Southern Africa: some older senior officers were from missionary backgrounds and had a pro-African if tribalist stance, while junior and technical officers generally kept the attitudes of their white settler origins. Beginning in 1935, and particularly after the Second World War, a new breed of junior officers with university qualifications was recruited, often directly from Britain. It was such a third party of colonial officers that revolted against their

---

[12]Another prominent young democrat then outside the country was M.T. Chiepe who died in the 1950s; his sister G.K.T. Chiepe rose to prominence in post-independence politics.

administrative overlords in January 1952. In an unprecedented move, and to the fury of officials right up to the commonwealth secretary, three district officers at Serowe petitioned the high commissioner against British policy for disregarding the rights and wishes of the Bangwato. (Two of the three continued to associate themselves with local aspirations and remained as key administrators after independence.)

It was the moderates among the Bangwato who finally proved more problematic to the British than either the die-hards or the bright young things. What emerged in June 1949 and reached fever pitch in July 1951 and June 1952 was mass resistance by the Bangwato against Tshekedi Khama and the colonial administration. Tshekedi himself identified two reasons why common men resented him. The first (which became the favorite explanation of the colonial authorities) was his extensive use of unpaid tribute labor on public works: men were kept for up to nine months working on Tshekedi's dream project—an educational complex known as Bamangwato College, in the remote valley of Moeng. The second grievance Tshekedi identified may not have been his fault. He became the butt of resentment for late payment of government resettlement grants to some five thousand Bangwato ex-soldiers demobilized after the Second World War.

Two other important groups of Bangwato made themselves conspicuous demanding Tshekedi's replacement by Seretse. One group of Bangwato was Kalanga-speakers who resented the peremptory expulsion of one of their leading headmen, John Nswazwi, into Southern Rhodesia (1947). Nswazwi had spoken out against Tshekedi's strict rule and as a result suffered as a scapegoat. His case became a burning issue among young educated Bakalanga, who looked to the rule of Seretse to right the wrongs. The other group of Bangwato that showed strong support for Seretse was one of the migrant workers working in the towns and mines of South Africa around Johannesburg and at Kimberley and Cape Town. This may be understood against the background of the radicalization of the African National Congress in South Africa as a mass party in 1949, leading up to the Defiance Campaign in June 1952.

Leadership for the mass of Bangwato towards ever greater militancy, however, came from the moderate royal uncles and headmen who supported Seretse. The most prominent of them, such as Keaboka and Peto Sekgoma, were intelligent men who had quarrelled with Tshekedi. These uncles and headmen were left in effective control by the withdrawal of the forty-two Bo-Rametsana households following Tshekedi. They led the passive resistance of the masses. Baring, the High Commissioner, in full ceremonial garb, was boycotted by the people voting with their feet when he visited the Serowe kgotla in March 1950 to officially announce the exile of Seretse. People then refused to pay taxes and local courts of law ground to a standstill until September of that year. The Bangwato refused to elect a kgosi in place of Seretse. Instead they named Keaboka as their "messenger" to the district commissioner who was acting as the native authority. But by the end of 1951 the third party of younger men had broken from the moderate royal uncles and headmen, protesting that they were now feathering their own nests with the spoils of tax and tribute collection. These moderates became frustrated feudalists–the "Keaboka crowd" or "Big Five" as other critics called them–who were subsequently prosecuted and convicted for either leading the June 1952 Serowe kgotla riot, or on charges of official corruption. Once the British had disposed of them, the way was open for the imposition of Rasebolai Kgamane as native authority in May 1953.[13]

The political agitation of frustrated feudalists is an insufficient explanation for the mass resistance to autocratic and colonial rule that burned between 1949 and 1952. The spark makes no fire unless the tinder is dry. In particular the most remarkable aspect of the mass resistance was the role and determination of ordinary women. It was women who had flocked

---

[13]Relations between Seretse Khama and the "Big Five" were strained after his return in 1956. Ironically after Seretse Khama's death, Keaboka and Peto Sekgoma appear to have been behind the "Bamangwato Democrats" who regarded President Masire as betraying the heritage of Sir Seretse Khama. In 1984 they joined the Botswana National Front.

to Seretse's side in November 1948, and then to Ruth when she arrived in July 1949. In August 1949 the women of Mahalapye petitioned the resident commissioner on behalf of Seretse as chief: "We are women, and we also put forward our request as such because a chief is for us all and not for men only who speak in Kgotla." In April 1950 hundreds of women surrounded Seretse and Ruth, when he was briefly permitted from exile to visit her at Serowe: "All women and children want Seretse! To-day we do not mind if the Government kills us all!"

Women broke through previous barriers on political participation in kgotla during the Bangwato succession crisis by attending important political assemblies from February 1951 onwards. In the July 1951 disturbances at Serowe and Mahalapye, "women took over the running from the men" in molesting and expelling known Bo-Rametsana (Tshekedi's supporters). Tshekedi was said to be in "acute personal danger, particularly from women." In the June 1952 Serowe kgotla riot women took the lead in attacking the police with rocks. Forty were arrested, and six were sentenced to a year in prison. To what extent were these women the amplifiers of general peasant grievances and to what extent were they expressing grievances particular to women? The main peasant grievance against Tshekedi's rule centered on the "warlands" scheme of the Second World War. Tshekedi had utilized the traditional royal right of *masotla* (fields cultivated by collective tribute labor) for extensive warlands to produce grain in support of the war effort. The burden had fallen disproportionately on women, old people and children, as adult male labour was serving in the army overseas or in South African mines. This would have been less unusual elsewhere in Africa where women were the main cultivators. But Bangwato society was extraordinary in that ox-plowing by men had replaced hoe-cultivation by women in the later nineteenth century. Women plowing with oxen has since become a common sight in Botswana, but was a novel feature during the 1940s.

With the partial exception of northeastern Kalanga-speaking areas, most of Bangwato country is marginal for agricultural production. Semi-arid conditions render soils unsuitable and make the plowing season short. The grievances of peasant cultivators are therefore rarely the stuff of Botswana history, and one must look elsewhere to explain the vehemence of the 1951-1952 women's revolt. The obvious direction in which to look is the long-standing aspects of women's position in society and their economic liberation of the 1940s, as well as the political opportunities of the early 1950s.

The blind fury of the Serowe kgotla riot in June 1952, with the stoning to death of three policemen, was a shock to all concerned—not least to the normally peaceable Bangwato themselves. It is not difficult to see, as the three young district officers at Serowe had seen, that the Bangwato had been endlessly baited and frustrated during three years of British drift and deceit. Finally their restraint had snapped. The British government attempted to explain the riot as an anarchic outburst provoked by women and drink. "Women and drink," retorted British member of parliament Jennie Lee, "were the women drunk?" A few days later the Commonwealth Relations Office learned that there was no evidence of drunkenness, only of women being in a state of extreme excitement. But the impression was maintained that the unnatural role of women in the riot had at least been an index, if not the cause, of the extraordinary collapse of the Bangwato moral order. The only hint as to why this happened is contained in a Commonwealth Relations Office observation on the militant women of Mahalapye: that they disliked Tshekedi because of his periodic campaigns to clean up the morals of the railway townships. Oral tradition also maintains that the Mahalapye women scolded their menfolk for inaction with the age-old taunt "Give us your trousers!"

Relathanye Ikitseng, the Mahalapye women's leader, interviewed in 1985, objected to this interpretation of moral looseness. Among the "Keaboka crowd" and the moderates there were many people just as puritanical as Tshekedi. (In teetotalism, no one could out do Tshekedi in fervor; but in broader questions of morality, wagging tongues catalogued the marital sins and divorces of Tshekedi and his forty-two followers.) According to Relathanye Ikitseng, the issue about which women demonstrated was quite simply the rightful succession of Seretse, which entailed the removal of Tshekedi and his followers. Yet, even if such issues were uppermost in the minds of the Mahalapye women, it is also true that under the rule of the Keaboka crowd at Serowe the strict control and even prohibition of beer brewing by Tshekedi was now relaxed. Mahalapye was the fastest growing urban center in Bechuanaland after Francistown, serving the needs of railroad passengers. Trains down the Cape-Rhodesia line stopped there for an hour or more for locomotives to be watered or changed. There was a growing market at Mahalapye for home-brewed beer and for the sale of delicacies collected in the veld, such as *phane* worms and *morula* plums, to the migrant workers from Bechuanaland, Angola, Northern Rhodesia, Nyasaland, and even Tanganyika who were shipped through by train from the Francistown labor depot to the Witwatersrand mines in South Africa.

Beginning in the later 1930s, with increased out-migration of able male labor to the South African mines, the 1940s and 1950s saw the growth of the rural phenomenon known to sociologists as the "female-headed household."[14] But such economic and social liberation from male domination was constrained by the marginal agricultural productivity of the land and the lack of oxen for plowing in female possession, exacerbated by the recovery of cattle prices in the 1940s after decades of market depression. Increasing numbers of Bangwato women were faced by the imperatives of how to feed the new "female-headed households." Mahalapye was the obvious center for such informal sector subsistence, and also the first stop on the train to domestic service abroad for which

---

[14]See P. Peters, "Gender, Development Cycles and Historical Process: a Critique of Recent Research on Women in Botswana," in *Journal of Southern African Studies* 10/1 (1983): 100-22; C. Kerven "Academics, Practitioners and All Kinds of Women in Development: A Reply to Peters," *ibid.* 10/2 (1984): 258-62; W. Izzard, "Migrants and Mothers: Case-studies from Botswana," *ibid.* 11/2 (1985): 258-80; I. Schapera, *Married Life in an African Tribe* (London: Faber, 1940) republished (Harmondsworth: Penguin, 1971).

Bangwato women with relatively widespread basic education were advantaged.[15] As a by-product of greater male agricultural activity and relative female inactivity, more Bangwato girls than boys were educated in school. Female consciousness of their status in society thereby arguably was raised. Tshekedi, like his father Khama III, saw himself as cleaning up the morals of the railroad townships. From another viewpoint, he had been holding back the self-sufficiency of women which helps to explain the vehemence of women's opposition to him in support of Seretse Khama's succession.

Conclusion

The Bangwato succession crisis of 1948-1953 opened up contradictions in Bangwato country and elsewhere. The political crisis, but not the problem of succession, was settled in 1953 by filling the vacuum of Bangwato chieftainship with the appointment of Rasebolai Kgamane—third in line in royal succession—as the native authority. Rasebolai, however, only gained popular legitimacy as interim ruler after Seretse Khama returned home in 1956. Seretse had renounced the chieftainship, but he remained the rightful kgosi in his peoples' eyes. In Weberian terms, Seretse had not only traditional legitimacy as kgosi of the Bangwato, but also gained in charisma because of his saint-like suffering for the sins of others, exile, and triumphant return in 1956. After 1966, as president of the Republic of Botswana, he could easily have also made himself legally legitimate as kgosi of the Bangwato. Yet he refrained from doing so, being content with what he saw as the greater legal-rationality of national rather than tribal leadership. The position of kgosi of the Bangwato was only filled in 1978 by formally recognizing his eldest son as titular rather than effectively ruling kgosi so as to give greater cover of legitimacy to the existing

---

[15]Female out-migration was a favorite, though not completely satisfactory, explanation for the anomaly of high masculinity (male:female) ratios in Botswana censuses up to 1956.

arrangements of rule by a so-called tribal authority after his own impending death.

The transmutation of traditional into legal-rational political leadership in a modern state separates Seretse Khama from nearly every other post-independence African head of government. Most political observers would point to this as an important element in Botswana's achievement of political stability and constitutional continuity since independence. But it was not just an automatic achievement. It was also a personal achievement by Seretse Khama: he consistently played down the traditional and charismatic elements of his popular legitimacy, and always stressed the legal-rational base of his presidency over the whole nation. As such, the political career of Seretse Khama provides an instructive contrast with other African leaders. Lawrence Peter Frank has compared the careers of Seretse Khama of Botswana and Leabua Jonathan of Lesotho. Having gained legal-rational status as head of a late colonial government, Leabua tried to achieve traditional and charismatic status after independence. He failed to do so while progressively losing his grip on the legal-rational mechanisms of statehood.[16] One could extend Frank's analogy to Lucas Mangope of Bophutatswana in South Africa, who explicitly took Seretse Khama for a role model but has reverted more to the model of Leabua Jonathan.

The Bangwato succession crisis of 1948-1953 illustrates the dangers of taking Weber's typology of legitimate authority too literally as a progression from superstition-bound tradition into the light of ever increasing rationality. The iron rule of primogeniture espoused by the Bangwato was based less on superstition than the externally imposed legal-rationality of the British which prevented Seretse Khama from royal succession. That "rationality" was ultimately based on irrationality—surrender to the shibboleths of white racial insecurity in Southern Africa. However, such legal-irrationality, though it remained the source of legitimate authority

---

[16]Lawrence Peter Frank, "Khama and Jonathan: A Study of Authority and Leadership in Southern Africa" (Ph.D. Diss., Columbia University, New York, 1974).

in South Africa, was superceded by a new kind of legal-rationality in Botswana based on a non-racial franchise and the fairer distribution of rising national income.

As this book emphasizes, succession to high office must be seen in the political context of factions jockeying for power and manipulating the rules of legitimacy in their own interests. It is possible in the case of the 1948-1953 succession crisis to trace back the history of various factions into the previous century.[17] But each faction is an exquisite and ever changing blend of personal ambitions and group interests. It is not possible to explain away the 1948-1953 crisis, as some British officials tried, simply as the product of "age-old bitterness, suspicion and intrigue" as if factions were fixed elements in the firmament. Factions rose, fell, adapted, and even swapped sides in the flux of political advantage and disadvantage. They were part of a much larger body politic. Their interest to political scientists and historians is as indicators of change in the body politic. For example, can we explain why some leading moderates (or frustrated feudalists) of 1948-1953 have become opponents of Seretse Khama's legitimate successors both as kgosi and as president since 1980?

The ultimate significance of the Bangwato succession crisis of 1948-1953 for Botswana political history is as the key-point in the transmutation of Botswana from tribalism to nationalism. Deriving good from evil, it enabled Seretse Khama to translate himself from tribal leader to national leader–the first president of the Republic of Botswana. Whatever his personal qualities, being hereditary ruler of the largest, richest, and most literate tribe in the country was obviously to his electoral advantage! The Ngwato state also set the pace for the other Tswana states that were combined into the nation-state of Botswana. The Ngwato state was converted from an autocratic (if progressive) state before 1949 to some kind of parliamentary democracy after 1956. The political

---

[17]See the Introduction to this volume.

perspectives of its leading figures, from Tshekedi and Seretse to Motsete and Koma, were turned outwards to national leadership.[18]

It is possible to argue that the Ngwato state, and by extension the Tswana states and Botswana as a whole, have always been a special case in Africa. As Fortes and Evans-Pritchard put it, in the introduction to their classic *African Political Systems* fifty years ago, the Ngwato state of all their African case studies most closely resembled a Western nation-state.[19] The Ngwato state had achieved the incorporation of a diversity of ethnic minorities within a common political structure, under the cultural-linguistic hegemony of a successful ruling minority. In that way, maybe the Botswana of today is merely yesterday's Ngwato state writ large. Yet is is essentially no different from the achievement of other traditional African states, or the aspirations of other modern African states. Botswana is only a special case in that it has not gone through the turmoil of post-independence socio-economic and constitutional experimentation. There has been much greater continuity between pre-independence and post-independence Botswana than in other modern African states, because important sections of the traditional establishment were forced to drastically modernize themselves during the later colonial period. This was at least as much due to extraordinary external intervention as to regular internal developments, as the 1948-1953 Bangwato succession crisis shows.

---

[18]See the Introduction to this volume and Appendices N-P for complaints of southern Botswana chiefs about Bangwato political activities in 1962.

[19]M. Fortes and E.E. Evans-Pritchard, eds., *African Political Systems* (London: Oxford University Press for the International African Institute, 1940), p. 22.

Chapter 4

SUCCESSION, LEGITIMACY, AND POLITICAL CHANGE IN BOTSWANA, 1956-1987

Jack Parson

Introduction

Seretse Khama, the first president of Botswana, died in office of natural causes on 13 July 1980. He was succeeded immediately by Quett Masire, a co-founder of the ruling Botswana Democratic party (BDP), sitting vice president of Botswana, and minister of finance and development planning. Quett Masire as president of the republic and BDP subsequently fought and won a regular general election in 1984, the fourth election since independence in 1966, remaining president of the republic of Botswana as well as his party. Constitutional and statutory law were observed in unremarkable and predictable detail throughout the process of succession and general election.

This last one of the three case studies on succession to high office is therefore the least fractious. Indeed, this succession hardly seems worthy of mention, its importance to the completion of Seretse Khama's life cycle notwithstanding. However, this smooth changing of the guard may indicate the presence of a successful process of parliamentary succession and its underpinning of legal-rational legitimacy. An exploration of this process *is* therefore of interest. In a review of continuity and change in the

Jack Parson

Bechuanaland and Botswana, political economy is a beginning point.[1]

Contours in the Political Economy of Change: 1956-1987

The crisis resulting from Seretse Khama's marriage ended with his return in 1956. The ensuing era unfolded in three periods. The most dramatic period began in 1956 with Seretse Khama's return and ended with the first post-independence elections in 1969. Constitutional principles changed from traditional to legal-rational ones resulting in the formation of political parties and the beginning of a new relationship between the chiefs and an elected national government. A state-centered mineral-led strategy of economic development produced relatively large-scale resources in the following decade (1969-1979). As a result, massive infrastructural facilities were built creating new services and jobs. This economic change underpinned the electoral popularity of the BDP government and the assertion of authority by the national government in general and in relation to tribal government in particular. The process of legally subordinating the chieftaincy continued although not without opposition. The electoral success of the main opposition party, the Botswana National Front (BNF), depended heavily upon ex-chief Bathoen's leadership.

The contradictions of continuity and change characterized the more mature 1980-1987 period. Economic change led to the development of new political factions and conflicts. Yet this did not result in familiar patterns of political instability. Multi-party competitive elections were held and political parties grew in their organization and activity. State allocated economic resources underpinned the folding of traditional authority systems into the legal-rational one and the hegemony of the latter over the former

---

[1]Some of the research for this chapter was supported by the Fulbright Senior Research Grant Program for Africa and was hosted at the University of Botswana (1984-1985) and by the College of Charleston (1987). The support of those agencies is gratefully acknowledged.

by 1987. While Seretse Khama's traditional status may have been exceptionally important to the establishment of national government authority in the early years of independence, it was much less so by the time of Quett Masire's succession to the presidency.

1956-1969: From the Bechuanaland Protectorate to the Republic of Botswana

By 1956 the British government was reconciled to the process leading to eventual independence (rather than incorporation into South Africa) for its High Commission Territories (Bechuanaland, Basutoland, and Swaziland). In Bechuanaland this reconciliation included the British government's capitulation on its exiling of Seretse Khama. He was allowed to return in 1956 and he then became vice chairman of the Bangwato Tribal Council as well as a member of the African Advisory Council, having foresworn his and his children's claims to the Bangwato throne.

The return of Seretse Khama in 1956 ushered in a decade of breathtaking political changes leading to the independence of the Republic of Botswana on 30 September 1966. During that same decade Seretse Khama went from being denied his chieftaincy, and his exile in Britain, to receiving an OBE from the British monarch, being named prime minister, and then elected first president of Botswana.

The essential details of the process leading to independence may be summarized easily. In 1959 the Joint Advisory Council recommended the creation of a Legislative Council, a recommendation accepted and announced by the colonial administration in December 1960.[2] Simultaneously, the Bechuanaland Peoples' party (BPP) was formally launched on a platform including the demand for independence. Its leaders were Motsamai Mpho, P.G. Matante, and K.T. Motsete. Legislative and executive councils were established in June of 1961. Seretse Khama, G. Mosinyi,

---

[2]The Joint Advisory Council (JAC) was created to bring together representatives of the previously separate African and European Advisory Councils. The JAC was created in 1951.

L.D. Raditladi, T. Tsheko, and A. Tsoebebe were elected to serve on it from the African Council representing the Northern Division and Chief Bathoen II, Chief Mokgosi, Quett Masire, Dr. S.M. Molema, and L. Mosielele were elected to represent the Southern Division. Seretse Khama and Chief Bathoen II were then selected to serve as nominated members on the executive council.[3]

The Bechuanaland Democratic party (BDP) was launched in January of 1962. Leading members of the legislative council (including Seretse Khama and Quett Masire) were among its leaders. It quickly became a virtual governing party. It was favored by the colonial authorities. The BPP was perceived by colonial authorities as being too radical, a perception shared by BDP leaders.

The resident commissioner announced a constitutional review for 1963 which resulted in the decision late in that year to bring Bechuanaland to self-government. The conference included representatives of the political parties and the chiefs as well as the European and Asian communities. By this time the BPP had split into two parties known at the time as the BPP (Motsete), at the conference represented by Motsete along with P.G. Matante and T.W. Motlhagodi, and the BPP (Mpho), represented by Mpho along with B.D. Macheng and M.M. Tlale. The BDP was represented by Seretse Khama, Quett Masire, and M.P.K. Nwako. Kgosi Bathoen II, Kgosi Mokgosi III, and Kgosi Linchwe II Kgafela

---

[3]See, "Lists of Members of Bechuanaland Protectorate Executive, Legislative and African Councils (as at 20th June, 1961)," in *The Constitution of the Bechuanaland Protectorate (1961)*, prepared by the Information Branch of the Bechuanaland Protectorate Government in co-operation with the Bechuanaland Book Centre (Lobatsi: Bechuanaland Book Centre, 1962), pp. 57-59, reprinted in W.J.A. Macartney, ed., *Readings in BOLESWA Government: Select Documents on the Government and Politics of Botswana, Lesotho and Swaziland* (Roma, Lesotho: UBLS Printing Unit, 1971).

represented the chiefs.[4] In June, 1964 the commonwealth secretary announced elections for March of 1965 at which time the BDP won twenty-eight Legislative Assembly seats while the BPP won three followed by the attainment of internal self-government on March 23rd.

A conference to discuss the timing for the achievement of independence was held in London in February 1966. Seretse Khama (now prime minister), Quett Masire (deputy prime minister), and P.G. Matante (leader of the opposition) represented the Legislative Assembly while Kgosi Bathoen II represented the House of Chiefs. Matante demanded further consultations on the constitutional proposals and the holding of new national elections before independence should be granted. He argued that the existing government did not have a mandate to bring the country to independence as such, only to self-government. Failing to persuade the other delegates, Matante left the conference and refused to endorse its recommendation to achieve full independence in 1966. The London conference was followed by local government elections and the achievement of independence on 30 September. Within the span of one decade Botswana went from being the neglected colonial Bechuanaland Protectorate to being the independent sovereign Republic of Botswana.

A change in the principle of legitimacy which underlay national political authority was at the heart of this political process of decolonization. This change was from an internal order based on traditional legitimacy controlled by an external colonial state, which was responsible to no one inside Bechuanaland, to one based on the principle of direct elections–from an order the central role of which was inherited to one controlled by universal suffrage elected by a representative legislature. This constitutional change did not eliminate the institution of chieftaincy. But the power of the chiefs was made subject to the authority of

---

[4]See *Bechuanaland Constitutional Proposals* (London: Her Majesty's Stationery Office, Cmnd. 2378), "List of Those Who Took Part in the Joint Consultations," reprinted in Macartney, *Readings in BOLESWA Government*, p. 85.

parliament and the president. The House of Chiefs was created to give the chiefs a collective voice in national political affairs but it was given no legislative power. In fact, while the constitution included the House of Chiefs in the section on parliament, the constitution's definition of parliament excluded the House. Moreover, the power to recognize, discipline, and even remove chiefs was by ordinary law to be placed in the hands of the president, a legal-rational role.

As the first elections approached, the chiefs were concerned about their future, but they did not jointly organize in opposition to the new order. As a consequence during the 1965 election their choices were limited.[5] They could (1) withdraw from politics, (2) individually campaign against the constitutional changes, or (3) come to terms with the political parties. The first two courses of action were untenable. To withdraw from the electoral arena entirely not only left the field completely open to the parties but would also be tantamount to an act of abdication: it would be an admission that there was a political order in which the chief had no role. The second course of action was equally unattractive. Chiefs who opposed the changes could be portrayed as opponents not only of progress but also as opponents of independence itself. Besides, a broad spectrum of dikgosana (those of high traditional status and royal blood) led by a chief (Seretse Khama) in the BDP were arguing the case for the compatibility, if not equality, of the legal-rational and traditional orders. How could a chief explain his opposition in such circumstances?

The chiefs individually, therefore, had to come to terms with the political parties. The idea of an open association with any of the BPPs was unappetizing. The national BPPs were viewed as hostile to the chieftaincy. In 1965, that left the BDP, the party of Seretse Khama. However, certain of the chiefs were skeptical about the intentions of the BDP toward the chiefs. On the one hand it *was* the party of a chief and much of its leadership was of royal descent, a feature of its leadership extending beyond the

---

[5]See Appendices N, O, and P.

boundaries of the Bangwato state. Moreover, the economic base of the chiefs in cattle, relying in part on traditional patron-client labor, seemed secure with the BDP. Its leadership shared this economic base and therefore could be expected to maintain those relations of production.

At the same time Seretse Khama had seemingly cut himself off from the chieftaincy and recruited to the party's leadership a large number of "new men" who could not be expected to automatically support the chieftaincy.[6] The economic interests of the new elements were potentially competitive, not complementary, to those of the chiefs. Chief Bathoen, for example, could not have easily imagined an alliance between himself and Quett Masire, one of the new men in Bangwaketse country, whose future was competitive with that of the chief and his "old men."

As a matter of policy, the BDP was cautious but unequivocal on the long-term surbordination of the chieftaincy. The election manifesto of the BDP in 1965 stated as follows:

> The Bechuanaland Democratic Party stands for a *gradual* but *sure* evolution of a national state in Bechuanaland, to which the tribal groups will, while they remain in existence, take a secondary place. This is an unavoidable development, an evolutionary law to which we must yield to survive, or resist and disappear as a people. Except in very vital issues such as the investing of mineral rights in the Central Government, the party does not, however, intend to force the pace in the process of subjecting local and tribal interests to national ones.

At the same time that tribal government would be subordinated, it would also be internally reformed. Councils to assist chiefs and to foster inter-tribal organization would be developed.

---

[6]See Adam Kuper, *Kalahari Village Politics: An African Democracy* (London: Cambridge University Press, 1970), particularly Chapter 3, pp. 49-60.

The evolution of democratic institutions and practices in tribal administrations must, however, be maintained and where possible the rate of their development must be accelerated. Likewise all moves towards closer inter-tribal co-operation will be encouraged, such, for instance, as the organisation of tribal and other groups into local councils, into which smaller tribal units will be absorbed for their own economic benefit, even if they retained a small measure of tribal identity.[7]

This ascendancy of the national government was to be not only political but also economic. The BDP Government was committed to transferring all but the most insignificant sources of tribal administration revenue to the soon-to-be-created district

---

[7]BDP, *Election Manifesto*, January, 1965, p. 5, reprinted in Macartney, *Readings in BOLESWA Government.* An answer to the question of what led the BDP to formulate its strategy toward the chieftaincy in this way is beyond the scope of this case study. Chief Bathoen, among others, in the very late colonial period argued that the reason was the fact that the chieftaincy was dead in the Bangwato Territory as a result of the dispute over Seretse's marriage and therefore the Bangwato were turning to parties. See Appendices N-P for these views. Alternatively, Larry Frank argues that Seretse Khama chose a legal-rational model for his own political career and the future of the country. See Lawrence Frank, "Khama and Jonathan: Leadership Strategies in Contemporary Southern Africa," in *The Journal of Developing Areas* 15 (1981): 173-98. In a broader historical context these policies were reminiscent of the attempt by the colonial administration in the 1930s to introduce similar "reforms," an attempt which was singularly unsuccessful because of the opposition of the chiefs. At that time the popular base supported the chiefs and held the colonial government at bay. See Michael Crowder's excellent book, *The Flogging of Phinehas McIntosh: A Tale of Colonial Folly and Injustice, Bechuanaland 1933* (New Haven: Yale University Press, 1988), for a discussion of this. See also Louis A. Picard, *The Politics of Development in Botswana: A Model for Success?* (Boulder: Lynne Rienner Publishers, 1987), particularly chapter 3, "Bureaucrats and Chiefs: Contradictions of Indirect Rule," pp. 46-69.

councils. Most important the party was committed to removing mineral rights from the tribal (and private company) to the national state level. The 1965 BDP Manifesto argued as follows:

> If discovered in good quantities and exploited to the full, minerals should ultimately serve to boost up the economy of Bechuanaland and take precedence over all other national products. Consequently leaving mineral rights vested in tribal authorities and private companies must necessarily result in uneven growth of the country's economy, as well as deprive the Central Government of an important source of revenue for developing the country.
> With this in view it will be the policy of the BDP government to negotiate with all parties concerned the takeover of the country's mineral rights by the Central Government, and subsequently expand the present mining operations and step up prospecting activities throughout the Territory.[8]

While the justification for this was obvious—to prevent divisive and capricious regional (tribal) disparities—it also removed the potential economic base for tribal independence and competition with the new national government.

The BDP stood for an "unavoidable" and "sure" process subordinating the traditional, tribal states. At the same time the process would be a "gradual" one characterized by the increasing democratization of tribal government through the encouragement of tribal councils directly representative of the people. The BDP, having determined the direction of change, would not force the pace. The chiefs, assuming that they in turn accepted the hegemony of the national state, could continue to exist.

For the most part the chiefs were reconciled to a BDP election victory. Most lent tacit support to the BDP. A notable

---

[8]Frank, "Khama and Jonathan," p. 6.

exception to this during the 1965 election campaign seems to have been in Mochudi where the BPP candidate, T.W. Motlhagodi, won the election with 2,163 votes in comparison with a BDP vote of 1,278 for its candidate, R.D. Molefe, and a distant third vote of 407 for Motsamai Mpho's Bechuanaland Independence party (BIP) candidate, S. Tladi. The BPP win was interpreted as a victory not for the BPP as much as a victory for Chief Linchwe II Kgafela.

The origins of the BPP in Mochudi appear to be related to a dispute between the then regent for Linchwe II (Mmusi) and a group called *Mphetsebe* (lend me your ears) led by Modisa Moremi and D. Seame. This faction, which later formed the initial membership of the BPP led by Moremi and Seame, seems to "have been speaking for Bakgatla who were removed from the royal circle and therefore wanted their opinions to be heard too." The faction then "used BPP politics to promote its local image, although it shared the party's broad nationalist aspirations."[9]

Mphetsebe alleged that Mmusi was inefficient and urged his replacement with Tshire Kgafela, Linchwe's elder sister. This did not happen. Linchwe was installed in 1963. However it appears that Tshire in turn strongly supported the BPP so much so that it is said that in 1965 she openly urged a BPP vote which stood for Linchwe and the chieftaincy. Linchwe himself opened a BPP conference in Mochudi in 1963 although he publicly remained politically neutral.[10] After the elections Linchwe was aligned with the BPP members on the Kgatleng District Council. His association with the BPP thus became an expression of a chief's autonomy. There may also have been a backlash of votes toward the BDP in Mochudi as a result of this history of the BPP. The royal family was not united and the anti-Linchwe factor may have given support to the BDP on these grounds. In addition, at least one minority community in Mochudi, the Bakalanga, appear to

---

[9]Monty Moswela, "Politics in Kgatleng: Parochialism versus Nationalism," University of Botswana History Department dissertation in partial fulfillment of the requirements for the B.A. Degree, 1980, p. 3.

[10]Moswela, "Politics in Kgatleng," p. 3.

have supported the BDP against the perception of their historical subjugation to the Bakgatla represented by the chief and the party identified with him, the BPP.[11]

Nationally the BDP swept the elections losing only two seats in the northeast (Tati West and Francistown & Tati East) in addition to Mochudi. In the Bangwaketse Tribal Territory, the home of kgosi Bathoen II, who subsequently became the leading public opponent of diminishing the power of the chieftaincy, the BDP easily won all three seats. Quett Masire for the BDP polled 3,700 votes handing defeats to both his BIP opponent (M. Ketshabile, 77 votes) and Matante's BPP candidate (P. Maruping, 89 votes).[12]

A result of the elections was a series of meetings among potential opposition leaders between March and October 1965. Chief Linchwe and Kenneth Koma appear to have worked independently to stimulate and sustain these discussions. While the debate did not lead to the creation of a united opposition to the BDP, it did lead to the creation of the Botswana National Front (BNF) paving the way for Chief Bathoen's eventual membership in the BNF and his entry into the national assembly as an elected member of parliament.

---

[11]This is, of course, a good example of the situational character of ethnicity and the fact that its politicization is circumstantial and not inherent. While in the northeast many Bakalanga supported the BPP, in Mochudi a significant number of Bakalanga supported the BDP. Both instances were related to an historical position of subordination. See Ben Mwalimu wa Nkosana, "Bakgatla/Bakalanga Relations: Politics of the Integration of a Minority," University of Botswana History Department dissertation in partial fulfillment of the requirements for the B.A. Degree, 1980, particularly pp. 7, 9, and 15. Concerning the situational relationship between ethnicity and class see Nelson Kasfir, ed., *State and Class in Africa* (London: Frank Cass, 1984).

[12]Vote totals from *Statistical Abstract, 1967*, (Gaborone: The Government Printer, no date). Candidate information from Botswana National Archives (BNA), "Botswana General Elections," Office of the President, I/10/3086, H 4/10 I.

After several years of academic training abroad, mainly in eastern Europe, Kenneth Koma returned to Bechuanaland shortly before the 1965 legislative assembly election. Early in March of 1965 a government intelligence summary reported that Koma was attempting to form a "united front" composed of the BPP and BIP to be led by Koma's "very good friend" Rydewell Molomo as president and Koma as secretary general. Matante and Mpho of the BPP and BIP respectively had, it was said, "overtly shown interest" in the scheme.[13]

In April 1965, a month after the legislative assembly election, certain traditional leaders–reportedly Chief Linchwe, Chief Letsholathebe (of the Batawana), and Seepapitso Gaseitsiwe (the son of and heir to Chief Bathoen)–held "secret discussions" with representatives of both the BIP and BPP. The result was reported to be an agreement in principle "to form an alliance of politicians and tribal leaders to provide powerful opposition to the BDP." The discussions at this stage did not seem to directly include Koma which the colonial government regarded as a setback for Koma.[14] These discussions widened at a meeting on 30 May 1965 when nineteen "prominent personalities and politicians" met under Linchwe's chairmanship. There continued to be a significant split, however, on the issue of Koma's proposed united front. Eight of those attending, including Linchwe and K.T. Motsete, were reported to have expressed interest in Koma's proposals while eight (including Seepapitso who was soon to go his own way in his short-lived Botswana National Union and Mpho of the BIP) opposed the idea. Three participants were non-commital. It was agreed to meet again on 27 June following "perusal by all concerned of a lengthy document prepared by Koma." The document was what became BNF Pamphlet No. 1 expressing the need to struggle against what was regarded as a neo-colonialist and anti-chief BDP government. The colonial authorities, for their

---

[13]BNA, Office of the President, I/6/2986, 23/2, Volume II.

[14]BNA, Office of the President, I/6/2986, 23/2, Volume II, Central Intelligence Committee, Report for the Month of April, 1965, pp. 3-4.

part, were optimistic that some, specifically Chief Linchwe, would think twice about forming an alliance with Koma after reading the document which in the view of colonial authorities was "couched in Communist dialectical gibberish."[15]

The national leadership of the established opposition parties refused to come into a united front coalition. A BPP national executive committee meeting was held on 20 June 1965 at which Matante was reported to have expressed his "unequivocal refusal to have anything to do with the united front proposals of Kenneth Koma." He also flatly rejected the suggestion of associating with an alternative opposition regrouping led by Seepapitso. The meeting on 27 June was held anyway in Mochudi at which time the BIP secretary general said he had been sent to reiterate that the BIP would not agree to Koma's plans. Seepapitso's plans to unilaterally form a new party were known by this time and the meeting ended with Koma's call to meet again at a later date.[16] A further meeting took place at the Mochudi Community Centre on August 25. Thirty-four persons were present including Koma, Seepapitso, Motlhagodi, Rydewell Molomo, Daniel Kwele, and representatives, but not national leaders, of the BIP and the BPP. Chief Linchwe was reported to have declared that he was not a member of any political organization but did chair the meeting. Koma discussed the document on "National Democratic Culture" and answered questions. Linchwe wanted to know Koma's attitude toward the chiefs and Koma reportedly said that they would eventually disappear. Molomo apparently advocated the establishment of the BNF while the existing opposition wanted to form a working committee of representatives. At the end of the

---

[15]BNA, Office of the President, I/6/2986, 23/2, Volume II, Central Intelligence Committee, Report for May, 1965.

[16]BNA, Office of the President, I/6/2986, 23/2, Volume II, Central Intelligence Committee, Report for June 1965, pp. 2-5.

meeting Linchwe proposed taking an additional three weeks to think about the matter.[17]

Linchwe's attitude of pressing ahead despite the assertion that the chiefs would disappear under a BNF government as well as under the BDP may seem incongruous. However, Koma's document actually provided significant concessions to the chiefs. While the BDP government was headed toward a quick elimination of the local power of chiefs and their isolation nationally in the advisory House of Chiefs, the "national democratic culture" and struggle would provide a very gradual elimination of the power of chiefs. First of all the House of Chiefs would be eliminated and the chiefs would automatically be members of parliament itself. Only later would those eight seats become special electoral constituencies which would be uncontested seats for the chiefs. At a much later date the chiefs would be removed from the assembly to a House of Nationalities to be composed of a variety of groups such as unions, youth, and others. From that point of view the BNF offered, at least on paper, a better deal than did the BDP.

The decision to launch the BNF was made at meetings in Mochudi on 2 and 3 October 1965. Linchwe was absent, having asked for a week's postponement which was not arranged. Having decided to launch the front, officers were elected including Rydewell Molomo as president, Daniel Kwele as vice president, and Koma as secretary for external affairs. Molomo, like Linchwe, was absent and despite his election seems never to have assumed that office. It was agreed to postpone a public announcement until 10 October. A closed meeting was held late in the morning of that day with eighty persons present. Linchwe took the chair for the final time and was reported to have explained that he, as a member of the House of Chiefs, was debarred from taking an active part in politics. Adding that he acted as chairman at previous meetings merely to ensure peaceful proceedings, Chief

---

[17]BNA, Office of the President, I/8/3035, Special Branch to Permanent Secretary, Ministry of Home Affairs.

Linchwe concluded by saying that he would withdraw now that there appreared to be some form of unity. He then left the meeting. Molomo continued to be absent and Kwele chaired the meeting. The Molepolole BPP defected to the BNF and it was accepted by certain BPP local notables in Mochudi but neither the BIP nor the BPP as political parties joined the BNF. That afternoon a public meeting gave the BNF an enthusiastic reception.[18]

The BNF thus came into existence with at least the tacit support of Linchwe and it continued to court others interested in maintaining the chieftaincy. But it did not serve to unify the chiefs in opposition to the BDP. Bathoen and Seepapitso continued to keep to themselves. The other opposition parties stayed away and the BNF was increasingly viewed by them as hostile, not as an umbrella to bring together those who opposed the BDP. The coming local government elections could be faced by the BDP, therefore, knowing that there was some chiefly opposition but also knowing that the chiefs' opposition and the opposition generally were badly divided. There was little prospect for the formation of a united opposition as the debates among its members in 1965 showed.

These discussions were evidence that certain chiefs recognized the marginalization of the traditional political order. This continued as district and town councils were elected in 1966 before independence. The BDP won control of all the councils except the North East district and Francistown town councils.[19] The jurisdictional boundaries of the district councils coincided where possible with the geographical boundaries of the tribal territories. The new councils were given functional authority over a range of local services including education, certain roads, and

---

[18]BNA, Office of the President, I/8/3035.

[19]Jack Parson, "The 1984 Botswana General Elections and Results: A Macro-Analysis," paper prepared for the conference on preliminary results from the 1984 University of Botswana Election Study Project, May, 1985, Table 12, p. 44.

the collection of local government tax. They also had some licensing powers. Although the chiefs were initially made ex-officio chairmen of the district councils, the basis of the councils' authority was their electoral mandate and national law. After independence the chiefs' powers were reduced further. The right of the chiefs to the proceeds from the sale of *matimela* (stray) cattle was transferred to the councils. Most of the staff and assets of the chiefs' administrative organizations were transferred to the district councils. The creation of Village Development Committees further obfuscated the situation. Their relation to the kgotla and the traditional process of decision-making as well as the councils was ill-defined. By 1969 the BDP election manifesto asserted that the district councils were "here to stay" and in combination with the Village Development Committees represented a reformed district administration which had gone a long way to replacing the traditional functions of the old tribal administration. The kgotla remained but its main function was seen to be that of an occasion for direct communication between the president and his ministers and the people of the villages. It was accepted that the chiefs still had a role but it was for them to demonstrate to the people that they were capable of discharging their responsibilities in a manner that was fully compatible with the best interests of the people and the nation. At the same time the BDP promised to continue eroding the resources the chiefs needed to demonstrate that capacity: "the next BDP Government will rationalise the present wasteful duplication, which still exists in certain areas, between District Councils and the surviving elements of the traditional administration," a rationalization which by no stretch of the imagination would be advantageous to the chiefs.[20]

The BDP paid a price for these actions after independence. Certain chiefs and a portion of the electorate understood and objected to the change in the basic principles upon which the

---

[20]Botswana Democratic Party, *Election Manifesto 1969*, issued by Q.K.J. Masire, General Secretary, Botswana Democratic Party, reprinted in Macartney, *Readings in BOLESWA Government*, pp. 224-25.

polity was based. Chief Bathoen of the Bangwaketse resigned his chieftaincy, joined the new BNF, and won a seat in the 1969 National Assembly elections. In that election he defeated the BDP candidate who happened to be Quett Masire, at the time deputy leader of the BDP, vice president of the republic, and minister of finance and development planning.

The rapid and far-reaching political changes in the period between 1956 and 1969 were not matched in the economy. The main industry continued to be the production of migratory, mainly adult male labor for the farms, factories, and particularly the mines of white South Africa. Nearly half of adult males were so occupied in 1943.[21] In 1964 more than one-third of males aged twenty to thirty-five were migrant workers. More than twice as many persons were working in South Africa as were recorded in employment inside Bechuanaland. The main domestic economy relied on cattle production but the ownership of herds was very unequal with the direct beneficiaries being large-herd owners. There were few good roads, little commerce, few primary schools, and no government secondary schools until 1966. Even the capital remained in Mafeking, South Africa until shortly before independence. Colonial Development and Welfare Funds increased in volume but were spread very thin. Most of this money was spent on infrastructure. In the period leading up to 1966 it was spent on building Gaborone in time to hold independence celebrations in a capital city inside the country. While mining prospects were promising, the overall condition of the economy and standard of living for the vast majority of people were poor and were improving only marginally.[22]

---

[21]Isaac Schapera, *Migrant Labour and Tribal Life: A Study of Conditions in the Bechuanaland Protectorate* (London: Oxford University Press, 1947), p. 39.

[22]Sources on the economy and its development during the period would include the following: *Basutoland, Bechuanaland Protectorate and Swaziland: Report of an Economic Survey Mission* (London: HMSO, 1960); Report of the Ministry of Overseas Development Economic Survey

The combination of economic promises but few direct benefits along with the political conflicts over the legitimacy of the national government created an unfavorable environment for the BDP as it faced the general elections in 1969. The formation of the BNF was a political focus around which could coalesce the disparate, sometimes contradictory, elements which were opposed to the national BDP government. As a result, in the 1969 National Assembly elections the opposition parties won seven of thirty-one seats, an accomplishment for the opposition not to be approached again until 1984. Mpho won the Okavango for the BIP, the BPP held its three seats, and the BNF won all three seats in the Bangwaketse district, including that won by Bathoen, beating Masire by 740 votes.[23] In the district and town council elections–held simultaneously with the National Assembly elections–the BNF won twenty-three seats including eleven of twenty-four in the Southern (Ngwaketse) council and four out of the eight seats in both the Lobatse and Gaborone town councils. The BPP retained its seats won in the Central district, Kgatleng district, and Francistown town councils and increased the number of its seats slightly in Ghanzi, the North East, and the South East.[24]

1969-1979: Continuity and Change

The subsequent decade (1969-1979) brought both continuity and change. The formal process of subordinating traditional to

---

Mission, *The Development of the Bechuanaland Economy* (Gaborone: The Government Printer, 1966); and Quill Hermans, "A Review of Botswana's Financial History, 1900-1973," in *Botswana Notes and Records* 6 (1974): 89-116.

[23]See *Report on the General Elections 1969* (Gaborone: The Government Printer, 1970).

[24]District and Town Council results from Parson, "The 1984 Botswana General Elections," pp. 44, 45.

national government authority continued and became routine through the "technical" process of development planning and project implementation. Chiefs were removed as chairmen of the district councils although they remained members and could be elected chairman if the elected councillors so chose. The chiefs were forced to share the power to allocate land with the creation of land boards. The land boards now had representatives from both the central Ministry of Local Government and Lands and the district councils, thus reducing the voice of the chief to one of three participants. In 1975 the Tribal Land Act was amended to give the president the power to alter any decision of any land board. Considering the fact that until land boards were created the chief had more or less unbridled formal authority to allocate land, these developments represented a substantial decrease in the power of chiefs.

Increasingly both the chiefs and the district councils found themselves at a disadvantage in the process of development planning and project implementation. They relied more and more heavily on the financial resources and technical personnel of central government departments. The central government created district development committees supported by new officials—district officers (development) and district officers (lands)—supervised by the district commissioners. The district commissioner's authority grew as he was given the power to inspect the books and otherwise directly intervene in the work of the district councils.[25] In the central government, "the principle of gradually removing the powers of the chiefs [was] one which command[ed] the general support of all ministries," although there was intra-bureaucratic

---

[25]The elaboration of the district administration and the role of the district commissioner is chronicled in William Tordoff, "Local Administration in Botswana, Parts I and II," in *Journal of Administration Overseas* 12/4 (1973): 172-84 and 13/1 (1974): 292-305.

conflict on the question of decentralizing functions to the district councils.[26]

By the late 1970s the chieftaincy retained its form but with greatly reduced functions. Vengroff concluded that "the prime source of 'formal' authority remaining in the hands of the tribal leaders is control over the Kgotla."[27] While this conclusion overstates the case–chiefs continued to have some authority over

---

[26] John Speed, "Developing Land Boards as Local Government Institutions," SSRC Conference on Land Tenure in Botswana, 1978, p. 4. An anecdotal but graphic illustration of the attitude of at least one district commissioner (DC) toward his role in relation to the chief occurred in 1974 when I was about to conduct research on the general election in Molepolole, the district capital of Kweneng District. During a courtesy call on the DC, I inquired as to whether or not the chief would be in his office and, it being during normal government working hours, the DC replied: "He had better be - he works for me!"

[27] Richard Vengroff, *Botswana: Rural Development in the Shadow of Apartheid* (Cranbury: Associated University Presses, 1977), p. 59. The following are among the more useful secondary sources on the recent history of chieftaincy and chieftaincy politics: John Wiseman, "The Organisation of Political Conflict in Botswana: 1966-73" (Ph.D. Thesis, University of Manchester, 1976); J.H. Proctor, "The House of Chiefs and the Political Development of Botswana," in *Journal of Modern African Studies* 6/1 (1968): 59-80; Simon Gillett, "The Survival of Chieftaincy in Botswana," in *African Affairs* 72/287 (1973): 179-85; Louis Picard, *The Politics of Development in Botswana: A Model for Success?* (Boulder: Lynne Rienner, 1987); the special number of the *Journal of African Law* on "Land Reform in the Making: Tradition, Public Policy and Ideology in Botswana," (edited by Richard Werbner) 24/1 (1980). See also the exchange between Robson Silitshena, "Chiefly Authority and the Organisation of Space in Botswana: Towards an Exploration of Nucleated Settlements Among the Tswana," pp. 55-67, and Sandy Grant," 'Reduced almost to nothing'? Chieftaincy and a traditional town. The case of Linchwe II Kgafela and Mochudi," pp. 89-100, in *Botswana Notes and Records*, volumes 11 and 12, and Silitshena's rejoinder, "Chiefly Authority and Organisation of Space in Botswana: Some Clarifications and Restatements," pp. 155-56 in *Botswana Notes and Records*, vol. 13.

land allocations, sat on district councils, and performed real judicial functions–there can be no doubt that the authority of the chiefs had been eroded. By 1974 the BDP manifesto, which was becoming a much more technically oriented document, dropped specific reference to the chieftaincy. Subsequent manifestos were likewise quiet on the subject, the BDP indicating that from its point of view a more or less successful conclusion had been reached.[28]

The political basis for continuing opposition from the chiefs was present but election results in both 1974 and 1979 indicated no appreciable change in support for their position. The BNF proportion of the total vote fell to 11.5 percent in 1974 and recovered to 12.9 percent in 1979 but in both years fell short of its inaugural appearance at 13.5 percent in 1969. As a result it lost one of its three seats, Vice President Masire winning his constituency for the BDP, although not against Bathoen who won a seat in Kanye, the district (tribal) capital, in both 1974 and 1979. The BNF retained its two seats in 1979. The BPP lost Mochudi in 1974, its perennial candidate, Mr. Motlhagodi, having died, and the BPP lost Francistown in 1979 subsequent to the death of P.G. Matante. After the 1979 election the BPP held a national assembly seat in the North East. Mpho held his seat in 1974 but lost the Okavango constituency to the BDP in 1979. In district council elections in 1974 the BNF won eleven seats (down from fifteen in 1969) ten of which were in the Southern district council. In 1979 it won only those ten seats. In town council elections the BNF won only one in 1974, a far cry from the fifty percent of the seats won in Lobatse and Gaborone in 1969. In 1979 it recovered only to two seats (out of eight) in Lobatse and one seat in Gaborone.[29]

---

[28]See Botswana Democratic Party, *Election Manifesto 1974* issued by Q.K.J. Masire, General Secretary, and Botswana Democratic Party, *Election Manifesto 1984* issued by D.K. Kwelagobe, General Secretary.

[29]Data on the 1974 and 1979 elections is from Parson, "The 1984 Botswana General Elections," pp. 39, 45.

Chief Linchwe II Kgafela's politics during the period were more subtle than Bathoen's bolt to the BNF before the 1969 elections. Linchwe appeared to become more amenable to the BDP, or at least wished to prevent too close an association with any party including the BPP. He served as Botswana's ambassador to Washington and gave at least tacit support to the BDP in both 1974 and 1979. The BPP proportion of the votes in 1974 in Mochudi declined to 21.8 percent and the BNF captured 18.0 percent of the votes but the BDP won the election with 60.2 percent of the votes.

Far from embracing the BNF, despite his earlier involvement in the events leading to its formation, Chief Linchwe found himself in conflict with one of the BNF's local leaders. Rrapula Sello of Morwa attempted to speak in kgotla only to be told by Linchwe that he (Sello) should sit down, that the kgotla was not a freedom square. This was perceived as a personal humiliation for Sello and as a deliberate attempt to suppress the BNF. Later the chief's car was burned and Sello was accused of perpetrating the crime. The case dragged on in 1977-1978, Sello being convicted of burning the chief's car then winning acquittal on appeal. The chief's disengagement with the BPP combined with these events may well have played a role in the BDP's having increased its proportion of the votes in 1979 to 62 percent. It may also have been the important factor in the BNF's failure to sponsor a candidate at all in the 1979 national assembly election in the Mochudi constituency. It did lead to the perception that the chief was now an ally, if only tacitly, of the BDP.[30]

The decade from 1969 to 1979 witnessed a decline in the political salience of the competition between legitimate authority based on traditional versus legal-rational principles. A major factor underpinning this decline was the significant economic

---

[30] This account is taken from Jack Parson, "Elections and Politics in the Mochudi National Assembly Constituency, 1984," a paper prepared as part of the conference on preliminary results from the 1984 University of Botswana Election Study Project, May, 1985. See also *Botswana Daily News*, June-July, 1977.

growth which took place. This growth lent credibility to the central government's claim to legitimate authority superior to all other levels and principles of governing.

Decisions to exploit the copper/nickel ore deposits at Selibi and Phikwe and the diamond deposits at Orapa in the Central district began the process of economic change. The resulting investments, which contributed to the generation of substantial government revenue after the renegotiation of the Southern African Customs Union Agreement in 1969, created jobs and new resources.[31] The earlier decision to remove mineral rights to the central government and the insistence upon joint government-private investor ownership insured a paramount role for the national government in determining the allocation of economic resources.[32] This was one of two key elements in the emerging mineral-led strategy of development. The second element was the policy of "re-investing the proceeds of these investments to promote labour intensive activities and improve services in rural areas."[33] Domestic resources generated from capital intensive mining combined with substantial in-flows of foreign assistance, both channelled through the central government, were supposed to be used for the purpose of rural development.

The Selibi-Phikwe mine did not meet expectations. The diamond mines, however, were successful and substantial resources and employment became available. By 1980, 7,200 persons were

---

[31]See P.M. Landell-Mills, "The 1969 Southern African Customs Union Agreement," in *Journal of Modern African Studies* 9/2 (1971): 263-82.

[32]The Government initially owned 15 percent of both the Selibi-Phikwe and Orapa mines. However in the mid-1970s the diamond mining arrangement changed, with DeBeers agreeing to a 50-50 deal. In addition, the Botswana Government purchased part of the equity in the Jwaneng mine in the southern part of the country near Kanye.

[33]*Rural Development in Botswana* Government Paper No. 1 of 1972 (Gaborone: The Ministry of Finance and Development Planning, 1972), p. 2.

employed directly in mining. The contribution of mining to gross domestic product had increased from 6.5 percent in 1974/75 to 34 percent. The direct contribution to government revenue from mining amounted to P 47.7 million or about 28.9 percent of total revenue, an increase from 13.5 percent in 1974/75.[34] From 1973 to 1981 approximately P 343 million worth of domestic funds and foreign aid were spent by the central government on development projects. About three-quarters of this went for the building of roads, urban development, primary and secondary education, rural water supplies, administrative infrastructure, and health services.[35]

For the most part these expenditures were uncontentious and their impact more or less evenly distributed from district to district. Schools existed where none had been previously. The government committed itself to free primary education for all children. Roads were built which carried people and goods more cheaply and in greater quantity than before. Safer water supplies made life both more secure and healthy for substantial numbers of households. These improvements were the work of a central government which had not existed a few short years before. The message sent to the population at large and to the factions of which it was composed was that the central government did matter, it delivered the goods, and popular acquiescence to it insured that this would continue. A vote for this was of course also a vote for the BDP insuring that it continued to be the governing party. While a chief and other local-level political leaders could associate themselves with these improvements, they could not claim direct credit for them. The credibility of the

---

[34]*Employment Survey (August, 1980)* (Gaborone: The Government Printer, 1981), Table 1, p. 10, and *National Development Plan 1979-85* (Gaborone: The Government Printer, 1980), pp. 184-85.

[35]*Estimates of Recurrent Expenditure and Estimate of Revenue and Expenditure of the Development Fund for the Year 1976/77* (Gaborone: The Government Printer, n.d.), pp. 159-215, and *National Development Plan 1976-81* (Gaborone: The Government Printer, 1977), pp. 365-66, and 369-84.

national government was increased. It improved living conditions and as a party government this improvement reflected on the BDP. The significance of this was not lost on the BDP for in 1974 the Accelerated Rural Development Programme was designed to ensure the completion of visible projects in rural areas by election day.[36]

At a mass level evidence existed of renewed support for the BDP in 1974 and 1979, and by implication of enhanced acceptance of the national government. The turnout of registered and eligible voters declined dramatically in 1974[37] but rebounded to 58.4 percent of registered voters in 1979.[38] A survey of rural households in 1974 indicated a significant proportion of the population who knew who the president was (81.0 percent), were registered to vote (63.6 percent), intended to vote (84.5 percent), and who believed that the government had helped a lot (43.6 percent) or at least a little (20.6 percent) in making life more comfortable since independence.[39] Politics seemed to matter and the focus of popular perceptions in terms of material life focussed on the central government.

The elite also presented a more or less united front. There was significant unity within the ruling BDP and between it and leaders in some opposition parties on the necessity of infrastructural development. No faction could argue that it had the capital or expertise to develop the mines. There was, therefore,

---

[36]See the review of the ARDP by Robert Chambers, *Botswana's Accelerated Rural Development Programme, 1973-76* (Gaborone: The Government Printer, 1977).

[37]A discussion of certain aspects of the 1974 electorate turnout is contained in Jack Parson, "A Note on the 1974 General Election in Botswana and the UBLS Election Study," in *Botswana Notes and Records*, Vol. 7, 1975, pp. 73-80.

[38]See Parson, "The 1984 Botswana General Elections."

[39]Jack Parson, "Political Culture in Rural Botswana: A Survey Result," in *Journal of Modern African Studies* 15/4 (1977): 644.

little criticism of the government's adopting this role in partnership with South African capital. Large-scale cattle owners as well as those with small herds needed better transportation and facilities at the Botswana Meat Commission in Lobatse. Civil servants and others welcomed a heavy expenditure on urban development where they lived. There were few voices of dissent among the elite and enough resources, internal and external, to benefit if not satisfy everyone.

The results of the survey of the electorate in 1974 indicated high levels of voter registration, intention to vote, and satisfaction with the performance of the state. These results were ironic: this voter survey was appended to the Rural Income Distribution Survey (RIDS) which indicated significant levels of poverty and a pattern of highly unequal ownership of cattle. Ownership of cattle was the most important agricultural asset. The RIDS indicated that 45 percent of households owned no cattle at all and that 83.8 percent owned twenty-five or fewer. Forty-five percent of households had incomes below the poverty line.[40] Given the fact that candidates for political office, office holders, and senior civil servants tended to be large-scale cattle holders, it was apparently inconsistent for there to be such a positive mass feeling toward voting and the services of the state.[41] This is especially inconsistent considering that the main policy initiative in the period, apart from mining and infrastructure, was the Tribal

---

[40]*Rural Income Distribution Survey in Botswana 1974/75* (Gaborone: The Government Printer, n.d.), pp. 111, 223. See also Carol Bond, *Women's Involvement in Agriculture* (Gaborone: The Government Printer, 1974), and Michael Lipton, *Employment and Labour Use in Botswana* Final Report (Gaborone: The Government Printer, 1978), two volumes.

[41]See John D. Holm, "Rural Development in Botswana: Three Basic Trends," in *Rural Africana*, 1972, pp. 80-92, and Dennis L. Cohen, "The Botswana Political Elite: Evidence from the 1974 General Election," in *Journal of Southern African Affairs* 4 (1979): 347-70.

Grazing Lands Policy (TGLP) the most obvious beneficiaries of which would be those who were already large-scale cattle owners.[42]

The TGLP did not prove to be a source of enduring conflict in the BDPs elite-mass relationship for four reasons: first, the opposition of interest between those with and those without cattle was cross-cut by traditional patron-client relations of employment on cattle-posts as well as traditional relations of lending cattle through mafisa arrangements. The relationship between cattle-owner and non-cattle-owner was therefore based on relations of seeming cooperation, not direct conflict. Second, the TGLP amounted to legalizing existing allocations of land (through water rights) rather than becoming a program of major new, disruptive land allocations; hence no new political antagonisms of national significance were automatically created. Third, the impact of any advantage to large-scale cattle owners was ameliorated by the improvements in rural life resulting from infrastructural developments including the creation of new employment opportunities. Everyone seemingly was better-off. Fourth, within the national political elite there was as yet little in the way of organized competition among diverse factions. The time had not yet arrived when intra-elite factional conflict required that faction leaders mobilize their own personal mass base.

In general, then, there *seemed* to be a congruence of mass and elite interests, underpinned by the economic changes which were taking place. The perception of this congruence was also an acquiescence in the role played by the elected national

---

[42]A selection of documents and analyses of the TGLP would include the following: *National Policy on Tribal Grazing Land*, Government Paper No. 2 of 1975, (Gaborone: The Government Printer, 1975); Jack Parson, "Class and the State in Rural Botswana," in *Journal of Southern African Studies* 7 (1981): 236-55; Lionel Cliffe and Richard Moorsom, "Rural Class Formation and Ecological Collapse in Botswana," in *Review of African Political Economy* 16 (1980): 35-52; and, *Lefatshe La Rona—Our Land: The Report on the Botswana Government's Consultation on Its Policy Proposals on Tribal Grazing Land* (Gaborone: The Government Printer, 1977).

government. To that extent its legitimacy was enhanced. This automatically reduced, but did not eliminate, the relative legitimacy of the traditional order reducing the likelihood of an opposition politics relying primarily upon that source for support. Seretse Khama's presidency personified this era of elite unity. He straddled the traditional and legal-rational systems, explicitly cultivating national elected authority while at the same time benefitting from the authority he inherited. He was the chief of the Bangwato. He had not abdicated that position in traditional terms. His not assuming that position was the result of an agreement with the British government whose legal authority was now defunct. He chose not to assume the position of chief. He gave no public indication that he would ever do so, and took no action to eliminate the Bangwato or any other chieftaincy. On the contrary, the government under Seretse Khama's leadership passed a law allowing a chief to take a leave of absence which paved the way for his eldest son, Ian, to become chief of the Bangwato in 1978 while simultaneously remaining second-in-command of the Botswana Defence Force. Furthermore, Seretse Khama's economic position as a large-scale cattle-owner created intra-elite credibility. A commitment to widespread distribution of new public services (combined with the money to pay for them) reinforced his own standing and authority. There were, however, consequences of this pattern of development as well as built-in contradictions in both economic and political terms in the years following 1979.

1980-1987: Consequences and Contradictions

Certain consequences of the mineral-led strategy emerged in the 1980s. The completion of a public infrastructure meant that it would not be as easy as in the past to paper-over conflict through dramatic improvements in basic public services. The impact of establishing for the first time a once a week health clinic in a village is much greater than increasing the frequency of its opening to two days a week. The introduction of free primary education and construction of a large number of primary schools had a greater qualitative impact than the extension of more universal education to the junior secondary school level, not that this did not add to the quality of publicly-rendered services. Incremental additions to the existing base, by this time, had become part of the public's expectations of its right to such services.

In addition, although government revenue continued to grow—particularly as a result of the new Jwaneng diamond mine and the appreciation of the United States dollar—the maintenance of the existing infrastructure was expensive. Moreover, the demands on government increased in their scope as a result of the emergence of new factions and the political maturation of existing factions. The managerial cadres in the national civil service demanded and won significant salary settlements including the introduction of a generous car allowance at the more senior levels. Civil servants, who already were allowed to be cattle ranchers, now wanted to take up other economic opportunities while remaining in the public service. National government salary adjustments had direct repercussions for local governments and in the private sector. Industrial class public sector manual workers and manual workers in the private sector demanded additional pay as well as, in urban areas, more public support for housing for low-paid workers. In the rural areas agricultural policy increased as an issue. TGLP had taken care of some of the needs of certain large-scale cattle farmers, but not all, and there were an increasing number of aspirant cattle and arable farmers requiring state resources to realize those aspirations. The promised benefits of the TGLP to small-scale cattle-owners in communal land areas had not materialized. The drought of the 1980s compounded existing problems in grazing areas and reduced or eliminated the possibility of growing crops in the land areas.

New educational opportunities had created a much wider and less homogeneous elite. The development of a more diversified economy had spread this elite into a number of new and competitive sectors: white collar positions opened up in the multinational corporate sector; managerial positions in the parastatal sector multiplied; the commercial sector mushroomed creating concomitant opportunities in importing, wholesaling, and retailing, the bar and bottle store revolution in the early 1980s being the most obvious manifestation; manufacturing (mostly of the light variety) grew rapidly often as joint ventures between South African and Batswana capital. Each of these sectors competed for state attention. Each had good reason to demand state subsidies for itself in the interest of "national development" just as the large-scale cattle-owners had been enjoying such subsidies for that reason for some years. Indeed there was significant articulation of the idea that it was time to help not only cattle-owners but also the more modern Batswana entrepreneurs.[43] Together these elites did not distinguish very clearly between their own and national (mass) development.

This differentiation and competition in society–intra-elite and between the elite and mass base–resulted in political competition. While this appeared to be a new fact of life, it may be best understood as the beginning of normal politics in a capitalist parliamentary democracy such as Botswana. Economic struggles over resources and labor relations created a political struggle played out ultimately in state allocations and laws. The legitimation of the allocation and enforcement of laws required popular majorities in regular elections. During the earlier periods such legitimation was more routine as the struggles were more muted.

These more normal struggles over resources emerged in the early 1980s. Seretse Khama's death in July 1980 is therefore a rather powerful symbol of this change. He represented an earlier era of homogeneity in elite circles as well as a politics in which legitimation still very importantly involved the circumstances of his own birth. He symbolized the unity, purpose, and real material progress associated with the historical moment of the early years in Botswana's post-colonial development. The success of this transitional position occupied by Seretse Khama would be tested

---

[43]See David Magang, "A Look at Botswana's Future Economic Prospects," speech made before the Botswana Society on 11 August 1981 (Gaborone: Printing and Publishing Co. Botswana, n.d.). David Magang is a lawyer and was elected to parliament as a BDP member.

in the persistence of regime and system stability in the ensuing period of normal politics.

The response of the post-Khama BDP government was to rely on expanding resources to meet new demands while maintaining existing services. In 1982 the Financial Assistance Policy (FAP) was created to subsidize new business ventures. Civil servants in 1984 were allowed to participate directly in certain private commercial enterprises in addition to their agricultural holdings, if any.[44] Licensing laws were passed limiting certain lines of business to citizens only. Joint ventures with foreign investors in other sectors were encouraged. In agriculture, large-scale cattle-owners continued to enjoy considerable subsidies and a new Accelerated Rainfed Arable Programme (ARAP) effectively subsidized the purchase of tractors for the better-off farmers.[45] As a result, small-scale arable farmers got their land plowed and also received some development in the Communal First Development Areas, a successor program to the TGLP in communal areas. An attempt was made to ameliorate the condition of low-paid manual workers in urban areas through expansion of the Self-Help Housing Agency. Still, by 1984, there remained demands from these factions and the potential for the development of new ones. The mass population defended the services presently provided and the elites' appetite remained insatiable.

The 1984 general elections were the first test of legitimacy and the BDP under Masire's presidency in this post-Khama era. Predictably the election was hard fought and the outcome more problematic than had been the case for some years. The 1984 election had the lowest proportion of uncontested National Assembly seats (one only–the Kgalagadi seat) and local government seats (53 out of 254 or 20.9 percent) in Botswana's

---

[44]See Personnel Directive No. 7 of 1984 issued by the Directorate of Personnel on 3 May 1984.

[45]See for example the ARAP annual report for 1986/87 issued by the Ministry of Agriculture, 1987.

electoral history.[46] The BNF fielded 27 candidates in National Assembly elections and 157 candidates for the 254 council seats. That represented 89.2 percent of all local government seats, nearly double the proportion of seats contested by the BNF in earlier elections. The BIP and BPP both increased the number of seats they contested but in a more incremental way. A new party, the Botswana Progressive Union (BPU) led by Daniel Kwele appeared on the scene in the north-central part of the country.[47]

In the 9 September 1984 general election more than three-quarters of registered voters and more than half of eligible voters cast ballots, levels of voting comparable only to 1965. The BDP won a clear victory with twenty-eight seats and nearly 78 percent of the total vote in National Assembly elections. But, the opposition won six seats, the largest number since 1969. The BNF won five of those with 20.5 percent of the total vote. This was the most seats won by a single opposition party and with the election of the BNF leader, Kenneth Koma, it became the official opposition. He became the leader of the opposition. The BNF was similarly successful in local government elections winning elected majorities in Gaborone and Jwaneng and coming within one seat of winning control of Lobatse.

The opposition parties in general capitalized on the continuing concerns of the mass base, in rural areas focused on agriculture, in urban areas on housing and working conditions. In both areas the issue of unemployment existed. Opposition parties also attracted disaffected members of the elite who could not find room in the circle of BDP leadership. During and after the election such defections took place, the most notoriety being given, perhaps, to Wellie Seboni's joining of the BNF. In earlier years he had been a BDP mayor of Gaborone and then assistant

---

[46]Unless otherwise noted the data on the 1984 elections is drawn from Parson, "The 1984 General Elections in Botswana."

[47]Kwele thereby achieved the position of having been in the leadership of three parties, the BNF, BDP and the new BPU which he created.

minister of finance and development planning.[48] The BNF was the most successful in capturing support from both the disaffected working class and disgruntled elites, the combination carrying both of the assembly seats in the capital for the BNF. Regions where non-Tswana communities were dominated historically by Tswana states continued to give support to parties other than the BDP: the BPP and to some extent BPU in the northeast and the BIP and BNF in the Okavango where in 1984 the BDP ran third behind those two parties.

The role of traditional leaders in electoral politics appeared to be more marginal than in previous elections including that of 1969, Chief Bathoen's re-election notwithstanding. Even in his case, there was a decline in relative support: he won 71 percent of the vote in 1969, but only 66.4 percent in 1974 and 58.9 percent in 1984. Clearly an automatic vote for the chieftaincy was a declining phenomenon and may have been a factor in Bathoen's decision to retire from politics and become the chairman of the Customary Court of Appeals.

Chief Linchwe II Kgafela was indirectly active in the 1984 elections but the outcome for him was very ambiguous. His seeming flirtation with the BDP in 1979 came to an end in 1984. Disenchanted with the incumbent M.P., it appeared that Linchwe backed Ray Molomo in the BDP primary elections. Molomo lost the primary and Greek Ruele was returned again as the BDP candidate.[49] Chief Linchwe made it clear that he was not

---

[48]Since that time there have been a limited number of defections. It was announced, for example, in January, 1988 that Raphael Sikwane, a former BDP member, would contest the next (1989) National Assembly constituency in Francistown for the BNF *Botswana Daily News*, January 22, 1988, p. 3.

[49]Interview with Chief Linchwe, July, 1984. In the 1989 BDP primary election in Mochudi Ray Molomo defeated the incumbent, Greek Ruele, thus increasing the perception that Linchwe was once again forging a close association with the ruling party. See Sandy Grant, "The human factor in Mochudi politics," *Mmegi/The Reporter* 6/14 (21-27 April 1989):

supporting the incumbent and although he remained neutral in public he seemed to give tacit support to the independent candidacy of Sandy Grant, director of the Phuthadikobo Museum and well-known long-time resident of Mochudi. Grant's posters were everywhere in Mochudi and elsewhere, his symbol–the eye–seeming to dominate the village from its perch on his house high on a hill. Even the choice of an eye as his election symbol illustrated the indirect tie between Sandy Grant and Chief Linchwe: Grant originally proposed a monkey, a symbol of the Bakgatla tribe, as his electoral symbol. The BDP candidate objected. The chief did not object but Grant relented and chose an eye as his symbol. By this time, of course, the point had been made that Grant had the chief's blessing, there having been considerable publicity about the dispute including an editorial cartoon in the *Botswana Daily News*. The BPP fielded a candidate but won only 14.8 percent of the votes. The BDP won and the BNF ran second. The electorate clearly did not do as it was bid by the chief. But undoubtedly the chief's open sympathy for Grant had an effect. Voter turnout in Mochudi was noticeably lower than elsewhere, for example, and it may have been due to the chief's views.

The relative marginalization of the competition between the traditional and rational-legal political orders therefore is indicated in the decline of explicit political conflict involving the chiefs. Additional indirect evidence is available from a mass survey of eligible voters in eleven constituencies conducted before the 1984 election. Table 1 presents selected results. High levels of the intention to vote, noted in 1974, continued in 1984. The act of voting appeared to be a valued one. Similarly in 1984, the population regarded voting as something which did have an effect on life; it was not viewed as merely a ritual, it was also instrumental. At the same time, at least in rural areas, engagement with the traditional system through the kgotla continued to be important, more important than attendance at political party

---

7.

rallies. Generally this data indicates a population clearly engaged in the national electoral system but still participating in an important aspect of the traditional political order. The maintenance of a Bangwato state, for example, continued to be on the agenda in the late 1980s. Although Ian Khama succeeded to the chieftaincy itself, the retirement of the tribal authority acting for him was an occasion for some to demand that one of Ian's brothers, Tshekedi Khama, should assume that role.[50]

Table 1. Selected Eligible Voter Attitudes Toward Voting and Politics, 1984

Voter Attitude	Proportion of the Sample (in percent)	
	Urban	Rural
Intends to vote	90.4%	83.1%
Believes voting has an important effect on life	80.1%	79.5%
Often or sometimes attends kgotla meetings	—	75.3%
Often or sometimes attends political party rallies	—	57.4%

Source: 1984 University of Botswana Election Study Project Eligible Voters Survey. See Louis Molamu, "Dimensions of Mass Politics: Results of a Sample Survey," paper presented at the University of Botswana Election Study Project Workshop on preliminary results, May, 1985.

---

[50]*Mmegi wa Dikgang (The Reporter)* 5/3 (30 Jan.-5 Feb. 1988): 1, and *Botswana Daily News*, 28 January 1988, p. 1; 1 February 1988, p. 1, and 3 February, 1988, p. 1.

Jack Parson

Factions, Elections, and Legitimacy in Botswana: 1956-1987

The broad outline of the post-colonial polity outlined above supports the view that the unremarkable succession of Quett Masire to the presidency was the result of the transference of ideas of legitimate constitutional authority from the traditional (tribal) to the legal-rational (national) political arena. But this recitation of events also argues that this transference was directly related to changes in the national economy creating a material and factional underpinning encouraging the acceptance of the new constitutional order. This acceptance of the constitutional order, at both mass and elite levels, corresponded to the pattern of economic development and its social and political consequences. The ideology of constitutional legitimacy—the practice of legitimate political authority—was therefore interwoven with the material conditions which underpinned it. It was not one or the other; it was both. In Botswana, respect for the rules governing the political order was reinforced by the material outcome of economic change. The system worked and it did so without disrupting the chieftaincy, the historical symbol of continuity and change.

This interpretation must be contrasted with those analyses of post-colonial Botswana which directly and indirectly attribute political stability and multi-party politics to either or both the personality and tribal position of Seretse Khama. Anthony Sillery, for example, generalizes that "in all emergent countries everything depends on the personality of the national leader, and Botswana is no exception. The position of Sir Seretse Khama appears at present [1974] impregnable, and it is well that this should be so, for there is nobody in sight who is capable of taking his place," although less than six years later Quett Masire did so.[51] Vengroff twice refers to Seretse Khama as a charismatic leader.[52] Colclough and McCarthy conclude that the multi-party system will remain so

---

[51] Anthony Sillery, *Botswana: A Short Political History* (London: Methuen & Co., 1974), p. 189

[52] Vengroff, *Botswana*, pp. 94, 97.

long as Seretse Khama is in power, however it has lasted longer.[53] John Holm emphasizes the ethnic dimension arguing that "probably over three-quarters of the vote in every Botswana general election can be explained by ethnic identification."[54]

These analyses cannot be dismissed out of hand. Certain facets of the Botswana political economy are explained by the personality and political culture of political leadership. However, those variables do not combine to create a sufficient explanation. The singularity of Seretse Khama's personality and traditional position cannot explain the uneventful succession of Masire and his continued prominence. Quett Masire is a less imposing personality and brings to the presidency *none* of the traditional status which may have contributed to Seretse Khama's authority. Moreover, while ethnic identification may account for a proportion of the support and votes for all parties, it cannot indisputably account for nearly all of it. Examples of voting support which cannot be accounted for in that way would include the large number of votes for the BDP in the Ngwaketse District, the urban multi-ethnic base of the BNF, and the BDP vote in Francistown. While Seretse Khama's chieftaincy undoubtedly did account for a large proportion of electorate behavior in Bangwato areas, this would not necessarily carry over to other places like the Kweneng where Seretse Khama had no claim to the chieftaincy let alone paramountcy over the Bakwena, the Bakwena tribe being "senior" to the Bangwato in historical origin.

Rates of voting turnout in 1984 are most interesting in assessing the idea that voting was a direct expression of the traditional order. There was a dramatic rise in voting by eligible and registered voters up to approximately the rates during the first

---

[53]Christopher Colclough and Stephen McCarthy, *The Political Economy of Botswana: A Study of Growth and Distribution* (London: Oxford University Press, 1980), p. 46.

[54]John D. Holm, "Elections in Botswana: Institutionalization of a New System of Legitimacy," in Fred M. Hayward, ed., *Elections in Independent Africa* (Boulder: Westview Press, 1987), p. 139.

election in 1965. In 1984 more than half of those eligible to vote, and slightly more than three quarters of those registered to vote, did so. The argument that a high turnout indicated a traditional "once and for all vote" attitude toward the presidency would seem to find support from these figures, 1984 being the first election after the passing of Seretse Khama. However, if that alone were true it was a most untraditional means through which to express traditionalism, for Masire had *only* a legal-rational claim to the position for which he stood. That must have meant that even if the high turnout was rooted in the belief in a once-and-for-all legitimation—as in the once-and-for-all recognition of the chief by the tribe—elections had become the mechanism for creating that regardless of the personal situation of the candidate for the highest of offices. If this were so it would argue for the view that legal-rational legitimation was in a process of being more or less accepted and entrenched.[55]

The process of folding traditional ideas of constitutionalism into the national parliamentary political order included protecting the institution and symbol of the chieftaincy although not its authority. This was one of probably two reasons for the willingness of the BDP to support the continued existence of the chieftaincy. The chiefs posed no threat to the national government in terms of their authority. The other reason was that while certain chiefs were able to use their formal legitimacy to generate a local politics in opposition to the central government, this opposition did not challenge the hegemony of the national state. Chief

---

[55]The analysis of rates of voter turnout, of course, is inconclusive. Changes in the rates over time are related to many factors including the political party and government administrative effort which went into voter registration and education, both relatively high in 1979 and 1984. James Polhemus discusses these efforts for both elections. See his "Botswana Votes: Parties and Elections in an African Democracy," in *Journal of Modern African Studies* 21/3 (1983): 397-430 and "Elections as Administrative process: A Survey of the 1984 Botswana Elections," paper presented at the University of Botswana Election Study Project Workshop, Gaborone, May, 1985.

Bathoen's resignation from the chieftaincy and subsequent parliamentary career in the BNF was a constant reminder of his opposition to being cast in a minor role, but it did not lead to a national coalition of chiefs in opposition to the government. Similarly, Chief Linchwe II Kgafela of the Bakgatla carefully cultivated his traditional authority in order to participate autonomously in the process of developing his territory even when that was in opposition to central government policy. He did not allow such conflicts as did exist, however, to reach the point of an ultimate confrontation. Such a confrontation would have left the central government no choice but to capitulate or remove him and abolish the tribal structure.[56] Collectively the House of Chiefs was a forum for criticism of the government in its treatment of the chiefs but the house did not go beyond its constitutionally mandated authority, which meant that *de facto* it accepted the constitutional status quo.[57] This approach to, but avoidance of, a

---

[56] A full account of the enterprising career of Chief Linchwe II Kgafela has yet to be written. An indication of his political career is contained in John Wiseman, "Conflict and Conflict Alliances in the Kgatleng District of Botswana," in *Journal of Modern African Studies* 16/3 (1978): 487-94; Monty Moswela, "Politics in Kgatleng: Parochialism Versus Nationalism," University of Botswana History Department dissertation in partial fulfillment of the requirements for the B.A. Degree, 1980; and Jack Parson, "Elections and Politics in the Mochudi National Assembly Constituency, 1984," paper prepared for the Workshop on Preliminary Results from the 1984 University of Botswana Election Study Project, May, 1984. Sandy Grant, "'Reduced to Almost Nothing?'" has done much to chronicle, among other things, Chief Linchwe's career.

[57] In 1987 certain chiefs including Chief Linchwe II Kgafela heaped criticism on the government over the passing of an amendment to the Chieftaincy Act which removed from the president to the minister of local government and lands the powers to recognize and discipline the chiefs. The chiefs viewed this as a demotion. From President Masire's point of view this meant creating an indirect rather than direct means for his dealing with the chiefs thus avoiding a debate in kgotla and villages about whether a commoner president can discipline a chief. While

direct (constitutional) confrontation left the legal-rational system as the winner. This also must have enhanced its legitimacy in the eyes of many people.

There is little doubt that the chiefs and tribal administration continued to generate loyalty particularly in the rural areas. The *Report of the Presidential Commission on Local Government Structure in Botswana 1979*, for example, was impressed by the overwhelming weight of popular support for the Tribal Administration and went so far as to recommend that the chief "should be regarded as the ceremonial leader of the district" taking "precedence on ceremonial occasions over all other office bearers in the district, including the Chairman of the Council and the District Development Director."[58]

The Presidential Commission reporting in 1979 had strong representation from those with traditional ties. The chairman was L.M. Seretse and its members included Chief Bathoen II and Chief Linchwe II Kgafela. That would account for some of the strong support lent the chiefs and tribal administration. The cabinet refused to endorse the recommendations, to no one's surprise. Still these sentiments represented more than special pleading. In a report to the Swedish International Development Agency in 1987, Brian Egner argued that

> the chiefs, sub-chiefs and headmen play a unique role in stabilizing the loyalties of the groups whose tribal identities they personify. As patriotic citizens with

---

Seretse lived this was not an issue but became so once Masire succeeded. See *Botswana Daily News*, 8 February 1988, p. 1, and, 12 February 1988, p. 1. See also *The Gazette*, 10 February 1988, p. 4. Ultimately the House of Chiefs did not press the issue which led kgosi Linchwe II Kgafela to resign as vice chairman of the House of Chiefs saying he had "lost confidence in members of the House of Chiefs," *The Gazette*, 17 February 1988, p. 8.

[58](Gaborone: The Government Printer, no date), vol. I, pp. 3 and 31. The commission advocated renaming the district commissioner the district development director.

special influence . . . they lend their traditional legitimacy to the national and local government systems which have absorbed many of their former powers. The tendency of some writers to dwell upon the loss of the tribal administration's statutory powers after 1966 has at times obscured the importance of the role the chiefs still play in the rural areas.

Egner concluded that "20 years after independence the councils in their political dealings with central government need the support of the chiefs more than the chiefs need them."[59]

Given the continued respect engendered for the chieftaincy by large numbers of the citizenry, the benefits to be gained for national legitimacy from its incorporation far outweighed the costs, which were the pinpricks of occasional local opposition. This was the primary reason why the chieftaincy was maintained. The costs of its elimination were counter-balanced by the benefits of its retention. The kgotla, for example, continued to be a venue respected and attended by a substantial segment of at least the rural population.

There are three important provisos to this commentary's assertion that national liberal-democratic legitimacy was created and the implication that it will continue. One proviso is that the evidence, although accumulating, is far from conclusive. The infrastructure of historical and political research and analysis on topics directly related to the question of legitimacy is in a formative stage. That infrastructure is developing, particularly with the emergence of a growing Batswana research capacity at the University of Botswana. Micro-studies of the politics of development need to be done nation-wide. More specifically, research needs to be done on the potential evidence that non-voting means legitimacy has not been established. On average less than half of those who could vote do so. Silence can mean consent, or support,

---

[59]Brian Egner, *The District Councils and Decentralization 1978-1986* (Gaborone: Economic Consultancies, February 1987), pp. 25-26.

but also can mean feelings of irrelevance or opposition. Without detailed research on that and on political life at a mass level, assertions about legitimacy will remain merely assertions.

A second proviso highlights the social and economic underpinning of political legitimacy. The political scientist Charles Lindblom once observed that "we understand liberal democracy so poorly that we do not know . . . why it is that liberal democracy has arisen only in nations that are market oriented, not in all of them but only in them. The tie between market and democracy is on many counts an astonishing historical fact."[60] The necessity of such a connection is clear. Market oriented—that is capitalist or private enterprise—societies are most efficient where employers are able to persuade workers that the wage relationship, which results in profits for capital and insecure and lower wages for labor, is natural, mutually beneficial, and therefore indisputable. If workers are persuaded that they, themselves, control the system, then this principle of efficiency is implemented easily. The problem is constructing such a system so that control does not slip from the hands of private property but at the same time convince those without property that the system works for them. The liberal democracies where this has happened (for example, in Britain, the Federal Republic of Germany, and the United States) all have in common the principle of legitimacy shared by Botswana, that of direct election. Universal suffrage creates law-giving legislatures which then by definition directly convey and represent the "popular" will. The sociologist Ralph Miliband argues that the House of Commons is by far the most important institution in the British political system not because it is a strong legislature or because it controls the executive but because "it enshrines the elective principle and thus provides the absolutely indispensable legitimation for the government of the country; nothing, for the

---

[60]Charles E. Lindblom, *Politics and Markets: The World's Political-Economic Systems* (New York: Basic Books, 1977), p. 5.

containment and management of pressure from below, could be more important than that."[61]

Historically it seems to have been possible to retain legitimacy by inter alia making concessions to the popular classes at moments of crisis. The extension of trade union rights, the widening of the franchise, the introduction of social welfare programs are all examples. This was possible in part because of an expansion of resources to be used in this way. Similarly it was possible to maintain the unity of the governing economic elites at least on fundamental issues.

Repeating this pattern of liberal democratic legitimacy in market-oriented (capitalist) Botswana is not a foregone conclusion. It has been possible to "purchase" mass support in certain respects through massive infrastructural development. However the resources to do so have resulted from capital intensive export-oriented diamond mining with few backward or forward linkages. The question has always been whether or not that growth was sustainable. The very real prospect of additional mines[62] means that it can be sustained but if so then legitimacy will also be sustained only so long as new mines are developed and markets are found for their produce.[63] The uncertainties of this scenario highlight in particular the external orientation of Botswana's political economy. The limits of its independent economic and political life in this scenario depend greatly upon forces beyond national control.

---

[61]Ralph Miliband, *Capitalist Democracy in Britain* (Oxford: Oxford University Press, 1982), p. 20.

[62]See "Diamond finds for Falconbridge," in *Mmegi Wa Dikgang (The Reporter)*, 30 January-5 February, 1988, p. 1.

[63]The governor of the Bank of Botswana, Quill Hermans, in early 1988 expressed concern for the future if Botswana remained dependent on uncertain mineral prospects. See a report of his speech to the annual general meeting of the Botswana Employers Federation, *Mmegi wa Dikgang (The Reporter)*, 5-11 March, 1988, pp. 1-2.

In addition it is not crystal clear that elite unity can be maintained. The factions which are contained within the BDP and across the party spectrum have become increasingly competitive. Their need for state subsidies, which they perceive as their right, is not easily satisfied. This has led to the fracturing of the unity apparent in the 1970s. If there is a slowdown in the generation of resources, then factional competition can become a "do-or-die" affair. When it does there is the possibility of a systemic breakdown and for more dictatorial solutions, for example, a military or a civilian/military cabal becoming arbiters of factional and popular demands at the point of a gun. That kind of solution is far from inevitable, as this survey of post-colonial Botswana shows, but it is possible.

The third proviso highlights the fact that sovereign political independence is not a purely national question. Botswana's economic and political past, present, and future is deeply touched by its geopolitical situation in southern Africa. The struggle over apartheid in South Africa in 1988 is an international one. Botswana has become part of South Africa's policy of destabilizing the political and economic integrity of its neighbors. This means that internal Botswana politics, ultimately the continuation of its system, is subject to outright invasions, terrorism, and more secret and covert intrigues perpetrated by the white South African state. It is not in that state's interest that Botswana's polity should gain in strength.

Conclusion

Successions to high office in Botswana have taken place within the precepts of legitimate political order. In the colonial period a powerful sense of constitutionalism existed in the Tswana states around the central political role of the kgosi, the succession to which was based on male primogeniture. Political factions formed and were active but within the rules of legitimate political combat. The case studies around the illness and death of Sekgoma Khama in 1925 and the succession crisis around the marriage of Seretse Khama illustrate that conclusion.

A strong sense of constitutional legitimacy has also played an important role in the politics of colonialism and nationalism. Adherence to a strict rule of male primogeniture sharply limited the extent to which the British colonial administration could intervene in the choice of a ruler. It also meant that colonial administration could not simply replace a recalcitrant ruler once in office. This gave the Tswana states more room for manoeuvre–still narrowly constrained by the imperial power–than was the case in many African colonies in the British Empire. In the 1925 succession involving Sekgoma, the colonial administration was compelled to deal with the factions of the royal family involved in the decision about his treatment. The autonomy resulting from the legitimacy extended to the kgosi was used to the hilt by Tshekedi Khama during his regency on behalf of Seretse Khama, the legitimate successor to Sekgoma. And it was this strong sense of constitutional legitimacy which lay at the root of the 1948-1953 crisis. Had not the population of the Bangwato state insisted on Seretse Khama's succession, the British government simply could have dismissed his claim to office and met their objective of placating white opinion in South Africa and Rhodesia by anointing a compliant successor.

Constitutional continuity in the Tswana polities during the colonial period created some autonomy in relation to Britain. This continuity was also an expression of nationalism. The political struggles between the chiefs and Britain in the colonial period were nationalist struggles. Chiefs like Bathoen II and Tshekedi Khama were nationalist politicians in terms of the Tswana state constitution.

Nationalism as an expression of constitutional legitimacy, therefore, was interwoven into the Tswana polities. There were, however, limits to state development based on this form of nationalism. It depended on the quality and character of the kgosi. In colonial Bechuanaland these varied tremendously and arguably tribal nationalist leaders like Bathoen II and Tshekedi Khama were exceptions rather than the rule in comparison to their peers. Moreover, the Tswana constitution did not admit a supra-national (pan-tribal) Bechuanaland government; there was no paramountcy of one kgosi over another let alone one over them all. There was an acknowledgement of genealogical "seniority" but seniority did not create authority. A kgosi from one tribe might mediate a dispute in another but by invitation and convention, not as a right of his authority. Finally the Tswana constitution could not accommodate or incorporate easily influence and power based primarily on achievement. The "new men" of Kuper's Kalahari and the "nationalists" in Bangwato country and beyond in the 1950s quickly came up against the limits of political organization within the Tswana constitution.

These limits, combined with the post-World War II and post South African 1948 apartheid election environments, called into question the adequacy of the prevailing constitution. The resolution of the 1948-1953 crisis created a context for constructing a supra-tribal political organization, the nation-state. Seretse Khama's leadership in the new nationalist movement allowed the bridging of the old with the new. The achievement of independence in 1966 created a new political order which was based on a different concept of legitimacy, that of elected representative parliamentary government. Its creation required the subordination of the traditional polities to this government. Popular participation suggests that the legitimacy of the new order was maintained. Factional politics have been played out within the rules of parliamentary government. The succession of Quett Masire to the presidency indicates that this legitimacy was perhaps systemic and not just a contribution of the tribal position and personality of Seretse Khama himself.

APPENDICES

Appendix A

LETTER FROM SEKGOMA KHAMA TO J. ELLENBERGER, RESIDENT COMMISSIONER, REQUESTING THE BANISHMENT OF PHETHU MPHOENG FROM SEKGOMA'S COUNTRY, RECEIVED ON 18 JANUARY 1924

(Botswana National Archives, S 3/6)

18 January 1924 (received)

His Honour J. Ellenberger, I.S.O.
RESIDENT COMMISSIONER

    I expect you will not be surprised at receiving and reading this pathetic letter from me, but I feel it is my duty to write to you again, and I hope you will pardon what may seem presumption or interference to your Honour's duty and consideration but believe me when I say that nothing but maintaining order and peace amongst the Bamangwato and my subject tribes is meant.
    It is the repeated request that Phethu with the other malcontents are undesirable and must leave my Country at once.
    Your Honour knows the dire necessity which compels this strong measure.
    My late father had placed Phethu at Madinare as hut-tax-collector and headman, but his power was gigantic and his rule henceforth was one of oppression, and misery followed in its train.
    Makalaka headmen were heavily fined, severely flogged in the public, some being very old men sixty to seventy years old.

Appendix A

These men presented themselves before Lieut-Colonel Daniel at the first enquiry which was held at the Kgotla.

Women as well suffered the same fate, goods were looted and other articles [taken] without just cause.

Men and Women were made to plough and weed vast lands for himself, [while] myself as Paramount Chief have none. Some men were reported to have died through the cause of severe thrashing.

School children were made to work for months at Phethu's brother's cattle ranches. [W]hen punished they had to be severely thrashed thirty to forty lashes irrespective of their age.

This case was once or twice brought before my late father and Phethu's brother was warned of the dangerous consequences but to no avail.

Certain headmen of Tobane Village had from time to time appealed to my late father to be emancipated from the system of oppression and were promised to be redressed, unfortunately my father died before anything was done to this effect, and therefore they had to make further overtures to me.

[T]hey were made to understand by Phethu that he was their chief and to nobody else could they appeal. Privately they came to Serowe to lay their grievances[. Here], they met Phethu who became very indignant and aggressive.

So when these Makalaka section made known the conduct of Phethu and his brother to me there was a general dissatisfaction throughout the Bamangwato.

On November 12th 1923, a big Letsholo was summoned. At this Letsholo Phethu showed indecent behaviour towards me.

By his action he defied the laws of the Bamangwato who placed him in authority over the Makalaka.

Phethu has with his supporters sullied the nation's honour and tradition.

My rights as Chief of the Bamangwato, they have trodden under foot and have brought order into chaos.

And why should I as Chief of the Bamangwato not preserve my interest and dignity of the seat on which Providence has placed

Sekgoma Requests Banishment of Phethu Mphoeng, 18 January 1924

me? The seat on which His Majesty the King has also approved to be legal.

Was it not the King's hand that installed me through his Servant Sir James Macgregor?

Phethu's action is now an obstacle to the happiness of the Bamangwato by depriving the tribe of her right of being ruled direct by me.

Is it therefore not high time that I should exercise my power when this is being undermined to a putrescent state by the agitators who seek nothing but to disturb the peace of the country?

Are the agitators in every land not punished by exile? May I say to Your Honour that I have been very patient but now I have had enough of these agitators and any serious action I am about to take, I feel myself to be justified by both Native and Government law.

I thought myself to have acted rightly when I telegraphed to Your Honour on the 12th November, for in anything serious I would not take action without first refering to you.

What about the acts of fiendish cruelty committed by Phethu at Madinare and Tobane?

Are the words of His Royal Highness Prince Arthur to me at Mahalapye mere talk?

Did he not speak about the ill-treatment of the Mabirwa, and that I must see that all my subject tribes are well treated by those who are placed in authority over them?

Is cruelty and torture now to be supported by both the Chief and the Government and left without being severely punished? Is it legal to be deprived of my hereditary rights when exercised lawfully and according to the wishes of His Royal Highness the late High Commissioner?

The British Government is strong enough to deprive me of my rightful Chieftain-ship without making an entrance through Phethu's scheme. With this revolt which is intended not only to ruin me of my rights, but to flood my Country with false allegations and to agitate my peaceful people to undermine my

Appendix A

laws, I shall not only have to blame Phethu and his supporters for, but also the Government.

Night secret meetings to assassinate me were discovered by some of the witnesses.

Remember that an ordinary native is an imitator, if Phethu is supported by the higher authority without just reason chaos will reign and the question is: who will then be responsible for what is apt to come?

Surely, should Your Honour fail to support my attitude, all honour and chieftainship will be lost and I will be bound to abdicate, for there will be no nation at all, every one will be on his own and that is what Phethu is clamouring for.

In conclusion I respectfully beg Your Honour very earnest consideration, I assure you the position has become very grave indeed owing to so much delay in settling this grievous matter, I have only dealt briefly with the position and feel that a personal interview would make matters considerably clearer.

I am,

Your Honour's friend,

Sekgoma (his signature)

Appendix B

PETITION TO THE RESIDENT COMMISSIONER FROM PHETHU MPHOENG AND OTHERS COMPLAINING ABOUT SEKGOMA KHAMA'S RULE, 21 JANUARY 1924

(Botswana National Archives, S 3/6)

The Resident Commissioner

Your Honour:

We the undersigned beg to acknowledge that we have the following words of plea, and ask that you should help us.

We belong to the royal blood of the Bamangwato, descended from Sekgoma the father of Khama.

We have been very much grieved and oppressed by our people and our chief. Therefore we have found it to be our duty to appeal to the Government, because our chief kills us without having done any wrong.

Your Honour, we think that under the British flag we are justified to bring forth such grievances as below mentioned as all British subjects should. They are as follows:-

[1] Whereas our chief has openly declared that he cannot separate with the sons of Ratshosa under any circumstances, they are known to be always the source of strife in the tribe, and who have aroused a spirit of conspiracy against us in the tribe, and the tribe have been convinced through ignorance, we therefore humbly ask that they be removed from all duties connected with the tribal administration and Government service.

Appendix B

They are the cause of all disputes and destroyers of the peace of Bamangwato.

2) Whereas the power of the witchdoctors is growing a good deal now among the tribe, and our chief and tribe believe in them, and we have found that they are the cause of this trouble, we therefore humbly beg to ask the Government to enforce a law against them as in all other civilized countries.

3) May it please your Honour to allow us to state that our chief should not be despotic, cruel, and revengeful, and our rule not sanguinary like the rule of the Matebele.

4) That our education be protected by the Government. The missionaries have no plans of progressing education, and the tribe no voice on education, the education is under control of the Ratshosas, but they are a blockade in the way of education. But we want progress and education.

Teachers have been turned out of schools by the chief without any wrong being committed by them, therefore we do not see how education can advance under the chief's control without him being its defender.

5) Whereas we think that we are the right people to speak to the Government, we humbly ask that from today and henceforward Your Honour should permit us to say our grievances to him and to our chief.

6) That we be granted our rights in our country as children of this our tribe, and be allowed to work in the land.

7) That the habit of banishing people be utterly abolished, because this habit destroys man's property, wells and habitation. It would be much better that a man is killed and finished with.

8) That all good laws of Khama be preserved.

Petition from Phethu Mphoeng, 21 January 1924

9) We also humbly ask that the Government should exercise the same authority in Bamangwato reserve as in all other Protectorate countries, and that we join the Protectorate Council which is attended by members of all other tribes.

Finally we beg to ask that Your Honour pay attention to these our words, and convey them to the High Commissioner, because there cannot be made any change, there can never be progress and no peace. We also ask that Your Honour should see that we are guarded at the request of all.

Your most humble servants,

(signed)

Phethu Mphoeng Sekgoma
Nwako Nkobele
Lekgoba Lekgoma
O. Mphoeng Sekgoma
L. Raditladi
K. Raditladi

Appendix C

MINUTES OF A MEETING HELD AT THE KGOTLA, SEROWE, AT 8 A.M. ON THURSDAY, 29 OCTOBER 1925 TO DISCUSS WHETHER CHIEF SEKGOMA SHOULD BE TREATED BY A EUROPEAN DOCTOR OR A TRADITIONAL DOCTOR

(Botswana National Archives, DCS 4/6)

PRESENT: Major H.D. Hannay, Ag. R.M.; Dr. D. Drew, M.O.; Revd. R.H. Lewis, L.M.S.; A.J.D. Germond, Esq.; The Ag. Chief (Gorewan), several of the Headmen and about 800 or 900 of the Tribe.

Major Hannay: The matter to be discussed this morning is this. Is the Chief Sekgoma to be treated by a European Doctor or by a Native Doctor?

I understand, Mathiba, that prior to the Chief's departure for Cape Town, while at a Cattle Post, he was treated by a Native Doctor named Mathobe. Is this true?

Mathiba: I do not know whether the Chief was actually under the treatment of Mathobe, but this I know that while at the Cattle Post the Chief was subject to several fits, and that he became so ill that the Doctor (Dr. Drew) was sent for. The Doctor ordered him to be taken back to Serowe.

John Ratshosa: I also was present at the Cattle Post and saw the man Mathobe, but as to whether he treated the Chief I cannot say.

Appendix C

Magistrate–to the people: I know there was a Native Doctor at the Cattle Post with the Chief, but whether he treated the Chief or not I do not know. I also know that the Chief had several fits while at the Cattle Post in company with the said Mathobe. I understand that ultimately a European Doctor was sent for. Why, if you have so much faith in your Native Doctors, did you send for the White Doctor?

I admit that some Native Doctors have a good knowledge of various herbal remedies and are able with the help of these to cure wounds, colds, stomach troubles etc. But I know your Doctor is going to make use of the 'Bones' and in this I have no faith whatsoever and am strongly opposed to it. I warn you that the day a Native Doctor enters the Chief's house Dr. Drew leaves, and the two European nurses are withdrawn. Also please understand that if anything happens while under treatment of the Witch Doctor, you and you alone, Bamangwato, will be to blame.

Your late Chief Khama disapproved of Witch Doctors for he had them chased out of the country.

One thing more. I want you to understand that the Acting Chief is not stopping you from having a Witch Doctor. I am the one who is opposed to it, and this because I am afraid that he will treat the Chief for a week or so, then, if matters do not show any sign of improvement or, which is very likely, get worse, he will blame Dr. Drew for it and leave. It will be of no use then to come to Dr. Drew for I shall refuse all help.

I wish to let you know that owing to the fact that the Chief has been very restless of late, especially during the nights, the two European Nurses find themselves unable to cope with the work, and it has been decided to send for a third Nurse.

My last word is a word of warning. I believe that a certain man has been spreading the story that the Government is sending for a third man to help to kill the Chief. This is a serious charge and if I am able to get sufficient evidence this man will be prosecuted. The man is lying and he knows it too. His whole idea is to put the people against European Doctors.

Serowe Kgotla of 29 October 1925 to Discuss Chief's Treatment

The Acting Chief: We have heard you. All I wish to say is in connection with the Deputation which interviewed you at your Office on behalf of the Bamangwato people. I was present and I know that both yourself and the Doctor were opposed to having a Witch Doctor treating the Chief.

In the afternoon I called again at your Office and heard the Chief's daughter saying that she also was strongly opposed to having a Witch Doctor called.

I then went in company with the Magistrate to the Chief's house and interviewed him on the subject. The Chief made us understand that to him all Doctors whether White or Black were the same, but if the Magistrate was not willing to have a Native Doctor called he was quite willing to remain in the hands of Doctor Drew.

Personally, I have nothing against Witch Doctors but I do not wish to have the Chief treated solely by a Native Doctor.

Headman Baipidi: We want to know who is the man who spoilt matters, for we were led to understand that the Magistrate had agreed to allow a Native Doctor to treat the Chief for a few days, and now we understand from what he has just said that he is opposed to it.

Magistrate: I was opposed to it from the very beginning. The Acting Chief and the Headmen who were present at the interview know it.

Headman Baipidi: We, as a Tribe, wish to have the Chief treated by a Witch Doctor.

Magistrate: Are all your headmen in favour of this?

Tribe: YES

Headman Disang: I, for one, am not in favour of this motion being carried out. I have great faith in European Doctors and very little in Native Doctors. I do not wish to see the Chief in the hands of

Appendix C

Witch Doctors for I realize and fear the great responsibility we take on ourselves by doing so.

Headman Oitsile: We were told that the Magistrate had been interviewed in connection with this matter, and that he had agreed to place the matter in our hands.

Magistrate: Five men came to my Office as the representatives of the Bamangwato Tribe. At the last moment one of them was turned away. Why? I begin to doubt whether these men did represent the Tribe.

Headman Oitsile: I do not know to what man you are referring, but this I know that the Bamangwato, as a Tribe, are begging you now to let them have their way in this. It is our custom to have a few men detailed as representatives of the whole Tribe and in these men we believe and put our trust. Thus, when our chosen representatives reported to us that though you had at first rejected their proposal you ultimately gave in, we had to believe them. But now it seems you have changed your mind. Why?

Magistrate: I have already given you my reasons. The Chief's daughter and relatives are against it, and I am bound to study their point of view before that of anyone else.

Headman Oitsile: You agreed to let us try one of our own Doctors for a few days.

Magistrate: Did you hear me say so?

Headman Oitsile: No. I heard it from one of the messengers.

Magistrate: The Acting Chief was present at the interview, did he hear me say I was in favour of a Native Doctor?

The Acting Chief: No. You said that you would refer matters to Headquarters.

Serowe Kgotla of 29 October 1925 to Discuss Chief's Treatment

Magistrate: Yes, that is what I said. I also tried my best to explain to them how much superior a White Doctor was to a Native Doctor. If your own Doctors are so good why did Khama send them away? Khama had no faith whatsoever in Witch Doctors. I can quote two instances. When I was here in 1912 he reported to me that a child suffering from pneumonia had been treated by a Native Doctor who had applied some form of ointment to his head with the result that the whole of his scalp was blistered and he had lost all his hair without obtaining any benefit from the treatment. Another instance. A Native boy was badly gored by an ox, and when brought into Serowe his intestines were actually hanging out. The Chief, having no faith in Native Doctors, placed the boy in the hands of Dr. Black, and it was Dr. Black who saved his life.

I wish all these men present here to understand clearly that I am strongly opposed to Native Doctors and have been so from the beginning. Doctor Drew wishes me to tell you that he made an offer to the five Headmen who came to the Office the other day, to operate on the Chief with the help of Doctor MacRae. He also explained to them the dangers of Chloroform and of the operation, but he told them that the operation was worth the risk. He tells me that the day a Native Doctor enters the Chief's house he will leave.

I, personally, do not care what Doctor treats the Chief. I gain nothing by refusing the Chief a Native Doctor. I am merely a representative of the Bechuanaland Government and am here to carry out their instructions.

Headman Baruti: Tribe of the Bamangwato. I have heard your words and desires. Remember that our whole Tribe is a mixture of several tribes and we, Bamangwatos, are only part of the Tribe, and have therefore no right to risk the life of the Chief without the consent of the rest of the Tribe. The Chief must have the best Doctor. Our Native Doctors, as you all know, are useless, so let us not give them so much as a single thought. You have told the Magistrate that the whole Tribe is willing to have a Native Doctor. Well, I for one am not willing.

Appendix C

Headman Oitsile: I wish to tell the Magistrate that we have nothing against the white doctors. We only wish, for the sake of the Chief, that you allow us to try one of our own men. He may perhaps be able, with the help of god, to do more for the Chief than has been done up to the present.

Revd. Lewis: Yesterday the Chief asked me what my ideas were on the subject. I answered that being a White man I was not in a position to answer his question for I had no right to interfere in matters of this nature. All I did was to show him the evils of Witch-craft. To-day he called for me again and told me that he had given up the idea of having a Native Doctor and that he would remain in the hands of Doctor Drew.

J. Ratshosa: I do not know what has happened to us Bamangwatos. In Khama's time no Witch Doctors were allowed in the place but to-day not only are they allowed among us but they are allowed to practice. I have been brought up by Khama and know that he hated Native Doctors. As a boy when I fell ill he placed me in the hands of European Doctors.

Native Doctor Boiditswe: Your words are false, for I, Boiditswe, was once called by Khama to treat the Chief's children who were suffering from ear-ache–the Chief's wife can bear me out in this. What is more, I am firmly convinced that I am able to cure the Chief himself. I have treated similar cases before and have been successful.

J. Ratshosa: Now that Khama is dead it is easy to lay such a charge against him, but this I can say that it was generally known that Khama was opposed to all Native Doctoring.

A Headman: The whole Tribe wishes for a Native Doctor. We beg that you our Magistrate, who has the power to grant our request, should give us what we ask for. I believe in both European and Native Doctors, for the Native, like the White man, is the child of

Serowe Kgotla of 29 October 1925 to Discuss Chief's Treatment

God, and why should God give wisdom to his White child and not to his Black child.

Magistrate: I think that too much time has been spent already. We shall now proceed to vote. Those who are in favour of a Native Doctor please step back.

> (The whole gathering falls back with the exception of the Acting Chief, S. Ratshosa, J. Ratshosa, O. Ratshosa and half-a-dozen Headmen.)

Magistrate: I see that you are all in favour of a Native Doctor. Now let it be understood the matter is now in your hands and that you take all responsibility. The day the Native Doctor visits the Chief, Doctor Drew and the two European Nurses leave.

I will report to-day by telegram to the Resident Commissioner what has happened here, and will tell him that you, as a Tribe, are all in favour of a Native Doctor.

Appendix D

MINUTES OF A MEETING HELD AT THE RESIDENT MAGISTRATE'S OFFICE, SEROWE, AT 10 A.M. ON THE 19TH DECEMBER 1925 TO DISCUSS THE FUTURE OF THE TRIBAL ADVISORY COUNCIL FORMED AFTER SEKGOMA'S DEATH BUT PRIOR TO THE ASSUMPTION OF POWER BY THE REGENT, TSHEKEDI KHAMA

(Botswana National Archives, DCS 4/1)

PRESENT: Captain H.B. Neale, Resident Magistrate, Mr. A.J.D. Germond, Ag. Chief Tshekedi, Gorewan, the Council and Headmen of the Tribe.

Subject for discussion: The subject for discussion was as to whether the Council should be abolished or not.

Tshekedi: On my arrival here I had an interview with the Magistrate and he broached the subject of a Council which was formed during my absence at Fort Hare. He explained to me what the duties and the functions of this Council were, pointing out clearly that the Council was purely an Advisory one. This morning I gathered the Tribe at the Kgotla in order to find what views the people held on the subject. I discovered that not only was the majority of the Tribe opposed to this Council but that all Members save three were dissatisfied with it. After discussion I decided that the matter should be brought this day in front of the Magistrate.

Appendix D

Magistrate: As far as I am able to see the whole trouble is that the People do not understand clearly what this Advisory Council really is, and are, therefore, rather suspicious of it. This new Council is much the same as your old Advisory Council. Its duties are similar, i.e. 1. To help and advise the Chief in the ruling of the People. (2ndly) To express the views and wishes of the Tribe as a whole on matters concerning the Tribe. The only difference is that the Members of the Council in this case are known to, and recognised by the Resident Commissioner. Let it be clearly understood that the Government has no wish to interfere in the government and customs of the Tribe, nor does it wish to weaken the power of the Chief or the Acting Chief. Remember that your Chief is young and inexperienced and is therefore in need of such a Council from which he could obtain reliable advice. If there be any Member of this Council or Headman of the Tribe who feels dissatisfied with the present state of affairs I shall be glad to hear what views he holds on the subject.

Mathoame: I am a Member of the Council. How I became one I do not know, but this I know that my name is written on the List of the Members chosen. I am opposed to this Council for it was hurried through and formed without consulting either the Headmen concerned or the Tribe. Its Members were apparently not elected but nominated. It would have been quite a different matter if the Government had waited for the arrival of Tshekedi and then in his presence and with his consent formed the Council.

Phethu: I am a Member of the Council. I was absent at the time the Council was formed. On my arrival in Serowe I was informed that I had been made a Member. I also am dissatisfied with this arrangement. I think that if there was to be a Council it should have been formed when Tshekedi was present. I am also dissatisfied with the hurried way in which it was formed; that which is done in a hurry is never satisfactory and always comes to a sudden end. At present the Council is not in favour for not only the Tribe but most of its Members are opposed to it. We wish to have Tshekedi's opinion on the matter.

Meeting of Resident Magistrate and Tshekedi, 19 December 1925

Mathiba: Let us remember that the reason why our Council was formed in a hurry was simply because it was formed under pressure of the grave events which followed the death of the late Chief. At that time the idea was, and still is, that the Council was to protect and advise the Acting Chief Gorewan. Gorewan as we all know is a weak Chief and was in dire need of such a Council. The arrival of Tshekedi has to some degree altered matters and all I can say now is that as far as I am concerned I wish to act entirely according to Tshekedi's will. If the Chief is opposed to the Council I am prepared to take up the same attitude.

S. Ratshosa: I am a Councillor and I am a strong supporter of the Council because it answers my every wish and desire, and also because I am convinced that if run on the right lines it would prove a great help in the government of our country. I do not blame those men who are against it. They have their own views and I have mine; every man is free to hold and express his own views. The Council does not as some of you seem to think eliminate the Chief's power, but, in my opinion it strengthens it. Let our young Chief Tshekedi follow in his father's footsteps and I, as a Member of the Council, will always be ready to help and advise him. Gorewan, if you wish to rule this Tribe, give up drink. If you wish to rule Simon, give up drink. If you wish to act as Regent, give up drink, for as long as you drink you will never have any beneficial influence over our Tribe and Chief.

Gorewan: The Council, as we all know, was formed in time of trouble, its sole object being to help me. My grievance is that the way in which our Council should function was never thoroughly discussed and explained; even I do not understand its position and duties. Now that Tshekedi has come his wish and not mine is to be considered. Yet though the Tribe may be opposed to this Council let us not do anything rashly but let our final decision result from a thorough discussion of the matter.

Magistrate: Tshekedi, I wish you to realize that it depends on you whether there shall be a Council or not. This matter is no small

Appendix D

matter and I would advise you to think carefully over it before you give me your answer.

Tshekedi: Before we disperse I wish to ask the Magistrate a question. Is the Council to carry on as usual while I think the matter over?

Magistrate: Yes it must until I receive a definite answer from you, and the sanction of the High Commissioner to the abolition of the Council has been obtained.

Appendix E

LIST OF THE BAMANGWATO COUNCIL, 1925 ATTACHMENT TO THE LETTER FROM THE RESIDENT COMMISSIONER TO THE HIGH COMMISSIONER, 21 NOVEMBER 1925

(Botswana National Archives, S 11/4)

The Acting Chief Gorewan

1. G.O. Mathiba
2. J. Ratshosa
3. D. Raditladi
4. Edirilwe Seretse
5. Oitsile
6. Simon Ratshosa
7. Mathoame
8. Phethu Mphoeng
9. Baipidi
10. Moloi Sekgoma
11. Pelaelo Tiro
12. Leburu
13. Mogomotse Morwe

Appendix F

LETTER FROM THE RESIDENT MAGISTRATE, SEROWE, INFORMING THE GOVERNMENT SECRETARY, MAFEKING, OF THE RESIDENT MAGISTRATE'S VIEW IN FAVOR OF RETAINING THE BAMANGWATO ADVISORY COUNCIL, 21 DECEMBER 1925

(Botswana National Archives, DCS 8/6)

The Government Secretary,
Mafeking

I have to report that Tshekedi Khama returned to Serowe on Saturday the 19th instant. In an interview which I had with him that morning he informed me that he had seen His Honour at Mafeking on his way home and that various matters connected with the Tribe had been discussed including the establishment of a Council at Serowe. He stated that His Honour had told him that the Council was elected for the purpose of helping and supporting the Acting Chief, but that if he did not desire it, it could be abolished.

He later put the matter to the Tribe in Kgotla and the following day appeared at the Office with the majority of the Headmen present in Serowe. Notes have been taken of the various speeches made at that Meeting, for future reference, a copy of which I will forward for His Honour's information as soon as it has been transcribed.

In effect, the general attitude was, that the Council having been elected in the absence of the Chief, should be abolished. Most speakers admitted that it had served a useful purpose, and stated that if the Chief wished it they would support one. All the

Appendix F

Members of the present Council resigned with the exception of the Ratshosas. The attitude of the retiring Members of the Council being that as the Chief not wishing to have a Council they did not wish one.

Tshekedi on the other hand stated that he had nothing against the Council but that he followed the wishes of the Tribe.

There would appear to be no advantage in attempting to force a system of Tribal control under the circumstances and from what His Honour said to Tshekedi I presume the Council is to be allowed to dissolve.

I regret that this should have happened. I feel sure that in course of time, when the idea has had time to be considered, something of the kind will be found to be necessary. There are many progressive Natives in the Bamangwato Reserve, who, apart from the Ratshosas, wish the old style of autocratic rule to be definitely finished with. There seemed to be an excellent chance for a more progressive system to be tried upon the young Regent's accession. Tshekedi himself, I think, is open to argument and states that the idea is not discarded but that time must be given them to consider a departure of this nature from their customs. In the meantime the position is as I have outlined.

Serowe,

RESIDENT MAGISTRATE
21 December 1925

Appendix G

'REX VERSUS S. AND O. RATSHOSA': EVIDENCE GIVEN BY THE REGENT TSHEKEDI KHAMA ON 22 AND 23 JUNE 1926 IN THE TRIAL OF SIMON AND OBEDITSE RATSHOSA FOR THE ATTEMPTED MURDER OF TSHEKEDI KHAMA

(Botswana National Archives, DCS 8/6)

Evidence given by the Regent Tshekedi in the trial of Simon and Obeditse Ratshosa for his attempted murder before Captain Robert O'Malley Reilly, Magistrate, with Mr. S. Minchin appearing for the Crown, and Dr. Lang for the Defence. 22 June 1926.

Chief Tshekedi having been sworn states:

Mr. Minchin: What is your position in the tribe? I am the 7th Chief of the Bamangwato tribe. The proper Chief is the Chief's son who is about 3 years of age.

How is your appointment made and who is it made by? I am the only brother of my late brother.

Was the appointment confirmed by the Government? The Resident Commissioner came along and confirmed it.

Do you know the accused? Yes I know them.

What relation? They are my nephews.

What are the relations between you and the accused. Are they friendly or otherwise? No we are not on good terms.

Since when? Ever since I was appointed Acting Chief from the 19th February last.

Why are the relations strained? Because they fired at me.

Appendix G

Since your appointment as Chief you say the relations have been strained? Yes.

Why, what is it all about? I cannot explain it.

Court: Can you give any reason why the Ratshosas and yourself are not on good terms? Before I was appointed Acting Chief of the Bamangwato tribe the Ratshosas used to attend the Kgotla in the morning, and since my appointment as the Acting Chief they have never come to the Kgotla; they come very seldom. And also before this trouble started, and when I called a meeting they used to delay and come as they liked. On one occasion I had called a meeting and at that meeting I had to discharge Johnny from my office.

What was Johnny's position then? He was my Secretary. Before I gave permission for them to go back to their homes Simon left. There were very many occasions when I called up the regiments to do something and Simon never attended them.

Mr. Minchin: Tell the Court what you know about this shooting business. On the 4th April last I notified my Magistrate that I would have a meeting on the 5th day of the month and I would be speaking to the Ratshosa brothers, and at the same time I advised the Magistrate to attend that meeting so that he could hear what I was going to say to the Ratshosa brothers. I also asked the Revd. Lewis to attend that meeting and requested him to act as Interpreter. On the afternoon of the 4th of the month I sent a man to report to the Ratshosa Brothers to inform them that I would have a meeting on the following day and that the Magistrate would attend that meeting.

What was the meeting about? There were some differences about two girls who had been taken away from Oratile (Simon's wife). They had been taken from their mothers. I had given orders that these girls be returned to their mothers but they refused to do so and I took them by force and returned them to their proper mothers.

You say you sent Kalipe? Yes. When I sent him to the Ratshosas about this trouble it was to inform them that the meeting would be held on the 5th April. On the morning of the 5th the meeting gathered together and the Magistrate and the Reverend Lewis attended the meeting but the Ratshosas did not attend. I sent a man Gadishwane to inform them that we were still waiting for them to come. This man returned and informed me that the Ratshosa Brothers said they were going to a dance; so I dispersed the meeting. About 4 o'clock on the same day I sent some men to go and call the Ratshosas. He returned and informed that they had said they were coming. After some time they came. When they came I told them that I had called them but that they had disobeyed my orders. On hearing that I threatened to beat them they said they could not be beaten. They all stood up—the three Ratshosas—and when my people saw that the Ratshosas were disobeying me they caught hold of them, and Johnny hit someone with a stick. He threatened or struck a stick at Ooitsile. When I threatened to beat those men my people saw that I was being disobeyed they got up and then Johnny struck with a stick and the row started. This row started by hitting one another in the Kgotla. I remember seeing my men catch hold of Johnny and thrashing him but the accused were not hit by anyone as they had run away. Sometime after this when the two accused had gone away there was no row of any kind. While I was still sitting there I saw Simon and Obeditse returning with guns, and from the place where I sat there are some poles about 100 yards away. I saw them and they fired and the bullets hit between them and myself. Two bullets were fired in the first place. Then they fired again.

Court: Where did the bullets strike? I did not see them.

Mr. Minchin: And then? Then the people came and lifted me from the ground and advised me to go away as I was in danger. While I was being pushed away I heard another explosion behind my back and I felt very sore on my side. I went into a shelter place, and at this place, on looking down, I saw that the man who held me had been wounded on the hip. This was Kgosidintsi. I was also wounded and can show the scar made by the bullets on

Appendix G

that day and the hole through the jacket which I was wearing. (Jacket produced and inspected by the Magistrate.)
 Where were you wounded? On the right side above the hip.

[....................]

Mr. Minchin: When this happened what happened then? After that I called my men and I informed them that I had wished to punish the Ratshosa brothers and instead of which they had shot me with a rifle, and I informed them that I wanted to see the Ratshosas alive or dead, and from that time the men went to fetch their guns. After I gave those instructions they went away to find the Ratshosas. After a time my men returned.

[....................]

Dr. Lang: How old are you? 21 years of age.
 Where were you educated? I was educated at Lovedale and Fort Hare Institution.
 How long were you away from here? The first time was in 1917 when I went away until 1920.
 And then? I returned home. I again returned to the School in 1923. I was absent 5 years altogether.
 You were quite a young boy when you went away? Yes.
 Now you have come back you are a man? Yes.
 All this time you have not been in direct touch with the Bamangwato affairs? No.
 You were not present here to know what was taking place? I used to come home.
 Yes for holidays? In 1921/2 I was all the time at home.
 How old were you then? I was 17.
 Did you take much interest in the tribal affairs while you were here? Yes I used to be instructed in some affairs but not in them all.
 You mean like regiments being called up to do some work for the Chiefs? Yes when I was called I used to go.

Did you belong to a regiment when you were 17? The regiment wasn't formed.

But how can you do work with a regiment that was not formed? It didn't matter even if we were not given a name we used to do some work. It is the work of a regiment still to be formed.

Did you attend the Kgotla in those days? I used to go sometimes but not always.

Still all this would not give you ideas as to native custom? I was speaking with some people who could instruct me in native custom.

When was that, when you were 17? All along when I was at home and afterwards.

Who instructed you? Not one man but several.

Tell me the names? One man is Malepi, he is here.

Anyone else? There are too many to mention.

Can you give me one or two names of native headmen? One is Malepi.

Can you give me a couple of names? Another one is Maramoqui.

When you came back from Lovedale you were sent for weren't you? At what time.

The last time you came from Lovedale? Yes I had been sent and it was time for me to go home on holiday.

When did you come back? It was on the 17th December 1925.

Who sent for you? It was already time and the headmen also called me to go home. It was Gorewan who called me.

Did he write you a letter? Yes.

What did he say, "that you must come home and be a Chief" or what? He reported that my brother had died, the late Chief Sekgoma. That is all I remember.

He didn't say that you must come home and take his place as Acting Chief? No he would not say that as the bereavement was too recent.

Did you expect to be acting Chief when you heard the news? I had no expectations at all, I was grieved at my brother's death.

Appendix G

    Surely you must have thought that someone or other was going to be Chief? I did not think of anybody because I was the brother of the late Chief. Therefore I knew that I was the second man.

    Is it a custom that the second brother automatically becomes acting Chief? No answer.

    Of course the late Chief left a child, a small boy? Yes.

    Is it an invariable custom that the brother of the Chief becomes acting Chief? Yes if the late Chief has no child full grown his brother must take charge.

    What about Gorewan? Yes if the Chief had no brother.

    If the Chief had a daughter does she come in at all? It was never done in our tribe that the Chief's daughter must take the chair.

    Do you know of any case of the Bamangwatos or any tribe where there is a queen, or, in other words, has any native tribe got a queen? No answer.

    There are several tribes in the country, have you heard that there is a Chieftainess over them? I have heard that at Kenya [sic][1] there is a Chieftainess.

    Is she any relation to the Ratshosas? Yes she is married to one of the Ratshosa brothers.

    How are they connected with the Bamangwato, are they related through marriage? No answer.

    What is the name of the tribe she rules? The Bamaketsi.[sic]

    Is that a tribe or an offshoot of the Bamangwato race? I do not know.

    But you should know? I do not know.

    But you must know the history of these people, that is the least you should know? I have said I do not know the history of the native tribe. That question you had better refer to the old people and not to me, I do not know.

---

[1] Kanye.

Not even what language they speak? They speak Bechuana. It is not quite the same language, a different dialect.

According to your custom there can be no Queen Regent? I never heard Sir that there was one among the Bamangwato tribe.

[....................]

Dr. Lang: You arrived at Serowe early in the morning did you? Yes.

You then saw Gorewan? Yes I met him.

You asked him to explain what he had done while you were away? No I did not ask him at the time.

What happened at this interview? According to the native custom it was his duty to report to me that my brother had passed away.

What else happened? I do not remember anything more that happened.

Court: Did anything else pass between yourself and Gorewan about the tribe? Not when I went to greet him, but sometime afterwards he mentioned something about the tribe.

Dr. Lang: Now you held a Kgotla meeting after seeing Gorewan? Not the same day as he arrived.

Didn't you call together your tribes that morning? No I did not call any on my return.

When did you hold the Kgotla meeting? On the third day after my arrival I held a meeting.

After that you had a meeting of some Council or other? The meeting with the Council was held before the general meeting of the tribe.

You attended the meeting of the Council? Yes.

What was this Council? The meeting was to suggest how to help Gorewan in connection with the Tribe.

You came back from Lovedale and to your surprise you found a Council? Yes when I came I found that the Council had been formed.

Appendix G

This Council was elected by your tribe? That is how I heard it.

You were told that? Yes.

It was a suggestion of the Resident Commissioner, Colonel Ellenberger? Well, I only know that the tribe elected a man.

Who were the men that were on the Council? Johnny and Simon Ratshosa, Phetu, Moloi, Disang and Edirilwe.

When you first heard of this Council you were dead against it? No that is not true.

Were you in favour of it? I didn't say anything, I simply said I would watch and see what the tribe would do.

Gorewan was the head of this Council? Yes.

You asked him "What does all this mean, why was it formed"? Yes I asked him those questions.

What was his reply to you? His explanation was that the Council wanted me to assist him as owing to the death of my brother there was a great row and he was unable to control the people.

Didn't that Council apply to you? I cannot say.

Do you think this Council was formed as a permanent institution, or was it to support Gorewan, a weak acting Regent? According to what Gorewan said they were elected to help him. He mentioned that in the meeting.

Of course you knew all about this Council as you met the Resident Commissioner in Mafeking? Yes he had informed me about it.

Didn't the Resident Commissioner give you the impression that this Council was of a permanent nature? No.

Do you deny that? No, he didn't say so.

You see, Chief, according to the accused you addressed the members of the Council and said "The question of the Council is a very important one and it is very important to know exactly what took place, and I have now come among you and I want to know the position of the affairs of the tribe and how they have been controlled since the death of the late Chief Sekgoma"? That is not correct.

You admitted just now what had taken place? No I didn't ask anything at the meeting of the Council. I remember one question that I asked during that meeting of the Council.

What was this question that you asked? I asked the Councillors how they ran the tribe. I spoke this during the meeting of the Council

You said "I have heard that you have put up a Council to support the Acting Chief Gorewan whom I understand you have found to be too weak to manage the affairs by himself"? I did not say that he was too weak.

You said I have just met the Resident Commissioner, Mafeking, on my way here? Yes I said that.

He told you that the Chief was dead and that Gorewan had been appointed as Acting Chief? Acting Regent.

Have you any reason for making a distinction? Yes because I was supposed to be acting Chief myself.

Aren't you Regent over this boy? Yes.

Didn't you say something about Gorewan having been appointed as acting Chief and that the Resident Commissioner had suggested Gorewan as acting Regent? No I didn't say that.

You further said that the Resident Commissioner had said that the Bamangwato nation had confirmed the arrangement? Yes I said that.

You went on and said "but if you find it to be against your wish you can do what you like"? Yes.

The Resident Commissioner further went on and he said "You can destroy the Council or allow it to remain, you can do just as you like"? Yes.

Then you went on and said that the High Commissioner had already approved of the Council and that it was a very good thing for the nation? I do not remember saying that.

Did the Resident Commissioner tell you that? I do not remember that.

Did you know that the High Commissioner had approved of it? Yes I knew that the High Commissioner had approved of that Council.

Appendix G

Then you went on and said "I have come among you Bamangwatos and I want you to tell me what the exact position of this Council is now. I understand the Council was meant for Gorewan and not for me"? That is not what I said.

You admitted that you thought yourself that the Council was not for you but for Gorewan? No answer.

Then you finished off by saying "Members of the Council I want to hear your opinions in connection with this matter"? Yes I remember that.

The Court adjourned at 5.10 p.m.

The Court resumed at 9 a.m., 23rd June 1926

Chief Tshekedi being warned that he is still on his former oath states:

[....................]

Dr. Lang: We finished last night with your speech when you arrived at the Council meeting. There were quite a number of Councillors there were there not? There were a few.

What did they say then? They spoke of different matters.

Didn't they say that the tribe was being managed in new ways which they didn't understand? Some of them said so.

And that it would have the effect of depriving you of autocratic power? No.

But you have autocratic power? I have got a power, but I have to consult the people before I do anything at all.

Didn't they point out to you that if you allowed this Council to exist you would command the respect of your predecessors? No Sir, they did not suggest that.

And that your orders would be undermined by your own subjects? No.

And the Council being in existence the Council would have the say in tribal matters? I do not remember that.

Surely they must have told you what their objections were? Yes they did say something.

What did they say? They said that they were not in favour of the Council as it was a new thing and they did not understand it.

Anything else? I only know that they said they did not understand the idea of the Council.

Somebody else said that the formation of the Council was suggested by cunning people who wished to deprive you of your Chieftainship? I do not remember all that.

Court: Do you remember any of it? The principal point that I remember is that some of the Councillors said that they did not like it.

Dr. Lang: Didn't they suggest that there were some people behind this Council who intended to deprive you of your Chieftainship? No I did not hear that.

You deny that was said? I do not remember it.

Simon was present? Yes.

Simon is going to say that all this took place and that somebody said that the effect of the Council would be that all power would be taken away from you and given to the white men? I do not know what he is going to say.

I must tell you so that you have a chance of denying it.

It was also said that you should rely on the old men and be guided by them, and not by the young men? That was not said at the meeting, and I deny it.

You know Phetu? Yes.

Who is he? He is Mphoeng's son.

Is he related to you? Yes.

How? Mphoeng is old Sekgoma's son.

What relation? Phetu's father is my uncle.

Since you have come back you have been in close touch with Phetu all the time? Yes like anybody else of my people.

Isn't he your Chief Adviser? Just like any of my uncles. He has the right to advise like the others.

Appendix G

He has been exercising that right quite a lot? I am not sure of that.
Don't you know who has been advising you most of all? I do not remember.
I say to you that Phetu is the man who has been giving you more advice than anyone else since you came back? No.
Would you like to say that he has not been advising you at all? He has advised just like all the other uncles.
Do you deny or not that Phetu is your Chief Adviser? He can advise me like all the other uncles.
Is he the Chief Adviser or not? I have replied already that I am not sure that he is the Chief Adviser.
Can't you give me a direct answer? I am not sure that he is the Chief Adviser.

Court: What you mean to say is that he has an equal footing with the other Councillors? Yes.

Dr. Lang: In your dealings with the Ratshosa Brothers he has taken a leading part? I am not sure of that.

Court: Has Phetu advised you in connection with the Ratshosa Brothers since you returned? No he was not the Chief Adviser. He has advised me like the others and has not given any more advice than the others.

Dr. Lang: Has he consulted you privately about it? No.
But couldn't Phetu come and consult you in a secret or private way? No.
Phetu was banished by the late Chief Sekgoma? Yes.
The people voted for this? Yes.

Court: How many years ago was it that Phetu was banished? In 1923.

Dr. Lang: Do you know whether the Ratshosas took a leading part in his banishment? No.

You know that it was done by the Bamangwatos? Yes.

That he was properly banished according to your custom? Yes.

He was pardoned afterwards? Yes.

Since he has come back he has always agitated for the removal of the Ratshosas from the high positions they have up to now occupied in the tribe? I do not know anything about that.

Are you going to tell me that since you came back you have never heard Phetu agitating against the Ratshosas? During the meeting they often quarrel about tribal matters.

Have you ever heard Phetu say that he has come back to wreck (sic) his vengeance [sic] on the Ratshosas? No I have never heard him saying so.

If other witnesses, members of your own tribe, say that will they be telling lies? I do not know what the other people will say but I am telling you what I know.

The evidence will be that in your presence Phetu on numerous occasions said that he was there for one thing and that was to get his revenge on the Ratshosas as they were the cause of his banishment, and that he was going to pay them out for what they had done? No I have never heard them say so in my presence.

Phetu is back now and he is entirely reinstated? Yes.

And the Ratshosas, who have played the leading part in the affairs of the tribe up to now, are standing here accused? Yes.

The position is reversed? Yes.

Coming back to the Council Meeting, Phetu was one of the speakers, is that correct? Yes he did speak.

According to the evidence that will be given for the defence Phetu said that he quite agreed with what had been said by the other members of the Council about the Council. No answer.

Court: What date was this Council Meeting? It was 3 days after my arrival.

What date? I returned home on the 17th February.

Appendix G

Dr. Lang: Phetu said that he quite agreed with what the Councillors had said about the Council: that he wasn't present when the Council was formed; that his name was proposed and confirmed by some of his friends; that he agreed to his nomination subsequently in spite of his views as to the Council? I remember all that you have said with the exception of the last sentence in which he agreed.

He was a member of the Council so he must have agreed to be a member? Yes he was agreeable.

Phetu at this meeting said that he agreed to be a member of the Council against his own views? I do not remember him saying that.

He expressed his opinion at the meeting that he was against it? No I did not hear him say so.

He spoke as to the advisability of keeping this Council on, that was the object of his speech? No I did not hear him say so.

So all he said was that he was a member of the Council? Yes I remember him saying that he was a member of the Council.

Do you mean to say that all he said was that he was a member of the Council? He also said that the Council was formed during his absence and that his name was proposed amongst others and that he must become a member of the Council.

And that he was against it? I do not remember that.

You remember little matters but not important things as to whether he was for or against the Council? On that particular day most of the members of the Council said that they did not understand the Council.

Did Phetu say that? Yes.

So that Phetu was against it? I cannot say.

Court: Do you mean to say that they did not understand why the Council was appointed? The Bamangwato people did not understand why it was formed at all.

Dr. Lang: You stand by it that Phetu did not advise the abolition of the Council? Not during that meeting.

Of course there were other men that supported the Council too? During that meeting I heard some of them saying that they like it.

Who? One was Simon.

Any others? Johnny.

Anybody else? The members didn't all speak as they did not understand it.

What about Disang? Yes.

Court: Did Johnny and Simon support the Council? Yes they were the only two that supported it as the others did not understand it because it was a new thing and a thing for the white men.

Dr. Lang: Did Edirilwe speak? Yes he did.

Wasn't he in favour of the Council? I cannot remember.

Simon made a long speech didn't he? Not very long, he made a speech.

Simon is going to say in evidence that he spoke as follows: "This Council was suggested by the Resident Commissioner at the Kgotla after the late Chief's funeral. The headmen of the tribe confirmed it in the presence of the Resident Commissioner, and the members were elected and the names were handed to the Resident Commissioner to confirm them in their appointment, and then the Resident Commissioner explained that it would be further submitted to the High Commissioner for approval. The Resident Magistrate, Mr. Neale, subsequently received a letter to say that the Bamangwato Council had been approved by the High Commissioner." This letter, according to Simon, was read before the tribe and "nobody complained, and now this morning I, Simon, hear that the people who agreed to the institution of the Council are now against it because they see your eyes and they are angry. It is a mistake to think that the Council was meant only for Gorewan; no it was meant specially for you, meaning the Chief, who was the Regent for Sekgoma's young child. It is a good thing to have this Council so that the affairs of the nation can be properly discussed in such a Council, and that there must be no

Appendix G

mistake about that, and you must always bear in mind that you are not the Chief but that you are the Regent and that you are acting for another man just as Gorewan acted for you while you were in School. Now the Council was appointed to look after the interests of the young infant child of the late Sekgoma and that it would serve the purpose." Johnny also spoke in a similar strain didn't he? Yes Johnny spoke like Simon.

The Council was not abolished at that stage was it? No.

What happened after that? Seeing that some of the members were not in favour of the Council and the others did not understand the idea another kgotla meeting was held.

You pointed out at this meeting that the members of the Council were against it? I informed the tribe that the members disagreed.

You told them that you would go and see Mr. Neale and point this out to him? Yes I did say so.

Did you go? Yes I did go after the meeting.

Accompanied by whom? With several people.

What did you tell him? I told him that I had come to see him about what the people had said about the Council and that the people would give their views about the Council.

What did he say? He listened.

Didn't he say anything? Yes.

Some gave their evidence? Yes.

Phetu was present? Yes.

Didn't he object to Johnny interpreting? Yes.

He objected to Johnny interpreting for him? Yes, not for the tribe, but for himself.

At Mr. Neale's office Simon spoke again? We were under some trees.

Yes, but in Mr. Neale's presence? Yes.

Did Obeditse speak there? Yes.

They still advocated the Council in Mr. Neale's presence? Yes that was what Simon said.

Then eventually Colonel Ellenberger arrived sometime in February? Yes on the 19th February.

You pointed out to him that in your opinion the people were against the Council? Yes.

And that the majority of the people were against it? Yes I said so.

He told you that he would convey what you had said to the High Commissioner? Yes he promised that.

After that the Council was never heard of again? No.

So the net result was that the Ratshosas all along advocated for this Council? Yes they like it.

The others were against it? Yes.

Including yourself? I wished to be led by the tribe.

Yes but what was your view? The only thing was that I would follow the people.

The Ratshosas say that you yourself were against it? No answer.

From that day you were antagonistic towards them because they advocated the Council? Nobody can stand up and say that it was so.

Did you treat the Ratshosas badly after that? No I did not treat them badly.

After that when there was any meeting of the Kgotla you asked people who had complaints to come up and speak them to you? Yes I did say so.

Were there any people that spoke up and said "all the people who had been employed before, especially the Ratshosas, should be sacked"? Some men spoke and said that some of those employed by the preceding Chiefs should be discharged, meaning the Ratshosas.

Court: Did the people say that? The people said that in the meeting.

Dr. Lang: As a result of this you sacked Johnny didn't you? Yes after the tribe explained as to how they didn't like Johnny and the Ratshosas I sacked him. They explained to us how they didn't like Johnny.

Appendix G

Johnny had been working for the last two Chiefs for a very long time? Not a very long time.

Well he worked for Sekgoma as Secretary? He didn't as Secretary after the death of Sekgoma. Before the death of the late Chief he was not employed as Secretary.

Court: After the death of the late Chief there was an acting Chief appointed, did he employ Johnny? I do not know.

You didn't employ him at all? Yes I employed him.

Dr. Lang: Well he also worked with Sekgoma? Yes.

It was a very hard thing for him to be dismissed in this way? It all depends on the Chiefs.

Now as regards the question of regiments, you have quite a lot of regiments in your tribe? Yes.

The Ratshosas are all members of various regiments? Yes.

I understand that when these regiments are formed all members are of a certain age or more or less of one age? Yes.

Of course these regiments are not employed in warfare? No because there are no wars.

What is the object of these regiments? The object of the regiments is that they are working parties.

Are members of the Royal Families also members of these regiments? Yes.

Have they to obey the orders of the Captains of the regiments? All the royal blood are the leaders of the regiments.

Since you have come back has there been a lot of work to do on the roads? Yes.

What regiments were doing the work, were they regiments to which Simon and Obeditse belonged? Simon's regiment belonged to the roads.

Where were they working? On the roads outside Serowe.

Did all the members of that regiment attend? I cannot say whether all of them attended as some were at cattle posts, but all those who were present were on the roads.

They had to go? The custom is that when a man is asked to go to join his regiment he must be asked by the head of the regiment. A certain regiment is summoned to go out and the men are instructed by the leader. I call the head of the regiment and instruct him to go out and do some work.

In the case of Simon a regiment came along in March? Yes during March month I called that regiment to go out and make a fence outside at Serowe at the zoo.

Court: Simon is not the head of the regiment? No, Edirilwe.

Dr. Lang: Is it the duty of Edirilwe to call upon Simon and ask him to join his regiment? Yes if Simon was not among the regiment he would go and fetch him. He could send anyone to call him.

Wasn't the object of getting him to attend this regiment really to get him out to be beaten? No that wasn't the object.

In fact Simon refused to go? Yes.

When Simon refused to go what happened then? I was informed that Edirilwe gave instructions for some people to go and call him. I was told this.

But do you know this yourself? I do not know, I only heard it.

[....................]

[**Tshekedi is cross-examined by Dr. Lang** as to his order that the Ratshosas should be punished:]

I sent a messenger to call them and that they had refused to obey me and therefore I would punish them by beating them. So I ordered them to lie down. They refused.

Did they say anything? They stood up and told me that they would not lie down.

Who stood up? All three.

What did Johnny do? The people rushed towards them and tried to catch them, and Johnny started to strike with a stick.

Appendix G

Didn't he make a speech then? I only heard them saying that they were not going to lie down, after that there was an uproar.

Didn't he give a reason? He said was one of the royal blood, he was the son of a Chief.

Simon said the same thing? No there was an uproar.

He spoke during the uproar? I didn't hear when he said.

Is that correct what Johnny said? No that is not correct.

Is it a custom that even Chief's sons are thrashed in the Kgotla? Yes it is a custom.

What sons of a Chief that you know have been thrashed? My uncle Moloi was thrashed in the Kgotla.

How long ago? During the lifetime of my father. He was thrashed by his regiment.

Yes but I am asking about the Kgotla. Who also was thrashed? Johnny's grandfather was also thrashed at the Kgotla.

You cannot say that as you were not alive then? I heard it.

The only man that you know in your time was Moloi. Do you know of your own knowledge that Moloi was thrashed or did you hear it? I heard it.

Have you seen anyone thrashed? No I have not seen anyone thrashed but I know it is a custom.

It must be a very great indignity for a son of a Chief to be thrashed in that way? They are all supposed to be thrashed in the Kgotla.

Is it an insult? No.

Not considered an insult? No.

If you were punished by your father in that way you would not have considered it a great insult? No.

You would not have punished a man in this way for a small matter? According to the gravity of the offence the punishment is meted out.

What did the Ratshosas do to offend you? By not coming that morning.

Is that a very serious crime in your country? A very great offence.

You always thrash people for it? Yes I have got the right to thrash or fine them.

Why did you thrash them? I wanted to thrash them and teach them a lesson.

You were advised to do that? I am their Chief and I do as I want.

When Johnny refused to be thrashed what happened then? The tribe, who were present, caught hold of him and hit him.

How many? I do not know.

Didn't they all come on top of him? No.

Didn't one man hit him with a stool? No.

Did you watch him very carefully? Yes.

Very carefully? Yes I watched, but I did not know much that took place. I was close by.

Johnny was left almost unconscious and it appeared that he was dead when they finished with him? No that is not true, they threw him on the ground and I commanded them to leave him alone.

Did he appear unconscious? He walked away.

Did you see a man striking him with a stick in his body? No.

What happened then? Simon and Obeditse went away without being touched by anyone. After Johnny and Simon went away we remained in the Kgotla.

Court: Did Simon and Obeditse run away? Yes.

Dr. Lang: Of course you were going to give them a hiding too? Yes.

You were satisfied that Johnny got his hiding? Yes I was satisfied since he was thrashed.

[....................]

Dr. Lang: The people were very angry of course? Yes because the Ratshosa brothers said that I had no right to thrash them.

Appendix G

Did they show their anger in any way? No they didn't do anything to show it.

[....................]

The position is this, the people may have been very angry with the Ratshosas, and you know your people and the Ratshosas say that people were armed, and they might have been without you knowing anything about it. Knowing your people as you do know, and knowing that they were angry, it is quite possible that they were armed? I did not see anyone.

Court: It is quite possible that some of your people were proceeding to a cattle post when it is usual to take their arms with them? Yes it is quite possible.

Dr. Lang: There may have been people with arms? I do not like to say what I have not seen. I like to tell what I have seen.
The next thing that you know was that you saw the Ratshosas with guns? Yes.

[....................]

After [. . . being treated by a doctor] did you hold a meeting of the Kgotla; I mean that afternoon? Yes on the evening of that day I called my men and said that I wanted the Ratshosa Brothers. I said that I wanted the Ratshosa brothers "dead or alive."
Had you any right to kill them? Well they having fired first.
So you thought that you had every right to do that? If a person shoots at you you can do so.
You instructed them to go and kill them if they could? I said "Bring them dead or alive."
You also instructed them to burn their houses? No, the houses were burnt during the night; then the following morning I gave instructions that they must burn the remaining houses.
That is why the Ratshosas are in custody? Yes this was after the Resident Commissioner had detained them.

Rex Versus S. and O. Ratshosa, 1926

So far as you are concerned they are finished altogether? No it was a fight between ourselves.

Did you look upon it as a war? Yes because firearms had been used.

So you retaliated by burning down their houses? Yes.

So this was a war and you retaliated by burning their houses? Yes it was a fight.

Now after the white men have finished and tried them you will probably punish them again being the defeated party? No that cannot be said here.

But you are going to deal with it? That is for me to say.

But you are going to see about it? Today I am waiting to see what the Government does.

You are always talking about your tribal customs and your right to deal with your people. As a result you punish them by burning their houses down one day, and for the same act they come before the white man's Court, and it all depends what the white man does whether you punish him again for the same act? I do not speak much about these things, and some of our men have no fingers.

Court: Is your punishment of the Ratshosa brothers complete? If they were still under my control I would not have finished with them.

Dr. Lang: So that under your native custom even though a man is punished in a white man's Court you can punish him again for the same thing? No.

[....................]

Mr. Minchin: You have been asked about native customs. What is the punishment for attempted murder? In accordance with the old customs they would be killed.

Appendix G

Court: And under the present custom? We take them to the Magistrate. When a man has committed a certain crime it must be taken to the Magistrate.

You hand him over to the Government? Yes.

Have you the right to fine these people for any crime like attempted murder, take their cattle or anything like that? As far as I know I know that the Chief has all the power except life and death.

Mr. Minchin: Since the Ratshosas have fallen from their high estate, lost their prestige, what has been their attitude towards you? They despise me and do not obey any of my orders.

They do not go to the Kgotla? Both accused do not go to the Kgotla when called.

When you meet them in the Stadt do they greet you? Yes they did.

Politely? Yes they appeared to be polite.

I want you to tell me who was the Ratshosas' father? He was an ordinary man.

Was he a headman? Yes a headman under another headman.

Whom did he marry? He was married to Bessie, the late Chief's daughter. She was the eldest daughter.

Did he get any particular rank then? No.

Did Bessie bring any property to the father's estate? I only heard it.

Did the Ratshosas' father have any property before he married Bessie? No answer.

You say that Simon and Johnny and a whole lot were the principals in the tribe at one time? They became well known and Johnny was Secretary to the Chief.

What I mean is that they all held positions of trust in the tribe. Johnny, wasn't he the Chief Secretary? Yes.

What was Simon? Once a teacher at the School.

What School, a tribal School? Yes.

Appointed by Khama? Yes.

These two held responsible positions under Khama? Yes.

This endured for several years? Yes.

When did the majority turn against them and didn't want them anymore in those positions? The majority decided that they were not to be trusted.

Give me the reason? There was once a dispute between Modisaotsile and the late Chief Sekgoma. The tribe suspected that the Chief did not receive letters from Modisaotsile. This was during the time when Johnny was Secretary.

What you are talking about is common knowledge in the tribe? This was said by the tribe.

I want to find out how that enmity arose and I am going to do so. This is for my own information and guidance[.] He only received letters when Edirilwe was acting in the office.

The whole matter is this, that the tribe suspected that the Ratshosa brothers were not playing the game and that is why they wanted to remove them from their positions of trust? Yes.

I understand that Johnny was on this Council? Yes.

Was Simon on the Council too? Yes.

Did they ever express publicly to your knowledge that they were very incensed about the Council being done away with? On one occasion at a certain meeting I heard Simon declaring that if that Council was done away with there would be no Chief that would be over him.

Did Johnny make any comment? No.

What did you understand from Simon's remark? From what he said I understood that he could only be controlled when the Council was still existing, otherwise no Chief could control him.

Dr. Lang objects to this question.

Have you ever done the accused any harm? No.
Have you oppressed them in any way? No.
Have you deprived them of any property? No.
The only thing you have deprived them of so far as I know is the two Masarwa girls? Yes.
That is the only thing? That is all I know.

[....................]

Appendix H

REPORTS OF THE PROCEEDINGS OF THE THREE
KGOTLAS HELD DURING THE PERIOD FROM
NOVEMBER 1948 TO JUNE 1949 TO
DISCUSS SERETSE KHAMA'S MARRIAGE
TO RUTH WILLIAMS

(Botswana National Archives, DCS 37/2)

The First Kgotla

Extracts From Notes Taken of Some Speeches During Tribal Meetings 15th to 19th November Held to Discuss the Question of Seretse's Marriage.*

Kgotla Speeches 15-17 November 1948

After several speeches had been made condemning the marriage, the Chief asked those in favour of it to speak.

Rajaba: [I have] no objection.

Kwagoean Mokganedi: Seretse is Chief. Does it matter about his wife?

Ramosamo (Sefhare Headman): We want Seretse to stay but we don't want his wife. If we drive him out, how will he live? If he

---

*Notes written by S.V. Lawrenson.

Appendix H

does go, it will be interpreted that Tshekedi conspired [to get rid of him]. If Seretse goes to England, he will have no love for the Tribe.

Serogola (Deputy Chief): We are all agreed we don't want the wife. If he takes this wife, he is not fit to be Chief. We must ask Government to see the marriage is dissolved.

Seretse: You are hiding something from me. The only objection I had had so far is that I have taken an European wife. Native Custom has been changed before. Under Native Custom you could have several wives. Khama changed this and adopted Christianity and had only one wife. We now worship God. You are hiding things from me. If I am not Sekgoma's son, tell me. People have been pardoned before, why not pardon me? Is this a conspiracy? I want to stay here and serve the tribe. I don't like German [i.e. Nazi] methods and this is like it. I want to stay here. Why is my fault so great?

P. Mphoeng: Quoted examples of people who were punished because they did not comply with customs of tribe regarding marriage. He knew of four civil wars caused by Chiefs not consulting their people, and if it were not for British Protection there would be one now.

Booditswe: If a Chief takes a wife without consultation with people there is always a dispute and a fight. Quotes examples of split between Khama and Sekgoma because Sekgoma took a wife without consultation.[1]

---

[1]During the 1890s Sekgoma II divorced the wife, Mma-Oratile, given him by his father Khama III. He then took a series of consorts not recognized by his father, or by church or magistrate, as lawful wife. Finally, in 1920, he married his father's choice, Tebogo Kebailele–who gave birth to Sekgoma's legitimate heir, Seretse, in 1921.

Seretse: Is the intention to cause a split in the tribe and then blame me? Is there to be a fight because I took a wife without consultation?

Chief: Nobody wants to suggest a fight.

Seretse: I think I am right. I want freedom of speech.

Chief: Seretse is under no compulsion. I am only giving him advice.

Seretse: Whether the Chief speaks loudly or softly I will always regard it as a reprimand and a stifling of freedom of speech.

Tumiso: The only thing that will split [the] tribe is a woman. The Batawana hived off from the Tribe because of a woman. Quotes case when Mathiba, Chief of Batawana, wanted to marry a girl and was not allowed to.

Gorewan: Withdraw from the woman, otherwise there will be war.

Motalaote: In old days there would be war. What is happening now is more painful and the trouble will be drawn out indefinitely. Seretse's wife knows nothing of Native Law and Custom. When he is in the Kgotla, Seretse will be called by his wife at 11 o'clock for tea [she] not knowing that kgotla meetings go on indefinitely. When women want to see him at night to bring complaints, she will not understand. She won't be able to go to lands etc.

[To Seretse:] Withdraw from the marriage. I was instrumental in bringing Sekgoma back to Khama. You married this girl without the consent of her parents. There are lots of girls here. Why pick an European. She will object to your talking to other women.

Moremi of Mobele Kgotla: Seretse should hear what the Tribe says. If [the] European woman were concubine it would be alright, but the Tribe cannot regard her as [the] principal wife.

Appendix H

Kgosetshu: Seretse should not have mentioned his forefathers. He should have treated his case on its own merits. Seeing everybody is against him in this issue, he should withdraw from the stand he has taken. Otherwise he will cause [a] split in the Tribe.

Manyaphiri: There are two [alternatives]. One: Seretse stays. Two: Seretse returns to his wife. We must find out what line he proposes to take.

Peto Sekgoma: We must get down to what is to be done. If there is a way to do so, Seretse must be separated from his wife. Seretse must not be allowed to return to England.

G. Mathiba: The Ratshosa affair was to secure Seretse's rights. Seretse seems by his attitude to be discarding his people. I am not agreeable [that] Seretse should return to England. I love him. He says he likes this country, but how can he if he wants to return to his wife. The disturbance which will result from this sort of thing can only result in one thing–direct rule by the British Government and not indirect rule.

Chief: Has anybody in this gathering ever heard [it said that] Seretse should be driven away?

Seretse: I object very strongly to Mathiba saying he loves me. I hate him.

Kgosidintsi: I never heard anybody say Seretse should be driven away.

[Unidentified speaker:] There was someone who said Seretse should return to England.

Nwako: I did suggest at one time that Seretse should be found a spot in Ngwato Territory in which to stay.

Nthebolang: You said Seretse should be sent back to England or be given a piece of Ngwato Territory in which to stay.

Kgosidintsi: I have no intention of advising Seretse to discard his uncle, nor advising Tshekedi to discard Seretse because he has taken an European wife.

My decision is that Seretse should not return to England, [neither] should he retain [his] wife.

Chief: I want further statements by Ramosamo, Serogola and Peto Sekgoma. Malope suggested Seretse [would] be deceived by [our] bringing him out [from England] and then not letting him return.

Ramosamo: [I] do not like Seretse to be deceived. But he should not be allowed to return to England and so will take responsibility [for "deceiving"him].

Serogola: I never said Seretse should be deceived. I[simply] said he should be allowed to come.

Chief: I sent telegrams and reported to the Tribe that he would only come on condition that if people did not want his wife, he would be allowed to return [to England].

Peto Sekgoma: The Chief can say that the Tribe is refusing to let him go.

Mopedi: The Chief paid Seretse's passage out. If Seretse returns it will be construed that the Chief has allowed him to return.

Elijah Mokgwathi: [I am] critical of [the line of the] Chief's questions. It would be better if Seretse had asked what [the] tribe would do. Seretse must not be allowed to return home.

Chief: Seretse's wife should be allowed here?

Mokgwathi: I now agree with what all the others have said.

Appendix H

Gasemore: Seretse should be allowed to return [to live?] with his wife.

Peter Sebina: I advise you to weigh the demands of the Tribe carefully. In private you will hear many tales. In public you will hear the truth.

Mothabane: [We should] refuse definitely to allow Seretse to return. The authorities should be so informed.

Ketareng: [It] does not matter who Seretse married, European or African, but he should have consulted the tribe. If Seretse returns, Tshekedi will be criticised.

Ikuku: I originally thought Seretse should be left alone but now I agree with the majority.

Panziri: Everything possible has been done, but if Seretse insists on bring his wife here there is nothing that can be done about it. The Chief has done his best. If Seretse's wife['s coming here] ruins the tribe, Seretse will be responsible.

Diahile: Let the wife come. In course of time he will discard her.

Masetsane: I first agreed that Seretse should have an European wife but in view of the discussions, I agree now with the majority. If the wife comes, mosquitoe etc. will drive her out.

Ontiretse: People must be unanimous, particularly the Royal Family.

Chief: Some people are inclined to contradict themselves.

Mathiba: Masetsane is not straight.

Obeditse Ratshosa: Seretse has taken a woman legally [in European Law] and the only thing left is for us to give a verdict on Native Law and Custom. Consult Government and let them assist. The deed has been done and he has married an European.

Motshumi: Seretse should be pardoned and the woman allowed to come here. Seretse has admitted his wrong. It has been said the tribe would be split, but this cannot be said with certainty until it happens.

Several other speakers: All opposed to the marriage. Suggestion of keeping Seretse here [was deemed] impossible. [We] have got to abide by the undertakings. The Tribe has not [yet] come to the point. If Seretse goes what will the Tribe do?

Oteng Mphoeng: If Seretse goes he must be assisted financially.

Maoto: We want Seretse to stay. If he goes it is his [own] affair.

Mosinyi Segotso: If Seretse goes back it is his own affair and he can't blame anybody but himself.

Phetlo Mphoeng: Even if we are like Germans, we feel you should not be allowed to go. [We] implore you to stay. [But we] can't keep you in a cell. You must abide by Native Law and Custom and obey. [Then] later when you rule, you will be obeyed.

Gaolebale: Very fact Seretse came out shews he was obeying. But he had an argument the other day about the marriages of his grandparents which shews something was put in his head after his arrival here.

Seretse says European law is written, Native law is not. Yet how does he think people can talk about incidents regarding his grandparents? It is because they come to kgotla while Seretse does not. He has only been once since his arrival. I have heard of no division [of the Bamangwato] yet, but the way we are going on [we] will cause one.

Appendix H

Seretse: I love the Chief and, although people are suggesting that there is trouble between us, it is not so. I wrote to the Chief about my marriage in order that there would be no complaint about lack of [prior] consultation. If I am against the Chief, I must be against the tribe, and that is not so.

Chief Mokgosi Bamalere: [We] implore Seretse to hear what the people say.

Chief Kgari Bakwena: Seretse has done this contrary to Native Law and Custom. There are duties expected of a wife which Seretse's wife would not be able to perform, e.g. going to [the] lands, receiving strangers, giving people hospitality etc. etc. Seretse should listen to what the majority say.

Kgotla Speech, 18 November 1948

Chief Bathoen (Bangwaketse): Chief Bathoen stated that Seretse had married the European girl with the premeditated intention of abandoning the Chieftainship, and that Seretse was a coward in that he was evading the responsibilities of a Chief. He requested Seretse to be frank and say that he declined to take over the Chieftainship. Seretse's version that he was for the tribe and the Bamangwato Territory was not true, because he could not do so while he adhered to his intentions and while he was unwilling to abide by his uncle's instructions. Seretse has no intention of residing in the Bamangwato Territory. Seretse has made his first appearance before the tribe [in kgotla] over such an important and unpleasant issue. Seretse was undoubtedly working up to something and Chief Bathoen demanded that he be frank and state his case if any. Seretse has brought trouble on the tribe and on his uncle. By his action he has driven us (Bathoen and Bangwaketse Tribe) from this village and not until such time as he withdrew and obeyed his uncle's order, would Bathoen accept any invitation from Seretse. Chief Bathoen stated that he would be wary of Seretse as he had brought great scorn on Chief Tshekedi. The people who tell Seretse that Tshekedi is not his uncle and father were deceiving him and leading Seretse astray. Moreover those who incited Seretse were now quiet and silent.

(Transcript of Notes of the Closing Speeches in
the Kgotla at Serowe, 19 November 1948)

(The Chief reminded the meeting that yesterday he had adjourned to give Seretse a chance to consider what had been said, especially by Chief Bathoen and so that he too might consider how he should give judgment).

Seretse said: When we parted, I was told to go and consider. I now tell you my feelings regarding the words of [Bathoen] the Chief of the Bangwaketse and the others. The Mongwaketse Chief has said he regards me as hard-hearted; that I am afraid of taking the Chieftainship; that I do not love my country and people. He would have me think about my actions, and my refusal to leave my wife.

I can try to contradict his thoughts and the lengthy statement which he made. Maybe you do not all agree, maybe you do agree in thinking that I am deceitful in denying what is attributed to me—that my love of my country is words only, that in fact I want to return to England. If you suspect me of evil intent, then everything one does you attribute to that, whether it be so or not. These evil thoughts which are said to be in me—lack of love while asserting it in words—are not mine. I have not yet learned such things, nor have I got used to people and their evil ways as they have been described by the Chief of the Bangwaketse. I cannot suspect you of deceit; I must take what you say at its face value. It has been said that I am a football, pumped up by other people with bad air (spirit) (*moya*). It is said that someone has inspired me to refuse [i.e. resist]; that there is some ulterior motive behind it. But if you love each other, you will understand. Nobody has suggested to me, either by letter before I came, or verbally now, that I ought to refuse to leave this woman. And now I will say exactly as before, I do not want to leave my wife; I hear the requests that are made and the prayers prayed, but I am unable

Appendix H

to leave here, because as I have said, I do not think God would wish it.

It has been said that I am a coward, that I ought to say outright that I do not want the Chieftainship, that my heart is not with you or with this country. But I cannot say so; it is not in my thoughts, it is not so; I cannot say it in order to be thought a man. You are not satisfied with me because I refuse to leave my wife. You say I refuse to leave a woman whom you do not want. I cannot compel you. I admit that I have taken her against your will, that I refused to refrain. You say that if I will not part with her she cannot come here. You have the power; had I had it, she would have been here. I love my country and my people. I told you that although there has been this disagreement, I can do the work of the Tribe and I am willing to do it. You say that because I will not part with her, I cannot do the work of the Tribe.

Were I to part from her now, and to take her again tomorrow when I shall be already Chief, you would not then tell me that I must leave the Tribe. I would be on the throne, but I will not cheat you so. I have given you the opportunity to rule me, to reprove me. Were I already Chief, you would have to be silent, though you might be dissatisfied.

I have taken a wife without proper announcement, this is not custom; this is my fault and you reprove me for it, and you will judge me for it. You think I should admit that I do not want to serve you. It is not true. I do not know people, I do not know you. I do not know who is speaking his own thoughts and intentions and who is speaking those of others, who is speaking without thought. You all say you do not want the woman–though a few say they want her, they are a small minority and they must not be heeded. I have told you, I tell you now, I cannot leave her. I cannot leave her.

Chief Bathoen said: The child of my uncle has said that I counselled him. I did so, I do so now, and I brought forth evidence for what I said. I said yesterday that people have led you astray in suggesting to you that Tshekedi is not your father.

There is no Motswana who has no father. Though perhaps not physically, Tshekedi is your father in deed.

You have suggested that we refuse you this woman because you are not yet Chief; that we could not do so if you were already Chief. You are mistaken. Were you doing this if you were already Chief, we would all be absent from here; you would have nobody to rule. These people do not belong to you [as an individual], they belong to a Chief whom they can love and respect. You are quite mistaken.

I said you fear [to take on] the Chieftainship. I say so again. Nobody can cast fire among people whom he loves. Even though in this matter the Tribe might be afraid to tell you what they think, they would scatter from you. I take back nothing that I have said. Do not think that a Chief cannot be answered [back]. The humblest servant can call the Chief to him. If the people go from here [Kgotla], who would be Chief of these poles?

Chief Tshekedi: Bamangwato, first of all I thank the District Commissioner, because when I invited him to this meeting he did not refuse to come, nor did he plead government business. I thank him because he has borne with it to the end. I thank him for his patience. He is the first District Commissioner in the Protectorate to come to hear how the people speak. Mostly they stay apart, not knowing how we speak, how we act and feel. So we perhaps despise you for not knowing the feeling of the Tribe, you know only those who bring their complaints to your offices. Had the trouble you have taken been taken before, you would have known how we feel. I hope that now you will understand that we do not fear to speak out.

I also thank the Chiefs of the Bamalete, Bakwena and Bangwaketse. A fire is burning in Gamangwato and you have come to pour water on it; so I thank you.

I do not know, perhaps I ought to address the Tribe, but in truth I have nothing to say to you. The Chief of the Bangwaketse made us take time, so that Seretse might think, and I too considered what I should say. I have nothing to say to the Tribe, I speak to this child. To you (the Tribe) I have listened carefully.

Appendix H

The Bamangwato are in the same distress as I am, at least the great majority. Nevertheless, as I have listened to some, even you agree with me that we refuse [reject] the woman, all the same we differ. It seems that you are perhaps thinking "This person [Tshekedi] has long been a burden on us; you (Seretse) would have released us. So I am glad that some new voices have spoken, apart from those whose ways I already know. What I would specially say is this; let there be trifling [with] other matters, not in a case like this. To you, child, I say; "*Motho ga a itsiwe senaga*": a person is not known like the veld. This is the first time you have heard it said, but the Chief of the Bangwaketse has said you have long transgressed. I did not say it, but as I hear it said I can now say [to the Bamangwato] "Your child has long doubted me." I shall give evidence; I do not conceal things.

I have looked after this place since I was a child. I have been tried by many things, some of them big things. I have had responsibility for a big Tribe, of many septs [clans], more divided than any [other] in the Protectorate. I have done this for twenty years. You come here ruined by others; you have not been ruined by Tshekedi. Although you speak as you do, you are not my equal nor are you experienced as I am. You might have spoken to me about your doubts when you were qualified to do so. Then I should have answered you. I shall not answer you now.

If I have cared for the Tribe, I will not say how I have done it in words, my actions shall tell. Have I love or not? I shall not speak, my actions shall speak. If I change in this, my actions shall show it.

When your child came, I told you that I should speak to him privately and I did so. I told you (Seretse) overseas, that if you want to split the Tribe, you have succeeded. There are the two of us, but you will not bring a lawsuit against me. Though we go to argue a case, my heart is clean. I shall be ruled by the Bamangwato.

Had I found the Bamangwato divided, with a majority agreeing to this marriage; had they been evenly divided, or even had there been a minority worth considering in favour, I should have said that I refuse to agree to her being married to my child.

I have no white blood [i.e. I am no saint], but all the same, if the Tribe agrees, I will not split it, I will say farewell. I will go to be a member of the Bakwena or Bangwaketse tribe. (I have refrained from suggesting the Batawana, [because] if I suggested going there you might think I want to be a Chief [again]—as there is nobody there my equal in rank and at present they have no Chief. This word [i.e. idea] of [my] going has not had to be said by me. But if it had, I should go. You (Seretse) would stay and you would scatter the Tribe. I tell you you are wrong, you began this wrongly. When you began, you told me that you had already put up the banns [of marriage in church], that you wanted me to hear [of it] from you yourself and not from another. You said "I am marrying; I know you will refuse, you cannot like it, nor the Tribe, I did not want to tell you before as I knew you would not like it."

There is nothing would hurt a parent more than when You stood and said "You are like the Germans, to drive people out." That could only mean me. You know who kept your town [i.e. state] for you. If you had doubted how I was doing it, you should have written, or spoken before you went away, that we might argue it out. Do you mean me or the Tribe when you say "You are like the Germans". I am amazed. You believe I am hardhearted in my dealings, yet you have hardly lived in this town. If I am hardhearted, the Bamangwato would know: I cannot [again] say it.

You say that the suggestion of your refusing to serve your country is a calumny. But you say you want the woman. We hear your words, but we see your actions. What are your first actions? I have held this town for you and I have no quarrel with the Bamangwato, possibly excepting a few whom you could count on your fingers. But I am amazed that you say I am a German to them. When we came from the kgotla [yesterday] and I sought to advise your child, I said to him "In kgotla your younger brother [i.e. a paternal cousin] told the people he found [contacted] you overseas, that you said you did not want to cause Tshekedi sorrow. You did not know your father, you had heard of the greatness of your grandfather, but you knew only Tshekedi; you wondered if you could manage affairs as he did." I did not answer it. This saying may please some; me it does not please. I am your father,

Appendix H

everything I do I do for you. I have looked after the Tribe for you. It was handed over to me; I found it without life, because of how your father [Sekgoma II] had been away (in the veld). I have moulded it. Some [people]will speak against me in private, they fear to do so in public, not for fear of me but for fear of the truth. To suggest that you are afraid to take on this work because you cannot manage it will arouse jealousy [i.e. public resentment]. How can you say you cannot manage [it, when], you have me to help you if you want. You said the other day that you were afraid of me, could not speak freely in kgotla because I reprove you. But you were not afraid to say such a thing as this. You spoke yesterday as if you were already Chief, and said that had you the power you would bring her.

My heart is rent. I thought I was serving you; I had no ease in order that I might serve you; now I am heartbroken.

I am afraid because of you. Apparently you plead a case about the throne as if you were already Chief. Had you just said you had nothing more to say this morning, it would have been better. But you answered the Chief of the Bangwaketse as if you were his equal. When you asked for it, you were told the facts about Khama's marriage and how it divided the Tribe. Your father was refused by the Tribe when he wanted a woman. But those women spoke with their own people [relatives] present. The cases are not parallel [with yours]. You have nobody at your side and you have nobody to plead against [i.e. and/or you?].

I would have been content to ask you where you would put me had I been given a separate village [to live in] and you stayed here. I would have overcome you, because the people would have left you for me. But I will not contest the town with you; I will not divide it with you, nor will I be here with your woman. I will not divide the Bamangwato. I would have taught you [when you became Chief]; then afterward if we did not agree, I would have gone away quietly.

I do not want the woman; if you marry her, you do so elsewhere. I say this before giving the Chieftainship over to you with the consent of the people. Would there have been such a gathering as this if an ordinary person had married a white woman. We should have merely laughed at him.

I tell you Bamangwato that I am leaving it to you, I do not judge. You Bamangwato refuse the woman, even as I do, so I am acting according to your words. There is a custom among the Batswana when a new Chief is to be installed, to call you to say that he has arrived. Then there is a time to teach him his duties, after which I must call you again to hand over the power to him. After that I can give him a wife, having secured him in his position.

He says he is married according to English custom, but I deny that she is a wife according to Sengwato custom. He does not know either English or Setswana custom properly. I am not afraid of this marriage. The missionaries opposed it, and it was not celebrated in Church. The white race ruling us respects our customs, but you Seretse have not done so.

The Government have power to refuse a Chief. He can be sent a letter saying he is causing a dangerous disturbance in the tribe, and he must go. We say that if this woman comes, she will divide the Tribe. There is a special law for Royal marriages. Had I had proper help [i.e. from Government], he would have been prevented from marrying before we could speak together. Therefore she cannot come to this country. Of those who have spoken [in Kgotla], 85 spoke against it. Only 7 spoke in favour—and when those spoke there was audible dissent in the kgotla. Since [even] a Chief can be exiled, I ask the Government to refuse her entry.

As for you Seretse, I cannot prevent you going [back to England]. If you insist on going you can go.

To those who say let him take her . . . There is no law forbidding it. But we are not considering law; we are considering the well-being of the country. He insists on doing it; I cannot do anything about it. If he could change his mind and leave the woman [that would be] well; but if he comes to rule with her, I cannot be under her.

Setswana law is not yet written, but yet it is law. We thought you Seretse might be the one to write it, but you have poured earth on it. Your grandfather altered the law, abolishing

Appendix H

bogadi and *bogwera,* but he did so as Chief. You would do so when you are not Chief. I will not alter the custom by which the Chief's wife regulates the [royal] courtyard.

I have asked that the woman be prevented from coming. If he [Seretse] stays here, I am glad; if he wants to go, I must give him the money for his journey. If he marries her, let him do so at the home of her relatives. I shall hold him [back] only as I have done before. If he goes, I shall call those of you who are here, telling them he bids them farewell. We shall remain. The Tribe may scatter after I have left it, but not while I am here.

The District Commissioner: Chiefs Tshekedi, Kgari, Bathoen, Mokgosi, and the Bamangwato, I greet you. First I should like to express my sympathy with you in this great trouble of yours, a trouble in which you have the sympathy of the Government and all people. Just now in my own country the people are celebrating the birth of a new Prince [Charles], the first son of Princess Elizabeth, whom you met at Lobatsi. I should have been inclined to ask you to join in these celebrations but I realize this is not possible because of the shadow on the Tribe.

The history of the Bamangwato tells of troubles from time to time, but I doubt if there was ever such a one as now, and it behoves all to keep this well in mind. During the past few days I have listened carefully to the speeches and I would congratulate you on the thoroughness and the restraint of all. A full report will be made by me to the R.C. [Resident Commissioner]. At this stage I prefer not to comment on the merits of the case, but observe that the Tribe has made its attitude perfectly clear. It remains now for me to appeal to you Tshekedi, Seretse and the Tribe, not to allow this trouble to cause division, for the sake of the freedom which you cherish so much. I make this appeal to you and I know you will not disregard it. To you Seretse, one word of advice. You have heard your fathers speaking to you. Do not disregard them.

The Kgotlas on Seretse Khama's Marriage, 1948-1949

The Second Kgotla

Seretse's Marriage to Ruth Williams in London
Notes of Kgotla Discussions 28th to 29th December, 1948[*]

Kgotla Speeches, 28 December 1948

Kgosi Tshekedi: As we have a large gathering I request those who wish to speak to speak loudly. In the first place I wish to inform you that we have the Government Secretary in our midst this morning. I requested that he should be present at this meeting as there appears to be no ending to the last discussions. The Government Secretary is not here to preside at this meeting but is merely here as an observer. As this is not the first time we have had a similar meeting discussing the same subject we all know what was discussed at the last meetings. It is not necessary for me to repeat what was said. At the conclusion of the last meeting which was on a Saturday, it was either on that Saturday or next Sunday evening that Seretse came to me and said that he was asking for my forgiveness, and secondly that he wished me to arrange for his passage to return to England. I suggested to him that he should not return immediately as it was probable the officials would like to have a talk with him before he returned, and that I was preparing to leave Serowe for the purpose of preparing my representations to Government on the decision arrived at, and I asked him to wait for me until my return.

It is not usual for me to read to the Tribe my representations to Government in decisions arrived at at tribal meetings, but as this is an extraordinary matter I decided to read my written representations to the people to get their confirmation before such representations were handed to government as an official document. Consequently I called a meeting of the headmen of "*Batlhanka ba ga Kgari*" after which I called a meeting

---

[*]Notes presented to the Bechuanaland Protectorate Government by Chief Tshekedi Khama.

Appendix H

of the royal headmen and sub-chiefs. To these meetings I read my written representations with the request that they be amended, altered or added to where it was found the statements were inaccurate. Previous to these meetings I had handed a copy of my representations to my nephew Seretse.

At all these meetings my statement was accepted as a correct representation of facts.

After I had handed Seretse a copy of the statement he again asked me when his passage to England would be arranged.

After I had convened the above meetings Seretse complained to the District Commissioner, and when we were both at the District Commissioner's office he stated that he was dissatisfied because two meetings had been convened to discuss a matter which concerned him but at these meetings he had not been called. I had replied to him that I did not call him because there was no new matter to consider, but I merely wished to have a confirmation or a correction of the representations I had made. At this meeting it was ultimately arranged to have the present meeting as it was the wish of Seretse that a meeting should be convened. Seretse will now speak.

Seretse Khama: I am also pleased to see that the Government Secretary is here as an observer. After the previous meetings I made a request to my uncle that arrangements should be made for my return to England, to join my wife and also to go and complete my studies which I hadn't had time to do. I consider it necessary that I should complete my studies because I understand it is not possible for my wife to join me here, and consequently I would have to work for my living. After this I was told my father was convening a lot of meetings discussing my affairs. He convened two meetings, one for the royal headmen and the other I understand for the headmen of the *Batlhanka*; and I complained because these meetings were held to discuss about me and I was not asked to attend. It was for this reason that I complained to the District Commissioner, and the District Commissioner asked my uncle and me to go and discuss things together. I now wish to hear from you people whether it is your wish that I should join my wife in

England and that she should not join me here. I do not wish to know the views of my uncle, because I know these; he says if my wife comes here he will leave the place. I wish to know the views of the people. I also understand that I am not permitted to reside in the Protectorate if I am with this woman, and as the officials are here I want everybody to speak freely. I ask that my uncle should not speak nor my uncles next to me namely Rasebolai, Phethu, Oteng, nor Serogola. I want to hear the views of the people first. My uncle has told me that this is a serious affair which might result with somebody losing his life—either himself or me. I want to hear from you as to whether you want to expel me from this country, and I say I am not going to be parted from my wife. Further I want to know from you. You are making this law as a result of my case—the law of driving me from my village because of my marriage.

Tshekedi Khama: I do not stand up to reply to various points raised. I just wish to make two points. Seretse says he does not wish to hear my views but wishes to hear those of the Tribe. I say Seretse is my son and it is not possible to silence me when his marriage is being discussed. Secondly I have already informed Seretse that this is a matter which can lead to serious trouble. In the case of any disturbance arising, Seretse will not be held responsible, nor the District Commissioner, but I will be held responsible—and consequently it is out of the question that I could remain silent. You say also that I should not speak because the tribe will accept my views because I am the Chief. I say to you that I am the son of Khama and you are the son of Sekgoma, and therefore the Tribe will accept the views of either of us according to their convictions.

Perhaps my nephew is of the opinion that I will deny having convened meetings at night-time. Far from [denying] that the meetings have been convened, I have full liberty to convene meetings anywhere and any time. I have not handed the administration of the Tribe to you. When a meeting is convened it is convened with the people, and those people are the Chief's people. You cannot expect to say bad words against a Chief of the Tribe

Appendix H

without those words getting known to the people. Another word which the Chief's son has forgotten to make known to the people is that he said in front of the District Commissioner that I was chasing him out of the country. My reply to this charge is my actions will speak for me.

Seretse Khama: Yes, I have said my uncle is chasing me out of the country. I do not want to leave this country and he does not want to. I understand that people can pay heed to my words. I do not think so because I have not ruled them yet. I say my uncle is chasing me out of the country because he says if I were to bring my wife he will himself leave the country. My uncle has told me that I was trying to fight against him before I became Chief whilst he was Chief. I am not claiming the chieftainship [but] I say it is the people who should tell me to leave and not my uncle.

Rasebolai Kgamane: I just wish to make a comment on one word which the Chief's son has stated. This matter was debated here at length. The decisions of the Tribe were recorded and a copy of such record was handed to you by the Chief. Not one in this meeting has said to you that you should go. All that the people have said is we do not want a white woman to be your wife. When the meeting dispersed this was the decision, and I do not think it is correct that the subject should be reopened. I say if there are any further difficulties this is not the place to re-examine them. The re-examination must go to a higher place. Seretse says he loves his country. He must; it is his father's country. But I do not believe that he loves his people, because from the time we had the meetings in this place Seretse has never come to the Kgotla. I have been the Chief's deputy ever since the first meetings but I have never seen him attending the Kgotla.

There must be something else to cause this meeting to take place. If the people have gone back on their first decision they must let us know why.

The Kgotlas on Seretse Khama's Marriage, 1948-1949

Seretse Khama: I want to hear from you people whether you [would] like me to live in England. This question of not attending the Kgotla can be discussed at another time.

Government Secretary: Chief Tshekedi has told you that I have come to listen to your discussions, but there is too much noise and I cannot hear what you are saying. Noise and fights will not help you [at all], and unless there is better behaviour I may go back to Mafeking without having listened to anything. You should speak like men.

Oteng Mphoeng: We have our customs. We may have our discussion in this place or elsewhere privately, but I know our customs. We have our four divisions Ditimamodimo, Maaloso, Maalosoanyana, and Basimane. We had a big meeting here and this matter was discussed, but today there appears to be a fifth division. I understand from Seretse that he does not expect us to speak today nevertheless—we shall talk. Now I shall address myself to the Tribe and say to them that before a decision made in Kgotla can be reversed there must be a reason for that reversal, and the matter must have been discussed at some meeting. I shall now call [upon] certain people to put questions to them. I call upon you members of Basimane Division. Will Boiditswe and others stand.

Seretse Khama: I see that you are calling people out by names. You have called out Boiditswe who is a senior *Motlhanka* to look after my interests. Ever since I came here I have never seen him once. He has never come to see me. I do not know whether that is in accordance with custom.

Boiditswe Nthuthu: Yes the Chief's son speaks the truth. I have never gone to see him at his house because I had heard that he had arrived and we always see him at the Kgotla. I came several times [to Kgotla] but have never found him.

Appendix H

Khumo Mothonami: We know of the record of the decision arrived at the last meetings, but the purpose of this present meeting I know nothing about.

Phuthego Moseakena: We have made one decision: we say we do not accept this wife, and we have had no other meeting except the last in this Kgotla.

Gabolebye Dinthi: Our views have not altered from those expressed previously.

Ramarula Mathodi: Ever since we left the last discussions we have had no others. Our views remain the same as recorded.

Tshoene Maudi: We have had no meeting apart from the meeting we had here. We still say we do not accept this woman.

Kgosi Tshekedi Khama: Today we shall probably discuss what should be discussed, and when this meeting disperses firm decisions should have been arrived at. This is a matter concerning the Chief-to-be and therefore there is no reason why the discussions should not be frank. Oteng correctly according to custom made certain leaders of various divisions to stand up. If it is the wish of the Tribe that a white woman should be their Chief's wife that is in order, but there is no reason why this statement should not be made frankly. It concerns the Chief's son. If it is necessary to reverse the decision previously made, then we have customary procedure to do so. There are various Kgotlas belonging to *Batlhanka Ba Ga Kgari*, and Seretse is going to carry his administration through this [Great] Kgotla. You have heard him say to Boiditswe that he has never come to see him ever since he came, and they gave replies to one another. When we speak of Basimane Kgotla we do not mean Boiditswe. That Kgotla composes many people and if it was their wish that the decision previously made should be reversed there is no reason why this section [division] should fear to say so. It is a customary procedure for this section to have deputed say four of their men to come and interview me, to tell me why they feel the previous Tribal decision should be reversed. I could receive people perhaps from another section of the Tribe. Headman Ramarula Mathodi could send other delegates to interview me. If I should chase these people away and not receive them . . . then procedure would have been followed and in a meeting like this you would have strong reason to raise the matter publicly because I had refused to consider your representations. This procedure has not been followed and I am surprised that this matter should be raised at this meeting. We have our big senior Kgotlas such as Ditharapa. If attempts to re-open this matter through Batlhanka Kgotlas had failed why not go to Ditharapa. Failing that why not go to the sub-chiefs of the allied clans such as Botalaote, Sebina, Bakhurutsi or even go far out to Maboledi to get those headmen to interview me that the matter should be reopened. This has not been done because ever since we left the previous meeting not a single person has interviewed me to say they wish the matter reopened. It is therefore incorrect for any attempts to be made to open this matter at a meeting of this kind. As far as I am concerned I have not altered my opinion that I do not accept this woman and I say nobody has ever on any day told me that they wish to reverse the decision. I shall be glad to see who is able to arrange the acceptance of this marriage without doing it through me. This matter concerns a chief of the Tribe and there is no reason why it should be discussed secretly. My son is no longer with me. He stays with Serogola. This puzzles me because I should be discussing this matter with Serogola. Allegations have been made that I have been arranging meetings at night-times. I suppose it is expected I am going to deny having arranged these meetings. The meetings were arranged when I heard that Serogola was collecting a number of discontented people to raise this matter again and I arranged night meetings to give instructions to the people to look out for this group which was being collected. The night meetings had immediate effect as I had expected and the other people got scared. The four say people who were being collected to raise the matter again are men who have had sentences passed against them. I do not know whether it will be

Appendix H

possible for Serogola to arrange the acceptance of this marriage without me.

Serogola Seretse: I hear from the chief that I have taken his son away from him and I want a clear statement to be made asserting this allegation.

Kgosi Tshekedi: The explanation you require will be given by those who attended your meetings.

Ramaselwane Boepego: I am the person who was deputed by the chief to attend Serogola's meetings. I met Rajaba Monaheng and I said to him that I am one of those who want this woman to come here. Rajaba said to me that it was well and we would have a meeting at Serogola's place. I asked Rajaba who the leader of this meeting was and he told me it was Serogola. And then I said if the chief's son is insistent that he must have this woman we will do our best. Rajaba Monaheng took our names down and sent them to Motamma Resheng who is the person deputed to collect the names of those who want the marriage accepted. They told me that I should listen hard to what the chief Tshekedi was saying so that I could report this to them. Serogola said to me that he will only believe those who will express their views in public. But we did not have any meetings. Serogola found us at Motamma Resheng's place. He had been sent to meet us there.

Serogola Seretse: The Government Secretary knows me and I have never gone to him when I was aggrieved with anything. But today you see that people are spying on me in this place.

Oahale Mathuba: The Chief came to me and told me that as I was a man who has various sentences passed against me it was probable that I would sooner or later be approached by people who were being collected to raise the question of Seretse's marriage. Shortly after this Rajaba Monaheng came to me and asked me what I felt about Seretse's marriage. I said to him I want the woman to come here. Rajaba asked me whether I knew of any others who held the same views as I did but I told him I knew of none. Then I asked him if there was any man of standing who held the same views as we did and he told me it was Serogola Seretse. I asked him if there were any others he told me Masetsane Ikitsing, and that two Motalaote's sons Gosiame and Bebeso were also with us. I said to him we seem to be few. After this I went to Motamma [and] I told Motamma Resheng that I was one of those who wanted this marriage to be accepted. After this Motamma took me to Serogola and asked me to state my views to Serogola. I told Serogola my grievances but Serogola made no comment. Motamma Resheng told me that report had already been sent to the District Commissioner by the chief. I also learned of other names of people who were of the same opinion as ourselves. These names are Serogola, Masetsane, Gosiame, Sebeso, Elisha, Tumelo, Legopelo, Ramasolwane, Oahile, Motamma Resheng, Rajaba. Serogola told me that he will listen to my views in a public meeting if I was at all grieved.

Masetsane Ikitseng: When we had a private meeting with the Chief a meeting being of Seretse's uncles I gave my views then that as Seretse was not prepared to give up this marriage he must be let alone. I feel now we are discussing the question of chieftainship because I see no harm in the marriage of Seretse. I understand a certain document was read but I have not seen it and I should know of its contents. What I should like to know is what are our views in connection with this marriage? The people in England do not seem to have any objection. It is we here who are objecting. I say let this woman come.

Rajaba Monaheng: The two men who have spoken namely Ramasolwane and Oahile speak my words. Oahile got out my views because he was spying on me. And I say let the woman come here by air. I am not going back on any word which I have said before. Serogola's name was given out by me. And if you are to be killed for this put the blame on me.

Appendix H

Serogola Seretse: How did my name come to be mentioned in this affair?

Rajhaba Monaheng: It is me who have mentioned your name that you are amongst those who want the marriage accepted.

Setshogo Kaochawe: I personally went to Serogola and asked him what his feelings were and told him I wanted the woman to come.

Lechokao Madikwe: It was plain to me that this matter will be as I see it now it has reached another phase. The previous debate was on the marriage but today we are debating another subject. This matter is not discussed in accordance with our customs and we do not know the truth of the discussions. I see that it has been twisted around. It is true that we had not gone to the Chief to voice our views personally. I want the Chief's wife to come. And I do not want her to be called Missus she must be known as the queen. When the Chief is given a "regimental" name is that not the time to signify that he is now of age and must be feared?

Dintwe Kakabali: When a chief's son is given a regimental name he must be feared thereafter.

Goitsikgosi Kekobile: When I refuse my son permission to marry any woman that signifies I am chasing him away.

Radisigo Goepamang: You have two sons Goitsikgosi and in both their cases you did not accept the woman they proposed to marry? Have you chased them away?

Goitsikgosi: Yes I have two sons and I did not accept the woman they proposed to marry but Tshekedi induced me to accept th[ese] marriages and they have married them. I did not chase them away.

Kgosi Tshekedi: You seem to be rushing up fighting to speak first. There is no intention of curtailing the discussions. Give each other time to speak[. T]he Government Secretary will not understand what you are talking about if there is so much noise.

Swaneng Modibetsane: Ever since these discussions started it is only Seretse who is being made to stand. Why do you want to bring us at loggerheads. I feel that you should discuss this matter with your uncles and then take it to the District Commissioner.

Kgosi Tshekedi: I say if there are any people who had any grievances about the last discussions they should have come to me especially you Swaneng headman of Maiketso Kgotla.

Swaneng Modibetsane: We are afraid of telling plainly that this marriage must be accepted.

Nwanaampe Mokibe: I say you should speak plainly and say Seretse must be installed in his position. I say you should accept the marriage.

Legomela Molefe: I heard Seretse say that his uncle and his other uncles should not speak but that the people should speak. He asked whether we were chasing him out. We say we are not going to agree that you must marry this woman in England[. W]e want you to marry her here. If anybody says you must go to England to join your wife there we will reply to him.

Mojuta Mabeo: I speak as Legomela has said; I say that you have come and we do not agree you should go back even to complete your education. We do not want your wife to be termed Missus [.T]his [form of address] is an insult. She must be known as queen. I say your wife should join you here. Chief Tshekedi has said that the marriage can only be confirmed through him. This is the truth[;] we can only accept this marriage by discussing it with him.

Appendix H

Lenyeletse Seretse: I stand up in connection with the allegations made about Serogola having meetings. I want the witnesses to speak.

Kgosi Tshekedi: I say my son is not with me but with Serogola. I am not concerned with meetings. You heard what Rajaba said and what Setshogo has said. I do not know why anybody who has a grievance concerning my son should go to Serogola. This meeting continues and you will get more evidence.

Oabona Ntobatsang: I say we want this woman, when we are in your presence we do not speak the truth. We are afraid of you but we want this woman.

Motamma Reshengg: I have heard my name being mentioned in this matter; when this matter was discussed first I was not present and after I had arrived I did not visit Seretse. Complaints and talks are brought to me in my hut. But these people come here to spy on us to extract our views, to collect evidence against us. The views of the people today are not the same. I blame Seretse for marrying without any consultation. But he was away from his home and lonely and naturally succumbed to temptations and got married to a white woman. The white people are our rulers today and it is an insult that we should not accept their daughter whom they themselves have no objection that we should marry. I do not know whether because of this marriage it is right that Seretse should lose his position. I have not heard it said that any chief has not been accepted because of his marriage. I do not know of any meetings convened by me and Serogola.

Lekhutile Motalaote: I agree that Seretse's father speaks the truth that when we changed our views that Seretse's marriage should not be rejected we should have informed him of such views. I said to Seretse that he was committing suicide when he married a white woman. You have asked Seretse to hear from us whether it is our wish that you should leave this country. We say such is not our wish. We want you to stay here. But I say you have persisted in your marriage and we are giving in. We say let this woman come. But you must know what you are doing. If you marry a white woman then you must know their custom. I have heard my son's names being mentioned but I was not present when any discussions were had.

Dikgakgamatso Kebailele: I see that all eyes are looking at me because I am the maternal uncle of Seretse. Ever since this matter commenced I have not said a word. But today I give my views. I say I see no fault in this marriage. I am the person who has to be killed first if Seretse is to be killed because I am his uncle. The Chief called me yesterday and asked me where I had gone to with Seretse. I told him we had gone to Lenyeletse and we followed him to Tshosa village. And I am sorry to hear that we were with Dingalo because I was not with Dingalo. I say if Seretse is chased out of this village I will go with him.

Kgosi Tshekedi: I have never asked you what your feelings were. I advised you to be cautious in your actions and not to rush on without the strength of the supporters of your views? With regard to your going out with Seretse to dances I do not wish to say anything thereto.

Phethu Mphoeng: I am surprised with you Lekhutile Motalaote. You seem to talk lightly on a matter of such serious concern. I do not agree that you know nothing of this attempt to reverse the decision. You were present when we had our previous discussions and you spoke against this marriage. If I were you I would remain silent. There was nobody being pressed to express any particular views. I understood you to say you do not want some of us to speak and I say to you the chief is subject to the wishes of his people and I do not see anybody who has a greater right to speak in this matter than Tshekedi who has brought you up. He is the only man who can protect you and none above him. When we have any dispute between father and son the father and son debate the matter. Personally I have said no to this wife and I

Appendix H

will continue to say no. I will only accept her after a donkey develops horns.

Manyaphiri Ikitseng: It was not my intention to speak now but I do so in view of the words made by Phethu. When Seretse was in England we said we did not accept Seretse's marriage because we have never inter-married with white people. Seretse arrived and the Chief told us to consult with him freely. We did so and at a subsequent meeting the tribe expressed its views that they did not accept this woman. I admire my brother Masetsane for his courageous stand in the last discussions [for] he said that he accepted Seretse's marriage. We were gathered to discuss this matter being sons and grandsons of Sekgoma and we all said we do not accept this woman and if there are any of us who today say they now accept this woman there is nothing reliable which they are saying. They are merely jumping from one decision to another. Regarding the document which was read to the sections of *Batlhanka* and *Dikgosana* I was not present at those meetings but accept the decision of those who were present. With regard to Serogola I know him to be a man who says one word and sticks to it. It is obvious that various members of the Tribe are most unreliable and I say to you Seretse pay particular notice to this change of decision. This attitude cannot help you in any way. I maintain what I said that I do not accept this woman. I have heard nobody in the meetings say that they do not love you. Regarding the Chieftainship there has to be real consultation before it passes from one person to the other. Seretse has nothing to say regarding the Chieftainship of the Tribe. You sent Seretse to school fulfilling his own wishes and not your wishes.

Lekhutile Motalaote: Replying to Phethu I say it is sometimes helpful to change one's views as it once helped Phethu. At one time he condemned the powers of the chiefs but he afterwards supported them. We are fighting and in every battle one must protect himself.

Phethu Mphoeng: Replying to Lekhutile I say conclude your statement by saying I am fighting my own battle.

Ookami Sedimo: I stand up because of confusion in my mind when the last meeting dispersed and decisions [were] reached. Such decisions were to be conveyed to Government and today we were expecting to be told of a reply from our Government but that is not the case. We are trying a new step. I expressed the same views as my other tribesmen that we do not accept this woman and I do not accept the views expressed this morning by those who spoke in favour of the marriage that they did not express their views last time because of fear. There is no reason to fear to express their views in a matter of this description. What they are really doing is merely to create agitation. I have not heard a single man saying Seretse is not our chief.

Goaletsa Segwesabone: This is the first time for me to give my views and I say Seretse's wife must come here and Seretse should not go anywhere. I hear that you do not accept this woman. I also complain of the meetings which the Chief has been making such as the one he made at Ramere Kgotla.

Ookame Sedimo: It is proper for the Chief to take any step to discover secret plots being made against him.

Gaofhetoge Mathiba: I am very pleased that it was you Sir, the Government Secretary, who has been deputed to attend this meeting because you know our customs. You are aware that no young people can arrange a marriage without the knowledge of the parents. I say as I have said before that I do not accept this woman. Nobody has ever gone to Seretse's father to plead with him that the marriage should be accepted. I have never heard before that the Chief and his son were not living peacefully together but today I see it is other people who are bringing them to loggerheads. I do not know whether his father has now changed his views. Tshekedi makes no claim to the Chieftainship.

Appendix H

All that he says is he does not accept the woman as a fitting wife for the Chief.

Nwako Nkobela: I am surprised because at the last meeting I made a suggestion that Seretse could be given a place to live in outside of Serowe. Serogola was very angry with me and accused me of trying to separate Kgama's sons but today he is trying to cause a division in the Tribe.

Serogola Seretse: During the last discussions Phethu said Seretse was dead and Tshekedi was alive, and Mathiba said he himself had parted with his own son and that Seretse must be thrown away. I cannot accept these things.

Kwagoean Dimeku: If I have got any views which I expressed secretly I ask somebody to stand up and express these views. In the first meeting I said openly that we were not going to lose Seretse on account of the white woman; why the white people are our masters today and they protect us. Further I want to know of the alleged meetings convened by Serogola. If Seretse's wife is coming to create trouble in this country let her come and do so. This is Seretse's country. Let him destroy his own country. You people are trying to create a misunderstanding between the Chief and his son. We are not chasing you away.

Mashako Mosarwe: We say let this woman come. We want her. We are not going to speak like the old men who are afraid of you, and who speak what you tell them to say.

Kwagoean Dimeku: I say let the subjects of the two meetings, those held by Serogola and those held by Tshekedi, be made clear as we do not know them.

Kgosidintsi Kgari: Your Honour, I am very pleased that it should be you who is present at this meeting. I speak as a member of our royal families. I am a descendant of both Sechele and Sekgoma. I say it is taboo that a Chief's son should marry without prior consultation. The parents of the Chief's son are the Tribe. It is [an] unknown thing for our Chief's son to have married a white woman. This is [an] evil omen. The Chief's son has asked whether anybody was chasing him away. Nobody has said to you go and nobody will say to you go. I heard somebody say it was an insolent expression to say Mrs. Seretse. I do not think so. I can call Chief Tshekedi's wife Mrs. Tshekedi. Regarding the question put by Dimeku I wish to tell him we were merely discussing the record of the decisions arrived at during the last meetings. It is true Seretse was not present at these meetings but I did not feel his presence was necessary.

Kammogo: We say we like the decision expressed here at the last meeting and if there are any difficulties this is not the place to re-open this matter.

Kgosi Tshekedi: Replying to the last speaker I wish to state that your decision of the last meeting has been passed on to the Government.

Edward Rakgole: I agree that the Tribe feared to express its views but personally I understood at the last meeting that our son's marriage has not been in accordance with custom but nobody wishes to expel Seretse. Personally I feel he is unable to part with this woman for fear of the contract because afterwards the white people may take him to be a Chief without any definite views. I belong to the Basimane section and it is our section which should be pleading for the return of our son. It is Boiditswe who should plead. They are those who say the procedure is to approach Seretse's father and plead with him and why should we be at loggerheads.

Rasebolai Kgamane: Seeing that a number of speakers have said Seretse's marriage should be accepted, I wish to know whether it is the intention of the Tribe that this marriage should pay no regard to our customs.

Appendix H

Motamma Reshengg: I say we should plead with the parent of Seretse to agree to this marriage.

Oabona Nthobatsang: According to modern practice young people can marry whom they wish. We should all be saying the same thing to the parent of the son but we are afraid to do so.

Rayaba Monahen: I say forgive Seretse. Let his wife come.

Rasebolai Kgamane: I say I do not understand what the speakers are saying. If it was necessary to reverse the previous decision, it would have been customary for people to approach the Chief and state their views. Someone might have at least approached one of the Chief's uncles to discuss the merits of the marriage. As a Tribe we said we do not accept this woman although opinion has been expressed that today anybody can marry whom they wish. I do not accept such opinion. It is wrong.

Kgosi Tshekedi: It is my wish and request that the discussions should not be curtailed. Many speakers today speaking for the marriage have said they were afraid to express their views during the last meetings and I should like to know from them whether what they feared then has been removed. I was interested in a remark made by Moata to the effect that people would kill me and I say to him only my actions can enable them to kill me. They cannot kill me for no reason. That remark has no effect on me at all. My actions will speak for themselves. I say to you that far from weakening my convictions you have strengthened them. I see no reason to change my views. I say I do not accept this marriage. I say also my son does no longer live with me. He lives with Serogola. If there was in effect any alterations of the views previously expressed how is it that nobody has come to me to tell me so. If I in fact want to chase Seretse out of this country my actions will show it. Right from the commencement of this talk, Seretse has never ceased to attack me but I have refrained from replying to his attacks as I do not wish to have any discussions with him. All that I say to him is I do not accept this woman.

My reason for saying that you have strengthened my views is that in spite of the unanimous decision made that the marriage was not accepted some of you did carry this decision into effect, but in actions you supported the marriage. Therefore, no real attempt has been made to carry out our convictions and therefore Seretse has not been opposed but has been supported. How can you therefore say he has remained resolute against tribal opposition. Many of the speakers have now said the woman must be allowed into this country. Personally [, however] the discussions may be prolonged [,] my views remain unchanged. I wish to point out that the people who have spoken in support of the marriage are people who have been convicted or an administrative action taken against them.

Kgotla Speeches Resumed, 29 December 1948

Kgosi Tshekedi: Before the discussions continue I have two remarks to make. At the conclusion of the previous meetings there was one decision made. I am not suggesting that such a decision can never be altered because the decision is the action of man and not of God. But it is important to know of reasons which have caused a change in the decision. I listened to this reason yesterday but could not get it. The second point is all the speakers who spoke in favour of the marriage yesterday are without exception men of no standing in the Tribe. They are mostly young people. When I said this matter was beyond the understanding of young people I was quite sincere. Yesterday many speakers spoke in favour but what is the position of these speakers in the Tribe [–] were those men respectable people even as individuals? It is not the numbers which count in a discussion of this nature. It is the quality of the speakers which matters. The Native Administration is carried through by means of well known people. I have not selected such people when I became Chief but they are the people whom my father Khama and my brother Sekgoma carried the administration of the Tribe through them and I did likewise. None of these people spoke yesterday

Appendix H

and I should be glad to receive their views today. Let this matter be discussed properly.

Phethu Mphoeng: It has been stated that I have said the King is dead long live the King. I agree that these are my words. The Chief's son is like a tiger [*nkwe*, i.e. leopard] which can never change its stripes [spots]. I do not go back on the words I said and I ask permission to explain them. There used to be a tribe known as Hottentots. I think here the nearest description would be the Bushmen or Masarwa. This tribe was in the Cape and they inter-married with the white people. That tribe is dead. They have got no definite race. Their descendants are either known as Coloureds or Bastards. I call this death. The Matebele in Rhodesia at one time killed every child born of a union between a white person and a black person. The Cape Coloureds today call us kafirs. To marry a white woman is merely to finish our tribalism. The coloured child born of the union will only regard us as kafirs. I weep over Seretse and I cannot be blamed for weeping over the death of my race. My fathers when they opposed anything made no pretence over it but they went straight to the point and I do not think that I shall go back on the word which I said. I shall never do so. When the Chief dies another Chief always succeeds him. We were all looking forward to Seretse taking over the Chieftainship from his uncle but to do so customary procedure would be adopted but Seretse is merely walking over us. Personally the Chief who will be my Chief will be a true descendant of the race of Sekgoma. We cannot be ruled by a Chief who looks low on the people, a Chief who will probably call the black people kafirs. That chief I do not want. I had expected Seretse to be supported by his uncle. I cannot accept a woman who will probably send dogs after me when I attempt to go to her house. I end by saying the King is dead long live the King.

Seretse Khama: Even though Phethu does not like my wife I have married her but be careful of using insolent expressions. You will soon blame me for following your example. I have married this woman and no insolent words should be used against her. Even if I had children I would speak as I speak today. Phethu indulges in speaking insolently. You speak of your tribalism only in meetings but you don't practice it outside of the meeting. You despise one another. You call people *Makalakanyana*, *Makgalagatsana*. I am not pleased with these words. Perhaps even Phethu himself has used these expressions.

Kgosi Tshekedi: I do not stand up to say anything against what has been said by the Chief's son. He might have felt hurt by the expressions used by his uncle Phethu because they are capable of several interpretations. To speak insolently is not nice and we would make better progress without insolent remarks being made. For example one speaker said yesterday that only Seretse was being made to stand and not Tshekedi. Another one said only the old men can have words pushed into them and not him. I therefore say if we speak respectfully we would make better progress.

Peto Mokhutshwane [Sekgoma]: I heard yesterday that this meeting was called by the Chief's son to get the views of the people and I want to know whether Seretse has got these views.

Seretse Khama: Yes, I said yesterday that I wished to get the views of the people from the tribe itself. There was a meeting of *Batlhanka* and *Dikgosana* but my uncles were not there as I understand they represent nobody. I say only the Bamangwato can drive me out of this village and my uncles can't. I understood that it is required that everybody should be angry with me but I want to know from you Tribe as to what you say. I am not going to abandon this marriage and I am not going to live away from my wife. When I leave this place you must know I won't come back again. The record of the decisions of the Tribe as submitted to the Government will stop me from coming here. Those have been written by a lawyer, but I haven't understood the views of the Tribe though it has been said that people who spoke yesterday are people of no account.

Appendix H

Mosinyi Tshwene: I stand up to ask for the reason which has reversed our previous decision because we are waiting to get reply from the Government to the representations we have made, namely that the woman should not be allowed to come into this territory, and that Seretse should remain in this country whilst waiting for the reply of the Government.

Elisha Keeditse: In reply to your question it is true we are still waiting for the government's reply to our representations. I understand that our representations were reduced to writing and forwarded whilst we were expecting such written representations to be read here. We understand that the Chief's son was given such written representations to read for himself and that these representations were read to certain headmen but I was not there.

Mphithetse Matheo: We are waiting to get reply to our representations and we have not received such reply.

Edumile Mogalakwe: The statement was read to us for the purpose of having this corrected if necessary. We found representations correct and we are still waiting for the reply.

Gaeemelwe Sebedi: I heard the Chief say he wishes the speakers who spoke yesterday to give chance to others to speak today. I ask that they should be allowed to proceed with their talk because they have not explained to us why they have found it necessary to change their views. We must find out how these people came to change their views.

Mosinyi Tshwene: I would perhaps have something further to say if reply to the representations we have made had been received but before receipt of this I do not find it necessary to say anything else.

Tsogang P. Sebina: Replying to Edumile Mogalakwe I think what the speakers want is to find out how representations went forward. They want to know why the statement was not read in public.

Lebati: It seems as if there is suspicion that at the meeting we had the statement was read to us we were there to discuss the affairs of the son of a Chief without him being present.

Peto Mokhutshwane [Sekgoma]: I am sure that during the last discussions no written record was taken and I cannot agree that what was presented to the officials is a correct record of what was said. I can only agree after I hear what I personally said being recorded. We said that now that Seretse was here he was here to stay and not to go back and that we do not accept his wife. We have also asked the Government to help us to achieve our wishes and nobody wants Seretse to go back. We said all effort must be made to effect a separation of Seretse from his English wife. We want this said record to be brought here to be read in public. At one time as Seretse's uncles we decided that all effort must be made to effect the required separation but afterwards some of us Seretse's uncles considered this matter and felt that if Seretse remained firm there could be no alternative but to agree to marry that woman. You Manyaphiri should not go back on your word. The last words I spoke were not made in a meeting but we just happened to meet and were having a general chat.

Serogola Seretse: When we speak of consultations we refer to a meeting convened for the purpose. We cannot regard a general chat as consultation.

Manyaphiri Ikitseng: Yes, I agree with what you say Peto.

Mosinyi Tshwene: I say we cannot open discussions before we get Government's reply to our decisions.

Serogola Seretse: It seems to me that in that document there is something which Seretse did not like.

Oten Mphoeng: When we see people bring father and son to loggerheads we say this is not proper.

Appendix H

Elisha Keeditse: If Seretse is Chief and convenes private meetings we will know that he wants to kill Tshekedi.

Chiliwa Mbaakanyi: I should like to know now what is being discussed whether it is the marriage of the Chief's son or he is claiming the Chieftainship. Seretse said if you do not accept my wife let me know and I will go back to England to join her there. They are people who should discuss affairs with the Chief but we do not see such people today and only see those who are creating trouble. Why do you mix up subjects? Tell us whether you are speaking for the marriage or for the Chieftainship.

Twaelan Boiteto: I ask that the document presenting our case should be read to the people in public.

Setohile Kgamane: I support what the last speaker says. I know what we said at the last meeting and today it looks as if we are discussing something else, not what we set here to discuss previously.

Kgosi Tshekedi: There is nothing confidential about this document. In fact, I have it here with me and before reading it I ask those headmen to whom the statement was read for confirmation to stand up. (The headmen asked for stand). Seretse was handed this document to read for himself so that if he wished to make any comment thereto he could do so. I reduced the decisions made here to writing. This procedure was not unusual but it is my duty to see that correct representations are made. It is not my duty however to read any representations in public. My representations to Government are merely my business. When I got to Mafeking I handed the report to the Resident Commissioner but I told him that I wanted to be very careful with every step that I took in this matter and therefore decided to have the statement read to the people for confirmation before forwarding it officially. There was nothing private about this. I emphasized that the statement was read for the purpose of correcting it if found incorrect. The people to whom the statement was read all agreed that it was a correct representation. After this Seretse went to the District Commissioner to complain and the two of us had a talk in the presence of the District Commissioner and both of us asked Seretse to point out any statement in the document which he considered incorrect and Seretse accepted the statement as a correct representation of what was said at the Kgotla. Seretse further asked that the statement should be read to a public meeting but I told him this was not necessary because it had not been challenged. I was merely giving an explanation to why this statement was not read in public.

Seretse Khama: It is true the document was given to me to read and I was asked whether it was a true account and I agreed it was, but there are other words which my uncle says were not said in the Kgotla but that such words were his advice to the Government that my wife should not be allowed to come here and I want the document read. I want to understand from you Tribe that you say I must join my wife in England.

Goareng Mosinyi: We want to hear this document read. Some of us were not present and those of you who were present have forgotten what was said.

Kgosi Tshekedi Khama: It is not my intention that the District Commissioner should be a witness in this matter and it is fortunate that he wrote down what was said with Seretse and I will ask him to read what Seretse said but no questions should be put to him.

District Commissioner reads:

> "In reply to the District Commissioner, Seretse admitted he had ample opportunity to study the memorandum and he did [not] challenge anything in it."

> "*Seretse* asked if memorandum were final.

Appendix H

Chief–it was unless it were challenged. It was a public document."

Kgosi Tshekedi: I shall now ask Reverend Seager to read the required document to the people. (Document read and translated.)[2]

Manyanya Molefi: I speak as frankly as the previous speakers have spoken. I say our Chief is not going to marry a woman without proper formalities being observed. I affirm what I said before.

Kgosi Tshekedi: The document has been read and I want those that wanted it read to comment on it.

Seretse Khama: Yes, the statement read was given to me to read. I said to the District Commissioner that I did not hear some of the statements made in this document said at the Kgotla and my uncle replied that some of the statements in the document are advices to Government giving what steps can be taken to help the Tribe's decision and I want to know from you whether you agree to these statements. I want to find out from you whether it is possible for a Chief's uncle to rule whilst the Chief himself is alive.

Olekile Koofhethile: Why does the Chief say that if Seretse's wife were to come here he would leave the country?

---

[2] The Memorandum in question was titled "Presentation of the Position Arising from the Political Crisis Occasioned by the Marriage of Seretse Khama to Ruth Williams in England: Case presented by Chief Tshekedi Khama of the Bamangwato people and their legal advisor Adv. D.M. Buchanan," originally dated 8 December 1948 (copies in BNA, S.599/11; and PRO, DO 35/4113). Presumably only the main text was read–up to ten folio pages typed in single spacing–and not the additional pages of annexes.

The Kgotlas on Seretse Khama's Marriage, 1948-1949

Kgosi Tshekedi: Seretse does not know his father. I have brought him up and I have arranged all his education. Seretse is my son. If Seretse was not a Chief I would have said to him that he could not marry this woman in my home. If it was Leapeetswe there would not be this talk because I would have told him that he should marry that woman in England but as Seretse is the Chief and I could not send him away from home I told him I would myself leave this place if the woman came in. I do not want coloured children. We say we do not accept this woman as Chief's wife. All marriages can be dissolved. Seretse must be given his position in true formalities and I repeat again that if this woman comes here I will leave this place but the matter has so far not been impossible.

Seretse Khama: I still say I am addressing myself to the Tribe. I ask if they too say I must marry my wife in England. If I go to live in England I will have children and I cannot throw away these children and therefore it would get more difficult for me to part with this woman. I say I am not going to give up this marriage.

Seretse Khama: You say you are waiting for the reply. What will you do when the reply comes.

Mosinyi Tshwene: If the decision should be the woman cannot be stopped from coming here we will make our comments and if the reply should be that the woman has been stopped in England we will also know what to say.

Tumiso Nkhukhu: I am one of those who stood up in protest against your marriage and I re-affirm my decision. I want to follow up what the Chief has said namely that if the white woman was to enter the country he would leave.

Kgosi Tshekedi: I say my actions will speak for me if I in any way hold fast to the Chieftainship and do not pass it on to Seretse. I say Seretse does not attend the Kgotla. I say I do not know what a son can say to his father that his father was speaking very

Appendix H

proudly. Further, no representations have been made to me after the previous decision that it was necessary to reconsider the matter. Many unpleasant words have been said to me by my son but I have had no single rebuke from you people. He has adopted a defiant attitude and again I have had no rebuke from you people. How can you expect me to live with him.

Tumiso Nkhukhu: We say we do not accept this woman. Seretse says if we say so we are chasing him away but we say we cannot accept a white woman. Two opposite protests have been made. The Chief says if the white woman comes he leaves the country. Seretse says if we refused the white woman he also leaves the country. What do these men mean? Do they both intend to leave the country? Who is to be the Chief of this large country? Our decision is we do not want our chiefs to turn Coloureds.

Seretse Khama: You have addressed your remark to the Tribe and if it is said I am not to marry a white woman then I leave and my uncle will remain.

Tumiso Nkhukhu: Your uncle is in charge of this village with our full support. You are emphatic that you cannot be parted from your wife and I also stress that we cannot accept that woman. We always bring our disobedient children before you to get your support to restore the obedience of the children. You are throwing away the Chieftainship. Those who are encouraging you in your wishes only want you to be at loggerheads. Our words have been previously expressed. Those who say they were afraid to express their views nobody stopped them from expressing their views and you Chief if you insist on leaving this country you will be a coward and you will not be opposing the marriage alone. There will be something else in your mind. This is your son. You must talk about him without tiring. My last word is we do not want this woman, only when his father declares that he is unable to do anything further will I then give in.

Motamma Resheng: I stand up to comment on what Tumiso has said. If Seretse dies could our white woman be our Chief. If Tshekedi dies would his wife be our Chief. We know Chief's wives have been appointed to the Chieftainship in Basutoland and Ngamiland but it has never been so amongst us.

Tumiso Nkhukhu: Yes, it is not possible here for the Chief's wife to become the Chief on the Chief's death.

Pelotona Kuate: Referring to the statement made by the last speakers I say amongst the Banwaketse and the Batawana the Chief's uncles were there but they refused to take over the Chieftainship but it can't be so amongst the Bamangwato.

Oraten Makwatse: Seretse wants to know whether we want him to marry the white woman in England and I say to him we want you to marry her here.

Molefhane Taukobon: The Chief's son has put a question which we want. Only Serowe people have been talking up to now. We who come from outside districts maintain the same view as we held at the last. Give us a chance to express our views. Tshekedi is Seretse's father. He has every right and liberty to give his views. You young people who have been carrying on discussions want to create trouble in this village with your agitation.

Kgosi Tshekedi: Molefhane speaks well when he wants room made for people from outside to speak, but even the local people have not spoken apart from those who expressed new views yesterday. Those who expressed previous views have not had a chance to speak.

Radisigo Goepamang: I belong to Serogola's village and I was displeased yesterday to learn that spies have been sent to Serogola and I have not been asked.

Appendix H

Kgosi Tshekedi: At the last meeting we had here Serogola spoke to me insolently in public. After this incident there was an important meeting here and Serogola and Pheto did not attend and these are the senior men whose presence was necessary. I drew the attention of Manyanya to this behaviour and Manyanya is the member of your village.

Radisigo Goepamang: It is wrong for Serogola to speak insolently to you and for him not to attend the meeting is also improper. I do not know what the discussion is about when the father and the son discuss the subject of a marriage. If the son has done wrong is it usual for him to be chased away? I say let us agree to this marriage, and add a white woman to our tribe. Seretse is our chief and it is difficult for us to chase him away because of this marriage.

Koobusitse Ntoeagae: We say we are protesting against this marriage. We do not chase Seretse away. If he wants to go on his own free will to join the white woman in England I say to him go.

Nonofhan Motshwaedi: I speak as I did on the last occasion that I do not accept this woman. You have done a grievous thing Seretse not to pay heed to our representations, and I ask the Government not to give permission to this woman to come here and Seretse should not be permitted to go to England and he must not be given any money. This will be tantamount to expelling him.

Olerile Lethemane: Tshekedi informed you that his son had disregarded all custom and disobeyed all wishes and asked you to assist him. But you do not reply to these facts. In reply you seem to say Tshekedi refuses to hand over the chieftainship. Previously you said you did not accept this woman and now you say you accept her but no representations have been made to Tshekedi in connection with the misbehaviour of his son.

Ramosamo Kebonang: Seretse and Tshekedi are the sons of Khama.

Motheo Mokubong: At the previous meetings I said to you that Seretse was like a football. People are just pumping air into him. Whether we were accepting or refusing Seretse's wife there should still be unity amongst us but today because of Seretse's presence there is disunity. Just from the commencement of the discussions Seretse is unmanageable and that he must be given his will. We are causing a division amongst the children of one man. How pleasing it would have been for both Seretse and Tshekedi to be at the head of our tribe. But if I begin to discuss matters to either of these people secretly I do not love any one of them. If you agree to the marriage let there be unanimity. In conclusion I say I do not accept this woman.

Mosinyi Segotso: I listened to these discussions yesterday. A request was made for a written report to be read. The report was read. And now nobody is making any comments on that report. Do you confirm it or reject it? We were waiting for a reply to these representations from the Government and now we are having fresh debates on different matters. Seretse has not yet been impossible. I will speak when I get the reply to our representations.

Peto Mokhutshwane [Sekgoma]: I am one of those who said the report of the decision should be read. The record is correct except that we said that Seretse must be stopped from going to England. I shall await the reply of the Government to our request before proceeding further.

Ramarula Mathodi: During the first discussions after the arrival of Seretse it was open for any man to express his view either for or against the marriage. Seven people spoke in favour of this marriage. The rest of the people did not want this marriage. With all my heart to this day I object to this marriage. After our unanimous agreement people turn their views secretly. The

Appendix H

subject is centered round the marriage. And we do not accept this marriage. We sent Seretse to England for his education. What he has ultimately done has grieved us. If there is any change of views from the views last expressed the proper way to bring this out is to approach the Chief himself but not to do so secretly. It was my wish that the white woman would not enter this country.

Olebogeng Legopelo: There are two ways to take one of which leads to death and the other to life and I follow that road leading to death. Seretse's father had made me a man and after his death I have gone down again. I say to Boiditswe that if you wish to extinguish this fire you could have done so. You could have consulted with Ramarula but you have done nothing.

Elisha Keeditse: I want to deal with the written report of the previous decision. In the report we said Seretse should not leave this place. That we do not accept his wife. This report has two parts. In the second part the Chief says he was strengthening what the people said. But that was really meant to pre-judge the case so that no other decision could be possible. We have said Seretse was not to leave us and we may have the right to stop him here. With regard to the white woman I do not see how we have any right to decide any case involving a white person. And I should like to have a reply to this point.

Kgosi Tshekedi: It is unusual for me to read to the tribe my written report to the Government but you people insisted that I should read the report and if you wish to put any question on this report I hand this report to you to do so to read me specific words which you want me to reply to but I shall not answer any general questions. Regarding the question of the power of the chief to decide cases involving white people that is the very point I fear. The English woman is to be married to my son and the Chief will have no jurisdiction over her hence our protest to accept her into our society.

Elisha Keeditse: Our words were we do not accept this woman but I was surprised at Phethu's words to the effect that he will only accept this marriage after a donkey develops horns. Does he mean that he will only have a chief above him when one of the chiefs has been killed? He also said that the Chief's son is like a tiger, it can never change its stripes. Isn't Seretse true to the saying? That in spite of the consequences he is not going to turn on his actions.

Phethu Mphoeng: When I used the expression the chief's son was like a tiger which never changes its stripes I mean by that I could not go back on the words I had said at the previous meeting but the tiger's colours may not be the same as those you have in mind.

Kgosi Tshekedi: At the last meeting you said you objected to Seretse's marriage. Have you now changed your views?

Elisha Keeditse: I have said we do not accept this woman and following the expression of the tiger which has been used does that mean Seretse should not give up this marriage?

Raselwane Boipego: You put a question as to how your name was mentioned amongst those who were holding secret meetings in support of the marriage. Your name was given to us by Rajaba Monaheng asking him how he came about it.

Rajaba Monaheng: Oahile was given your name by me. I gave the name to Ramaselwane and Oahile.

Elisha Keeditse: I realised that my name would be mentioned because I was not in the meeting of the headmen.

Manyaphiri Ikitseng: I just wish to point out that the behaviour of these people who have been speaking, particularly when they refer anything to the Chief, is very bad and it is painful to us.

Appendix H

Ramarula Mathodi: You Elisha your manner is very unseemly when speaking to the Chief. He is not your brother but your chief.

Tshilwane Batshuhile: I stand up to say the Chief's son Seretse cannot have a wife without the Tribe knowing about it. I defy all statements made yesterday which seemed to blame the Chief for refusing to accept his son's wife. This is a common practice amongst us and no parent has ever been blamed before. If what you are discussing today is truly the marriage all that I can say to you is you can only arrange such marriage with Tshekedi and not without him. When that woman arrives here who else will be responsible for her welfare except Tshekedi. To you Seretse the people who are supporting your marriage are men who cannot help you in anything at all. I have said before and I say again that I do not accept this marriage. The words spoken yesterday are new to us perhaps these men who express new views are visitors amongst us. And to you Seretse my Chief's son I say if you are not careful with the attitude of these people, they only want to create trouble between you and the Tribe. We look to you as our chief. All that we say is we do not accept your marriage. We do not hate you nor do we want to fight you. All that we want is submission to the wishes of the people.

Seretse: You say in the previous meetings that only seven people spoke in favour of the marriage. And now you say those who spoke in favour of the marriage are men who cannot help me at all. I do not accept these views with all my heart. It has also been said people who say the wife should be accepted are small boys and that it is the old men who should speak. During the first discussions I heard my uncle tell me that Serogola would lead me into trouble. And that Serogola and Peto if they came to the meeting there might be a disturbance. I heard yesterday a man from Mathuba village say he was sent to spy on Serogola so as to get information. This is a dangerous thing. I hear also that people who spoke in favour of the marriage are men who have been convicted or have administrative actions passed against them.

This proves that those who are against my marriage are those who are satisfied with the administration; that is they hate me. When I was in England I understood that my uncle had said if people wanted to go after me he would not go and that if my wife came he would divide this country. These are things I fear. It has been alleged I stay at Serogola's place but I don't. You speak as men who know the law. You say if a chief's son marries not in accordance with custom his children cannot rule and this should apply to everybody and not to me alone.

Baraabatsile: I was not present when you had the first meetings but I heard that representations had gone forward on the last decision we made, and I say we should wait for the Government to reply. There are always two sides to the story and we may hear from the parents of the woman in question and we do not know Government views.

Malokwane Phalalo: We have had long discussions over this matter and we have persistently refused to accept this woman but today I see a division amongst us. This is not unusual with the Bamangwato people. In ancient times Chief Kgari was killed by the Mashona people. Sekgoma Kgari's son was a young man and Sedimo ruled the Tribe in the meantime and when Sekgoma became of age the Chieftainship was peacefully handed to Sekgoma by Sedimo but you Seretse come into this tribe with big trouble which we know nothing about. And now there is this division. When Tshekedi sent Seretse to school it was with the full knowledge of the Tribe and I do not think it is right that no regard should be given to Tshekedi in what Seretse is doing. Tshekedi is Seretse's father. Fingers have been pointed at the Chief during this discussion and this is insolence and contrary to our custom. We say to you Seretse be obedient to your father. Nobody disputes your Chieftainship and nobody can claim it from you. Only seven people stood up at the first discussions to speak in favour of the marriage but today many people have. This is hypocrisy. I say to you pay heed to what your father tells you. Later on he may agree to your marriage. I am very disturbed

Appendix H

about these talks. We all love you. We are having no case against you. The truth is we weep for you. We don't want you to hold your position without dignity and respect.

Gaefhiwe Setshwantsho: When we heard of the second call to discuss the marriage we expected to continue the discussions as we left them the last time but today we are discussing a different matter. I say Bamangwato this is not the discussion of the marriage. You are discussing something else. I understood the Chief to say nobody has ever come to him since the last meeting to discuss with him the acceptance of the marriage but today many of you have spoken to that effect. I say be plain in what you want to say. It is unusual for a parent to be told to be obedient to his son. That's what you say and this will have the effect of making Tshekedi more stubborn in his decision because we do not discuss this matter in accordance with our customs.

Mosoyane Lebada: I do not accept a white woman. I want my Chief to marry a woman of my colour. We were unanimous at the last meetings in this view only seven speaking in favour. You Chief's uncles are always people who cause trouble. As a tribe we say no to this woman.

Potoko Motsholapheko: I was not present at the last meetings. Tshekedi has not changed his views. He asked you yesterday whether you have changed your views and had so informed him but you said you had not been to him. I say Seretse is your son. Seretse has been warned against this marriage. He has persisted. Let him get into trouble (*E are go lelela bogota e lesiwe e boyo*).

Olweleng Ntsaga: At the last meetings we said we could not accept the marriage of which we were not consulted. We do not know what this discussion is about today because we are waiting to receive reply to our representations. To Seretse I say you are here to stay. We don't want you to go to England. Stay in your Kgotla and let that woman stay in England.

Manyeapelo Osahile: I do not see that we are discussing this matter truthfully. The Chief has said his son has been repeatedly disobedient but he also says he came to him and asked for forgiveness but I do not know whether his father was unable to forgive him because of repeated disobedience. Something has been said about colour. Kgama enjoys the inheritance of England and how can Seretse be prevented from marrying a white woman because we owe our protection to the white people.

Ogopotse Selaelo: We discuss this matter and at times we fear to express our views. Originally we all said we only want Seretse and not the woman and that we did not like the woman. We were asked as to what we would do if she just came amongst us. No reply was given. We say we do not like this woman. We were also told that Seretse might come or Seretse might not come, and we said we could go and get him. It is surprising that we should have gone back on our decision that we do not accept this woman. I say Seretse will not pay heed to the protest we made because he is now being supported in his attitude. I do not think this matter will be settled. We, though, were being called to receive the reply to our words but we are unable to proceed because no reply has been received.

Makwati: This matter has several additional issues. Some speakers are not definite in their expressions. This matter must be concluded. You Phethu, you are unable to restore peace between your sons. Will you accept the Government's decision that the country be divided. I say let us accept this marriage we will protest against Seretse's second action.

Nwako Nkobela: We thought Seretse had gone to school and we were surprised to learn that he was married. That is the cause of this talk. At the time when suggestions were made for this installation he said he wished to go and continue his studies. Today we are not discussing the question of marriage. There is no feud but it is the members of the Tribe who are creating the trouble. The son is in the wrong and he should be so told and

Appendix H

this matter should be discussed with his father. We wanted his father to arrange the marriage in a customary and proper manner, but this matter is contrary to our custom.

Sekwakwa Mbe: This matter is weighty. Is this the life of the Tribe or the death of the Tribe. We were waiting to receive the reply to the decisions made but I see we are creating war between the sons of Sekgoma. We should take this matter properly and not try to create trouble. No parent can be pleased if his child is disobedient to him. We were waiting to receive reply to the last representations but I see that people are creating trouble because others are now saying Seretse must marry the white woman and others say he must not. To me I say we just want to create trouble between Tshekedi and Seretse.

Mpeo Mabuaaeme: This matter is grievous. Today at the first meeting we were a united people but that is not the case today. We were told whilst the Chief's son was in England that he had said he would marry whether his father and people agree or not. Our reply was we do not accept the white woman. We have been expecting the reply to representations made but not what we are discussing today. I do not know whether you were with the Chief's son in England consulting and arranging about this marriage and further the Chief Tshekedi stated yesterday that since the last discussions nobody had come to him to say we should agree to this marriage. These actions are contrary to custom. The Chief has repeatedly said that he was making no claim to the Chieftainship and now you want to create trouble between them. You profess to like Seretse. You don't like him. When he becomes Chief you won't like him. No doubt you are saying Tshekedi has ruled over you for a long time. For the Chief's son to return to England, we object to; if we find that we just cannot turn him away from this marriage [then] let him marry this woman.

Gaoakelwe Ntshwali: During the first discussions we said we wanted Seretse but objected to the marriage. I emphatically protest to this marriage today and will not turn back on my views.

Motsomi Sankoloba: I am ashamed of what has been said. The son is being disobedient to the father and people are urging him on. I agree with his father when he says he objects to this marriage. My views are very far removed from accepting this woman. We sent him to England to get education and not a wife. He says if we object to this woman he will leave us. I say it does not matter. Let him go. We were not consulted on this marriage.

Joel Baitswi: I am glad that when the views are expressed at this meeting I be present. When we spoke during the last discussions we professed to be expressing the truth and today we are giving evidence to the Government that we are not people of our word. We say one thing today and completely change the following day. We do not agree to this marriage. It seems as if some people did not express their views clearly. The Chief said at the previous meeting that if the woman came what would you do because we could not throw stones at her and we made no reply. We lay low like fish in the water. It is clear that when trouble begins we will say it was only the Chief who protested against the marriage but some of us express our views and we do [not] like this marriage.

Seretse Khama: I do not want the Chief to leave this country. If the people say they do not accept my wife I will go and join her elsewhere.

Modiro Ramosesane: Here is our trouble. Here Seretse says he wants to marry this woman and his father says bring her along and I go. Seretse replies, if my wife is not accepted here I go. This is our trouble. This matter should have been discussed in our villages first. We don't want to create trouble between them and we are unable to unite them.

Appendix H

Kgosi Tshekedi: It is the wish of the Government Secretary to leave to-night and I am compelled to cut discussions short.

Kgosi Bathoen: The Government Secretary, the District Commissioner, Chief and my fathers it has well been said that the matter differs from the last. The position is very serious today.

Seretse Khama: My uncle has said if my wife comes here he goes, and I am stubborn because he is also stubborn. I don't say that he is making this an excuse to drive me out of the country but that is what I suspect. Yes I did say the Tribe would not accept my wife but that my uncle would and I say if the Tribe accepts my wife my uncle will not.

Segotso Sethoko: The proverb that the village is found in the home (*Motse o lwapen*) means that it is the woman who looks after the village because she bears children, looks after the man, and cares for visitors.

Kgosi Bathoen: I deliberately asked the explanation of this proverb for it has been said that Seretse's wife will have nothing to do with the Chieftainship as she remains in the house and Seretse conducts tribal affairs. You have left off discussions on the marriage of Sekgoma's son. You are now concerned with personal grievances, jealousies, and misunderstandings. One speaker has said everybody loves a young chief but the moment he rules he begins to be hated. The truth is you have got enough of Tshekedi's rule and you are creating excuses to put him out. Names of people have been given who hold secret discussions on this marriage and this cannot create a settlement of this matter. During my first talk at the last meetings I said to you that I was not going to make any attempt to say to you that you should give up this marriage because you had given full consideration before you acted as you did. I told you that nothing will go well with you if you insisted and now those who have been conducting the affairs of this country have expressed their determination to leave you. I told you also that when I had occasion to come, find me another place to stay in and not in your home. When we speak of your marriage you say people are insulting you and you forget the disrespectful remarks you made about the marriages of your grandfathers, matters which it was not right for you to have raised. Your people have not told you that you were wrong to raise such matters. It was not proper for you to do so. Somebody has asked whether a woman cannot rule. At Kanye the daughter of Bathoen became chief and amongst the Batawana the tribe decided the Chief's wife should rule and not the Chief's uncles. I say to you, you decided on this so as to avoid the Chieftainship. You want to be in a position to say you are driven away by the Bamangwato people. We know of no case here of a white woman being married by a black man. I support those who say the woman is not accepted. If you leave this place you will do so at your own free will. To the Tribe I say your chieftainship has been disrupted. You were a strong tribe but you are now broken up. I say Seretse is driving himself away. Tshekedi has worked so hard for Seretse wherever you may be and there is no peace amongst the Bamangwato[; you should] realise that such disturbance is your creation. What made you consider marrying a white woman? Your habit is a white man's habit; they have no settled home. Their home is wherever they are with their wives. Seretse wishes to go; I say to him you have destroyed your chieftainship.

Kgosi Tshekedi: Firstly I express my thanks to the Government for having deputed the Government Secretary to be an observer in this discussion. Secondly I thank the Chiefs for attending this meeting even though some of them said nothing. Their presence is just as expressive as words. I do not wish to speak at length at this juncture. A few days ago I warned the District Commissioner that a disturbance was likely at the asked for meeting. My suspicion has proved correct. The Government Secretary witnessed the disturbances yesterday and was compelled to stand up and to restore order. What I said has been misrepresented. I did not say small boys were discussing this matter. What I said was people of no standing in the Tribe and of no character spoke yesterday. These men who spoke yesterday are not the type of people who

Appendix H

can assist Seretse's administration in any way. I made this statement at the beginning of the discussion this morning and my words have not been challenged by anybody. This morning you said I should read the written report of the decisions arrived at during the last meetings. This report was read in public and it has not been challenged as misrepresenting what was said at the last meetings. I have nothing further to say. Perhaps the Government Secretary may wish to say something.

Government Secretary: Chief Tshekedi and the Bamangwato, for two days I have listened to your discussions. I have warned you that talks of war will not help you in any way. Remain in Peace (*Ka Pula*).

Kgosi Tshekedi: I forgot to make an important announcement. Twenty-four people have spoken in favour of the marriage and 37 against the marriage, adding this to the previous results we get 115 against the marriage and 31 in favour of the marriage.

Addresses Given by Seretse and Tshekedi on
30 December 1948 Prior to Seretse's
Return to England

Seretse Khama: No doubt it will be difficult for you to understand what I am going to say. Others may even be afraid of it but I ask you not to be disturbed. I intend to leave you tomorrow to return to England but I am not leaving for good. I shall return. I have decided to wait for the decision whilst in England, and to fill up the time by completing my studies. I will be back here in May. If I was going for good I would tell you so. You Bamangwato people do not misconstrue my intention. If the decision can come to say I must go and live in England with my wife I would have completed my education and I would earn my living. I have not come to bid you good-bye but merely to let you know that I have decided to wait for the decision in England.

The Kgotlas on Seretse Khama's Marriage, 1948-1949

Kgosi Tshekedi: Yesterday afternoon the Government Secretary asked me to arrange a meeting between him and Seretse; they had their discussions the two of them in my absence and later he notified me that arrangements have been made for Seretse to return to England immediately, and later in the evening Seretse came to me to inform me of the arrangements made. When Seretse made proposals to go to England for his studies on the first occasion, at a meeting of the headmen, I said that Seretse was of age to take on the administration of the Tribe and that if it was decided that he should go to England to further his studies the people must permit this at their own free will. During this month he would have completed his studies and I had notified him either in September or October that soon after sitting for his examination he was to return but before his return, however, he became involved in the present difficulties. While Seretse was in England prior to his coming here he said that if he was not allowed to bring his wife with [him], he would join her in England. The Tribe definitely agreed that he should not bring his wife along and that if we could not persuade him to stay here he would be allowed to go back to England to join his wife there, but when you saw Seretse you went back on your decision. Nobody is chasing Seretse out of the country. He has accused me of driving him away from this country. I am not worried with that accusation because my actions will speak for me. If Seretse likes this country as he states, his actions will show it. Other statements were made to the effect that if Seretse was provided with funds by me to enable him to go to England this would be a sign that I was chasing him away, but I commented to this that I could not chain Seretse or imprison him and that if he wished to go he would go. Your made a further suggestion that I should at least delay his departure and in spite of repeated requests by Seretse which he made soon after the first meeting I respected your wishes and delayed Seretse's departure. It's now over a month since Seretse made his first request and he is still here. What I said that it was beyond my power to stop Seretse from going to England has now been proved by Seretse himself because in my absence he himself arranged his departure to go to England. I do not place any

Appendix H

blame on him for this action because if he had made the request to me now I would have likewise arranged for his immediate departure.

We had meetings here and arrived at definite decisions which were later reduced to writing and having done so read the statements to you for your confirmation or correction. You confirmed this written decision but during the last two days attempts were made to prove it false but it was a factual statement and the truth could not be reversed and so it stood as submitted.

Recent events have now proved that you had some ulterior motive when you suggested that Seretse should be stopped from returning to England in spite of your previous decision. The purpose of this suggestion was that he must be delayed here so that it should be possible to rally discontented elements around him to start an opposition against me.

I have full liberty to convene meetings in my village, private and public and today I am being told that I was acting improperly.

I have openly been insulted in public by Seretse himself and his supporters but I held my peace and made no comment thereat. My silence did not mean that I was unable to defend myself.

I had a bitter experience yesterday which everybody witnessed when people wished to raise certain questions they did not do so directly but were trying to raise these questions by making Seretse raise them. I refer to Serogola and Peto, this was an obvious action to get Seretse to oppose me. This grieved me very much and it gave strong evidence of the secret consultations which Serogola had been organising. I should inform you also that whilst the secret consultations were being carried on I received information that a meeting of those who purported to support the marriage would be held at night time at the Ratshosa hill[. T]his spot was found unsuitable it being in the centre of the village and it was suggested that the meeting should be held out of the village beyond Metsemaswau river. These meetings did not however take place because I organised counter meetings to find out the intended attendants of these meetings. Those concerned got scared and the meetings did not take place.

Regarding the question of the marriage I have said before that I could not accept it and my decision is not changed even today. My objection is not based on sentiment but on facts which can be stated and continue to be given.

Evidence was given by certain people whom I had deputed to attend Serogola's secret meetings. These people did not go to Serogola on their own. They were advised that the leader of the organisation was Serogola and were told to contact him. These witnesses alleged above information was supplied them by Rayaba Monahen and on being asked Rayaba confirmed it and never denied it. I am impressed with Rayaba's sincerity[.] I am convinced with his genuineness that he is fighting the cause of his Chief. He is the type of a man who can fight for the Chief.

But of the other people who spoke in favour of the marriage yesterday I only saw one tribal section namely the Batalaote section which spoke as a section because it was their chief who stood up to speak and in a matter of such a nature he must have had consultations with them. The rest of the people who spoke in favour were individuals and mostly men of no standing in the Tribe both as regards their positions and as individuals.

In conclusion I wish to say that it is not my habit to say to the Tribe one thing whilst I mean the other. The Chief's son has said he was merely going away to await for decision whilst in England and has promised to return in May. I wish to say to the Tribe that I have my doubts about this declaration. I am convinced his return will be governed by the outcome of the representations which we have made to Government namely that we do not accept the wife chosen as our Chief's wife. I wanted to make this statement now before anything happens.

The Tribe can now disperse and I trust that all of you who have been called from outside districts will not feel that you had been summoned for no important purpose. *"Nelwan ke Pula."*

Appendix H

The Third Kgotla

Report on the Meeting of the Bamangwato to Discuss Seretse's Marriage

(Botswana National Archives, S.170/1/3)

Kgotla Speeches, Monday, 20 June 1949

The Chief Tshekedi Khama: I now go into the matter for which we have congregated. To start with I have to let you know that I have brought up your child, namely, Sekgoma's son assuming it was in order. It is not according to our custom that you should be assembled here today. The first meeting I should have summoned should have been that of introducing your child to his people, having first of all had a preliminary meeting with his uncles and made arrangements for such a day. This is not so. This meeting is not called by me. The trouble has been caused by his marriage to a white lady without having consulted us. All of us (Bamangwatos) did not know. The issue at hand has many branches. I shall start from the beginning in order to remind the Tribe before I express my own opinion. I told some of Seretse's relatives about a cable message which spoke about his marriage. We unanimously objected to the marriage. Seretse did not listen and got married and sent me another cable message to the effect that he had married. I called a few people who were then available and we sorrowfully asked Seretse to come home so that we might have the matter discussed in a meeting. After I had heard the views of the Bamangwato and also after consultation with heads of the Tribe in order to learn your feelings, although that was not a binding necessity on my part, I wrote out a memorandum. I knew that this affair was of paramount importance. I wrote the letter there (Cape Town) assisted by advisers. I had an interview with the Resident Commissioner about it and also told His Honour that I would not send it before the Bamangwato saw it. The memorandum was subsequently read and amended in the Kgotla and ultimately sent to the Government.

I received a reply to it just a few days ago, just before Seretse's arrival. I wish that the memorandum be perused and interpreted. I have not aired my views yet, I am merely reminding the Tribe about the proceedings of the previous meetings.

(Rev. Seager read and interpreted the Memorandum)[3]

Chief Tshekedi Khama: The Memorandum was sent under an agreement and we awaited the reply. We did not know whether the Government would agree. Here is the reply to the memorandum.

(Reply to the Memorandum read and interpreted)[4]

Chief Tshekedi Khama: The Bamangwato Tribe, I know that our previous discussions had ended thus. Your child [Seretse] had promised to be here [at Serowe] these days and I had aimed at having the discussions [about Seretse's marriage] resumed. A reply to our Memorandum has been received but this reply does not help us as much as we expected. It still leads us to continue the discussions. Those who wished Seretse to come with his wife and those who did not[,] anticipate[d] that the reply to this Memorandum would give a final decision.

As a result of an agreement with our leaders [Government] Seretse has left his wife behind. Now, what do we [the tribe] say? This is my question. The first meeting was stormy. The child stated that I was driving him away. I did not answer because I was concerned with the marriage only. At Mafeking he alleged that I wanted to usurp his chieftainship. No one amongst the

---

[3]This refers to the Memorandum originally drafted 8 December 1948, which was read out to the second kgotla on 29 December 1948 and was then revised and expanded from forty-one to fifty-three pages (copies in BNA, DCS 37/12 and S. 169/15/3).

[4]Since Tshekedi claims the reply was "just a few days ago," this presumably refers to the High Commissioner's letter copied to both Tshekedi and Seretse, 14 June 1949 (BNA S.169/15/4).

Appendix H

Bamangwatos has ever said that against me nor has anyone ever spoken to me about this marriage. Maybe I will hear these words said against me today. There are two main disputes. One is about Seretse's wife, another about the Chieftainship. I am prepared to answer for both. As there was great disorder at the previous meetings I asked the Government that when our child is about to sail to South Africa for the Bechuanaland Protectorate I should be informed so as to tell the people. The Government agreed on the understanding that there might be Civil War or any occurrence of a kindred nature. The District Commissioner informed you in the Kgotla that you (the Bamangwatos) would be informed as to when Seretse would arrive. Shortly later we heard that Seretse was already at Mafeking. I asked the District Commissioner to ask Seretse to remain in Mafeking for some time. The Government did not say much about his unexpected arrival and he too agreed to remain at Mafeking for a couple of days and to arrive at Serowe the following Wednesday. This arrangement was made by the Government, the District Commissioner, Seretse and myself. About Seretse's livelihood I have arranged with the Government to keep on sending him money and I would pay back the amounts involved. He gets his money from the Government. I had arranged with them that when Seretse is about to come they should send him money for his voyage. I asked where he got the money for his airfare from on his arrival as the Government said they did not know. They stated that he had traveled by aeroplane because the difficulties that existed during the war have improved. They [Government] did not know how Seretse came. He arrived unexpectedly. He said he borrowed the money in question but I do not agree. I heard from rumours that he would be drafted some money. I believe it is so. I said I am merely opening the discussions. If you wish me to answer anything in connection with this marriage or the alleged usurpation of the Chieftainship I shall do so.

The Chief's Son, Seretse Khama: As it has already been said that whoever stands up to speak should give his name I shall first of all extend my greetings to the Representatives of the Resident

The Kgotlas on Seretse Khama's Marriage, 1948-1949

Commissioner, those who have accompanied him and the Chiefs of the other Tribes. One of the Bechuanaland Protectorate Chiefs has not attended. I do not know whether he has been invited or not. Perhaps you know me or perhaps you do not. I may say we do not know each other. I am Seretse the son of Sekgoma, who was once a chief of the Bamangwato. I have been overseas for education. I have received very little education there. Presumably you will give me better education today.

My uncle has already informed you that I did not notify you about my coming here. I shall begin with my journey to South Africa. You sent me money i.e. the Government sent me money from your Treasury. I had insufficient money for airfare because the fare is £ 164. I requested the [Colonial] Government to inform you that I was desirous of coming home. I do not know whether the letter was received. I waited for the reply until I got impatient.

I asked whether a reply had been received, two weeks expired, and they informed me that a reply to the effect that I should be given some money and that the Bechuanaland Protectorate Government would pay back the loan had been received from the High Commissioner.

The High Commissioner asked me to leave my wife behind [in England. I, then, could return to Bechuanaland] to settle matters here first. I do not know whether you wish me to live with my wife at my parents-in-law. At the previous meeting it was said that if I returned to England I would not come back. This suspicion saddened me. I love this country just as much as anybody does. I got money from where I got it. It is suspected that somebody sent me the money.

I would not make it a secret if somebody did send me the money. Have I not [the] right to accept gifts from my people? If I hold no right to receive gifts from you like any of the chiefs that have ruled you this right will terminate when a chief other than myself has taken over the Chieftainship from me. If anyone had sent me money I should have accepted it. However, there are many channels through which you can make investigations as to how I got the money.

Appendix H

About my arrival: I went to Mr. Ellenberger. He was surprised to see me. He then took me to the Resident Commissioner. They both did not have anything much to say about my arrival. I am domicile[d] in this country. I have the right to arrive at whatever time it may be.

I was there in person when the Resident Commissioner said he could not stop me from coming. But when he heard that there might be civil war he said I should remain there. I asked whether I could not wait somewhere other than at Mafeking and this privilege was extended to me. I then left Mafeking with Chief Bathoen because he was there. Chief Mokgori came to see me at Kanye and then I paid him a visit. On Tuesday we left for Serowe by car and we arrived here on Wednesday morning.

About the Chieftainship: I said you want to drive me away from the Chieftainship. At Mafeking you advised me to see the assistance of a legal adviser. I refused and said the Bamangwatos would speak for me. I said I would speak for myself. If those who will speak for me will be exiled that's alright; I will do it.

When I heard that there might be civil war I concluded that we were fighting for the Chieftainship. When we were under that camelthorn tree you said: "if I like I can split the Tribe and divide the Country and have jurisdiction over one section of the people and you another." You said "if I brought my wife you would either go to and live with the Bangwaketse or with the Bakwena." This attitude proved to me that you wanted me to leave. Some people said "Seretse is dead and Tshekedi lives." One of Sekgoma's people said "that I should go and live with my parents-in-law." You have been persuaded to forsake me. I cannot part with my wife. You have something to do with me but not my wife. This is not a dispute about my marriage but about the Chieftainship. You say you are angry with me because I married on my own.

When you make reference to anything of importance you refer to Kgama but you refuse me the privilege to refer to Kgama. I am bound to do so. If you trace our History there is no one who has the right to succeed to Chieftainship of the Bamangwato. Kgama married against the Tribe's wish therefore Sekgoma is not Chief, when his wife died he married a second wife, Tshekedi's mother, who was a wife not selected for him by the people therefore my uncle is not Chief. It is said that my wife is a foreigner and as such any children born to me by her will not be successors to the Chieftainship. I now await the decision of the High Commissioner. I want to know whether you want me to go away. It is stated that the poor support me in this marriage and that I am treading on the footsteps of my father who fought with his father and went to Nyekati only to come back poor. The wealth of any chief comes from its people. However, riches do not worry me much. I say I have come and it is for you to decide whether you want to drive me away.

Chief Tshekedi Khama: I shall make a short speech before I proceed to answer Seretse. Seretse has said that one of the Bechuanaland Chiefs has not come. The Chiefs of the Bechuanaland Protectorate who are not present today are those of the Batlokwa, Bakgatla and Batawana. I had requested Chief Bathoen to invite the Batlokwas on my behalf, but I am informed that the Batlokwa had a function for the child today. I invited the Bakgatla at the previous meeting, and they did not attend. This time I did not invite them. This is the position regarding Seretse's livelihood. I started by sending him to school. I should have asked for assistance from the Tribe, but I did not even use the tribal funds; I used my own cash for his education. I did not ask the Tribe to contribute although I had the right to do so. Last year when Seretse returned to England I told the District Commissioner that the burden was now heavy for me, that is, I paid for Seretse's education for a long time now something must be done. It is said that a cable message was sent to say Seretse was coming home. I know that since Seretse returned to England he never wrote to me. I do not say he did write to the Government. I do not know anything about his coming and the Government people never told me he had written. As regards the question of my surprise about the money for his voyage, it is so. But I now leave it. Customarily and necessarily, you can give Seretse some gifts through me; and he too should let me know what he received during my absence. As Seretse has already

Appendix H

explained how he got the money, I have nothing further to say. I know it is a disgrace to the Tribe what he did because I had prepared the money for his journey. I said so that he should get a legal adviser; it was not a secret talk. I do not think this matter will end here as the Government says. Though you may say I am teaching the people the habit of seeking the help of legal advisers[,] I still say it because this case will be settled by these men [Government]. But they will do so with facts.

    I am now coming to the point raised by Seretse alleging that I am chasing him away. I have been waiting to hear anybody stating the facts to show that I am desirous to claim the Chieftainship of Sekgoma's son. I thought Seretse would say something different from what I have already said and which I still maintain that I am against his marriage of a white woman. I say my heart is sad. Perhaps some of the Bamangwatos do not realize that Seretse does not know his father. He knows me. I have educated and doctored him, knowing very well that the children who loose their parents through death usually lead a bad life. Today you will tell me if I ever ill-treated Seretse. I have shown him the ways and means of my living and how he should live in England. It is said the dispute is about the marriage. I say Seretse is my child, and he cannot marry without my knowing. His uncles and the Tribe should consult with me about his marriage. They should tell me that they have tried him but he is adamant to his marriage. None of you who will say came to me about the marriage and still say I am refusing the marriage. What I say will be confirmed by his letters. He wrote to say he was aware that the Bamangwato would not approve of the marriage. I still say none of you came to me to say Seretse should be left to marry as he would not change his mind. If Sekgoma were alive he would not settle Seretse's marriage without me. He would wait if I were absent. It is now said he should be allowed to marry against my will. I cannot deceive myself that I agree to the marriage. Despite all this talk I still refuse the marriage. His marriage [will] be conducted by those people who support him. This matter is very much disappointing and breaks one's heart. Seretse's supporters are silent. They have made him to take the lead. It is not our custom, it is a disgrace to me to hear Seretse telling the people whose son he is. When Sekgoma disagreed with his father he was supported by his uncles. I also want Seretse's uncles, who say I usurp his chieftainship, to speak before giving my own views.

About the woman[,] I am refusing because she is not suitable for him. I still say do what you can, those who support him. I am against it.

I have not come to the question of chieftainship even though it could suit me to dispute it with him customarily, but I am still waiting for anybody who can say I am disputing the Chieftainship. Seretse cannot put himself on the seat. His father was put on the seat by Mphoeng; when I took over I had no younger brother but I was put on the seat by Gorewan. I never put myself. If Seretse wants to put himself by force he is undertaking a big task. I would like my mistakes point[ed] out first then I will speak.

Kgotla Meeting Resumed, Tuesday 21 June 1949

Chief Tshekedi Khama: The discussion will start now, and I remind the speakers to give their names and Kgotlas [wards].

Manyaphiri Ikitseng: The Deputy Resident Commissioner and all who are here, before I speak I would like to point out this: it was said no meetings should be held at night in this connection. Last night some of my people came to me and said they were called by Gaofhetoge who asked them what I usually say to them and to find out their views on this matter. I said I would reply in the Kgotla.

We have discussed Seretse's affair for a long time. Last year we [uncles] were summoned by the Chief to discuss Seretse's marriage. Two things were at issue for consideration namely marriage without consulting with the Tribe, and marriage to a white lady. We dismissed without any agreement with Seretse. We again met on the 13th and 14th December on the same subject and still Seretse refused to agree with us. Among us there was only one person who agreed to the marriage. On the 15th December this matter was discussed in the Kgotla meeting but

Appendix H

Seretse would not agree. When the meeting dismissed we had different opinions on Seretse's affair. This was brought about by these facts: that Seretse should be forsaken and that he should be sent to England for good. Ever since we have no confidence in each other. This aspect of the affair created a lot of misunderstanding. The fact that Seretse should be chased away. We refused to chase Seretse away for marriage. The issue today is about Chieftainship; the question of marriage is put aside. The history of our forefathers makes me fear. I do not know anything about many meetings. When Seretse returned to England I said I would not like to lose Seretse because of his marriage and therefore I changed my mind and agreed to the marriage. Seretse asked for an apology from us in the Kgotla for having married without our knowledge. The question was put to him whether he would divorce with his wife and [he] replied, "no." What Chief Tshekedi said yesterday is about the Chieftainship.

Phethu Mphoeng: I thank the Deputy Resident Commissioner and all who are here. I would like to say something about Seretse's marriage which is the centre of disturbance amongst us. We sent him to school and we heard he married a European. He came to Serowe and we objected to the marriage. Even today we still refuse the marriage. We had sent you to school particularly as the Chief's son. You have done something which is not in accordance with Setswana custom. Yesterday I heard that the dispute is now about the Chieftainship which is Seretse's who is the only heir to the Bamangwato Chieftainship. Most of us were against the marriage. There were only seven people who agreed to it. It is today we hear that we are divided. It is surprising because we were not compelled, neither by Tshekedi nor Seretse, to give our views on the matter. I still say a Chief's son is controlled and put on the seat as Chief by the people like ourselves, Chief Tshekedi and the Tribe. The Chief's son changes his mind. I still say what I said before. Referring to what Seretse said yesterday, we mean that you should obey us and we will obey like your grandfathers who were advised. I have been telling you that a child never deliberately imitates his father's bad doings. He never follows the bad records like you. Your grand-grandfather, Sekgoma, told Kgama at the time when Tshukudu was killed at Mokwena that his house would not rule. Kgama also told your father the same thing and it was so. That is why I say we should not go into this, though some of you will not succeed to the Bangwato Chieftainship. I am speaking about the Setswana Law and Custom. It is not advisable for you to refer to Khama's ill doings. You have caused the dispute about your chieftainship. I would ask the man who has told Seretse that Kgama married Semane without the consent of the Tribe to stand and explain to us. We are told that the marriage was of a woman from whose family one of our old chiefs married some years ago. The person who was telling you that was misleading you. If you talk of recent events, perhaps you are thinking of Lenkeme's case, the Chief refused, saying the Chief never marries a servant, and the Tribe refused. We do not know of any Chief's son who is not obedient to his father and his uncles. The Chief never introduces himself as you did yesterday. You have degraded our dignity in the public. I am airing my views even if I am considered an enemy. You have already ignored us when you got married. You did not tell us. I said so that you were as good as a dead man because you have interfered with our intentions. These people who stand for you today will desert you soon. Sekgoma's son, you are a harsh Chief by disputing matters which you should not discuss, and by having power before you take over the Chieftainship. We regard Chief as God, it is not advisable for anyone to speak ill of him as you have been speaking about your grand-father. I have already told you that it is customary for us to correct the Chief if he is wrong. I would end my speech by asking you to tell me about Semane. I know about Mma Tshukudu.

Peto Sekgoma: I greet the Deputy Resident Commissioner, the District Commissioner and the Chiefs who are present. I am grateful that you have come to help us because we are in a very dangerous political situation. I say our political situation has reached its crisis and nobody has any power to put it right. I expect you to do so. The dispute was about Seretse's marriage

Appendix H

which, it was alleged, he did on his own. We were all for the marriage to be dissolved. I was one of those who were against the marriage when we spoke in the private meetings. I thought the Government would have power to end this dispute. I have changed my mind now because we are no longer disputing the marriage. I did so as a result of the letter which states that the dispute is now about the Chieftainship. The contents of that letter made me decide otherwise. Today I want Seretse to come with his wife[.] Though he married on his own, that is no condition to deprive him of his position as Chief. Marriage to a white lady would not spoil anything. Seretse is the heir to the Chieftainship of the Bamangwato. I thought as Seretse has now come he would be put on the seat and the question of his marriage to be settled later. Seretse is meant to be Chief. Nobody can dispute the Chieftainship with him.

Goaletsa Tshukudu: The Deputy Resident Commissioner and the District Commissioner—when this affair started I realized that in the long run this dispute would be about the Chieftainship. When Seretse returned to England I said I agreed to the marriage. The means by which Seretse could be driven away had been found as a result of his marriage to a white lady. Before this matter was settled Seretse's uncle went to the cattle post and on his return told us that all the oxen, strayed cattle and the elephant's tusks, and the Tribe, were his. These words strengthened my determination. The elephant's tusks should be the property of the Chief, not the Regent. As regards Phethu's words that we did not agree to the marriage, it is not so. The Tribe has always been alleged to have said or done something which is not true. The Tribe never said we do not want Seretse's wife. The people who were against the marriage were only twenty-six; those who said Seretse could go and stay with his wife in England we will ask them to stand as the discussion is going on. Nobody will chase Seretse away. This country is his and the people [are also his]. He is the Chief not Regent. This Kgotla is his. My father was born here. I agreed to the marriage from the beginning. I knew it would not be easy for Tshekedi to hand over the Chieftainship. Seretse could be put on the seat by his fathers only when there is peace. But in a dispute like this the Tribe and the Government should put Seretse on the chair. This has been so even in the olden days.

Mogwera Mogalakwe: I greet the Government Officers, the Chiefs and the Tribe. I am one of those who were against the marriage. I was against the cholera. We said Seretse should not be allowed to return to England to his wife. We approved the contents of the memorandum which was read yesterday, asking the Government to dissolve Seretse's marriage. We saw a letter saying Seretse should divorce his wife otherwise he would not rule as Chief. I do not know what this means. There are secret meetings. We never asked Seretse to divorce his wife if he wanted to rule us or to keep her if he did not want to. This might have been said in the secret meetings. Tshekedi said if we agree to the marriage he would leave the country, he then swore he would rather die. He would rather share the country with Seretse and split the tribe because he did a lot for this country. I say if Tshekedi could have some people to rule and part of the country to himself the Government would not be fair. I know Tshekedi, like any other Regent, did a lot for this country. If the Government should oppress he would not be making peace to us. Bathoen said Seretse has laid a bad example to the people. I do not agree with him. We made Tshekedi a Regent Chief and [he had] to bring up Seretse, who is the Chief. The question of the elephant's tusk drives us to the conclusion that we are now disputing the Chieftainship. Phetu said Seretse is dead and Tshekedi lives; when the London bell tolls, it reports his death and that Tshekedi rules.

Olweleng Ntsaga: The Deputy Resident Commissioner and the Chiefs who have come to listen to this dispute which has been on for a long time. We refuse Seretse's marriage because he did it on his own. The matter was first discussed at the secret meeting. We said it would be better if Seretse should come alone and leave his wife behind. I said, should Seretse come he must not be allowed to return to England. On his arrival I still said it. When he returned he asked whether the Tribe wanted him to stay in

Appendix H

England with his wife. He then refused his uncles to speak in the meetings. My reply was the same as before; but now I have changed my mind as a result of the appeal from Ramarula to explain that appeal he made to me. This appeal was in the form of a letter.

Ramarula Mathodi: I do not remember, you had better give me the name of that person.

Olweleng Ntsaga: I would ask the Government officials that the letter be read. Did you not write it? Here is the letter.

Tshekedi Khama: I would ask the Interpreter to read it.

(Another one produced and read)

Olweleng Ntsaga: Bamangwato, that is the appeal I received from my Chief in Maaloso Kgotla. I was very sad at this news, to note that the position had changed and was no longer the question of marriage, but we were now disputing the Chieftainship. For this reason I would ask that Seretse be allowed to bring his wife even if Seretse is not put on the seat yet. I was refusing the marriage but now I would rather agree to it.

Gabolebywe Mabebela: I greet the Deputy Resident Commissioner, the Chiefs, and the tribes who have come to listen to the dispute. I say in this matter every speaker must choose points on which to base his dispute. I shall voice my feelings which were originally your feelings or at least of some of you. I do not think there is anybody who can draw a comparison between Tshekedi's and Seretse's chieftainship, because it is obvious that Seretse is the Chief. No one can dispute it. Our cry is one that Sekgoma's son has broken his father's law. I feel that my child must not do what it likes. I am Seretse's servant with whom Seretse can do what he likes. I have not given Seretse anything to help him. I am disappointed to hear Seretse say he was brought up with the tribal funds. The Government officials, who are now here, know that there is no arrangement made to provide Seretse with the tribal fund. Everyone has a right to give Seretse anything provided that such a gift comes through the Chief Tshekedi. Yesterday Tshekedi said we should point out his bad deeds in as far as Seretse's treatment is concerned. He was saying this for the second time. I heard that what Tshekedi said, that if Seretse brought his wife he would go. It meant that Tshekedi wanted to usurp Seretse's chieftainship.

I have some evidence to prove Tshekedi's love for Seretse. When we first heard about this marriage Manyaphiri Ikitseng spoke with a trembling voice and I thought he would die. That was the first example for his love. All things pertaining to the Chieftainship are fine. Tshekedi wished Seretse every success by educating him. When Seretse was young Tshekedi chose Baruti as his tutor in order to give him a good foundation. This is another example of his love. In 1946 when we went to the Victory Celebration in London Tshekedi said before we left that Seretse expressed his desire to come home but he, Tshekedi, would be very sorry if that happened before Seretse could acquire the education that he wished him, because the great weapon these days is the education. When we met Seretse in England he said at one time he wrote to his uncle saying he wanted to come home. Subsequently he thought of the love Tshekedi had for him and how much he desired him to receive good education and as a result he wrote him a letter of apology. We are faced with the marriage question and it is difficult to chase away our Chief's son. I want you Seretse to stay with us. The matter about the Chieftainship will be settled by these Government officials. (Noise quote—page 9 of Setswana). [Tshekedi intervenes to quell noise]. It is now said the street talk will put us in trouble. Nevertheless, the rumours are that the idea in supporting Seretse's marriage is that the country should be divided into farms, and that the people will be under no chief. The dispute about Chieftainship is a new thing. I cannot change from what I said. I still refuse the marriage.

Appendix H

Gaolaolwe Manaheng: I thank the Deputy Resident Commissioner and officers to come and listen to the dispute which has now become complicated. We were refusing Seretse's wife whom he married without consulting us and well knowing that the Tribe and Tshekedi would not agree. We started by refusing the marriage and I still say so. We thought Tshekedi Khama would place Seretse before us without any trouble. I would ask the Deputy Resident Commissioner to listen to this case very carefully. We are expecting the Chief's son to bring us his education and nothing else. The dispute about the Chieftainship has suddenly sprung out as a by-subject, and Ramarula's words must be followed carefully. We are concerned with the marriage.

Seretse Khama: I have not much to say. I would draw the Deputy Resident Commissioner's attention to what my uncles said regarding the number of speakers, that four should speak on the affirmative and four on the opposition, and ask whether it would not be advisable to let the people speak as usual in their Setswana Kgotla custom.

Tshekedi Khama: I follow what the Chief's son says. I was suggesting that because of the nature of this discussion which is about the Chieftainship. I heard the heads of villages speak, such as Ntsaga and the Sekgoma's sons. I know the Tribe will be allowed to speak, but I wanted the important people and the Chief's uncles to speak first and to give each other a chance to balance both sides. But, as the matter has been put to the Deputy Resident Commissioner, I leave it to him.

Seretse Khama: That had been my request because this matter, even a few days ago, has been said to be difficult although the discussion at the time appeared to have been about marriage, yet it was connected with this. The discussion was carried out in the usual manner. The question was first put what should now be done because the marriage has been solemnised and finished with? If I heard correctly it was said "Do we accept Seretse with his wife or not." Even now I have come to hear the final decision whether

I am welcome with my wife or not. But I am not divorcing my wife. I do not want what has been discussed last because that will waste time. I would suggest everybody be allowed to voice out his opinion, not only the Sekgoma's sons or responsible Headmen.

Tshekedi Khama: I say I would not like to give out my views before the discussion is entered into by the majority. One of the speakers said there are only twenty-six people who do not want Seretse's wife. This is something we cannot follow. I am sad about the meetings which mislead the Chief's son. The dispute we are faced with is about the country, and it will eventually be dealt with by the Tribe in their Kgotlas. Usually before we do that we give the people a chance to discuss here. I would ask the Government officials to give us time not to hurry and end the discussion. I will stop so far at present. As the Chief's son has nothing to say I would like the matter discussed as I have explained i.e. four people to speak on one side and four on the other and so on.

Goitsekgosi Sekga: Shortly I would refer to what would appear to be your habit. It is said the Chief's son is given a wife by his fathers and the tribe. I say there is nothing like that, it never happened. Kgama had a wife whom he divorced and married the one he liked. This was the case with Sekgoma, Mphoeng and Tshekedi who divorced Bagakgametse. If anybody wants to dispute that let him stand. I will tell him.

Bakwena Mosarwa: I will speak at length. I have lived for some years during Tshekedi's rule as regent, but I never heard at any one time the rumours that Tshekedi wanted to usurp Seretse's chieftainship. We know Tshekedi has been acting on behalf of Seretse. We never thought there would be noise about the Chief's son. I have not much evidence about Tshekedi's love for Seretse as someone has already stated. The education given to Seretse is a proof for Tshekedi's love for Seretse. One word of love is this: When Chief Tshekedi Khama sent Seretse to school he said to me: "I want the Chief's son to exceed you [people] in everything" and

Appendix H

I realized he really loved him. When he sent him to England I believed that he is acting on his behalf in reality. When I was expecting Seretse to finish his education and come home to be shown to his people I heard the Chief saying Seretse had married a European. We [the Bamangwato] were very sad at this news. We asked Tshekedi to call Seretse for us. I thought he did it without intention, and also that when he saw us he would divorce his wife. We were allowed to interview him. I went to see him and spoke to him about marriage. I said Kgama did not gather the tribes to be scattered. I have come to tell you this. Before he went to England he said "I am glad if you send me to school. I will fail very much against my will." No negotiations have been undertaken about your wife by your parents. The chief's wife should be chosen and asked for because she is the mother to the tribe. I said this last time, and that if you didn't listen to me you would keep [rule] me. These words were not the slip of the tongue. I still say them. I am expressing but my feelings. If we were disputing the Chieftainship Tshekedi would be alone, but we are talking about the marriage. The Chieftainship is for the Ngwato to settle. It is said Mphoeng put Sekgoma on the chair. The Ngwato chieftainship is bestowed upon. Sekgoma did not rule long. Gorewan then took over when Tshekedi was still at school. He was put on the seat by the Bamangwato by agreement. It is difficult to say we don't want you, stay away. It is equally difficult to accept Seretse without his wife. You should make it clear that we don't want you with your wife. The matter will be easy.

Lesole Maporoso: I, as your servant, understand the dispute between our chief's sons. I stand to point out the division that the tribe is causing between the two. I can prove his [Tshekedi's] love for Seretse. Tshekedi and Seretse faced their difficulties alone and Tshekedi brought up Seretse who is now a grown-up, and suddenly you separate them. I do not know whether a man could bring up an enemy.

Rajaba Monaheng: I have long agreed to the marriage since the beginning of the dispute. There are many people who divorce their wives, not being asked but because of the misunderstanding in their homes. It surprises me today to hear that Seretse, the Chief's son, should be forced by authority to divorce his wife for the sake of the Chieftainship, which is his. What is wrong with this woman? God says "thou shall not attempt to undo what I have done." Khama said a man should marry the woman he loves. Seretse married in accordance with Khama's law.

Lekhulile Motalaote: To you, Government officials and the Chiefs. I stand for all the trouble you have come for. You should be patient. This matter was dealt with a few months ago, and only seven people agreed to the marriage. Most of us were against it. The number was sent to Cape Town. When are we going to know those who are against the marriage and those who agree? I would ask the people to vote. I was refusing but now I agree. Men are prophets who can foretell what the future has in store. I can also foretell. Khama, Bathoen, and Sebele, were not told to go to England to ask for protection. Seretse also comes from our seat of Government who knows that we are Seretse's parents as well as they are. This is what made me change my mind. Today we know their protection and we move about without firearms. In the past Europeans would not allow anybody to mix with their women, but today they have done so. I think they have done this from their sincere love; love, which is above all things. I am of the opinion that if there was no love they would not marry their daughter to the black man. We too no longer look down upon other tribes such as the Barotsis and Blantyres to marry our children. Khama said our children blamed us for marrying them; they should be left to make their own choice so that we could answer for ourselves when they disputed with their wives. I say Seretse has created a link of love between the white and black races. Setswana says *"Eare go loetsiwa bobe e bo e tswe Bololoi."* Why do you want to dwell long on this matter? A few months ago and yesterday you said "Do not ignore me and marry my child; nobody came to me to say if you do not pardon your child for what he did he would leave us." I would suggest we take a vote to end the dispute quickly. Let the woman come in peace.

Appendix H

(The Tribe—Pula!!)

Mosinyi Segotso: I am glad to hear the discussion about the marriage. Originally we all refused, but Seretse said he would not divorce his wife. Today we seem to be on a different subject; but Seretse still says he would not leave his wife. When the memorandum was read in the Kgotla I said I would answer when the parents of Mrs. Seretse had replied. Now I notice they have said nothing and I say Seretse should bring his wife. The Government officials seem not to have a guilty conscience and I think we are tools. We have diverted from the original dispute.

Mmereki Motshegwa: When the dispute started I was absent. I came when Tshekedi called us at the time Seretse returned to England. We agreed. He said he would be sorry if we had refused, because the white people want an educated man. Europeans are our leaders. Seretse has done well because his in-laws will listen to him when he speaks. If anybody refuses this marriage I do not understand what he means because we depend on the white people. I think it is in order that the white people have given their daughter to Seretse. I do not understand what is meant by the negotiations referred to. This child has acted like his grand-father, who went and asked for protection for us from England. Let rain come.

(The Tribe—Pula!!)

Oteng Mphoeng: I greet the Government officers. I am Phethu's younger brother, both of us are Chief's representatives at Madinare. Before I speak I would like somebody to answer me. Was there any dispute during Tshekedi's regency that Seretse would not take over the Chieftainship?

Dingalo Nthebolong: There was no dispute but because the dispute has arisen we have to go into it.

Masetsane Ikitseng: There was once a dispute during Dingalo's case. Tshekedi told me if he wanted he would not give Seretse his place as Chief. I opposed him.

Oteng Mphoeng: I do not agree with you. There was never a tribal dispute. We tried Dingalo for doctoring Seretse. We said he was not his son but the Tribe's child. Dingalo also doctored Seretse at Gaofetoge's yard and without Gaofetoge's knowledge. We then sentenced him to a term of imprisonment. Was it not so Manyaphiri? Can a man like Olweleng install Seretse on the seat without his father's knowing? Did we not discuss this matter in the secret meeting and refused this marriage Manyaphiri?

Manyaphiri Ikitseng: Yes, it is so.

Oteng Mphoeng: We said Seretse had put us in an awkward position, when we heard he was marrying. Manyaphiri and I had the same cry that we were now split. When did you differ with us in the secret meeting of Sekgoma's family [sons], or in the Kgotla?

Manyaphiri Ikitseng: I changed my mind when I heard you say your father was sent to Mokwena and Ngwaketse to call armies to come and chase away Macheng from home. Again you said Seretse was harsh; he could not rule us.

Oteng Mphoeng: You Peto, what letters do you say made you change your mind?

Peto Sekgoma: They were read.

Oteng Mphoeng: The letter was not written by the Chief. It should not have made you change your mind. It was a letter from a different man. None of us could be found guilty of writing that letter. Ramarula himself denies it. Tshukudu's son said there were twenty-six people who were against the marriage. Can he read out the names.

Appendix H

Goaletsa reads out the names of those who do not want Seretse's wife.

Tshekedi Khama: I would like to remind you of this. You take this dispute as a light matter. A man like Lekhutile said those who were for marriage should stand aside and those who were against it; because the dispute was now about the Chieftainship. I don't say Sekgoma's son is not Chief. In the Setswana Custom there would be civil war but now the white people have power, they could settle the dispute about Chieftainship. I saw a list of names of those who are said to oppose the marriage. I also gave the Government a list of names of those who hold meetings at night. I would like them to look at it and see if they would find the names of some of the speakers there. Do not make a noise when others oppose the marriage. As regards my words repeated by my uncles, I said so that a child is foresaken until he repents to his parents. I was not saying this as a secret. Even today I say so. This also applies to elephant's tusks and strayed cattle. I was pleased to see the letters produced in the meeting. We heard about them long before now. I shall say something about them later. As regards the inference to Macheng I am not answering for Oteng, but I know that it was said Bangwaketsi and Bakwena usually come to make peace amongst us when we are at loggerheads as it is today. There was no other inference. Mokaa (Headman Mosinyi Segotso) and Lekhutile say the Government knows all about this matter and it looks at us as idiots. I realize that this is my last year of my regency if there is peace. There is nothing wrong for the people to change their minds, provided they give reasons. I will hand over the Chieftainship to Seretse customarily, not otherwise. We follow the Protectorate law and custom.

Kgotla Meeting, Wednesday, 22 June 1949

Tshekedi Khama: I remind you what I said yesterday that we are too many. We cannot all speak even if the officials could be patient. That is why I say four people should speak and the other four to oppose them. I would like to make it clear to you that you would not settle this matter by making a noise. That is nothing. We are disputing the Chieftainship which in the past would be settled by civil war. Today the war is the verdict which the Government would give after following the discussion. I shall call upon Oteng to finish his speech.

Oteng Mphoeng: Yesterday I said nobody claims the Chieftainship. I still say I do not want a white woman. But if you, Chief's son, do not obey me, the Tribe and the Chief, you won't rule me. Lekhutile, Bakaa and Baphaleng, you came determined, but I say you will not marry him. On more than one occasion we fought for this orphan of Sekgoma.

Ramarula Mathodi: The Deputy Resident Commissioner, District Commissioner, Chiefs Kgari, Mokgosi, and Tshekedi, I have a short speech. Chief Tshekedi told us that Seretse was getting married, at which news we became cold blooded. Soon after we heard he had now married. We asked that Seretse be called home and he came. I said I was against the marriage and I still say so. I said to Seretse if you do not obey your father I won't obey you. You have broken the law which you should set as an example to the Tribe. I will refuse to obey you. Tshekedi is not claiming the Chieftainship, he cannot do it, because here is the rightful chief. Tshekedi was refusing the white woman. I do not know whether a child can be led to despise his [father]. Tshekedi will obey Seretse after he has been installed as Chief. If Tshekedi was for the Chieftainship I would have refused.

Seitshiro Mowen: I greet the Deputy Resident Commissioner, District Commissioner, Chief Tshekedi Khama and the Chiefs who have come to listen to this dispute. Because I am hurt, I shall speak at length. We are discussing Seretse's marriage, together with Chief Tshekedi Khama. If the marriage was negotiated by Tshekedi Khama and his son, then we would have very little to say. But Seretse married on his own without regard to the people and his father. We say it is Khama's law. Khama said when were

Appendix H

at Palapye that people should be left to make their own choice in marriage. Khama, however, did not allow his own child to do what it pleased. Bonyerile, for instance, was forced to marry Lekhutile Motalaote. She was married according to the father's will. If anything we are following the white man's way. Are we leaving our law and custom? We must manage Seretse in order to set an example to his people. I do not want that woman. You accuse us when you say we want the Chieftainship when we dispute the marriage. If Tshekedi said it, I would say something. I would not [say] Seretse has done well, even if I will be regarded to support the claim for Chieftainship. Khama never said we should do as we like.

Radisigo Goepamang: The Deputy Resident Commissioner, District Commissioner and Chiefs. I oppose Seitshiro. He actually agrees with the Tribe. He says Khama's child was forced to agree to the father's will and I would like him to say whether that is still standing. The child has returned home because he was forced. When Gorewan was acting Chief, he never went to count cattle before Tshekedi took over. Tshekedi never took the members of the Tribe with him when he went to check his cattle. He took a few people with him to check the cattle after the dispute on the marriage last year. He did so during Seretse's absence. I thought Seretse was to be installed on the seat when I saw all the tribes gathered.

Tumiso Nkhukhu: I thank the Deputy Resident Commissioner to come and protect us and the tribes who have come to make peace amongst us. The Chief is responsible for all the affairs of the Tribe. He is their eyes and ears. Seretse may be regarded as such. We started the dispute with the marriage. We called Seretse to whom we spoke about his wife but he would not divorce her. I said to Seretse, if there is no agreement between the Tribe and the Chief, usually the dispute is settled by civil war. He asked me if that would then happen. I said "yes." I still say so and I mean this dispute. I still refuse your wife, even those who say [they] have changed their minds are the same as we are: your people. Regarding the chieftainship, I don't say much. You started the dispute because you said, if you were a chief, you would marry the woman against our consent. It never happened where the Chieftainship was taken over by the other chief without regard to the custom. However, this never happened here in the Ngwato Reserve, because we have always had chiefs. I still refuse your white wife and I have written some of my speech in order to make it short: to oppose Goaletsa: (Chief Tshekedi Khama refuses the letter).

Tumiso: Our sub-chiefs from outside villages did not give due consideration to this matter–that is why they are involved in the dispute. Sub-chiefs and Sekgoma's sons [relatives] are responsible for this dispute. Should there be any misunderstanding; that comes from the marriage. There is nobody claiming the Chieftainship. Sekgoma submitted to his father. There is no father who is forced to yield to his child. You say, it was alleged your father was poor, there is no such a thing. Who is your father you are talking about? Look, all these people are yours. Do not worry yourself. I still say I refuse your wife.

Cassils Goletilweng: I do not speak like last speakers. People give their opinions on what they have seen. We should follow the matter before us and find out what is wanting. The people who discussed this matter in the secret meetings should have told the Chief that Seretse has defeated us and because we do not wish to lose him he should be left to marry. I would ask you Seretse to hold your peace and leave the matter for us to settle.

Tshosa Galiorutwe: I would like to know whether this matter is dealt with in European or Setswana custom, because Tshekedi is presiding and yet he is a party and Seretse. I oppose you Seitshiro. You say Seretse has no right to give orders before he takes over, yet Gorewan left the chair before Tshekedi's arrival. There was no chief whose installation was awaited. You, Mphoeng, you hate Seretse as you hated his father and your father

Appendix H

fought with his fathers. What Manyaphiri said about the night meetings conducted by Mathiba should be investigated.

Tshekedi said four people should speak on one side and the other four to oppose them. He said some people barked at him and these he calls drunkards. He forgets these are the people who do the work for him. Even now those who side with him are drunkards like Kgosidintsi, their chief (Leader).

Owabona Nthobatsang: The Deputy Resident Commissioner and Officials, the Chiefs and Tribe. I am grateful for standing here. I am aware I am not important, but I shall say my word. We are all Khama's people. Even we too (Bakalaka) because our fathers saw Khama's kindness. We are here today because of that. I feel small to hear that some are people of no standing. But I know we are all Bangwatos. I speak about marriage. When Seretse returned to England I said we should bear in mind what is meant by a European. Do you know what is meant by that? Remember this woman has parents. What do they say?

Tshekedi Khama: They refused.

Seretse: They eventually agreed.

Owabona Nthobatsang: What did the Government say (Marriage Officer)?

Tshekedi Khama: Government is impartial.

Owabona Nthobatsang: Did he marry in church or Government office?

Seretse: What we would call District Commissioner's office in this country.

Owabona Nthobatsang: Have we got any right to undo what the white people did?

Seretse: No.

Owabona Nthobatsang: If Seretse did that what effect would it have on the tribe? Would the white men not say we are hypocrites? Let us think of this that Seretse has signed an agreement with the white people and if he does not abide by it they will say he is a hypocrite. In days to come he will make agreement with them, but if they have known him to be so pliable they will leave him in the dark. I maintain the white woman should come because that is a confirmation of victory. No fault has been found with her. I think Seretse has done well. I wish this woman comes and if she should have a child I be allowed to give it a name. You are responsible for the misunderstanding between the Chief's son. We must not do this.

Kamnogo Mpolokang: I greet the Deputy Resident Commissioner and my Chief and Tribe. The dispute started when the Chief said we should send a letter. But today I have little to say. Seretse apologised for what he did without informing us. I pray that he be excused. Our Government Officials are here and they hear what has been said. If there is anybody saying the Government is not fair let him say so. I agree–the woman should come.

Tshekedi Khama: Gaofetoge will answer about the secret meetings, how it was done.

Gaofetoge Mathiba: With greetings to the Deputy Resident Commissioner and Chiefs. I shall answer Manyaphiri's question endorsed by Tshosa. There was no secret meeting at night. This refers to a few people whom I called on a different matter. I am of the royal family. As such I do not think Manyaphiri has any right to question me why I had called those few people. I shall call upon those three men whom I interviewed to come and say what I called them for.

Kenyafetse Dipao: Ramonyadiwa came to me in the evening to call us. I asked my uncle to come with me but he stopped him.

Appendix H

Ramonyadiwa was with Ditiro. We met Ketshabile Kodumatse. Ketshabile gave him something which I could not make out what it was in the dark. We were scared and wondered as to where we were going at night. We thought perhaps we were called by our headman, Manyaphiri Ikitseng. We went and got up to Gaofetoge's yard. Ramonyadiwa left us there and on his return told us we would be called singly. Ketshabile went first and he did not return to us, he went out through the other gate. I was then called and found Gaofetoge who asked me if Manyaphiri had not told me anything. I said no, I knew nothing. I do not know what was said by Kudumatse and Ditiro because we did not meet again. When I got to our camp I found no people and I went to bed. Shortly after, Thipe came and said Manyaphiri wanted me. I got up and went to him. I found him at the tent. He then said: I understand you have been called by Ramonyadiwa, I was told by Thipe. I replied Gaofetoge had called us and asked us what the news were. I said there were none. Gaofetoge called us one by one and we did not meet again. I do not know what Ditiro and Kenyafetse said. Manyaphiri then said it was alright that Gaofetoge called us to find out what he said to you. Ditiro will give account of what he said.

Ditiro Seduke: Ramonyadiwa came to me at night and said he wanted me. I followed him, accompanied by Kenyafetse, and Dipoiso, who returned on the way. We got up to Gaofetoge's place and Ramonyadiwa directed us to go inside the yard. Ramonyadiwa said I was wanted. I went with him to Mathiba, who said he had something to ask me. We went inside the house. He asked if Manyaphiri never called me. I said he called me when he was sick and asked me why I did not go to see him. He then said I should tell my brother that tax money was wanting. Mathiba replied "I thought he called you for something in connection with the Chieftainship."

Ketshabile Kudumatse: I will repeat what the last speakers said. We met Ramonyadiwa near the tent and he said our Chief wanted us, we thought he meant Manyaphiri, but he said it was Mathiba who wanted us. Mathiba asked me if I never had any private talk with Manyaphiri or Peto. I said only Manyaphiri who called me when he was sick and asked why I did not come to see him.

Gaofetoge Mathiba: What they have said is true except Itebatseng who said [. . .] had met Peto. I do not think Manyaphiri had any right to ask who sent me.

The District Resident Commissioner I shall now come to the point. I am one of those who refuse the marriage and I do not change. It is said I alleged the Chief's son should be thrown away like my son. I have foresaken my son because he was drinking beer, even today I won't accept him if he does not apologise. I gave him and his mother everything for their livelihood. Seretse must work in agreement with the Tribe. The Chieftainship is his and no one can dispute it. The Chief is for the people and the people for the Chief. It is alleged Tshekedi claims the Chieftainship, it is not so; a letter was read to that effect, but I, as his assistant, know nothing about intention. We would have asked him what he meant. I can prove his parental care over his son Seretse. He made wealth for him. The brands that were made long ago by Chief Khama are still in use. This is a good example of his care. As regards his works and health treatment for his son there is no one to surpass him. He sent for Doctors from Johannesburg by air. I agree with Goaletsa when he said the chief's uncles are responsible for dispute between the chiefs. It is true they caused a misunderstanding between Seretse and his uncle and as a consequence upon this very much mislead him. I would not be ruled by the Chief's uncles. Even the secret which Samson did not want to disclose was eventually known. Why is it not possible with Tshekedi? The Government would be knowing something about him now. But I say I do not want Seretse's wife.

Kgosidintsi Jakoba: I greet the District Commissioner and Officers, and Chiefs. I am of the Royal family at Mokwena, where beer is food. You, Tshosa, I am not a drunkard like you of Tshosa village, who shot me with a gun when you were drunk. Why have you written my name? Because you Tshosa, said Seretse should

Appendix H

go and live with his wife in England? Your Honour, these people are trying to retaliate for having been punished and Seretse is also still to punish them for their bad deeds. The dispute is now about the Chieftainship for which I went to Tshekedi and asked him how this was connected with the marriage. I am of the Royal stock and I must die for the Chieftainship. I have a bullet scar on my hip, by the people of Tshosa village. Tshekedi denied knowledge of claiming the chieftainship. I told him as a refugee I would like to be ruled by the chief who is installed in the chair. I am not like you Goaletsa whose father was thrown into a cafe—and if you are not careful I will do that with you. I will make Tshekedi suffer the same fate too, if he claims to be Chief. I am not a drunkard but I drink to live. I would be grateful if you could give me some drink after this.

Inyatseng Monaheng: Greetings. Do you not agree with me now Tshekedi in what I told you when we came from Mafeking? I abide by what I said. I am the son of a prominent servant, who, if it were according to Setswana Custom, someone would have been hurt. I said when you have brought up Seretse your rivals would work him against you. A few months ago I asked the Chief's son to bid us good-bye, but he deserted us. Nobody could give you a wife without our knowledge. Tshekedi is not a chief but the Chief's uncle. I hear the Chief's uncles say that they have now changed their decisions. I am very much disappointed at you because you did come and join us to go to the Chief and implore him to allow Seretse to marry a white lady. It is not our custom to desert others without notice. We would have pleaded for the Chief's wife to be accepted by the Tribe. I have nothing to say about the Chieftainship. Seretse is the Chief not Tshekedi.

Mokgalo Selepeng: I greet the Deputy Resident Commissioner, the Chiefs and the Tribe. I wish to thank our Government for the way it takes an interest in this matter, and that every word will be carefully noted. I thank Seretse and not forgetting his word that every speaker should not try to please him. I would say what Marobela has already said and which I consider is worth noting.

It is alleged Tshekedi is a greedy man and a thief, but who can what he did as Marobela's son has already explained. The young Marobela said Tshekedi had very [definite] aims when Seretse went to England. He placed the matter before the Kgotla and it was unanimously agreed. Nobody objected, but today we say he is greedy, and a thief. I would ask pardon from the Minister for quoting a few words from the Holy Book. It is said "They all stood and said crucify him" and the judge said "what has he done?" He has done nothing wrong. But they wanted him to be crucified and it was so. He died for them. When we say Khama's son be crucified, what has he done: before he is crucified let us point his faults. You have hurt me Sekgoma's son because I thought I would hear something about this greedy man, but Ramarula denied knowledge of the letters. I would direct my speech to you the Bangwato tribe and warn you about the split you are making among yourselves. I am not afraid of anything. My own views on the matter are that the Tribe should ask the parents of the Chief's son to persuade him to change his mind. But now the discussion is about the Chieftainship for which I have evidence to prove that Tshekedi is claiming it. Watch how you are splitting yourselves. I would also direct my request to Chief[s] Mokgosi, Kgari and Bathoen to take interest in this matter and see how the Bangwato tribe is splitting itself.

Kgolo Goitsekgosi: I am directing my question to you Edumile Mogwera. What did you say in the first meeting when you heard that our child married a European? I said if we agree he should be called home.

Goaletsa Tshukudu, were you present in the first meeting? What did you say?

I said Seretse's wife should come.

When a person stands for Chief Tshekedi he is considered to be enjoying presents from him, but I am not such. I work for my living. He hires me when he has work to be done. In the first meeting we unanimously agreed that Seretse could not marry a European. We did not hate the white person but we were following the custom. Referring to what Goaletsa said about the

Appendix H

change of decision this came about as a result of the nocturnal meetings of which I heard when I was at Moeng and I knew they would cause trouble. It is alleged Khama said we could marry as we wished, did he mean even when a child is sent to Lovedale he should bring home a wife? I refuse the marriage, not because I hate the white lady, but because it was not done customarily. My father refused when my younger brother married without his consent.

Ngwanampe Mokgadi: Do you now agree with me Tshekedi? I asked you to install Seretse in the chair when he was young. You Seretse do not listen to those who pull you away from your father. This is very common amongst your people. At one time some of them broke away. Then Khama allowed those who remained to drink beer as they wished, and some of those who broke away returned. I refused to take part in many organisations against the Chieftainship. Oteng should not say he is hurt by what Lekhutile said. I would ask Tshekedi about the marriage after the dispute is settled. If the tribe had agreed with Tshekedi about Seretse's marriage, Tshekedi would probably consider your request and Seretse himself would agree. I implore you Chief Tshekedi not to take to heart what Seretse said. Install him in the chair tomorrow. He will beat us here. You too, Seretse. I pray you, everything is yours, made for you by Tshekedi. You, Lekhutile, should be careful of the words you use. I feel pity for Serogola because he has been forced to allege that Chief Tshekedi claims the Chieftainship.

(The Tribe–Pula!!)

Serogola G. Seretse: I greet the Deputy Resident Commissioner and Government Officials, Chiefs and the Tribes. The dispute started a few days ago and the records were read. I shall begin where I received a letter to proceed to Lobatsi for the High Court session–on my return I heard Seretse was married to a European. I asked Masetsane and Badirwang. Both denied knowledge. Tshekedi was then at Mafeking and I was told he had taken the decision of the Tribe that if Seretse has married a European he would not enter their country. We discussed at length what Phethu and Gaofetoge said, that Seretse should come home. After his arrival we were allowed to interview him in private. Several times I was called by Tshekedi who said Seretse is determined not to divorce his wife. If he does not leave his wife I will not give him the Chieftainship and the [live]stock. He said Mr. Ellenberger showed him the will made by Chief Khama. I said Seretse should be given time to think over the matter. After this there were several secret meetings of Sekgoma's sons (uncles) in which I did not speak. In English silence means consent but in Setswana [silence] means the opposite. Therefore my silence meant I was not agreeable to what it was said. I said to Seretse: be steady when you speak. Tshekedi should not tell the Tribe that I am responsible for Seretse's behaviour. I suggested that a legislation be drawn which would nullify this marriage, but this has not been done, and the dispute is still referred back to us. I still follow what Tshekedi said about the Chieftainship and stock. I began to fear when I thought Seretse is leaving home for good. Seretse is a chief alone and nobody can dispute the Chieftainship with him. If it were not what Tshekedi said I would refuse the marriage. But because now I have been found a hypocrite, I want the woman to come. The letters were read. A man came from Maaloso Kgotla to say Sekgoma's sons (uncles) were siding with Seretse. I would ask your honour and the Chiefs that we should discuss the Chieftainship not marriage. I heard Tshekedi say he would hand over the chair to Seretse. The child will rule with rain [in peace].

(The Tribe–Pula!!)

Tshekedi Khama: If the speakers could speak like Serogola the dispute would be settled quickly. It is only now that I have heard what I wanted. I shall reply because I am not afraid of what I said. I would answer but I must keep my word about the number of speakers on either side.

Appendix H

Bathoen Pelaelo: We have discussed this matter for about four months now. In the last Kgotla meeting when the decision was drawn I was present, but now I have changed. I want Seretse to marry that woman and bring her to Serowe. We cannot undo what God did.

Ramosamo Kebonang: I greet his honour and his assistants. I am one of those who spoke in the previous meetings against the marriage. Last year I heard Tshekedi say he received a letter saying Seretse wished to marry and shortly another letter saying he had married. I asked him how they lived at home. I am complaining why has he done this. I asked that he be called home that we should speak to him personally. After his arrival some spoke to him in private. I would have spoken to him in private but refrained as I had no secret to discuss with him. I said I would speak to him in the Kgotla. When he was in the Kgotla meeting I asked him if he came on his own or whether he was on leave. He replied we called him. I asked Tshekedi where Seretse would get money for his journey back. I refused the marriage and said Seretse should know this. Today I have changed because Tshekedi told Seretse that he was Chief, all the cattle were his and the people. I thought of what Tshekedi said to Seretse that he should not attack him from outside, that all the stock were his and the people, further that if and when Seretse's wife arrived he would leave the country quietly and go to Mokwena or Ngwaketse, but not to Ngamiland because it might be considered he would claim the Chieftainship. He further said the Government does not allow anybody to leave his birth-land. These words made me conclude we were disputing the country and not the marriage. I have changed my mind and I accept Seretse's wife, because I see that this is an intrigue to end Seretse, and I will die with him. I had decided to speak to Chief Tshekedi that we would lose our child. When I reached him I felt I should come and meet Tshekedi but when I got to Mahalapye Manyaphiri told me that the Chief was not at home and I returned. I delayed to come on account of my ill health. I now want Seretse's wife to come because I do not want to lose him. I want him to be near when I die not to hear about my death when he is in England.

(The Tribe—Pula!!)

Where would I get Seretse if he is thrown away. I want him with his wife—with rain.

Kgotla Speeches, Thursday, 23 June 1949

Tshekedi Khama: Yesterday we dispersed when I still had to reply to some words but I would give Boiditswe a chance to reply to words directed to him.

Boiditswe Nthutang: I greet the Deputy Resident Commissioner and the Chiefs. Some months ago the Chief said Seretse wished to marry and shortly thereafter he said he was already married. We refused the marriage. Seretse says what I have said. I have never seen a dispute like this. I know that even in Sekgoma's case the Bangwato behaved in this manner. His uncles did the same thing like these. But none of them can say how far Sekgoma went. When they objected they had no intentions of saving Sekgoma, nor did they have any love for him, they merely meant to mislead. My father died at Nakati. None of them can say when Sekgoma returned. I am not mentioning the names of those who refuse and those who agree. They spoke yesterday and they were listened to. What they said leads to destruction. Ramosamo's father was one of those who went with Sekgoma. I know once a chief is taken away from his father it only means facing hardships. Chief Khama sent me to Nakati to build for Sekgoma after which I returned. I know what your people want to do with you. It is their habit, they will do nothing for you. When Tshekedi returned from the elephant hunt Goitsekgosi told me to hide Seretse away, saying Tshekedi would kill him. Dingolo said Gawetshwarwe should be installed in the chair as Chief and I refused, that there was a Chief for whom Tshekedi was acting. We fought hard for you when you were young but today you have fathers. I would like some one to stand and say where Sekgoma returned. Yesterday I heard Serogola say Khama's Chieftainship is now over, when he finished there was an applause and I want to know whether you were pleased at that. Again I heard Radisigo say he realized that Tshekedi wants the Chieftainship by taking a few people [headmen] with him to the cattle post. I was one of those who went with Tshekedi. I had known the Chief's cattle posts before, but after this visit with the Chief, I realized that Tshekedi did his best for Sekgoma's son. I will not keep quiet when I see the people who usually spoil for me. Tshekedi said yesterday that Sekgoma did not rule, and I am not going to allow this to happen again.

Tshekedi Khama: Yesterday when we dispersed I said if the speakers spoke as Serogola and Ramosamo did, it would be easy to end the dispute. I realize from the noise you make that you want Seretse's wife and when I speak you seem to think that I am not aware that you want her. I have a complaint which is not about what you say but how you brought it about, that the woman should come. We were many when we refused the woman, and I did not speak too much as I have done today. I stood time and again to stop the noise and maintain order when somebody said the woman should come. We assembled in the meetings and drew a memorandum which was amended and approved. I am drawing your attention to what was arranged after the discussion. The village and the people are all mine as I have not yet handed over to this child. I have the right to call you day and night in this matter, and I would like anyone to say I called him in private and said I wanted the Chieftainship. When I said the discussion should wait for a reply to our letter nobody stood to dispute the contents. I said there were some people who met at Serogola's place to be advised that they should say they wanted Seretse's wife. I still say so. It will take me some time to show how Serogola recruited the people. Sekgoma's son's chieftainship is used as an excuse to shelter what is intended. The allegation that I want the Chieftainship is a serious matter for which I should be put in prison or banished. I said I am quiet. Perhaps the people who insulted me think I will answer. You are making the Chief's son a shelter. When the dispute started before Chief Mogkosi and Bathoen II, I said to Seretse I would leave you alone. We are starting the marriage dispute. You are coming to the village which has always some dispute, you should be careful of yourself, the people would say they want your wife when it is not so. I warned you about Serogola, Masetsane and the people of Tshosa Kgotla. They would want to have a dispute against me through you. I said this in strict confidence to the Chief's son. Some of you spoke ill of Sekgoma to me but I kept it at heart. When I spoke to Seretse I did not mean he should neglect his people. I was warning him. Sekgoma's son went to his people and told them about my warning. I know what the two people said. Seretse will dispute it. At that time we lived happily as father and son. Our misunderstanding sprang out from the marriage. When I told him these things he said he would reply me in the Kgotla. It is said I am making accusations but I will mention one instance. Today Seretse uses Peto's car. In the past he used my car as he liked, and used everything of mine as he liked, I mean when we lived peacefully. I say some people had the chance of bringing up the personal animosity against me by using the dispute of the marriage of the Chief's son. You disputed Boiditswe's statement that Serogola said Khama's chieftainship has come to an end. He said so. I say there is nobody who has power or right to interfere with our affairs unless my bad ways can be proved. If proofs are wanted I did not know that this child was coming but Serogola knew. I heard Makgala was seen at Bourima saying Serogola said Seretse was coming. If Seretse fears me because I refuse his wife he should also fear Manyaphiri and Serogola because they were also refusing his wife. I called two night meetings in which I said a child is foresaken until he apologises. Mathwai, like Serogola, was refusing the woman but changed his mind after I fined. His uncles who say his wife should come are those whom I fined. Even if we give Sekgoma's son his chair, these people will never be happy until I am banished. But this will never happen. I have told you that the white wife is not suitable for the Chief's son. I told him I would be hurt if I would have your white child as my

Appendix H

chief. I said as soon as you come with your white wife I would go because if I stayed here, it would be considered I am looking for followers.   I heard that Peto and Radiphofu were seen at Mahalapye wearing shawls when they met Serogola.   I heard Serogola had gone to Phaleng and Kgatleng in connection with this matter.   These I did not call.   I tolerated their behaviour. Manyaphiri asked Gaofetoge about the people he had called and Gaofetoge explained. Gaofetoge was sent by me. I told him to ask them one by one.   Manyaphiri told me he was going to the cattle post on account of his illness–heart trouble–because the Dr. said he should rest.   When I heard the people say he has been calling some people I then thought probably it was in connection with this matter.   Manyaphiri never collected tax before.   The Chief's son is shown his duties and the people. I hear that Seretse went to Batalaote where the Batalaote gathered to see him. This child should be taken by some one if he goes to see the people. These things make me have complaints. I warned Seretse against the Tshosa people. I fought them for your sake, they had taken the servants for whom they had sent Oratile. They are the people who wounded me; I was fighting for you. We put Dingalo in Gaol, still fighting for you. He was not alone; he was with others whom I did not point out. Obeditse was with Dingalo but I did not want to bring this out because I did not want the child (Seretse) who told me to be a witness. I do not think we can install Seretse in the chair when there is a trouble like this. I have brought up this child and I never did anything wrong to him. Today he does not want to talk to me, not to eat my food which brought him up. Peto says, he is born in the third house. Is there anybody who ever saw him trying cases in this Kgotla or speaking in any tribal meetings during peace time? He is the one who says I must not come close to Seretse. Kgama's chieftainship is Seretse's. I have told him that we had enemies but today he sees for himself. I am deeply hurt to hear Manyaphiri and others say I claim the Chieftainship when I say I do not want a white chief. The dispute is not about marriage but something else and Seretse is used as a tool.

Serogola says he changed his mind when he heard me say I would not give Seretse his stock. It is not so. We discussed this matter first at home and Masetsane said we should leave Seretse. Peto said: could we not be allowed to speak to him in private and I said he should ask him, he replied though it would seem as if I am taught what to ask. They never sided with you at all in the marriage dispute. Serogola, when Seretse spoke angrily to us, he said he was now talking. When I spoke to him in the Kgotla he said (help Seretse). I said to Seretse, come alone, if you bring a wife with you it will put you in trouble. Serogola also spoke to him in similar manner, speaking as a father giving good advice to the child. As regards Sekgoma's cattle I said they wasted when he wandered. By this I did not mean I am cleverer than my father. I implied that I tried to increase the cattle that were wasted. I took some people to show them that I would not be ashamed now to put before the Tribe Seretse's cattle. I said so about the elephant's tusk and the strayed cattle etc., etc. I said the Bamangwato have left their custom; they do not give presents anymore. I was speaking on law and custom. Today we do not even see the strayed cattle here. Sub-chiefs and headmen eat them. As I am not used to cursing I will not mention the names. I said I would not give you Sekgoma's cattle if you refuse to divorce your wife. As regards Khama's will, I told you that Mr. Ellenberger, the father of his honour now here, showed me a letter of Khama's Will which he made in my name after his dispute with Sekgoma. I called a few heads of villages and put this matter before them. I said to Seretse if you do not decide to agree with me and leave your wife, I will do what Khama did regarding the inheritance. I will give Seretse the English proverb that "give a doctor his own medicine." If you teach him to know Setswana I shall give him his inheritance. I do not know a house [person] which attacks itself. This is a serious matter, and I shall call upon those who say: we do not want the woman, to stand before His Honour and beat their breasts, like Sekgoma's sons. I shall call upon Sekgoma's uncles who object to stand before His Honour to take their names (onto the stage). We also beat our breasts if the Tribe is split on account of our child who is being used as a

Appendix H

weapon thrown at us from outside. Those who say will take Seretse by force, I say to you in the presence of the Government Officials that the people you saw standing here are my successors if I should die. There are many heads [Headmen] who help me in the tribal affairs, and whom Seretse hates today. Should all the people leave the country because of Sekgoma's sons [uncles] who separate us.

(Forty headmen come forward and stand facing the Kgotla)

Twaelang: This dispute started on Monday and it should not have taken us long. The question was: do we accept Seretse with his wife or not?

Interval

Tshekedi Khama: I have forgotten something very important. I call upon Mophaleng (Sub-chief Olweleng Ntsaga). Did you hear yourself saying you changed your mind because of the letter from Ramarula?

Mophaleng: It is so.

Tshekedi Khama: I pray you to go into this matter of your child and not follow Ramarula's letter. I am almost sure it is not his.

Olweleng Ntsaga: I have not shown the letter to my people except to a few headmen. The Tribe has not seen it. I believe that it comes from Ramarula because I see his name.

Seretse Khama: Bangwato, I have not much to say. My uncles were made to stand up that you may see them as those who are against the marriage. The question was put up that if the people refuse the marriage, would I punish them for that when I am on the seat. If so I would not be following the custom. A few months ago some of my uncles would come and greet me but today they do not do it. This behaviour makes me believe there is something. I have no hatred, they are afraid of me. When I arrived a few days ago they never came to see me. I do not know what is in their minds. I hear that there are some people, who are hypocrites, who boast of their intentions. I have been using Peto's car. A few days ago I went to Batalaote, accompanied by Serogola and Mpedi's son. The people came to see me at Ramotalaote's yard, not at the Kgotla. I am beginning to hear for the first time that when I go about negotiations should first be taken. This makes me fear. I have been in the habit of visiting these Bangwato people in the past. Today I hear there are people who are at loggerheads with Tshekedi Khama. I would point out that the people who were standing here are those who work with Tshekedi. That is why they side with him. There are some whom I could ask to stand and I think they can do so. I am a person and I cannot force myself where I see danger. I use Peto's car to see the people, well knowing that Tshekedi has cars, but I did not know that Peto is an agitator. I know the people have been discussing the marriage and it is sad to note that those who accept the marriage are agitators and those who refuse it are good citizens. I would like to know whether those who refuse the marriage would be chased away if the woman should come. I am not teaching you. You know the tribal disputes. I warn you not to conclude that if a person does not agree with the Chief is an enemy. Refusal sometimes helps. A person can decide whether he wants me as his chief or not. Similarly, if you do not want me, I will go. My uncles are not agitators because they oppose Tshekedi. Does it mean that those who agree with him are good? A few days ago His Honour asked whether we accept Seretse and his wife or not. But now we are on something else. We should not suspect people. More often than not a person may say what he does not mean and might even be killed for it. I would show the people to know that I am not alone. All my uncles siding with me should come on the stage that His Honour may see them— seventeen uncles [join Seretse]. Some of them are not here. I meant to show you the "agitators" who interfere in the tribal affairs [and for] the District Commissioner to see them[. The uncles may now] get down. I did not start this but it is what my father

Appendix H

Ramotalaote suggested and it was refused; despite that, those who refuse the marriage were made to stand up. The discussion will continue. I am not conversant with the Setswana custom but I do not know whether you were not aware when you sent me to school that I would know the European Custom. Every young child who comes from school does not know the Setswana Custom. In order to show His Honour how many people want my wife I would ask you to sit down. This does not [text missing] I am closing the discussion. You saw my uncles who refuse and who agree. Now I would ask the Tribe those who do not want me to bring my wife. A mob wants Seretse's wife with rain (in peace). I said I am not stopping the dispute to continue. I say Ramotalaote suggested this and Tshekedi refused. He has now made the people to stand. I end so far.

Kgosidintsi Jakoba: Do you mean only those who want your wife or that you should not become chief?

Seretse Khama: His Honour has already asked if you take Seretse. Do you take him with his wife or not?

(Assembly rises and acclaims Seretse as Chief)

Kgotla Speeches, Friday, 24 June 1949

Chief Tshekedi Khama: There is not much discussion today. We will give the Chiefs and their people from the other Reserves a chance to say something if they have any.

Chief Bathoen II: Your Honour, Chief Tshekedi and Sekgoma's son. I greet you. I stand here for the second time to speak in this sad dispute of the Bangwato. Today the dispute has now advanced to a different stage from what we were discussing. A few months ago we left the dispute on the point of the Chieftainship. I said in Bechuanaland Protectorate tribes have their disputes but the Bangwato are leaders and I am speaking the truth. You have left the dispute about marriage. You are now disputing the Chieftainship. How you arrived at this I do not know. You have misled Sekgoma's son. You made him override his father. He does not speak to him as his father. I am not worrying about the two parents but Seretse. Tshekedi said he does not eat his food. I have noticed that Seretse does not agree with me. I was with him at Kanye. What I shall say now is not a secret. You may ask him what I said to him. I said I can see that you regard me as an enemy. Some people told you that Tshekedi and Bathoen are one thing and of course it is so. Tshekedi and I do not miss each other. Tshekedi is my father and also a chief, you too will soon be a ruling Chief and I will be with you. I will speak to you about the Tribe from my experience. I say "*Khutsana Malemela a peteke.*" The people who supported Tshekedi have now left him and you do not know what is in their hearts. Some are sincere, others only look for a chance to question Tshekedi's authority. Some who are not expecting you to give them something will violate your authority when they have failed to get anything. You have seen some who were against the marriage have now changed their minds. I was surprised yesterday to see the child commanding the Tribe to stand and they did so. I do not say he is not a chief but I am on the custom. You have misled him.

(Noise—Chief Tshekedi intervenes)

A few days ago when we were at Kanye I said to Seretse there were rumours that your chieftainship has been disputed. I said as far as I know there is nobody who could dispute your chieftainship; not even Tshekedi himself could do it. Should Tshekedi attempt to do so I would oppose him. I still say so. I have been listening carefully and I have not yet heard anybody explaining or pointing out the ways in which Tshekedi claims the Chieftainship. I have only heard the insults. I have said this to Seretse. That is why I say you have misled this child. The people seem to think that as we have gathered here with His Honour amongst us, Tshekedi has come to hand over the Chieftainship to Seretse. Though you may make a roar I will speak what I want to

Appendix H

say. I said whether you rule us or leave us remember you have created a lot of disharmony in the Tribe and I still say so. The Bangwato chieftainship used to be strong. Yesterday we saw your headmen namely sub-chiefs of the Ngwato. Seretse said stand up and some did so while others sat down. What he did was a new thing to me, for a child to order the people to stand up and sit down, and come round, and they did so. You have stated that after Sekgoma's death Gorewan acted with authority. When Tshekedi arrived from school he–Gorewan–gathered you and put Tshekedi before you to be installed in the chair. Let us talk of recent things. Tshekedi did not gather you and introduce Seretse to you. We are going, we have heard what you said. Wherever we are we will wait to hear the result of your dispute. As regards the marriage, some of us are sincere in accepting her and others are not, but merely wanting to cause misunderstanding amongst Sekgoma's sons [uncles]. You have explained how the Bangwato made the marriage law objecting the young men to choose their own wives. I notice the reason why you want Seretse's wife. It is because you are tired of Tshekedi's ruling–Seretse wrote to his uncle saying he intended to do something very great which Tshekedi and the people would not like; I want to marry a European. He managed and got married. He heard some of you say you accept the marriage and others say we refuse. Speaking sorrowfully we can see that the Bangwato chieftainship is ending. I mean your high repute is ending. Before I sit down I would say here is Sekgoma's son whom you have put above his father. You have made a dividing between Sekgoma's sons.

People say the village usually is split by the chief's uncles not the ordinary layman. When we listened Tshekedi asked that his cruelty to Seretse be explained but nobody did so, the excuse is that he usurps Seretse's chieftainship. I do not like the way you behaved Seretse. Your uncle never ill-treated you. Here in the Kgotla you said he warned you at Mafeking to get yourself a lawyer; and you refused because you do not regard him as your father. I felt very small at this news. You said these words not of your own will, but you have been dictated to. Yet you have no other father than Tshekedi. If Tshekedi is not your father you would not agree with this Tribe, and the Tribe itself would not agree with you, except on condition that you are the Chief and the Tribe is living in your country (Bamangwatos country). I said we respect our people (Headmen) if we make a law and the people refuse it we leave it. You are only casting a bad spell in your future by saying Tshekedi is not your father. Some of your headmen said you would not rule them. I honour the man who takes the Chieftainship with one word. Yesterday I gave up hope when you said Tshekedi was not your father. I felt small when you addressed the people who look at Tshekedi as your assistant. I do not know whose advice you will take. There is a saying in Setswana: "*Ngwana a sa utlweng malao wa ga iragwe o uttwa wa manong.*" (He that will not be ruled by his own dame shall be ruled by his step-dame.) The words that have been said would not go in vain. You will listen to others. I am speaking on the main points to which I do not know whether you are listening or not, that does not worry me. I will say what I have in mind. It is said: "*Lentswe gale boe go boa menwana*" "Like an arrow to its aim flies the good man's words." Lastly I say you have misled Sekgoma's son, you have made him leave his father, you have thrown away your high repute. You will agree with me. In a few days I will be leaving and I will tell the Bangwaketsi what I have seen. I thank you, Chief Tshekedi, for inviting me to come and listen to this dispute. I particularly thank Sekgoma's son with whom I will be sharing the burden of Chieftainship in the near future. I thank you for your honour. I thank our Government representatives for their presence so that we could refer this to them in future. You have separated Sekgoma's sons. If the Tribe splits it is a draw-back and once that has happened it will take a considerable time to repair.

Chief Kgari Sechele: Your Honour, Chief Tshekedi and other Chiefs, I greet you. I thank Chief Tshekedi for inviting us for this dispute from the beginning. Twice we came to discuss this matter on the marriage and nothing else. Today it has developed into something great. As regards the marriage I agree with the speakers, even Chief Tshekedi himself, when he said nobody came

Appendix H

to say the dispute was growing. He further said we had the right to urge him; and say could we lose Seretse for the sake of the woman. He would think over the matter and say: many hands make light work (Setswana "*ke mpya pedi gase thata*"). You will pardon if I say something out of place: "*Mmualege o bua la gagwe gore lentle le tswe.*" I would mention that we are defeated now. I do not want to mention anything in connection with all that has been said. If we dispute the Chieftainship, we all know that Seretse is the Chief of the Bamangwato. We know that Tshekedi is the Regent, nobody is wrong in saying Seretse cannot lose his chieftainship because of his wife. Those who said Seretse would not rule them, were only talking, he will rule them. Customarily when two people are involved in a case each of them expects to win. I do think whatever words have been said should make us hate each other. Seretse is a Chief but all the tribal affairs are Tshekedi's. For instance, if I send a message from Mokwena, it will be delivered to Tshekedi. We know that Tshekedi did for you and the Government. It is his duty to hand them over to Seretse when it is convenient for him to do so. There is no doubt that Seretse is a Chief. I would put the matter before you and mention, though we had different opinions on the matter, we should not take to heart that is common in any dispute. Let us forget such talks as what would he do. These would only make matters worse. If we fear there might be a split we should put ourselves together. I pray for peace; if there is none we are as good as dead. I refer this to you, Seretse, that you study your people very carefully and Tshekedi, they should not separate you and he too should do likewise. It is said we pray for evil not for good. Let us pray that the Ngwato Tribe should live in peace. "Pula."

Chief Mkgosi: I greet His Honour and Chiefs Kgari, Bathoen and Tshekedi. I have not much to say but endorse what Chief Kgari said. When this dispute started I came running to condole. I said to Tshekedi that if this dispute went and got complicated I would withdraw. Tshekedi said nobody disputed the Chieftainship. I am Chief Mokgosi's son at Maleti; I do not hate Tshekedi or Seretse.

I know Tshekedi is our father but I wish Seretse to rule with his wife. My words perhaps will annoy Tshekedi. It is not good to suspect a person and I do not suggest that Tshekedi is trying to usurp the Chieftainship. I pray for the senior house to rule. I pray Seretse to apologise to Tshekedi and he should also welcome Seretse whom he has educated. Seretse's weapon is Tshekedi.

Chief Tshekedi Khama: There are some people who have come with their Chiefs and we ask them to say anything if they have.

Sebolai Mokgweetsi: Your Honour and Officers, Tshekedi and Seretse, Chiefs and the Tribe, I greet you. I am sent by Lottamoreng, the son of Montshiwa, to represent him in the marriage dispute which is the only issue he knows and for which I have come. He knew nothing about the present dispute. I shall say the Chief's message to Seretse. He says you should not be misled by any person or people. You, the son of Tshekedi Khama, if you have done anything wrong you have aimed against him; should you apologise, do it for him. You are the Chief but speak to Tshekedi with respect. People usually intrude where they are not invited. People usually hurry to separate son from his father. That is the intention of weakening you and your father. He says Tshekedi Khama is a hard worker and if you can regard him as your father he will do everything in his power for you. There is no other pride than your tribe. Some people do not know their fathers are their pride. Though your father may be deeply hurt you will be snow-white. He says Tshekedi will give you your rights (intestines) namely the people. But when you work on the intestines you must have them on the stump. Tshekedi is like that stump on which to work your intestines in order not to have them dirty. He says you should apologise and your father will forgive you. To you Tshekedi, Chief Montshiwa says, there is your child, you are not alone, there are many parents who have been wronged by their children but they gave consideration to their grievance. But grievance does not mean father should forsake his son. He says think what your child did is not easy. But the child can be tried by others who have come to help. To you, Bangwato Chief,

Appendix H

Montshiwa says, there is Seretse having a dispute with Tshekedi and you should serve as a joining link between them, they should not separate. He refers to the previous meetings in connection with Seretse's marriage. He says make them agree. That is Chief Montshiwa's message. I followed the dispute since Monday and I will give the report to Chief Montshiwa. Even though he only sent on the marriage dispute. I cannot say anything regarding the Chieftainship. I am directing this to you, the Bangwato, that Seretse's and Tshekedi's dispute is not according to custom; I have never seen it anywhere when two people dispute and none of them is found on the wrong. Tshekedi asked that his wrong-doings be explained but you have failed to do so either with Seretse or Tshekedi. I stop there. *"Pula"*.

Makgasane Kgosidintsi: I greet His Honour, the District Commissioner, the Chiefs and the Tribe. These two are my nephews. I would not like to lose any of them. I was not present in the previous meetings. On Monday you said you did not wish him to marry in England. There was something which engendered your difference of opinions and that was to marry without regard to or consent of the Tribe. He asked for an apology and explained that he married out of love sentiment. I do not think you consider his apology. Some have seen that they would lose their child if they do not agree to the marriage. I am not disputing that he should be be reprimanded. What usually happens to the child who has done so? He is not the first child as far as I know. Here is the dispute, you should agree on it, you should not split Chief Tshekedi. Do not take them as enemies. Those who accept the marriage, I heard you say they should have come to you and say we have failed. Do not follow those people. To you Seretse, I say look out. I was pleased to hear you say that you would not have any grudge against those who refuse the marriage. Let it be so. Tshekedi is your father there is no other, there is no other parent. We have come to listen and pray that you listen to us, and God give you unity. Leave out splitting yourselves. There is no other position than to build up Chieftainship. There are abusive words, but even if Seretse is installed as Chief, Tshekedi will still rule. Seretse obey your father; he is the foundation. Let God bless these words. "*Pula*".

Martinius Seboni: It is the second time I attended this dispute. My Chief, Kgari, said all that I had to say. We pray for peace. Seretse is the Chief and so is Tshekedi. Anybody comes through Tshekedi if he wants to see Seretse on any matter and cases. Nobody will take a case without Tshekedi's knowing. A person can curb his ways and doings when he is alone but his children will take different ways and he will not throw them away. The child who has done wrong to his father is brought before the Chief for punishment but not to persecute him. Khama was famous because he maintained peace. Seretse, you should live in peace with your uncle. Let rain come. "*Pula.*"

Ketshwerebothala Ikaneng: Your Honour, the District Commissioner and the Tribe. I have very little to say. All that is worth saying was said by the Barolong Chief. What I would say has already been said by others. This dispute was very bad. I never thought it would be what it is today. I say Chief Tshekedi, that the mother never throws away her child when it has messed her hands. I say kill and throw in the shade. I would implore you to forget what Seretse said. Your Chief's son should have been punished for what you said. The son of the Chief, you have done wrong. You should apologise to your father. Tshekedi will forgive you if you do that. Tshekedi and his uncles should live in peace. We have brought you rain. Let there be peace. "*Pula.*"

Andrew Kgasa: I am a minister of the London Missionary Society. I am a Reverend. In regiment I am Phethu's comrade seventy-six years old. I greet His Honour, Officials and all the Chiefs. My first word in what has happened is this. I have listened up to yesterday. I would say to Chief Tshekedi that for a long time you have had such difficulties as this. When this dispute came to your hand you failed as [to] what to do. That is why I say you have faced such difficulties for a long time. Sleep on your wound and let the blood flow. You, Seretse, have done a very bad thing when

Appendix H

you look at it and think of it. It has been said no house attacks itself, but you have done so. If you think well, you will see that I am speaking the truth. I do not think many of you have considered carefully what Seretse did. I would therefore ask him to apologise to his father, Tshekedi. When we speak of what happened it is not that we despise the white people. We are thinking of our history. When God made us he had no doubt, and our customs etc. Our customs are different from the white man's, and it will take us a considerable time to make them agree. In life we have to put ourselves together and this usually happens. I implore the Government Officers to take great interest in this matter and think of our future. It would not be Seretse alone who will do this, even those who come after him will do the same. If that happens, what would become of our history, race etc. If this becomes a habit then we shall lose our personality and prestige. If provision is not made by the Government what Khama, Bathoen and Sebele did, will disappear. I was sorry and disappointed to see you abuse and tread the Chieftainship. Our custom is to respect our chiefs, not to curse. My last word is to make peace in your works and life. By this we can achieve our future personality. Those are my words of prayer and peace, my dear friends. "*Pula.*"

Chief Tshekedi Khama: When we dismiss after His Honour has left, you should come out through these gates (indicated). A few days ago we forgot to show His Honour the people. Serowe people, stand; Lesoso stand, Machana and Mahalapye, Letswapo, Sebirwa, Mogapinyana, Kgagodi, Mogapi, Diloro, Sefhophe, Tamasane, Malatsi, Madinare, Tonota, Sekalaka, Seteti and Macha.

Your Honour and the Tribe I have very little to say. I say, you have hurried me in such a way that I am nervous. We have discussed this dispute before at our leisure. The second meeting was called not according to my will. I would call this meeting and follow the usual procedure. I would settle up the dispute nicely or badly, by what I am. To the Chiefs, I take the dispute in the same manner. You had come to help in this dispute, but I did not have what I wanted. You think (Bangwato) that you have disappointed me but I say you have honoured me. His Honour also heard. Usually there are disputes between parents and children and when the disputes become complicated, fathers are oppressed. But you have not done so, to come to me and stop me in my dispute with Seretse about marriage. There are six months which Seretse took overseas after we started this dispute. That was sufficient time for you to prove my enmity in claiming the chieftainship but I saw nobody on that point. Today in this meeting you would be telling His Honour my unfaithfulness and mistakes. Seretse's great honour would have been to go to the Protectorate Chiefs or come to you seeking refuge. I would be ashamed now if I did not take your plea. But as it is now said that crucify him without stating his faults, I am not afraid. Seretse will say whether I do not respect him here in the Kgotla and at home, because you did not. What I would say in closing the meeting [is that] you should have waited to take control from me. But now you have taken control from me. Seretse is controlling now. The reason why I called the Tribe, His Honour and the Chiefs, I was afraid of this, it is not the Setswana Custom not to get the views of the people. A person is answered with reasons. We have two ways of tackling a big dispute like this, I usually put to the four main divisions (Kgotlas). But this time this would appear to have been avoided. The speakers who spoke in this meeting usually take part in those four divisions. I would mention this for the information of His Honour and the Chiefs, that I saw some people coming to me the whole day to ask why the people stood in the Kgotlas. Out of them ten were sub-chiefs from outside villages. I would not mention their names. You refused to allow me to give my views on the matter. You say you want the woman and Seretse to be installed as Chief. In both cases I would have no objection. The woman come without any trouble, we would say Seretse refused to obey us. I shall dismiss the meeting tomorrow; our Government Officials would be with us. His Honour will speak when I finish.

(Mr. Ellenberger's speech)

Appendix H

Tshekedi Khama: I say tomorrow I would say something when I dismiss you. I have asked His Honour and the Chiefs to be present and the Tribes. It would be the same as it is today, you should assemble as usual.

Kgotla Meeting, Saturday, 25 June 1949

Kgosi Tshekedi Khama: I have called this meeting to dismiss the Bamangwato Tribe to return to their homes after many days' stay here. I have something to say. I thank His Honour for taking interest in our dispute and for his words of good advice. If he did not help us we would have had no progress. I also thank the Commissioner of Police for helping us. Had it not been for their presence, even though they are few, there would have been trouble, but we obeyed them. I thank the Chiefs for coming to see how the Bamangwato country is going to waste. In future because the disputes are not only for us we shall go to them. I said if I speak, you would say I am not discussing the subject at issue. I have heard what you say and the Tribe. I heard how the Bamangwato want their child. You said, because Seretse would leave the country you now want his wife. I, for one, am still set and determined. I do not want to deceive you and Seretse. I said it after carefully thinking over the matter. I told Seretse before he married that he was spoiling. I am not starting the dispute. I have finished it. I say the woman is not suitable for him. She is not suitable to beget us a chief. At that time Seretse and I were in peace. There is nobody who has more love for him than me. Our misunderstanding sprang from the marriage that the woman was not suitable for him. There are two important factors: Chief and the Country. The Country comes first, the Chiefs die and pass like Khama. The protectorate forgets that the Country is the foundation and the Chief an overseer. There is a saying in Setswana (*Fa thako ea pele e gatang teng la eamorago e gata teng*). I say you have killed us. I would tell him the Chief is like a prisoner. The duty of a Chief is to bear all insults. My first law would be: listen to your people. If we had married white people there would be nothing wrong. I know several people who have married the whites in the Union where there is colour-bar. But Seretse's marriage has caused a great noise. He had no right to marry on his own. He has changed our custom that our Chiefs could marry as they wish—on their own. I am not going to say what pleases you. When you say Tshekedi is a hard nut to crack you would have a case to present. When a case is too hard for me, I give up and say it is alright. But in this case I say you are mistaken. This is weakening. You have weakened us. Usually when the Government is pressing us we ask for permission to interview the Tribe first. You have killed us and this child. The Tribe can think better if the leader has common sense. This child will be my Chief. You have given him the Chieftainship. I will put the matter to Seretse. Today the white people know that the Chief can play about with the Tribe. You agreed that you did not want the woman but today some of you have withdrawn that decision. This has killed us. It could be in order to change our decision without insults but reasons. You have proved to the white people that you can for the Chief. You should have forced me by following the custom, speaking to me at my house or in the Kgotla. It is a respect to the Government Officials. You did not do so. You followed a wrong way and made my child to override me instead of speaking to me and to him in private. You did not do so. You have made many mistakes. This is how you have weakened yourselves.

According to custom the chieftainship is given to the succeeding chief. I saw Seretse ordering the people, who are not doing tribal work, to stand. I was showing the people who are doing or holding the tribal government and those who could be sent on tribal duties. I have told this child that in the handling of tribal affairs these are the people who could perhaps help you:– stand, Setshile, Manyaphiri and Ngwato. I cannot accuse a person or damage his character like you. These are the persons who could help you in the tribal duties. The only trouble is that they are not straight-forward. I am not cursing. Ngwato has never done or said anything wrong. When Manyaphiri returned to Mahalapye we were in agreement against the marriage. It is today I see him having changed his mind. Serogola can be put on trying

Appendix H

cases but not on tribal duties otherwise you will have trouble. He is keen on trying cases. I am discussing the matter on its merits. My last word is that these people can carry out missions, but do not know the ins and outs of the tribal government. Whether six or any number of your uncles, tell them news but not your secret mind, do the same to the Tribe. When this meeting started I said I received a telegram which said we should try this dispute in peace, we should not think of ourselves. There is a curse that I am trying to usurp the Chieftainship of Sekgoma's son, when I refuse the white wife. If I were fighting for Chieftainship I should have taken it in two days time. Serogola incited you, but in the way I know him, if I had asked someone to reply to him I should have made a big noise which would mean a riot resulting in the chasing away of this child. I would escape. The meeting was mine, I have not yet given him the chair. He realized that I moved your hearts and they made him break the law, and they put up their hands that they want the wife. I know his temper as Serogola. I knew it would touch your hearts if I ordered Seretse to sit down. I said the Police were to stop the noise, but I had to stop it now and then. You have broken the law. I never intended to dispute the Chieftainship with this child. The allegation that I am trying to usurp Seretse' chieftainship, does not hurt me. I know you wanted Seretse but not according to custom. There are two things which were left out and I thought they would be discussed namely the call of Regiments and the soldier's money, which it is alleged I have eaten; I would answer: I say even if you were alleging that I was usurping the Chieftainship I would try to bear that insult. One of the chiefs said I thought you were usurping this child's chieftainship. I said I would not make a noise for this country. I said to Seretse if your wife comes I would go. I said I had done no wrong and you could not chase me away in any way. I said if the woman entered the village I would not ask the Government to allot any piece of land to me but would quietly leave the country. If I wanted the Chieftainship during the six months Seretse took after returning to England, I would have taken a few villages, two or three, in order that when the Government said what do you say? I would reply I am alone, knowing I have supporters. There are villages like Bokaa and Baphaleng. Baphaleng would drive me away after some days stay with them. There are villages on the east of the railway. I would have taken them. Twenty people–ten sub-chiefs–(Headmen) came to me singly to ask why were the people standing. This I would His Honour to know but I would mention their names. I bid you good-bye. I am afraid of you–as I said I would go alone as I am not disputing the country with Seretse. I shall become a subject to Mokwena, perhaps Mongwaketsi. I shall prepare myself at ease. I must hand over tribal affairs to your child and school work in a short time. I shall go alone. Kgama said he would not give me any people not even a servant. I also say I shall go alone. I will often visit you to show that I am not fighting for chieftainship. When things get spoilt on the arrival of the woman you would say it is this hypocrite. I say you have denied Seretse the Chieftainship. You have failed to become Chief, I am not cursing. What would happen, you should not blame me. The Raditladis split during Khama's time when he went to England. I am going. I have warned you against a few people that they are not speaking truly about the Chieftainship but against me.

Cassils Goletitweng: I object to the accusation. I object . . . (Tshekedi stops him)

I stand not to say I agree to the marriage or against the marriage. I ask what I said. I said where are you, with whom are you ruling, how do you take the Tribe? They say you are a lion–nobody answers you. I was not speaking in secret. These are not with you.

Ramatudung Bareki: Your Honour, the District Commissioner and Chiefs, I am just standing. Yesterday I was agreeable to the woman's coming. The question is did we say Seretse would leave the country? I went to Ramarula and said the fire is ablaze, I asked who are the (*batlhanka*) (headmen). I thought it meant those who could put out the fire. (Tshekedi stops him).

Appendix H

K.M.: I stand with a painful heart when I hear Tshekedi saying he is leaving the country. I heard Chief Kgari and His Honour pray for peace but now what is being said is not good. We were expecting the quieting of the dispute.

Seabe Setemere: I speak as the last speaker, we are expecting peace to take effect. As the Chiefs and the District Commissioner have asked for peace I do not see how Seretse who is alone could be left by the Ngwato Tribe (Tshekedi stops him, dismisses the meeting).

End.

Appendix I

THE BRITISH GOVERNMENT SECRETARY OF STATE FOR COMMONWEALTH RELATIONS' MEMORANDUM TO THE CABINET TITLED THE "BECHUANALAND PROTECTORATE: SUCCESSION TO CHIEFTAINSHIP OF THE BAMANGWATO TRIBE" ON THE SUBJECT OF WHETHER TO ESTABLISH JUDICIAL ENQUIRY, C.P. (49) 155, 19TH JULY, 1949

Bechuanaland Protectorate: Succession to Chieftainship of the Bamangwato Tribe

MEMORANDUM BY THE SECRETARY OF STATE FOR COMMONWEALTH RELATIONS

A difficult problem, to which some prominence has been given in the Press recently, has arisen from the marriage to an English girl of Seretse Khama, the Chief Designate of the Bamangwato Tribe in the Bechuanaland Protectorate. This is the largest and most important tribe in the Protectorate. Owing to Seretse having been a minor when his father died, his uncle Tshekedi has been for a considerable time the Acting Chief of the Tribe and has achieved the position of being one of the most prominent Africans in South Africa. Under the local native custom the Chieftainship is hereditary, descending from the father to the eldest son, but the local Native Administration Proclamation provides that, upon the occurrence of a vacancy in the Chieftainship, the tribe must designate the former Chief's successor according to native customs and cause the name to be submitted to the Resident Commissioner, with a view to seeking the High

Appendix I

Commissioner's recognition and the Secretary of State's confirmation of such designation.

2. Seretse, who is now a man of twenty-seven, has had an unusually prolonged education, which was arranged for him by Tshekedi at the cost of tribal funds. He was sent two years ago to England, where he spent a year at Balliol College, Oxford, and afterwards became a law student at London University. When in London he met an English girl—Ruth Williams—at some social function for Colonial students, and they were married last year, in spite of vigorous warnings given to both parties by interested friends that such a marriage would be resented by the Bamangwato tribe. Ruth Williams is, apparently, a fairly well educated girl, interested in Church matters, and there is nothing against her character personally.

3. Shortly after the marriage, Seretse proceeded by air to South Africa to discuss his position with the tribe. A series of meetings took place and the local Resident Commissioner reported that, although there was no opposition to Seretse's claim to be chief, there was almost solid disapproval of the marriage among the Bamangwato. This disapproval was based upon the following grounds:–

(*a*) General racial bias.
(*b*) Seretse's neglect to conform to the formalities required in an African marriage.
(*c*) Aversion to a possible half-caste heir.

The result was that Seretse returned to England to complete his law studies and the position remained unresolved.

4. Last month Seretse went out again by air to the Bechuanaland Protectorate and further meetings were held. Tshekedi and his chief followers reiterated their strong objection to the marriage which Seretse had made. At the final meeting, however, Seretse made an emotional appeal, which resulted in a

very large majority of those present acclaiming him as the hereditary heir to the Chieftainship. The High Commissioner states that it would appear that constitutional questions regarding the marriage were rather submerged in the process and that the implications of the marriage were not defined. Tshekedi subsequently made a formal statement to the effect that tradition was being so severely flouted, and native law and custom so abused, that he proposed, having wound up his administration, to leave the Bamangwato Reserve, and he declared that he would never concur in acceptance of a white woman as the Chief's first or principal wife.

5. In the ordinary course, the signification of approval by the majority of the tribe would be regarded as an adequate ground for proceeding to recognise Seretse. It appears, however, that the recent meetings were not very fully representative of the tribe as a whole, since those present included more than half the men of the tribal capital, but only about one-fiftieth of those in the country districts. There had also evidently been a good deal of propaganda by certain members of the tribe who nurse various personal grievances against Tshekedi. Nevertheless, it is surprising that there should have been such a sudden reversal of the opinion expressed by the great majority of the tribe last year. The High Commissioner states that the local administrative aspects are such that he feels great hesitation about the immediate recognition of Seretse. In his opinion, the doubts cast upon the representative character of the assembly, the indefinite nature of the decisions taken at it, the obscurities relating to the status and position of Seretse's wife and any children of the marriage, and the dangers of a split in the tribe and of a breakdown of native administration, are sufficient reasons for holding some further enquiry, which would allow time for a considered verdict.

6. There are, moreover, other wider considerations involved. The suggestion that we should recognise a chief who is married to a white woman has caused intense feeling among Europeans, both in the Union of South Africa and in Southern Rhodesia.

Appendix I

Representations have been made to me by the High Commissioner for the Union in London, on behalf of his Government, to the effect that the repercussions in the Union of a white woman becoming the Chieftainess in an African tribe will be extremely grave. Similar views have also been expressed to our High Commissioner, Sir Evelyn Baring, by the Prime Minister of Southern Rhodesia. Sir Evelyn Baring reports that information which he has received, from such a reliable authority as the Secretary of the Department of External Affairs, has convinced him that this matter is the gravest which has faced us since he first went to South Africa. It is suggested that the more extreme Nationalists will argue that the recognition of Seretse would demonstrate the folly of allowing the existence side by side in Southern Africa of two systems of native administration diametrically opposed to one another. They would say that South Africans should not and cannot remain associated with a country which recognises officially an African Chief married to a white woman, and they would make Seretse's recognition the occasion of an appeal to the country for the establishment of a Republic, and not only a Republic, but of a Republic outside the Commonwealth. Sir Evelyn Baring states that the South African Prime Minister is desperately worried and feels that he could not successfully oppose an extremist offensive on these lines. It must be remembered in this connection that the Union Government has a particularly close interest in the Bechuanaland Protectorate, since this is one of the territories which, in view of the provisions in the South Africa Act of 1909, they look upon as due to be transferred to the Union. The question of such transfer has been frequently raised by the Union Government and, quite apart, therefore, from the graver possibilities indicated above, the demand for the transfer of the High Commission Territories might clearly become more insistent if we disregarded the Union Government's views in a matter of this kind in relation to one of these territories. The fact that Dr. Malan is feeling extreme anxiety, rather than jubilation, at the present development, is evidence that the threat to the Commonwealth relationship must be taken seriously. Indeed, we cannot exclude the possibility of an armed incursion into the

Bechuanaland Protectorate from the Union if Seretse were to be recognised forthwith, while feeling on the subject is inflamed.

7. In all these circumstances it seems clearly important that a decision in favour of Seretse's recognition, if it is ever to be taken, should not be rushed, and that there should be due time for reflection and enquiry. In the Bechuanaland Protectorate Native Administration Proclamation there is a provision to the effect that, if any doubt arises whether a person designated as chief is worthy or capable of exercising that office justly, or for any other sufficient reasons is a fit and proper person to discharge the functions of chief, the High Commissioner may direct that a judicial enquiry should be held to enquire into the matter and to report thereon to the High Commissioner, who shall then decide the matter. The High Commissioner accordingly proposes that use should be made of this provision and that an enquiry should be held, presided over by the Judge of the High Courts of the High Commissioner Territories, to investigate Seretse's suitability for the Chieftainship and the true views of the tribe. During the interval the present Regency would continue. It is proposed that the Judge be assisted by two other officers, one of whom might be the Government Secretary of the Bechuanaland Protectorate and the other possibly a retired administrative officer from one of the other two High Commission Territories.

8. There appear to be two possible courses of action. We could declare now that we could not recognise Seretse in view of his disregard of the native custom in the matter of his marriage. The Local Administration, indeed, feel that if we are ever to take this line, it would be better to do so now. Sir Evelyn Baring has, however, explained that he has assumed that the United Kingdom Government would not be prepared to declare forthwith that Seretse cannot be recognised as Chief simply on the ground that an African married to a European woman cannot successfully perform the functions of a Chief. The other course of a judicial enquiry, which Sir Evelyn Baring has advocated as an alternative to immediate refusal to recognise Seretse, would at least

Appendix I

demonstrate both in the Union of South Africa and in Southern Rhodesia, that the Protectorate authorities and the United Kingdom Government were mindful of the gravity of the issues involved. It cannot, of course, be assumed that the enquiry would result in a report unfavourable to the recognition of Seretse. But the eventual decision would still remain with the High Commissioner and a careful enquiry into all the issues should have resulted in the presentation of a report which would set out fully the pros and cons, and would provide clearer material for a decision than exists at present.

9. I am still in communication with the High Commissioner on various aspects of the matter, and I will shortly be able to present a further report to my colleagues. This preliminary paper has been prepared in advance of further advice from the High Commissioner, since it is important that a decision should be announced as soon as possible. Seretse's wife is likely to leave for South Africa within a short time, and, if she joins him there before we have made any announcement, the position will have become much more difficult, since the press would sensationally represent this as the arrival of a white "Chieftainess." It would be very difficult to overstate the implications of this, and any subsequent announcement would look like a harassed rear-guard action. The High Commissioner is anxious therefore to be authorised to make an announcement by 23rd July, when he is visiting Mafeking, and will be able to see both Seretse and Tshekedi, and so could first inform them personally.

10. In the light of the above, and of the further report which I hope to make, a decision has to be taken between (i) declaring now that Seretse is not recognised, and (ii) announcing the appointment of a judicial enquiry.

Commonwealth Relations Office,
19th July, 1949   P.J. N-B.

Appendix J

REPORT OF THE JUDICIAL ENQUIRY RE SERETSE KHAMA, OF THE BAMANGWATO TRIBE, "THE HARRAGIN REPORT," 1 DECEMBER 1949, FINDING THAT SERETSE KHAMA SHOULD NOT BE RECOGNIZED AS CHIEF OF THE BAMANGWATO TRIBE

Report of the Judicial Enquiry Re
Seretse Khama, of the Bamangwato Tribe

APPOINTED BY HIS EXCELLENCY THE HIGH COMMISSIONER BY NOTICE NO. 204 OF 1949, OF THE 15TH SEPTEMBER, 1949

Report of the Judicial Enquiry

appointed to enquire into the circumstances attending and matters arising from the alleged designation of Seretse Khama as Chief of the Bamangwato Tribe at a Kgotla held at Serowe, in the Bechuanaland Protectorate between the 20th June and the 25th June, 1949.

To: His Excellency the High Commissioner for Basutoland, the Bechuanaland Protectorate and Swaziland.

May it Please Your Excellency:

We, the undersigned, have the honour to submit the following report:–

Appendix J

The appointment of the Judicial Enquiry, as contained in High Commissioner's Notice No. 165 of 1949, dated the 29th July, 1949, reads as follows:–

"It is hereby notified for general information that, in exercise of the powers vested in him by section three of the Bechuanaland Protectorate Native Administration Proclamation, 1943 (No. 32 of 1943), His Excellency the High Commissioner has been pleased to direct that a Judicial Enquiry, presided over by Sir Walter Harragin, C.M.G., K.C., Judge of the High Court, be held to enquire into the circumstances attending and matters arising from the designation of Seretse Khama as Chief of the Bamangwato Tribe at a Kgotla held at Serowe in the Bechuanaland Protectorate between the 20th and the 25th days of June, 1949."

"The terms of reference of the Enquiry and the names of those appointed to assist the Judge at the enquiry will be published at a later date."

The names of the Members, and terms of reference of the Judicial Enquiry were published in High Commissioner's Notice No. 204, 1949, dated the 15th September, 1949:–

"It is hereby notified for general information that His Excellency the High Commissioner has been pleased to appoint Mr. R.S. Hudson, C.M.G., and Mr. G.E. Nettelton, C.B.E., to be members of the Judicial Enquiry announced by High Commissioner's Notice No. 165 of 1949, which is to be presided over by Sir Walter Harragin, C.M.G., K.C., Judge of the High Court. The terms of reference of the enquiry shall be:–

(1) To report whether the Kgotla held at Serowe between the 20th and 25th June, 1949, at which Seretse Khama was designated as Chief of the Bamangwato tribe,

was properly convened and assembled, and its proceedings conducted in accordance with native custom.

(2) To report on the question whether, having particular regard to the interests and well-being of the tribe, Seretse Khama is a fit and proper person to discharge the functions of Chief."

"The enquiry will commence its hearings at Serowe in the Bechuanaland Protectorate in the latter part of October. The exact date will be notified later by the Chairman by notice in the *Gazette*."

Mr. F.G. Holmes, Assistant District Commissioner, Serowe, was appointed Secretary.

By Public Notice, dated the 6th October, 1949, published in the *Gazette*, the date and the procedure to be adopted were fixed by the Chairman. The Enquiry would commence its sittings at Serowe on the 1st November, 1949.

The procedure adopted was, as far as was practicable, similar to the procedure laid down for civil cases. Persons giving evidence were liable to be examined and cross-examined by interested parties, or their legal representatives. Any person (other than a person called by one of the parties to the enquiry) desiring to give evidence could communicate with the Secretary and a date was fixed for his evidence. Any person unable to attend the enquiry could submit written memoranda to the Secretary and these, when admitted as evidence, were read out at the Enquiry.

For the purposes of clarity and convenience, Tshekedi Khama was regarded as Plaintiff, and Seretse Khama as Defendant.

The events leading up to the present enquiry began with the marriage of Seretse Khama, heir to the Chieftainship of the Bamangwato tribe, to Ruth Williams, an English woman, in London, a little more than a year ago. A general history of the tribe and of Seretse Khama's marriage will be found in Chapter II but, to anticipate briefly, this enquiry was a result of a meeting of the tribe in June 1949, at which Seretse Khama was acclaimed Chief of the Bamangwato. At two previous meetings his European

Appendix J

wife had been found unacceptable. At this final meeting the tribe, by an overwhelming majority, demanded him as Chief, and accepted his wife. Tshekedi Khama, the Regent, voiced his protest at the decision of the tribe by removing to a neighbouring reserve, followed by some forty leading tribal personalities, and stated in a public declaration, which forms part of the record, that he found it impossible to accept Ruth Williams as Queen and mother of the tribe. Recognised tribal law and custom had not been observed, and the decision of the June meeting, if implemented, could only lead to the disruption of the tribe. He therefore requested the Government to hold a judicial enquiry to declare once and for all the final position of Ruth and her children. A report of the meeting, and the public declaration, were forwarded to the High Commissioner and to the Secretary of State for Commonwealth Relations. Their decision was contained in High Commissioner's Notice No. 165, which is quoted in the first paragraph of this report. This was read out by the Resident Commissioner to the tribe assembled in Kgotla on the 30th June, 1949.

During the last week-end of October, the members of the Judicial Enquiry arrived in Serowe, and on Tuesday, the 1st November, the Enquiry commenced its sittings. The proceedings were held in a marquee erected near the office of the District Commissioner and were attended by a large and orderly crowd of tribesmen.

Mr. A.C. Thompson, M.C., K.C., Attorney-General of the High Commission Territories, was present, acting on instructions from the High Commissioner, holding a watching brief for the Administration. Mr. P.A. Fraenkel represented Seretse Khama. Tshekedi Khama was neither present nor represented, but he had sent a petition, requesting the Judicial Enquiry to take the evidence of himself and his followers at Lobatsi, the seat of the High Court of the Protectorate. After due consideration, the Chairman decided that the enquiry would remove to Lobatsi to hear Tshekedi's evidence. As Mr. Fraenkel, on behalf of Seretse, was not prepared to produce his witnesses before he had heard those of Tshekedi, two independent witnesses, the Reverend Haile, of the London Missionary Society, and Mr. Ellenberger, First

The Harragin Report, December 1949

Assistant Secretary of the Bechuanaland Protectorate, were heard at Serowe that afternoon. The Enquiry then adjourned to reassemble at the Court House in Lobatsi on the 4th November.

On the 4th November, Mr. Fraenkel, instructed by the tribe, asked permission of the Chairman to stand down during the proceedings at Lobatsi, as a protest against Tshekedi Khama's attitude in refusing to give evidence at Serowe. His request was granted.

Tshekedi Khama, represented by Mr. D.M. Buchanan, K.C., then began his evidence. Ten witnesses were examined at Lobatsi, all of whom appeared for Tshekedi, including an African witness from the Union of South Africa. The Enquiry finished its sittings at Lobatsi on the 10th November and reassembled at Serowe on the 14th November.

Five witnesses appeared at Serowe on behalf of Seretse, including himself. Seven independent witnesses, including Mr. Ellenberger, who was recalled, and Mr. Sullivan, the District Commissioner of Serowe, also gave evidence. One African witness appeared to state the views of the Bamangwato who were working at the mines on the Rand. The written memoranda were read out by the Secretary. The evidence was finally closed on the 18th November. Evidence was given in both Tswana and English and was interpreted throughout the proceedings. A complete record of the evidence in English is submitted with this report.

The report of the Enquiry was written at Pretoria.

A complete list of all witnesses who appeared, the dates and places of their appearance, and on whose behalf, is given in Schedule A, and a list of the exhibits, and the witnesses who handed them in, is given in Schedule B. These Schedules appear at the beginning of the record of evidence. The written memoranda appear in the record of the proceedings. Certain letters were disallowed by the Chairman as being offensive or irrelevant.

Appendix J

Chapter II

The Ba-Ngwato, as their name indicates, are the people of Chief Ngwato, whom they followed after internecine warfare amongst the Ba-Hurutshe, from whom the Batswana originated, some time in the 18th century. In the fashion of the Batswana of today, a dispute arose over the chieftainship, and Ngwato, with his followers, moved from what is now the Southern Bechuanaland Protectorate, leaving his brother, Kwena, in possession, in the vicinity of what is now known as the Bakwena Reserve.

Following a fight between the rival sections, Ngwato finally took up his residence with his adherents at Shoshong, in what is now known as the Bamangwato Reserve.

The history of the Batswana tribes consists of a succession of internal disputes often arising out of the reluctance of the Regent to surrender his trust to the rightful heir at the appropriate time. For generations it is found that tribal life is upset at intervals by these disputes and, when there were no internal disagreements to engage the attention of the Chief and his men, the invaders (*i.e.*, the Matabele, the Makololo of Sebitwane, &c.) drove them from one place to another.

It was Sekgoma, the father of Khama III, whose despotic rule brought together the scattered remnants of the people who are the present Bangwato tribe, with its great mixture of what are termed "allied" peoples, who came to them for protection from their enemies.

Sekgoma was succeeded by his son, Khama III, who is regarded as one of the great African rulers and who is the grandfather of Seretse, the subject of this enquiry.

Khama III was born about 1827-28, dying in 1923 at Serowe after a rule of just over fifty years.

The reign of Khama III followed the same pattern as those of his predecessors. Khama III had himself been deeply suspected by his father, Sekgoma I, from whom he received drastic treatment and he, in turn, found himself in violent conflict with his son, Sekgoma II.

The Harragin Report, December 1949

Sekgoma II finally left his father in 1899 with a considerable following of men, who found in him a more generous and less severe chief. This estrangement between father and son was a serious one, which lasted until 1916 when in his declining years Khama received his son back into the tribe.

Sekgoma II had four wives, the last one, Tebogo, daughter of Kebailele, bearing him two sons, of whom the younger died in infancy, leaving Seretse, who was born on the 1st July, 1921, as his heir.

It is well at this stage to give a brief picture of the achievements of Khama III. He was a fanatic on the subject of drink of any kind, not only the white man's strong drink, but even the milder native beer brewed from Sorghum (kaffir corn). To this day there are many Bangwato who are total abstainers.

In 1896 Khama, accompanied by Chiefs Bathoen of the Bangwaketse, and Sebele of the Bakwena, visited England and had an interview with Mr. Chamberlain, then Secretary of State for the Colonies. A plea was made by the Chiefs for the preservation to them of their land and of their rights, and it was requested, among other things, that strong drink should not be sold in their respective countries to either white people or black people. These Chiefs had seen the ruination following the sale to their people of brandy and wines by concession hunters and traders.

One of the results of this visit was that the present Bamangwato Reserve, which is shown on the accompanying map, was created by Proclamation No. 9 of 1899. Certain portions of Crown Land have since been added by Proclamation No. 31 of 1933. Its area is approximately 40,000 square miles and its African population, according to a census taken in 1946, is 100,000. A striking feature arising out of population statistics is that there are only some 18,000 Bangwato proper, the remaining number of 82,000 being subject or "allied" peoples of whom the principal, numerically, are:–

Appendix J

Makalaka	24,000
Mabirwa	6,500
Makgalagadi	6,000
Batalaote	4,000
Matswapong (A mixture of small groups) ...	13,000

They are pastoral people and own large herds of cattle, totalling about 300,000 head. There are 500 Europeans and 150 Coloured persons in the Reserve and no Asiatics.

It is this inheritance which Seretse now seeks and which it is alleged Tshekedi covets for himself.

On the death of Khama in 1923, Sekgoma became Chief, but he was destined to rule for little more than two years, during the course of which the inevitable internal disputes were prominent, and Sekgoma died in 1925, leaving as his heir his infant son, Seretse.

The rule of the tribe was carried on for a time by means of a Council of Regency but in 1926 it was found more suitable to install as Regent, Tshekedi, the son of Khama and half-brother of Sekgoma. At this time, Seretse was at Serowe at the home of his mother, who died in 1930, leaving the full responsibility for him in the hands of Tshekedi.

In due course, Seretse was sent away to school, attending in turn Tiger Kloof, Lovedale, Adams College and Fort Hare. He came of age and normally should have taken up his position as Chief but instead came the fateful decision to send him to the United Kingdom to study law. Seretse himself expressed a desire to continue his education at Oxford. He had passed the examination for his Bachelor of Arts degree at Fort Hare and should have been well enough equipped to cope with the responsibilities of his position. It would seem, however, that the Bangwato wished their Chief to become a sufficiently learned person in law to be able to hold his own against all. So, in 1945, Seretse left South Africa for England and Tshekedi remained to carry on the Regency, with the full support and confidence of the Bangwato, for what gave the appearance of being an indefinite period.

The Harragin Report, December 1949

Seretse began his overseas academic career at Balliol College, Oxford, eventually finding his way to London, where he carried on his legal studies, achieving the first part of the Bar examination.

The Government of the Bechuanaland Protectorate played no part in the arrangements for the advancement of Seretse's overseas studies.

On the 20th September, 1948, an air mail letter came from Seretse to his uncle and guardian, Tshekedi, saying that he proposed to marry an English girl and that he feared his uncle and the tribe would not approve of his proposed action. He announced his marriage day as the 2nd October. Such steps as were possible were taken by Tshekedi to prevent or delay the marriage, but Seretse merely advanced his wedding day to the 24th September, and finally on the 29th September, in the face of all opposition, married Ruth Williams, an English girl living in London.

Seretse was summoned to Serowe to give an account of himself, arriving by air on the 22nd October, 1948, after an assurance that he would be permitted to return to his wife in England.

On the 26th October, a meeting of welcome was held at Serowe and, on its termination, the people were invited to discuss any matters they wished with Seretse informally. It was hoped than many persons would use their endeavours to persuade Seretse to give up his European wife. Various meetings of members of the Royal house were held, but Seretse remained unshakable in his determination to retain his wife.

On the 15th November, a large meeting of the tribe was held, lasting until the 19th November, at which Seretse was taken to task by the tribe for his breach of tribal custom. Prior to the meeting, he had been given the opportunity of freely discussing his affairs with whomsoever he wished. Strangely enough, he did not attend at the Kgotla in the customary fashion, but instead seems to have attached himself to the persons who are now his ardent supporters. At this stage the relations between guardian and ward were not entirely lacking in cordiality, for Tshekedi still hoped to wean Seretse from his white wife.

Appendix J

The tribe at this first meeting, with almost one voice, condemned the marriage and resolved that all steps should be taken to prevent Seretse's white wife from entering the Bamangwato Reserve. It was still, however, left open to Seretse to return to England in terms of the undertaking given him. It is shown that the tribe hoped for the aid of the British Government in destroying the marriage, or at least in preventing Seretse's white wife from coming to the Bamangwato Reserve. Doubts began to arise and it was whispered that Tshekedi had grasped what to him seemed the opportunity for keeping the chieftainship for himself. People began to say, "He talks of the chieftainship, not of the white wife." It would seem that support for Seretse was slowly growing in the tribe, not so much out of the desire for Seretse and his white wife, but as a means of ridding themselves of Tshekedi. Tshekedi affirmed, and continues to affirm, that the right of succession of Seretse is indisputable.

Seretse had been left by the tribe after the first Kgotla meeting in November to think things over, but it is clear that in the course of this space of time there was no change in Seretse's attitude, *i.e.*, he would keep his white wife or leave the country forever. On the 27th to the 29th December, the second Kgotla meeting was called by Tshekedi, being attended by the Deputy Resident Commissioner as a Government observer. It is recorded that there was a significant strengthening of support for Seretse. Seretse remained adamant and a certain amount of alarm arose amongst the tribesmen lest Seretse should be lost for ever and Tshekedi should become their Chief in his own right. Feeling was perhaps best illustrated by an elderly headman who said in Setswana, "I thoroughly disapprove of the marriage–it is a bad thing–but I see what it all means. You want to destroy the marriage, which will require money–that means another levy. Let the wife come, let the wife come."

At the November meeting, seven people had spoken in favour of the marriage and many against it. On the 27th to 29th December, at the second Kgotla meeting, the figures showed a significant increase in those in support of the marriage. The meeting was an indecisive one and, after a short discussion with the Deputy Resident Commissioner, Seretse willingly agreed to the suggestion that he should return to England and endeavour to complete his law examinations. This decision was conveyed to the Tribe which insisted on a guarantee that Seretse would not be prevented from returning and, in his farewell address, he told the people he would return in June.

The people dispersed and all remained quiet for the time being.

It was conveyed to Tshekedi in March that the Government was not prepared to take any step to prevent Seretse's wife from entering the Bechuanaland Protectorate.

Seretse arrived in Mafeking, unannounced, on the 8th June. It would appear that on his return his attitude was one of reiteration of his former statement, that he would in no circumstances give up his wife and that he had come to ascertain finally whether or not the Tribe wanted him and to make it clear that in this they would have to bear in mind that, in accepting him, they would also have to accept his wife.

On the 20th June, 1949, and on the following days, the third Kgotla meeting was held at Serowe, being attended, as Government observer, by Mr. V.F. Ellenberger, I.S.O., Acting Government Secretary.

The suspicion that Tshekedi sought to wrest the chieftainship from Seretse had steadily grown and the vast majority of the Tribe, realising that any hope they formerly had that the Government would destroy the marriage or keep Seretse's wife out of the territory had vanished, were prepared to accept Seretse under any conditions. Furthermore, they realised that even if Seretse's wife were kept out, he would return to her and be lost to them.

The result of the meeting was a popular demonstration in favour of Seretse. Events had taken a most unexpected turn and Tshekedi found his authority literally overthrown by the Tribe.

Following this, Tshekedi announced his intention of leaving the Reserve and he made a public declaration to this effect, which is embodied in the record of evidence. Further, he asked the High Commissioner to hold a judicial enquiry to declare once and for all the final position as regards Seretse's wife and her children.

Appendix J

The High Commissioner appointed this Commission with the terms of reference as set out in Chapter I of this Report.

Tshekedi, with some forty-five supporters, began to take active steps for moving from the Bamangwato Reserve.

Seretse's wife arrived at Serowe on the 20th August, 1949.

At the end of October, the Government of the Union of South Africa declared both Seretse and his wife prohibited immigrants. The Government of Southern Rhodesia announced that it would take such steps as it considered necessary, should the occasion arise.

The events following the meeting in June are not of great significance, but the opposition to Tshekedi grew daily and at the commencement of the hearing of this enquiry he had virtually lost control of the tribe, though still nominally Regent. He spent most of his time at his new home at Rametsana in the Bakwena Reserve.

Chapter III

In order to appreciate the problem that faced the Enquiry, it is of interest to consider the characters of the two contesting parties. We have already described the education given to Seretse, and it must be realised that his outlook on life is very different from that of the vast majority of his Tribe and all his so-called uncles, of whom he appears to have a large number.

It would be incorrect to think of him as an African well satisfied with a mud and wattle hut, and with crude sanitary conveniences. Though a typical African in build and features, he has assimilated, to a great extent, the manners and thoughts of an Oxford undergraduate. He speaks English well and is obviously quick to appreciate, even if he may not agree with, the European point of view. Thus he was an easy witness to examine, he immediately understood the questions and answered them without hesitation, clearly and fairly, and we have no hesitation in finding that, but for his unfortunate marriage, his prospects of success as a Chief are as bright as those of any Native in Africa with whom we have come in contact, provided that he shows himself to be as

The Harragin Report, December 1949

good a judge in the choice of his advisers as he is in other matters and that his industry and tact prove to be of as high an order as his educational qualifications.

His uncle and opponent is a man of very different character and outlook. Appointed Regent at the early age of 20, without the educational advantages that he has given to his nephew, he has driven his people hard for a period of 23 years. He is a dynamic character, shrewd, strong-minded and suspicious and we should imagine intolerant of opposition. He appeared to regard every question asked him by the members of the Commission as a carefully thought out trap and took every precaution to avoid falling into it, even where the answers were obvious and simple. Thus, as a witness, he compared unfavourably with his nephew. We are not, however, unaware of the difficult years through which he has guided his people with great skill and determination, a people brought up on dissension and intrigue, as is so clearly shown in their history. Seretse must have known that he was taking on a doughty opponent when he crossed swords with this uncle of his, who had been a father to him in every way from a very early age until his marriage.

The High Commissioner, in directing this enquiry to be held, has invoked his powers under Section 3 of the Bechuanaland Native Administration Proclamation 1943 (32/43) but nowhere in the Proclamation is there any indication of the procedure to be adopted at an enquiry, save in the interpretation section, which reads as follows:–

> "Judicial enquiry means an enquiry conducted according to the rules of evidence, and at which any party interested shall have the right to appear and to be legally represented."

It was not, therefore, surprising that neither Tshekedi nor Seretse were certain as to the order and manner in which the evidence would be elicited from the witnesses at the enquiry. The Secretary was, therefore, directed to inform interested parties that the procedure that would be adopted at the enquiry would follow, as far as possible, that of a civil case, save that the Chairman

Appendix J

would commence the proceedings by calling one or two witnesses to give a short resume of the history of the Bamangwato tribe, and put in the family tree of Khama. This evidence was to be followed by that of Tshekedi and his witnesses, as if he were the plaintiff in a civil action, followed by Seretse and his witnesses as the defendant.

The suggestion that he was to be regarded as plaintiff elicited a formal protest from Tshekedi, but in the event it turned out to be a satisfactory method of obtaining the evidence. It might be added here that, at the conclusion of the evidence of interested parties, the Chairman called two members of the administration to give factual evidence as to the state of affairs in the tribe at the present day, while certain written evidence, which had been posted to the Secretary was read *coram publico*, and copies were given to interested parties on application.

On arriving at Serowe, we received a petition from Tshekedi, requesting that the enquiry be transferred to Lobatsi, a distance of 250 miles, as he feared that his life would be in danger if he gave evidence in Serowe. This application did not come as a surprise to us, as a similar appeal had been made to the High Commissioner when the notice fixing the hearing at Serowe had been published, but it was none the less embarrassing, as this enquiry without Tshekedi might well be compared with Hamlet without the Prince of Denmark.

Whether there was any substance in the fears of Tshekedi and his legal adviser it was impossible to judge, as at that time we had no opportunity of assessing the temper of the 5,000 people who had assembled to hear the proceedings. We therefore decided to take no risk and, at great inconvenience to ourselves and everyone else, we adjourned the enquiry to Lobatsi and there took the evidence of Tshekedi and his witnesses, returning to Serowe as soon as their evidence was concluded.

In the light of our subsequent experience, we are satisfied that this move was probably unnecessary, for the behaviour of the crowd in Serowe was orderly and restrained throughout but, as we have said above, it was essential that Tshekedi should give his evidence and we were not prepared to risk an incident of which

The Harragin Report, December 1949

we had been warned, even if we could have persuaded Tshekedi to give evidence in Serowe.

Our decision to adjourn to Lobatsi was very unpopular with Seretse and his followers, who pointed out, with reason, that the matter was essentially the concern of the Bamangwato people, that their administrative centre was Serowe, that they had collected from all over the Reserve to hear the Enquiry and give evidence, that Lobatsi was outside the Reserve, and that Tshekedi had been moving freely in the Reserve up to a few days before the Enquiry started. They then proceeded to hold a meeting at which they, in turn, decided to take no part in the proceedings at Lobatsi, except to direct their legal adviser to attend and hold a watching brief. This decision was regrettable from our point of view, as it permitted Tshekedi to give his evidence without fear of cross-examination and obliged the Attorney-General and ourselves at times to appear in the light of cross-examiners whenever any matter within our knowledge required clarification, while it was a tactical error on the part of Seretse and his supporters, as Tshekedi and his witnesses could have been vigorously cross-examined in Lobatsi without fear of retaliation in Serowe.

Tshekedi gave his evidence at great length and with the aid of carefully prepared documents, but he regarded any questions by the Attorney-General or by ourselves with grave suspicion, thus his answers were usually more verbose and involved than the simplicity of the question appeared to demand. This attitude of mind tended to prolong proceedings, as can be shown in one very simple example. For hours Tshekedi impugned the validity of the decision of the June Kgotla to accept Seretse as Chief and Ruth as Queen, but in the last few minutes of his evidence he volunteered the fact that the tribe at a Kgotla in 1925 had designated Seretse as Chief, so that it was a matter of no practical importance whether they reiterated their decision in June 1949 or not. Tshekedi has, however, given some very definite and clear evidence as to Seretse's misconduct with regard to native law and custom, and it might be convenient at this point to set out *seriatim* the various allegations which, if proved, would in Tshekedi's submission unfit Seretse to hold the position of Chief. That:—

Appendix J

(a) Seretse, having married without obtaining the consent of the Chief and elders of the Chief's family, his wife could never under any circumstances become Queen of the tribe.
(b) The children of Ruth could never succeed to the chieftainship under any circumstances.
(c) Seretse, by ignoring native law and custom in this matter, has shown himself as irresponsible and therefore unfit to be a Chief.
(d) Seretse, by refusing to accept the decision of the November Kgotla and by pretending that the question before the Kgotla last June was a question of chieftainship and not one of irregular marriage, stampeded the tribe into an improper decision.
(e) According to native law and custom, no proposition could be placed before the Kgotla save by the Chief or Chairman of the Kgotla, and that therefore the question put before the June Kgotla by Seretse was improperly and irregularly voted upon.
(f) In any event, voting at a Kgotla is contrary to native law and custom, as only the Chief or Chairman at a Kgotla can give the decision of a Kgotla.
(g) Seretse, by drinking intoxicating liquor contrary to native law and custom, and in particular to Bamangwato custom, had barred himself from the chieftainship.
(h) Seretse had been levying or inspiring illegal levies and was therefore liable to prosecution, which should disqualify him for the chieftainship.
(i) Seretse, during the period that he was in England from January to May 1949 was conspiring through his agents to deceive the people into believing that the issue for the June Kgotla was one of the chieftainship and not the unsuitability of his marriage.
(j) The recognition by the High Commissioner of Seretse as Chief will cause disruption in the tribe.
(k) The recognition by the High Commissioner of Seretse as Chief will endanger the friendly relations of the Bamangwato

with the Union of South Africa and Southern Rhodesia, upon whose good offices the tribe is greatly dependent.
(l) The fact that the Union of South Africa had declared Seretse a prohibited immigrant makes it impossible for him to carry out his duties as Chief.
(m) The statutory laws of the Protectorate do not envisage a European as a member of a tribe.

We will now deal *seriatim* with these charges.

(a) and (b) There can be no question but that Seretse has in fact married without obtaining the consent of his uncle, Tshekedi, who was the Chief (Regent) of the tribe, nor did he place the matter before any of the other elders of the tribe. Before his marriage he informed Tshekedi of his intentions and Tshekedi made very effort, official and unofficial, to prevent Seretse carrying out his desire, which in the opinion of Tshekedi was a fatal mistake from every point of view. The only result, however, of the efforts made in England to prevent this marriage was to provoke Seretse into marrying at a Registry Office, at a date earlier than he had originally intended.

Tshekedi's immediate reaction to the news of the marriage was to have Seretse summoned back to Bechuanaland, where in due course his conduct was discussed in the November Kgotla, with the result indicated in the last chapter. The tribe was shocked by the marriage and the lack of respect shown by the Chief designate for native law and custom, and they clearly indicated that, in their view, Seretse should get rid of his wife. How exactly this was to be done does not seem to have been considered very carefully, and it would appear to have been assumed that the disapproval of the tribe would have been accepted as good cause for a divorce in England. At the end of the November Kgotla it was apparently decided to hold a further Kgotla in December. Why this was necessary is not very clear, but it seems to have been thought by Tshekedi and others that the matter might by that time have been settled for them by a kindly Government, who would have declared Ruth Seretse a prohibited

Appendix J

immigrant and have refused to permit Seretse to leave Bechuanaland to join her in England and they hoped that in this way Seretse's interest in his European wife would disappear and matters would right themselves eventually, by perhaps a divorce on the grounds of desertion.

In the meanwhile, local pressure was being brought to bear on Seretse by the senior members of the tribe to make him see the error of his ways, but time passed, and Seretse, still to his credit, refused to contemplate divorce and when the December Kgotla assembled public opinion was beginning to waver.

The real pattern of future events was becoming more clear. Seretse obviously had no intention of giving up his wife, even if it meant surrendering the chieftainship, and the Government had no intention of preventing the young couple coming together again, and we think that a fair interpretation of the feelings of the December Kgotla was that Seretse should return to England to his wife and there continue his legal studies, but that he should report back in six months' time, when they hoped that he would have got over the first blush of his infatuation. The majority of the Kgotla still made it clear that they did not approve of the marriage, and we do not think that the question of the chieftainship was seriously discussed. In May Seretse duly returned as promised, leaving his wife in London, and the result of the June meeting is recorded in the last Chapter. The first question then for consideration is whether there is any substance in Tshekedi's contention that Ruth Seretse could never become Queen of the tribe, which includes, of course *(b)*, Tshekedi's second contention that her children could never succeed to the chieftainship. A great deal of evidence was given upon this point and it must be realised that this is not a question of white versus black, but a straight issue as to whether, under any circumstances, a Chief or an heir apparent, who marries without permission of his tribe, could ever have his wife recognised as Queen. We have no hesitation in finding that this is, and always was, a possibility, and that Seretse's answer to this contention is the correct one, and it amounts to this: a Chief, even though he acts without the consent of the tribe, can subsequently obtain their forgiveness and ratification of his action, in which event the woman whom he has married will be recognised by the tribe as Queen and her children as lawful successors to the chieftainship. We are well aware that in the old days this matter would have been settled quite simply by the tribe in November either killing Seretse or driving him into exile. In fact, as the history of the Bamangwato shows, most chiefs seem to have spent years in exile for some misdemeanour, but if and when they returned and were accepted by the tribe, if their wife was also accepted, there is no doubt that their children were looked upon as the lawful heirs. In these days Seretse has won the battle for himself and his wife, not by force of arms, but by force of votes.

We would, however, point out that our terms of reference do not envisage a decision on this issue, nor is such a question contemplated by the particular proclamation under which we were appointed and we only touch on the point because much emphasis was laid upon it by Tshekedi. We agree with Seretse that it is for the tribe, and not for the Government, to decide who is to be recognised as Queen of the tribe. It should be realised that the word "Queen" is quite inappropriate for the wife of a Chief, and has no justification in tribal history, where she would be referred to as the principal wife, it being presumed that the Chief would have several wives.

(c) We have already indicated, and Seretse does not dispute the fact, that he ignored native law and custom over his marriage, the only question now for consideration is whether his conduct is such a serious breach of native law that he has unfitted himself for the position of Chief.

His defence on this charge is exactly the same as that put forward with regard to *(a)* and *(b)*. He admits ignoring native custom, but alleges that the tribe has forgiven him and that the matter is therefore closed, and he further points out that chiefs on many occasions in the past have ignored native custom, but that, provided they received forgiveness from the tribe, nothing further was heard of the matter.

With this contention we entirely agree; in our view, the matter is one for the tribesmen and for them alone, and if they

Appendix J

are prepared to forgive a chief who has ignored their custom, who are we to insist on his punishment?

(d) It is true that Seretse did not accept the decision of the first Kgotla held in November 1948, but it must be remembered that it was Tshekedi himself who summoned the subsequent Kgotlas, so that even he could not have considered that a final and irrevocable decision had been made in November, and the fact that the third Kgotla in June reversed the decision of the first Kgotla in November is, in our view, sufficient answer to this criticism; it is idle to pretend that any assembly is bound irrevocably by its previous decision.

We cannot agree that Seretse stampeded the tribe in the third Kgotla in June. Undoubtedly, the main issue that Tshekedi wished to put before the tribe was the marriage, and what was to happen as a result of the marriage, and we accept Tshekedi's statement that he had never claimed the chieftainship of right or raised that issue, but in practice the chieftainship did in fact depend on the decision to be taken by the Kgotla. Seretse had declared from the outset that if the tribe would not accept his wife he would not remain in the Protectorate without her, *a fortiori*, he could not become their chief, so that, if the tribe had reaffirmed their decision that they would not accept Ruth Seretse, it would have meant that Seretse could not be their chief, and we consider that it was a perfectly relevant question that Seretse put to the Kgotla when he asked them whether they would accept him and his wife. We are also satisfied that the tribe, when they voted in favour of Seretse, knew exactly what they were doing and why they were doing it and we are of the opinion that so unpopular had Tshekedi become with the tribe that they looked upon Seretse as their only hope of deliverance from their unpopular Regent, and they would have accepted Seretse under almost any circumstances and whether he had broken any or all the native customs connected with the marriage.

(e) In theory, there is no doubt about Tshekedi's contention that only the chief or chairman of a Kgotla may put the question to the Kgotla, and it was certainly irregular for Seretse to have jumped up and put the question himself. It must, however, be

remembered that this Kgotla was the third that had been held to discuss the same subject, it had already lasted several days without any result, and Tshekedi does not appear to have been anxious to put the question himself, presumably because he knew from the speakers that his cause was lost and he was playing for time. Further, Tshekedi, as Chairman of the meeting, made no attempt to prevent the question being put and we are satisfied that, irregular though the proceedings may have been, the result reflected truthfully the feeling of the meeting. It should here be noted that Tshekedi himself admits that no useful purpose would be served by a finding to the effect that the Kgotla, having been irregularly conducted, was a nullity. The only effect of such a recommendation would be that another Kgotla would have to be summoned, which would have the same result.

(f) Tshekedi in this allegation, which is to the effect that voting at a Kgotla is unknown and contrary to native law and custom, is relying on a mere technicality. We agree with him that in the olden days voting was unheard of and that all that happened at a Kgotla was that the Chief, having put the question before the people, listened to the speakers and, having heard all that they had to say, he himself announced the decision without any formal vote being taken; but it would have been a foolhardy chief who formally announced a decision which was contrary to the feelings of the meeting, and there is no doubt that the majority would have dealt with him, if the matter had been of importance, in no uncertain manner. In recent days, however, evidence was given, which we accept, to the effect that, although actual voting may not have taken place at Kgotla meetings, it is not unknown for the various parties at a Kgotla to collect in groups, from which the Chairman would judge of their strength. We are therefore of the opinion that there is no real substance in this complaint.

At this point we would like to quote from the words of Sir Herbert Stanley, the then High Commissioner, in his memorandum dealing with the 1943 Native Administration Proclamation, as we feel that they are even more true today than they were when they were written.

Appendix J

"In the affairs of men, nothing can remain stationary. As the years pass, conditions change, and institutions and forms of Government which do not adapt themselves to changing conditions, and progress with them, lose their vitality and sink into decay. Bechuanas are no longer the very primitive people that they were some 40 years ago. Contact with European civilization and the gradual spread of education have affected them appreciably, though in varying degrees. Many of their thoughts and ways of life, *and systems and methods which may have sufficed 40 years ago, must, if they are to survive at all, be brought into line with the changed conditions*, and must be rendered capable of further development in conformity with such further changes as the future may bring forth."

(g) The custom of the Bamangwato, as very definitely laid down by Khama, is to the effect that intoxicating liquor is forbidden. Seretse admits that he does in fact, from time to time, drink intoxicating liquor and to that extent is departing from custom. There is no suggestion that he drinks to excess and there is no doubt that there are many other Natives in the Reserve, and in the Protectorate generally, who do indulge in intoxicating liquor, wrong though it may be, and we are not prepared to find that Seretse is thereby unfit for the chieftainship.

(h) Tshekedi alleged that Seretse had been levying or inspiring illegal levies, but there was no evidence to support this accusation and, although it was evident that Seretse had been obtaining considerable sums of money from somewhere, we can see no objection to his friends voluntarily supporting him in his fight for what they believe to be his rights.

(i) The allegation that between January and May 1949 Seretse, through his agents, deceived the people as to the real issue at the June Kgotla, we have already touched upon, and not only do we find that there was no deception as to the real issue at the June Kgotla but we can find no evidence that Seretse was in any way disseminating false propaganda, as alleged. The change of heart that took place between December and June, as we have already stated, was due entirely to the realisation by the people that if they did not accept Seretse with his wife the rule of Tshekedi would continue.

(j) The recognition by the High Commissioner of Seretse as Chief would, of course, cause a certain amount of disruption in the tribe. Tshekedi and his followers have announced that, should Seretse's wife remain in the Bamangwato Reserve, they will depart elsewhere. Tshekedi's followers are not numerous but they are influential, they are probably the most experienced administrators in the tribe, possibly because they have been given administrative duties by Tshekedi in the past. Tshekedi himself is one of the most enlightened and experienced native administrators in Africa, and theoretically he himself should be a great loss, but the fact is that, so far as the Bamangwato tribe is concerned, he has outstayed his welcome and, in spite of all his good work, he is at present the most unpopular man in the tribe. It is, therefore, both in his own interest and in the interests of law and order, that he should pursue his resolve and remove himself from the Reserve.

Against his followers there appears to be little real animosity, and their wise counsel will be missed, even though Seretse is quite satisfied that those who remain will be well able to carry on the administrative duties, particularly as, he points out, the actual number leaving the Reserve is small and in due course may be expected to drift back.

We must find, however, as a fact that Seretse's recognition as Chief would cause a rift in the tribe, in any event to begin with, and if Seretse's declared intention to regard his uncle, Serogola, as his principal adviser is carried out, we certainly are of the opinion that the tribe would suffer. We had the advantage of hearing and seeing Serogola in the witness box and we cannot regard him in any way as a suitable adviser to a young chief.

(k) Tshekedi's next point is indeed a most serious one; he alleges that the recognition by the High Commissioner of Seretse as Chief would endanger the friendly relations of the Bechuanaland Protectorate with the Union of South Africa and Southern Rhodesia. We are aware of the attitude that has been

Appendix J

taken up by the Union of South Africa and Southern Rhodesia, for we have read the utterances of the Prime Minister of the Union and the debates in the Southern Rhodesian Parliament, and we are also aware of how dependent the Bechuanaland Protectorate is upon the good offices of the Union and Southern Rhodesia. It is only necessary for us to mention the association with the Union and Southern Rhodesia in such matters as customs, the railway, the posts and telegraphs, currency, and the assistance given by the Union in veterinary and medical matters. There is no need for us to expand or explain the facilities and services rendered by the Union (and to a lesser degree by Southern Rhodesia)–they are self-evident.

We have also noted the statement made by the Under-Secretary for Commonwealth Relations in the British Parliament in answer to a question put to him by Mr. Platts-Mills, which reads as follows:–

> "Could you give a solemn assurance that the attitude of the Government will be in no way prejudiced by the fact that Seretse Khama married a white woman? Will you convey that attitude to the Government of South Africa, which has looked with greedy and race-ridden eyes on this problem."

to which the following reply was given:–

> "I do not think there is any need to give such an assurance. The Government of South Africa does not come into this matter at all."

We are aware that, in theory, this may be a perfectly correct answer to the question but we also know in what straits the Bamangwato Reserve and Bechuanaland would be if, for some reason, the Union of South Africa ceased to co-operate, if only to the extent of finding it impossible to supply Bechuanaland with maize during famine months. There are, of course, innumerable other ways in which the Union and Southern Rhodesia could make themselves felt in the Protectorate if they ceased to be friendly, even though they might not resort to such drastic action as economic sanctions. The attitude of the vast majority of the European population and many of the Africans in the Union and Southern Rhodesia to this marriage cannot be ignored, and, in spite of the Under-Secretary of State's reply, we have no hesitation in saying that in practice an unfriendly policy in the Union or Southern Rhodesia would have devastating effects on the Bechuanaland Protectorate.

(*l*) And further in this connection it must be remembered that the Headquarters of the Bechuanaland Protectorate are in Mafeking, which is in the Union, and the Union Government has declared Seretse to be a prohibited immigrant. The immediate result of this declaration is that, if Seretse were recognised as Chief of the Bamangwato Tribe, the official representative of the tribe (representing almost half the Bechuanaland Protectorate and at least 100,000 people) would be debarred from visiting headquarters. We are quite unable to believe that, under those circumstances, Seretse would be able to carry out his duties as Chief. It is calculated that in the past the Chief has found it necessary to visit the Resident Commissioner once every six weeks, ignoring for the moment the occasions upon which it has been necessary for him to visit the High Commissioner, while all meetings of importance are held in Mafeking, *e.g.*, the African Advisory Council, and from all these Seretse will be debarred.

When we put these difficulties to Seretse, his only reply was to suggest that the meetings should be held on the border which is about 15 miles from Mafeking, a quite impracticable suggestion. We realise that it is unfortunate that the official headquarters of the Protectorate lie in a neighbouring territory, but it is a fact that has got to be faced, and we are quite unable to think of any practical way in which the difficulty could be overcome, short of moving the headquarters into the Protectorate which, apart from any other difficulties, might well cost £ 1,000,000 and take a very long time.

In all these circumstances we are bound to find that it would be impossible for Seretse Khama to carry out his duties as Chief.

Appendix J

(m) The last point made by Tshekedi with regard to the statutory laws of the Protectorate, which do not envisage a European as a member of a tribe, has of course some substance; as for example the fact that Seretse's wife would in the normal way be able to obtain a permit for intoxicating liquor but she would be committing an offence if she gave any of it to her husband is true, but we do not consider this to be an insuperable obstacle to Seretse's recognition, for it is always possible to amend the statutory law to meet hard cases.

In the course of the enquiry, two legal points were raised, one on behalf of Tshekedi and the other on behalf of Seretse. Counsel for Tshekedi submitted a memorandum in which he argued that, although Seretse might have been legally married in England, for certain purposes his marriage was invalid in the Protectorate. We do not consider an enquiry of this description a proper place in which to record judgment on a point of law. We will observe, however, that if in fact Ruth Williams is not married to Seretse for certain purposes when in the Protectorate, it is strange that Tshekedi should take such violent exception to his nephew living in sin with a woman, a practice by no means unknown according to native law and custom in the Protectorate. In any event, we are assured by our Chairman that there is no substance in the legal point raised.

Counsel for Seretse took, in our view, an equally ingenious point, which we find it difficult to believe he wished us to consider seriously. He argued that, because in 1925 a Kgotla had designated Seretse as Chief and as in 1930 the Secretary of State, in conversation, referred to Seretse as "Chief Seretse," therefore he had been confirmed as Chief and came within the purview of Section 2 of Proclamation No. 32 of 1943, which reads as follows:–

> "Every Chief, who at the commencement of this Proclamation is lawfully holding the office of Chief, shall be deemed to have been recognised by the High Commissioner, and confirmed by the Secretary of State."

The Harragin Report, December 1949

Seretse's legal representative argues that, as Seretse was designated Chief in 1925 and accepted as Chief in 1930 by the Secretary of State, he was automatically confirmed in his office by the 1943 Proclamation. Our only comment on this is to say that, because the Secretary of State refers to someone as a Chief in the course of conversation, this cannot be regarded as a formal recognition of his position, and moreover the words used in this section are, "holding the office of Chief" and it can hardly be argued that Seretse was holding the office of Chief when pursuing his studies at Fort Hare, Witwatersrand or Oxford University.

Our conclusions on the questions referred to us in the terms of reference can therefore be recorded as follows:–

1. We are of the opinion that the Kgotla held at Serowe between the 20th and 25th June, 1949, at which Seretse Khama was designated as Chief of the Bamangwato Tribe, was properly convened and assembled, and its proceedings conducted in accordance with native custom.
2. That having regard to the interests and well-being of the Tribe, Seretse Khama is not a fit and proper person to discharge the functions of Chief.

Both these findings are subject to the comments which we have made earlier, when dealing *seriatim* with the charges. Thus, although there may have been technical irregularities in accordance with native custom in the proceedings of the above-mentioned Kgotla, we are satisfied that it did record faithfully and correctly the feelings of the Tribe, which are even stronger today than they were on the date of the Kgotla, and no useful purpose would be served in recommending the assembling of another Kgotla, which would only record the same decision even more emphatically.

In finding that Seretse Khama is not a fit and proper person to discharge the functions of Chief, we wish to emphasize the fact that, should conditions change, as they well might in a variety of ways, Seretse Khama should be allowed to assume his duties as Chief. He is admittedly the lawful and legitimate heir and, save

Appendix J

for his irresponsibility in contracting this unfortunate marriage, would be, in our opinion, a fit and proper person to assume the chieftainship.

We realise that our finding with regard to Seretse will be unpopular with the Bamangwato Tribe, who are very loyal to the reigning house, and we wish to make it clear to them that we are not disinheriting the house of Sekgoma forever, and it may well be that the time is not far distant when Seretse Khama will be able to assume the chieftainship. We would point out that it is not without precedent in the history of the tribes of the Bechuanaland Protectorate that a Chief has, for a period of years, been unable for one reason or another to carry out his duties as Chief.

Our findings may therefore be summed up shortly as follows:–

We, with regret but with no hesitation, are unable to recommend the recognition of Seretse Khama as Chief of the Bamangwato Tribe because:–

(1) Being a prohibited immigrant in the Union of South Africa, he will be unable to efficiently carry out his duties as Chief.

(2) A friendly and co-operative Union of South Africa and Southern Rhodesia is essential to the well-being of the Tribe and indeed the whole of the Bechuanaland Protectorate.

(3) His recognition will undoubtedly cause disruption in the Bamangwato Tribe.

Chapter IV

We have found that in the present circumstances Seretse is not "a fit and proper person" to be Chief of the Bamangwato. If this finding is accepted, the administration will be faced with the problem of devising such arrangements for the conduct of the business normally performed by the Native Authority as appear to be in the best interests of the Tribe. While it is not within our terms of reference to make recommendations to this end, it

The Harragin Report, December 1949

appears to us appropriate to mention some of the problems which will arise from our findings and, with diffidence, to suggest a course which might meet the immediate needs of the situation. We would emphasize that we are, advisedly, making no attempt to suggest any fundamental change in the basic structure of the Native Government other than that which must, it seems to us, inevitably flow from our finding.

Section 13 of the Bechuanaland Protectorate Native Administration Proclamation 1943 (No. 32 of 1943) prescribes that the Chief of a tribal area shall be appointed to the office of Native Authority for the tribal area, and Section 17(1), as amended on the 7th November, 1949, provides that:–

> "Where the office of Native Authority constituted under this Proclamation is for the time being vacant or where in the opinion of the High Commissioner it is desirable in the interests of peace, order and good government in the area, the High Commissioner may appoint any person or body of persons to such office."

The position at the time of writing this Report is that Tshekedi is still nominally Native Authority, though he has left the Bamangwato Reserve and has admitted to us in evidence that he is no longer able to perform the functions of Native Authority.

In fact the Tribal Administration, as such, has broken down completely and the District Commissioner is carrying on the essential Native Administration without, however, possessing the power of a Native Authority. We understand that it is the Government's intention to make the District Commissioner the Native Authority in place of Tshekedi under Section 17(1) of the Proclamation (as amended) which we have quoted above. With respect, we consider that this is the only course possible in the interests of peace, order and good government in the Bamangwato Reserve.

An alternative procedure which might be followed in such circumstances would be that laid down in Section 7 of the Proclamation which provides *inter alia* that where a Chief (which

Appendix J

term includes Regent) becomes incapable of performing adequately the duties of his office, the tribe in Kgotla should "designate the person or persons who, subject to the approval of the High Commissioner, shall exercise the functions of the chieftainship or shall assist the Chief in the exercise of his functions." We are, however, satisfied that this procedure would yield no satisfactory result in the present circumstances, where Seretse is desired as Chief by the vast majority of the tribe, and where no other member or members of the Chief's family would be generally acceptable as Regent or as a Council of Regency.

Our belief is that a satisfactory solution to the immediate administrative problem can only be found in arrangements whereby the District Commissioner is the Native Authority in place of the Chief. Acting in this capacity he would, no doubt, be assisted by an advisory council selected from the tribal leaders and would continue to use the existing agencies of administration. We have in mind such agencies as the Chief's representatives in the districts, the regimental leaders, headmen and committees which have been set up for special purposes, such as education. We suggest that this arrangement should not continue for longer than is necessary in the interests of the orderly good government of the tribe. Circumstances may alter so as to make the recognition of Seretse as Chief practicable or, alternatively, it may be found possible successfully to employ the procedure set out in Section 7 of the Proclamation, to which we have referred, to select another Regent or a Council of Regency.

We are satisfied from the evidence before us that a period of direct rule would be in the immediate interests of the Bamangwato, not only because it seems to us the only satisfactory way out of the impasse which has arisen in connection with the chieftainship, but also because it would afford opportunities for healing tribal dissensions and for the reformation of the tribal administration. It is clear from the evidence of the District Commissioner, Serowe, that much work is required in this latter direction, especially in regard to the working of the Native Treasury.

The Harragin Report, December 1949

Parallel arrangements would no doubt be possible in respect of the hearing of those court cases at present falling under the jurisdiction of the Court of the Chief of the Bamangwato, and some consequential amendment to the Native Administration and Native Courts Proclamations may be required. In addition to the powers conferred upon him as Native Authority or by virtue of his judicial powers, the Chief has certain customary social and administrative functions to perform, such as giving the word for the annual cultivations to start. How such duties are to be discharged in the absence of a Chief will be for the Administration and Kgotla to settle in consultation.

If it is decided to introduce a period of direct rule on the lines suggested, the position of Seretse and Tshekedi will require careful consideration. While we have found that in the present circumstances Seretse is not "a fit and proper person" to be Chief, he remains the Chief designate and the person to whom customary allegiance is willingly accorded by the majority of the tribe. In the present unfortunate circumstances we believe that his continued presence in the Bamangwato Reserve would be an embarrassment to the Administration and not in the best interests of tribal tranquility and of the orderly conduct of business. At the same time we feel that, as Chief designate, he should be enabled to maintain himself in a manner fitting to his status, so long as he conducts himself as not to embarrass the Administration of the Reserve.

We accordingly hope that the Administration will be able to arrange that he be paid such subsidy as will enable him to live in appropriate style, provided that he lives outside the Bechuanaland Protectorate, or until the High Commissioner is satisfied that it is in the interests of the Tribe that he be permitted to return. We have suggested that such subsidy should be dependent on Seretse leaving the Protectorate because we believe that condition to be essential to the peace and good order of the Bamangwato Reserve. We would go further, and suggest that if Seretse does not voluntarily leave the High Commissioner should consider using powers to ensure his removal. If it should become necessary for Seretse to attend sittings of the local High Court, as is possible,

Appendix J

special permission could no doubt be granted to him to proceed to Lobatsi, where the High Court normally sits.

Tshekedi will, we understand, soon cease to be Regent. He has stated quite clearly that he would in no circumstances agree to become Chief in the future, though he has stressed that he would be willing to continue to serve the Tribe in some other capacity. In the meantime, he has removed himself and his belongings to Rametsana in the Bakwena Reserve, which is adjacent to the Bamangwato Reserve. It is not for us to judge Tshekedi's action in leaving the Bamangwato country with his followers or to speculate as to the motives which caused him to do so. Whatever the merits of the matter, the result has been to cause some considerable tribal disorder, and his presence adjacent to the Bamangwato Reserve no doubt constitutes a potential focus for intrigue and malcontents. This energetic and forceful personality has, however, borne the main burden of the tribal administration of the Bamangwato for the past 23 years and we hope that, for so long as his conduct and activities do not interfere with the orderly administration of the tribe, he will receive some adequate pension, provided that enquiries now being made into the Native Treasury affairs do not indicate that the grant of such pension would be inappropriate. In any event we suggest that any pension granted should, at any rate for some years, be dependent on Tshekedi remaining outside the Bamangwato Reserve. If he is not prepared to remain outside the Reserve of his own volition, the High Commissioner will no doubt consider using powers to order him to do so. If he remains peacefully in retirement for the present, it may be found possible for his undoubted ability, energy and initiative to be employed in the future in the service of the Bamangwato people.

Inevitably a period of difficulty, reorganisation and adjustment lies before those administering the Bamangwato country. Recent events have given the traditional system a rude shock, but history shows that it is well accustomed to withstanding such a shock, and we believe that by adopting some such course as we have suggested the essential features of the tribal administration will survive unimpaired and may indeed emerge with renewed vigour when the present difficulties have disappeared. Had the tribal government consisted of a Chief and Council, on the pattern now familiar in many parts of Africa, it might well have been possible to carry on indirect rule or African local government, without the District Commissioner assuming the duties of Native Authority; but in the Bamangwato country power to govern is vested in the Chief himself and he governs subject to the usual overriding authority of the Administration, in consultation with the full tribal meeting or Kgotla. His position was aptly described by the Hon. Mr. Justice E.F. Watermeyer, presiding over a special court in the Bechuanaland Protectorate in 1936. He said:–

> "Under native custom the Chief resembles a Saxon King more than a constitutional monarch. He is a representative chief, with wide discretionary power; he is the legislature, executive and the final Court of Appeal. In exercising these functions he takes advice from whom he pleases, but he is to some extent controlled by tribal opinion because he has to make his decisions in public in the Kgotla where he is bound to listen to anyone who cares to speak. In that way he feels the pulse of the tribe, but the decision is his and he can disregard the opinion of the majority. In practice, however, he follows tribal opinion, because the security of his position as Chief to some extent depends upon the character of his rule. . . . "

It is because the Chief of the Bamangwato plays such an important role in tribal government that we believe that during the temporary eclipse of the chieftainship there must be resort to the modified form of direct rule which we suggest, a direct rule which will, no doubt, be combined with a progressive development programme.

Appendix J

Chapter V

In conclusion, we should like to express our appreciation for the arrangements made in connection with this enquiry, and our most sincere and grateful thanks to our hostesses and hosts upon whom we have been billeted for so long. Their unfailing hospitality and good nature under trying circumstances will long be remembered by us. While to our hard working Secretary and his staff we are deeply indebted, not only for the able manner in which they carried out what might be called their normal duties, but for the innumerable ways in which they have managed to make the days spent on this enquiry a pleasure rather than a duty.

WALTER HARRAGIN, *Chairman.*   F.G. HOLMES, *Secretary*

R.S. HUDSON, *Member.*   G.E. NETTELTON, *Member*

Pretoria
  1st December, 1949

Appendix K

THE BRITISH GOVERNMENT SECRETARY OF STATE
FOR COMMONWEALTH RELATIONS' MEMORANDUM
TO THE CABINET RECOMMENDING THAT
SERETSE KHAMA NOT BE RECOGNIZED
AS CHIEF OF THE BAMANGWATO,
AND CABINET CONCLUSIONS
C.P. (50), 13, 26 JANUARY 1950

United Kingdom Cabinet Conclusions
C.M. (50) 3, 31st January, 1950

BECHUANALAND PROTECTORATE:
CHIEFTAINSHIP OF THE BAMANGWATO TRIBE
(Previous Reference C.M. (49) 47/8)

1. The Cabinet considered a memorandum by the Secretary of State for Commonwealth Relations (C.P. (50) 13) on the succession to the Chieftainship of the Bamangwato Tribe.

The Secretary of State for Commonwealth Relations recalled that the Cabinet had agreed on 21st July that a Judicial Enquiry should be held under the provisions of the Bechuanaland Native Administration Proclamation into the suitability of Seretse Khama for the Chieftainship of the Bamangwato Tribe. The Judicial Enquiry had now completed their work and a copy of their report was annexed to C.P. (50) 13. Their main findings were that the tribal meeting (Kgotla) at which Seretse had been designated as Chief had been properly convened and assembled, and that its proceedings had been conducted in accordance with native custom; but that, having regard to the interests and well-being of the Tribe,

Appendix K

Seretse was not a fit and proper person to discharge the functions of Chief. The reasons given for this second finding were that, as the headquarters of the administration was at Mafeking and Seretse was a prohibited immigrant in the Union of South Africa, he would be unable efficiently to carry out his duties as Chief; that the friendship of the Union and of Southern Rhodesia was essential to the well-being of the Tribe and to the Bechuanaland Protectorate generally; and that recognition of Seretse would disrupt the Tribe. The Secretary of State said that, while he accepted the conclusion that Seretse was not a fit and proper person to discharge the functions of Chief, he did not consider that the reasons given by the members of the Enquiry in support of this conclusion could be endorsed by His Majesty's Government. In his view there were three main reasons for refusing to recognise Seretse as Chief. First, those closely acquainted with the Bamangwato Tribe were agreed that the Enquiry had underestimated the risk that his recognition would result in the disruption of the Tribe. At their previous discussions, Ministers had expressed the view "that the principal objective of policy must be to safeguard the future well-being of the Bamangwato themselves" and he was in no doubt that a decision to recognise Seretse would be incompatible with this objective. Indeed, various passages in the report showed that, in supporting Seretse, the members of the Tribe had been actuated by fear of Tshekedi, and the decision of the tribal meeting should not therefore be regarded as an endorsement of Seretse's claims. Secondly, Seretse had shown an irresponsibility, both in his marriage and in other matters, which made it doubtful whether he could safely be entrusted with the duties and responsibilities of Chieftain. Thirdly, liberal European opinion generally was convinced that Seretse ought not to be recognised as Chieftain, and this view was shared by a strong body of native opinion in Africa. He thought that these considerations would in themselves justify a decision not to recognise Seretse; but it would not be realistic wholly to ignore the effect which recognition might have on South African opinion and on future relations with the Union Government. From the point of view of African interests, the paramount need was to safeguard the position of the South African High Commission Territories. For the first time, there was a strong body of opinion within the Union itself which considered the Union's claim to these Territories ought not to be actively pressed at the present time. Recognition of Seretse would weaken this opposition and strengthen the position of those who favoured the transfer of these Territories to the Union. In these circumstances he recommended that Seretse should not be recognised as Chief, and that the Government's decision should be announced in a White Paper on the lines of the draft annexed to C.P. (50) 13. In the first instance, however, he suggested that Seretse and his wife should be invited to come to England, so that a further attempt might be made to persuade him to relinquish voluntarily his claim to the Chieftainship. Finally, he recommended that the administration of the Bechuanaland [sic. Bamangwato] Reserve should for the present be conducted directly by the Bechuanaland Protectorate Administration, and that the system of native government in the Reserve should, by gradual stages, be made more representative.

The Secretary of State for the Colonies said that he was in general agreement with the recommendations made in C.P. (50) 13. The decisive consideration was that the recognition of Seretse would undoubtedly endanger the stability and well-being of the Bamangwato Tribe. Although opinion in Africa was divided on this issue, it was clear that a substantial body of opinion was opposed to the recognition of Seretse. He also endorsed the proposals for reforming the system of native government in the Bamangwato Reserve; and he thought that every effort should be made to transfer the headquarters of the administration from Mafeking to some place inside the Protectorate.

In discussion there was general agreement that the handling of this problem had been seriously complicated by the terms of the report of the Judicial Enquiry. It was impossible for the Government to endorse the reasons on which the second conclusion of the Enquiry was based; and, if it became necessary to publish the report, the Government would have no alternative but to make this

Appendix K

clear. There were other passages in the report which were likely to give rise to damaging controversy in this country or in Africa. On the other hand, there could be no doubt that Seretse's marriage had introduced into the affairs of the Bamangwato Tribe a persisting element of controversy and unsettlement, which would be further aggravated if he should have children. Indeed, the United Kingdom High Commissioner and his advisers considered that insufficient weight was given in the report of the Judicial Enquiry to the stimulus which recognition of Seretse would give to the disruptive tendencies already inherent in the Tribe. In these circumstances Seretse's continuance as Chieftain would involve great risks for the Tribe. It seemed likely that Seretse himself was not unaware of these considerations and that he might therefore be responsive to suggestion that, by relinquishing voluntarily his claims to the Chieftainship, he would serve best both his own interests and those of the Tribe. The general view of Ministers was therefore that, as a first step, Seretse and his wife should be invited to come to London for discussions with the Secretary of State. In these talks an offer of an allowance and other appropriate forms of help should be made to Seretse on condition that he should not return to the Bechuanaland Protectorate. Ministers hoped that it might then be possible to avoid publication of the report of the Judicial Enquiry.

Ministers considered that it was unnecessary to decide at the present stage what action should be taken if it should prove impossible to persuade Seretse to relinquish the Chieftainship.

The Cabinet–

(1) Invited the Secretary of State for Commonwealth Relations to invite Seretse Khama and his wife to visit London with a view to persuading him to relinquish voluntarily the Chieftainship of the Bamangwato Tribe.

(2) Agreed that their consideration of the recommendations made in C.P. (50) 13 should be resumed in the light of the results of the talks held in accordance with Conclusion (1) above.

(3) Instructed the Secretary to recall all copies of C.P. (50) 13 from circulation.

Cabinet conclusions denying Seretse Khama his chieftaincy, 1950

United Kingdom Cabinet Memorandum
C.P. (50) 13, 26th January 1950

BECHUANALAND PROTECTORATE: SUCCESSION TO CHIEFTAINSHIP OF THE BAMANGWATO TRIBE

Memorandum By The Secretary of State
For Commonwealth Relations

My colleagues will remember that on 21st July (C.M. (49) 47th Conclusions, Minute 8) I laid before them the question of the recognition of Seretse Khama as Chief of the Bamangwato Tribe. The Cabinet decided that, before recognition was granted or withheld, a judicial enquiry should be held under the provisions of the Bechuanaland Native Administrative Proclamation into Seretse's suitability for the Chieftainship. The minutes of that meeting summarised "the general view of the Cabinet" as follows:–

"It could not be supposed that the recognition of Seretse would provide a satisfactory or lasting solution of the problem. The issue was not one of the merits or demerits of mixed marriages, and the Government should vigorously rebut any suggestion that their attitude to this question was in any way determined by purely racial considerations. The principal objective of policy must be to safeguard the future well-being of the Bamangwato themselves, and there could be no doubt that the recognition of a Chieftain with a white wife might have consequences gravely prejudicial to good government and to the stability of the local native administration. As a matter of tactics, no attempt should be made to reach a hasty decision; and the holding of a judicial enquiry would afford time for reflection by all the parties concerned."

2. The Judicial Enquiry has now completed its work, and the Commission have now presented a report. The two main findings of the report are as follows:–

Appendix K

"(1) We are of the opinion that the Kgotla held at Serowe between 20th and 25th June, 1949, at which Seretse Khama was designated as Chief of the Bamangwato Tribe, was properly convened and assembled, and its proceedings conducted in accordance with native custom;

(2) that, having regard to the interests and well-being of the Tribe, Seretse Khama is not a fit and proper person to discharge the functions of Chief."

Reasons why Seretse should not be recognised

3. I have examined most carefully both the report and the evidence taken by the enquiry and have discussed them with the High Commissioner, Sir Evelyn Baring, and I accept both the findings. The more important is of course the second finding, and for the following reasons I am fully convinced that Seretse should not be recognised:–

(a) The decision of the Kgotla was influenced by the strong feelings of the Tribe against the Regent Tshekedi (see paragraph 4 (a) below).

(b) Recognition would be contrary to the best interests of the Tribe. It would, I am advised, certainly lead to further disintegration. Already Tshekedi, who has had a fine personal record, has left the Reserve and has taken with him a number of the ablest and most important leaders of the Tribe. It seems inevitable that, if Seretse remained, faction feeling would grow within the Tribe, and so would opposition to him from neighbouring tribes.

(c) Seretse himself has shown evidence of irresponsibility which makes it doubtful whether he would, in fact, prove a wise Chief. He married Ruth precipitately and ignored appeals from the Bamangwato to return home first and discuss the matter. He has declared his intention to choose as his principal adviser one of his uncles whom the Judicial Enquiry regard as quite unsuitable– if this intention were carried out, they say, "the Tribe would certainly suffer." He has been drinking liquor, although this is contrary both to Protectorate law and to the Bamangwato custom; the Judicial Enquiry say that this is not, in itself, enough to make him unfit for the Chieftainship; but, in view of the past importance of prohibition in the life of the Tribe, it adds something to the other evidence of irresponsibility.

(d) There is a strong body of African opinion outside the Bamangwato Reserve which is against the recognition of Seretse (see paragraph 4 (b) and paragraphs 5-8 below).

(e) A decision to recognise might unite and inflame public opinion in the Union of South Africa. This might lead to either or both of the following results:—

(i) Dr. Malan's proposed demand for transfer of the Territories, the presentation of which, at this particular time, is opposed by a large section of white opinion in South Africa, would receive the warm and solid support of all sections of white opinion in the Union. Recognition would, therefore, play directly into Dr. Malan's hand in the matter of the transfer of the Territories.

(ii) If the demand for transfer were resisted and Dr. Malan attempted to apply economic pressure, South African Europeans would, in the event of recognition of Seretse, give him far more wholehearted support in these measures than he could otherwise obtain.

4. On the first finding of the enquiry (see paragraph 2 (a) above) I think that the following considerations should be borne in mind. The decision of the Kgotla which accepted Seretse in June does not necessarily mean that native opinion in southern Africa, or even native opinion in the Bechuanaland Protectorate, approved of his marriage to a white woman, or considered that he should be recognised as Chief. Thus—

(a) It is not clear that, by its decision of June last, the Kgotla was committing even those who took part in it to any firm view in favour of Seretse's marriage. This issue was in fact brought before them on three different occasions, in November 1948, December 1948 and June 1949. At the first meeting the marriage was almost universally condemned. At the second there was rather more support for Seretse. On the third occasion the

Appendix K

opinion swung heavily in his favour. But the report of the Judicial Enquiry makes it plain that this change of view was inspired, not by a changed view about the marriage, but by the fear that if Seretse was rejected his uncle, the Regent Tshekedi, the next legitimate heir, would become Chief. Tshekedi has already as Regent administered the affairs of the Tribe for 23 years. He has proved himself to be able, honest and progressive; but in the words of the report "he has driven his people hard," and has become very unpopular. It seems clear that it was rather fear and dislike of Tshekedi than approval of Seretse and his marriage which decided the issue in June.

(b) There is strong evidence that much African opinion in the rest of the Bechuanaland Protectorate is against the recognition of Seretse. The second largest tribe in the Bechuanaland Protectorate is the *Bangwaketse*. Their Chief Bathoen, who is well educated and progressive and who is well supported by his people gave evidence to the Judicial Enquiry against the recognition of Seretse. The third largest tribe in the Bechuanaland Protectorate is the *Bakwena*. Their Chief sent a representative to give evidence against Seretse. The Tribe of the *Barolong* live partly in the Union of South Africa. A certain Mokgaetsi, who frequently acts for the Chief, gave evidence against the recognition of Seretse.

Thus while no doubt some Africans in the Bechuanaland Protectorate support the Kgotla's decision in favour of Seretse, it is clear that there is a strong body of opinion on the other side.

5. The High Commissioner has obtained information concerning African opinion in the other two High Commission Territories of Basutoland and Swaziland, and in the Union. The Paramount Chief and his leading Counsellors in Swaziland informed him that they will support a decision by the United Kingdom Government to refuse recognition to Seretse.

6. Owing to recent events in connection with witchcraft and murder trials, it was considered inadvisable to make a direct

Cabinet conclusions denying Seretse Khama his chieftaincy, 1950

approach to the African Chief of Basutoland, but there is reason to believe that the Basuto would acquiesce in a decision of this nature.

7. Enquiries made by the High Commissioner in the Union indicate that the most prominent Africans there are strongly opposed to the recognition of Seretse. The editors of the two vernacular papers with the widest circulation, and the Chairman of the African political association with the largest membership, have spoken to the High Commissioner strongly against recognition.

8. Moreover, discussions with West African representatives at a Conference in Nigeria recently suggest that African opinion outside southern Africa would either welcome, or at least acquiesce in, a decision not to recognise Seretse. A copy of the relevant telegram is attached.

Reasons Adduced by Judicial Enquiry

9. I have given above the reasons why I accept the findings of the Judicial Enquiry: the reasons adduced by the Enquiry itself are as follows:–

"(a) being a prohibited immigrant in the Union of South Africa, Seretse would be unable efficiently to carry out his duties as Chief;
   (b) a friendly and co-operative Union of South Africa and Southern Rhodesia is essential to the well-being of the Tribe and indeed the whole of the Bechuanaland Protectorate;
   (c) Seretse's recognition would undoubtedly cause disruption in the Bamangwato Tribe."

10. The first reason given by the Enquiry cannot be accepted as valid; since, if Seretse were otherwise suitable, ways and means would have to be found of enabling him to perform his duties as Chief without requiring him to visit Mafeking. It is, of course, eminently desirable, as stated in the second reason,

Appendix K

that the Union and Southern Rhodesia should be friendly and co-operative, and the point is particularly important at present for the reasons given in paragraph 3 (e) above. But if the recognition of Seretse had been desirable on other grounds, the views of the Union and Southern Rhodesian Governments would have had to be carefully considered.

11. I have prepared a White Paper, which gives detailed reasons for my decision, together with copies of the relevant documents. A copy of the draft White Paper is attached.

12. In July, on the advice of my officials, which was endorsed by that of Senator and Mrs. Ballinger,[1] I suggested to the Cabinet (C.M. (49) 47th Conclusions, Minute 8) that Seretse should be asked to come home and relinquish his Chieftainship. The Cabinet rejected the suggestion of such action at that stage, on the grounds that it was open to misrepresentation. If, however, we are now to refuse recognition, it seems eminently desirable that Seretse should not be in the Territory when the decision is announced. I am advised by the Office of the High Commissioner for Basutoland, the Bechuanaland Protectorate and Swaziland that Seretse has indicated in recent conversations that an adverse decision would not surprise him, but that he would in such an event be very hard up. The local authorities consider that he may agree fairly readily to go to London for discussion, and accept the offer of a generous allowance. The local authorities also stress the advantages of an early announcement, since they state that a decision could be announced without serious trouble now when the people are working in their fields and Serowe is comparatively empty, and on the assumption that Seretse is not in the Bechuanaland Protectorate at the time. In view of these advantages I propose to cable to Seretse asking him and his wife to come to this country. On his arrival I would inform him of the

---

[1]Elected by natives of the Union to represent them in the Senate and the Legislative Assembly respectively of South Africa.

decision and offer him an allowance and also help in finding useful employment.

13. In order to make this decision more acceptable, it is also necessary to announce that Tshekedi will not become Chief, nor continue to be Regent. He has, in fact, already indicated that he would give up the Regency once a decision had been announced. The administration of the Reserve will be conducted directly by the Bechuanaland Protectorate Administration for the time being. It is not yet possible to foresee when it will be safe to reconstitute the Native Authority.

14. Before this is done, I think we should have to examine the existing system of native government in the Bamangwato Reserve with some care. At present it leaves much to be desired. The total number of Africans who live in the Bamangwato Reserve and who are under the authority of the Chief of the Bamangwato is 100,000. But the Bamangwato themselves number only 18,000; the rest are so called "allies" who are not represented in the administration. The inhabitants of the Reserve are widely scattered over a territory of 40,000 square miles. In fact very few of them take part in a Kgotla except those who live in the capital, Serowe. Of the 4,000 who attended the Kgotla which endorsed Seretse's Chieftainship in June last more than 90 per cent were from Serowe. I am hoping to introduce a more representative system on the following lines:–

(a) to each of the Chief's representatives in the various districts of the Reserve, a small Council might be attached, the members being drawn from the so-called allied tribes;

(b) there might be regular arrangements for the representation of the outlying districts, at the more important tribal meetings held at Serowe; and

(c) some steps might be taken to explain that the Chief should act on the advice of his Council and not on his own authority.

Appendix K

We have been carrying out some similar reforms in Basutoland and Swaziland. But the Bechuana, like some other African tribes, are intensely conservative and it would be fatal to try to introduce wholesale reforms very quickly. The changes must be introduced gradually, and for this reason it would be unwise to publish full proposals at the present time, since to do so might jeopardise the chances of their eventual acceptance.

15. Immediately after I have seen Seretse, I will make a suitable announcement and publish the White Paper. If Seretse refuses to come, it will be necessary to announce the decision as soon as local arrangements for simultaneous announcement can be made, and for the High Commissioner to remove him from the Bechuanaland Protectorate.

16. It is of the utmost importance that the decision should be announced without delay since:

(a) Dr. Malan has announced his intention to present a demand by the Union Government for the transfer of the High Commission Territories. It would be deplorable if the announcement of our decision not to recognise Seretse should follow this demand and should thus appear to be taken, not on its merits, but under Dr. Malan's pressure. On the other hand, an early announcement might possibly result in a demand for transfer not being presented at all.

(b) Seretse's wife is due to give birth to a child in May or thereabouts. Seretse is unlikely to leave Serowe willingly without her; I am most reluctant to leave them both in Serowe for much longer. An offer of the best medical attention in London in her confinement may prove a strong inducement. If action is not taken in the next two or three weeks it will for this reason have to be postponed until the later summer, and I am convinced that the situation in the Reserve could not be more propitious for the announcement than at present, and may very well become much worse.

(c) The danger of minor disturbances (such as friction between Tshekedi and Seretse over the possession of the Chief's cattle) and possibly of a major outbreak of violence, increases as time goes on.

For all these reasons it is imperative that a decision should be reached immediately; if we delay we may find that the position has deteriorated very seriously and our task may be made much harder.

Summary of Conclusions

17. I, therefore, ask the Cabinet to decide–

(a) that Seretse should not be recognised as Chief;
(b) that Tshekedi should not become Chief and should not be re-instated as Regent;
(c) that these decisions should be published in a White Paper, of which a draft is attached;
(d) that before they are published, Seretse should be invited to come with his wife to London, should be informed of the decision, and should be offered an allowance and other help, provided he does not return to the Bechuanaland Protectorate without the leave of His Majesty's Government;
(e) that the administration of the Bamangwato Reserve should, for the present, be conducted directly by the Bechuanaland Protectorate Administration;
(f) that the system of native Government in the Bamangwato Reserve should by gradual stages, be made more representative.

P.J. N-B.

Commonwealth Relations Office, S.W. 1,
 26th January, 1950

Appendix K

Copy of Telegram Dated 24th January, 1950,
to Sir Evelyn Baring From Clark

While in Basutoland I learned from King, Director of Livestock and Agricultural Services in Basutoland, that at recent conferences at Joss, in Nigeria, he found great interest displayed by West African delegates in question of transfer. It was frequently raised in informal conversation and impression he gained was that they regarded United Kingdom Government's action in the matter as a test of good faith which was very relevant to United Kingdom's promise of eventual self-government for West African colonies.

2. By contrast they did not refer at all to Seretse question until King himself brought it up. Even then they displayed only mild interest, but more than one remarked that Seretse appeared to have acted rather foolishly and irresponsibly.

Appendix L

REPORTS OF MEETINGS WITH THE EXTERNAL "OBSERVERS" AND VARIOUS PUBLIC GATHERINGS DURING AUGUST 1951 ON THE QUESTION OF THE RETURN OF TSHEKEDI KHAMA TO THE BAMANGWATO RESERVE

(Botswana National Archives, DCS 38/2, Ngwato Affairs)

Meeting Held at Sefhare on Tuesday, 7th August, 1951

Brief greeting Ramosamo. District Commissioner introduces Mr. Lipson, the observer, and states that [the] point to be settled at the meeting is that of Tshekedi's return as a private citizen.

Mr. Lipson greets his friends[,] congratulates [them] on beautiful surroundings[, and] states he is not [a] member of Government, but an independent member of Parliament. He stressed that he is an independent member and therefore did not take sides in differences between [the] three parties[.] [I]f he thought a thing right he gave it his support. He hoped that Kgotla would appreciate his independent position. He took no sides for or against Tshekedi Khama. He would not argue with the Kgotla. He wished to find out what their opinion was. He wanted the opinion of all as it was unlikely in an English meeting that all would think alike[.] [I]t might be the same here. They should make it clear, and Observer wished to hear the minority also. In England every one had the right to hold his own views and respected the views of those who differs from it. A man who claims the right to hold a view should give the right to others

Appendix L

whatever views they held they should realise how unfortunate it was that such a quarrel exists. To-day they had to express their views on one question only—Whether Tshekedi Khama should be allowed to come back or not. The shorter the speeches the more would be able to speak. He appealed for a calm spirit, [and] reason as a guide.

Kobe Selika: Greets [the] District Commissioner and guest from [the] British Government. He asked whether they could speak freely.

Observer: Yes.

Kobe Selika: Spoke in the name of Queen Victoria and the tolerant Khama [III].
 I did not expect questions to be approached from this angle. He expected same procedure as in August 18th. Tshekedi Khama explained that he was going to give us Seretse or his bones. That was at Gaberones when Seretse and his wife left for England. He asked whether Seretse or his bones had come. It was difficult for underlings of the tribe to make peace. Tshekedi Khama could only be forgiven by Seretse. The matter was beyond them. The Bamangwato were like bees. The chief was the queen. When the queen was away the bees scattered. The Tribe have scattered. All the people wanted the chief. If one day they could hear that the chief had returned all would unite. If Seretse returns to Bechuanaland Protectorate the church would be in order in peace and church offerings if Seretse were back. He would take the taxes to the District Commissioner and the church collections to the Minister.
 It was difficult to forgive Tshekedi Khama in absence of Seretse. Only the chief could extend forgiveness.
 What they said was let the chief return. Where could they see a good Government, they wanted peace.

Makubu (From Ratholo): I greet our District Commissioner and guest. We are pleased they are before us to-day. We hope the

Observer is listening to the cry of the Tribe. Mention has been made about forgiveness to Tshekedi Khama. I do not feel we are competent to discuss this. Only Seretse can do this. If Seretse is here all this reserve will be in peace. Seretse is the father of the land and of the people. He alone can bring an end to all the noise. Let the Government give a very good ear, we are in difficulties without our chief. He is a born chief. He alone can agree to [the] entrance of Tshekedi Khama. Who are we to be called upon to say anything about forgiveness to Tshekedi Khama. Seretse should deal with Tshekedi Khama's predicament.

Thapelo (from Mangadi): I am glad we can speak freely. This is the practice of the black people. If I have offended my elder brother, what I do is to go to my uncle and tell him to ask for forgiveness from him. Then my uncle goes as intercessor. If a person of no standing acts as intercessor this is regarded as an insult. Tshekedi Khama should ask Seretse for forgiveness and we here do not see how it can be done if Seretse does not agree. All that we want is the chief–Seretse. The fountain of this reserve has dried up. Seretse will do as Kgama [did]. We cannot lay out our feelings regarding Tshekedi. I would be pleased if Tshekedi and Seretse were here and Tshekedi [was] asking forgiveness from Seretse.

Malele (from Rasesa): I greet the District Commissioner and the honourable guest.

District Commissioner: says you have not been asked to forgive Tshekedi Khama. The point is do you wish Tshekedi Khama to come back to the Reserve to live as a private citizen or whether you do not agree [to his return]. That is the point.

Malele: I do not agree. I am not competent to forgive Tshekedi Khama. I want Seretse. Seretse alone is competent to forgive Tshekedi Khama.

Appendix L

Rrakedibeile (Machaneng): I greet the District Commissioner and guest. I am [a] private citizen. I regret [that it is] the Government Officials [who] are here to-day. It would be a good thing if they were put forward by Seretse. If Seretse said my uncle is returning asking for forgiveness–to-day we do not know where these two people are. If they were here we would have something to say. To-day we only speak to the Government. We wish to talk with Seretse to-day. There is nothing we can say [in the absence of Seretse].

Masoka (From Lerala): I am a sub-chief. I greet our District Commissioner and guest. There are two points of issue. They are should Tshekedi Khama come as chief or a private citizen.

District Commissioner: There is only one point. Will you allow him to come as a private person? We cannot say anything different. Tshekedi Khama has been an acting chief and we do not know what happened to bring them [Seretse and Tshekedi] to loggerheads and what took them apart and left us in this chaos. Now I feel I want Tshekedi to come back and bring him to court and ask him what he has done with Seretse. I cannot find out which side to take. I am not swamping. I do not know how they quarrelled. Unless these two [are] brought together and thrashed out it will never be understood by anyone.

Philemon Dipholo (Bobirwa Village): I am a private citizen. I thank our District Commissioner and guest. Concerning Tshekedi and Seretse we love the two of them. Regarding [the] question I say he should be allowed to come. We note here he is not a chief. We want Tshekedi Khama to come to the reserve. We have never said Seretse is not a chief. We know he is chief. Nothing can be said about his claims to the chieftainship. Now we want both of these people. Whether Tshekedi Khama should come as a private individual or not, I say he should. As some people press that he should not and charge laid against him we say we want him as a private individual and not as chief. I do not see why he should be exiled.

Public meetings with the "Observers" on the return of Tshekedi

Boitsheko from Ratholo: I am a sub-chief. I greet the District Commissioner and Government. I come from Batswapong people and follow Tshekedi Khama. I follow Tshekedi Khama because I objected to the European woman; yet I knew Seretse was the chief. Now that the European woman is gone Tshekedi is to come back. He never claimed the chieftainship. No one in this gathering has ever told what Tshekedi Khama has done wrong.

Gontsi of Maefale: I am a private citizen. I greet the District Commissioner and the one who has been delegated by Government. We are here in sorrow. We cannot plough without rain. We die because we are without our chief. We do not want Tshekedi Khama. He went away of his own accord. [Why are we] asked about him[?] He went away of his own accord. Now our administration is at a standstill because of Tshekedi Khama. Now he went of his own accord.

Chupelo of Ratholo: I am the son of the sub-chief. I greet the District Commissioner and the observers. We want Tshekedi Khama to come back. We do not know his fault. I know he left because of the white woman. I followed him because I felt that I did not like the white woman. Now I think he should return because what he went away for is gone, but he should not be back as a chief.

Ramosamo (Chief's Representative): I never heard that the return of Tshekedi was connected with Seretse's wife having left this reserve having been divorced.

Lekgoanyana (Sub-chief from Serowe): Greetings to the District Commissioner and honourable guest. My personal view is that Tshekedi should not be allowed to enter this Reserve without Seretse. We do not know where Tshekedi will settle if he is allowed to return to this reserve. Only Seretse can show Tshekedi the spot where he should settle. It is my first experience that a man is made to come and settle in the land without reference to his Senior.

Appendix L

Modise, Sefhare, Commoner: Greetings to District Commissioner and guest In this affair there are those who have followed Tshekedi as well as Seretse's supporters. Generally we have meetings separately. Seretse has not chased Tshekedi from this reserve. It is surprising that we should speak of a man who left the Reserve of his own accord.

Poison Taunyane, a Commoner: Greetings to District Commissioner and guest from overseas. I did not expect this gathering could be in this form. We expected comfort from our guest i.e. bringing our chief with him and presenting him to us. Tshekedi cannot come before Seretse comes. Tshekedi left this Reserve on his own and we have been discussing this matter for a lengthy period. If Seretse comes, meetings and unrest will come to. Exercise patience in discussing this matter otherwise we will lose our case.

It is not right that we should have been combined with Tshekedi's supporters when discussing this matter.

Keatsile from Mangodi, a commoner: Greetings to the guest from England and Officer Commanding Police.

Ever since the beginning of this talk we never discussed the matter being combined with Tshekedi's supporters. The matter should be settled by vote and not waste time having each and all to speak. Then the guest would be in a position to gauge the feelings of the people by comparing the numbers.

I was present when Tshekedi bade farewell to the tribe at Serowe–and Tshekedi said he was leaving alone although when lorries left some people were loaded.

Kobooatshwene–from Lerala–Junior headman: Pleased to see commoners who have come to us. Sub chief of Lerala died at Rametsana and the village is now in [a] chaotic state.

Tshekedi is the cause of the land being in this state and he left on his own having not been chased by anyone. We can discuss Tshekedi's affair only if Seretse is amongst us.

Public meetings with the "Observers" on the return of Tshekedi

Gaofhatoge Mathiba, Royal Headman: expressing his own mind. I am Tshekedi's follower. Even when we are together and we discuss chieftainship—he renounces having any claim to chieftainship as Seretse is still alive. Our custom is [that] not all things are decided by the chief—all of us have no chief—we are all looking forward to our chief Seretse.

Maun Chief's wife [is] ruling on account of there being no chief yet she is a Morolong. We all want our chief Seretse. We have not followed Tshekedi because he is a chief.

Generally we [can] go and come back and be forgiven.

Quote—Ikitseng left for Bakwena Reserve on his return he was forgiven by Chief Khama. We should not have followed Tshekedi if it had been the question of chieftainship.

Selaelo Madibela, from Mokobeng—Headman: Greeting to those in authority.

Tshekedi has not been chased from this reserve. He has his Senior Seretse—It is regretted that today they are enemies. Tshekedi should have scolded Seretse and then allowed him to come back and be chief. Tshekedi's uncles pointed out that the whole thing was that Tshekedi was arguing [about] chieftainship and not the question of the wife. We pointed out that we are not chasing you but that you are leaving on your own accord. When the Commissioner came to Serowe Tshekedi refused to come and give evidence because the Bamangwato would kill him. The tribe assured the Commissioner that Tshekedi was their child and nothing could happen to him, but he refused. He and Seretse are our Gods.

Owaleng—Rasesa—Commoner: Greetings to District Commissioner and guest. I do not object to Tshekedi but do not want to see Tshekedi before I see Seretse.

Ofhentse, Mangodi, Sub-chief's brother: Greetings to District Commissioner and guest.

I heard some one mention a vote—that man knows that Tshekedi's supporters are in the minority. We stand for the truth

Appendix L

and we all supported Tshekedi [in] that we did not want the white woman. In the process of time there was a division and we stood behind Tshekedi. We should decide and reason and not just because we do not want him.

I am aware that Seretse is my chief. We all want Seretse including Rametsana people. We have no intention of leaving this reserve without having been shown Tshekedi's fault and thus would like Tshekedi to be allowed to return to this reserve.

Tshotego Khumanego, Sub-Chief Mokubeng village: Greetings to District Commissioner and guest.

In my opinion it is difficult to accept Tshekedi. We are underlings and the only person to allow him to come back is Seretse. We do not know what chased Tshekedi from this reserve. It is his duty to bring back Seretse before he returns.

Kganyo, Mangodi, a commoner: Greetings to the authorities. Question—whether Tshekedi to return as chief or private citizen? I say that Tshekedi should return because he was not chief but acting for Seretse. Even when he comes he can still take up his position.

Sebetlela Maifhala, Sub headman at Maifhala village: Greetings to authorities. Rametsana people did not attend the two previous meetings. It is the first time they have come to say they want Tshekedi to come back—Rametsana people are an annoyance to us.

Meeting With the Observers Held at Palapye on 15th August 1951 (Approximately 400 People Present)

(Botswana National Archives, DO 35/4142 74039)

Chairman. Nwako Kederetse, Headman of Palapye Village.

Present. The three Observers, Mr. Bullock, Mr. Lipson and Professor MacMillan and the District Commissioner, Mr. Germond.

Public meetings with the "Observers" on the return of Tshekedi

Before opening the meeting the Chairman informed the observers that he could not proceed as there were 5 Rametsana people present. A discussion ensued between the Chairman and the three observers and it was eventually agreed to ask the Rametsana people to remove themselves which they did without further trouble.

District Commissioner: Mr. Germond introduced the three observers and explained the reason for their visit.

The Observers: Each spoke in turn after which the Chairman asked the meeting to give their views regarding the return of Tshekedi.

Obeseng Dinte, a Headman of Lecheng: Said everything would be wrong if Tshekedi returned. If Tshekedi returns Seretse must be present. He said he wished to emphasize the fact that they wished Seretse to return.

Maruming Maunatala, Headman of Maunatala: It would not be right if Tshekedi returned. It would only be right if Seretse were present to pardon Tshekedi. Our wish is that Seretse should have been present at these discussions and there would have been no trouble which is caused by people saying that Tshekedi will return. We did not drive the Rametsana people away. They can stay where they are and allow us to remain and weep for our Chief.

Morobolo Kebafodile of Palapye: Asked if the Observers knew the Bamangwato Law and Custom. Tshekedi left the Reserve through an argument. He did not leave because of trouble and he left of his own accord. It would hurt if Tshekedi returned without Seretse. Tshekedi is the son of Khama and was a Regent. He started this trouble and left us. To whom will he apologize if he returns. Seretse is the only one to whom he can apologize. This would not be difficult if Seretse were present. If Seretse were present there would be no trouble. There is no one above

Appendix L

Tshekedi except Seretse and we cannot therefore allow him to return as a private person.

Kederetse Nwako, Headman of Palapye: Said I have to second what the previous speakers have said. We have heard what will happen if Tshekedi returns. If a man is born a Chief nothing can prevent him from becoming Chief. If the Chief is not present no one can overlook his brother. If Tshekedi came he would be Chief as he was born as such. Nothing will remove our custom. This is why we ask for Seretse to be present. If Tshekedi returns without Seretse there will be further disturbances and there will be no peace.

Ranaou Ramojarabo of Palapye: If Tshekedi came as a private citizen there would be no peace as Tshekedi was born a Chief and he would have to be recognised as such. If he is allowed to return there will be trouble. You stressed that we should agree to the Rametsana people being amongst us. If we allow these people to come I do not know what they will do. Our view is that both Seretse and Tshekedi should be allowed to return. Seretse is the only man to whom Tshekedi can apologize. You do not speak of Seretse. Our main object is to have Seretse returned to us.

Oetsile Maele, Headman of Gotsu: We want Seretse to return and he can decide upon the return of Tshekedi. Tshekedi can then apologize to Seretse.

Tshupelo Malebelo of Gotsu: Tshekedi cannot return as a private individual, according to our law. He cannot be sent out with a regiment. The only person who can give orders to Tshekedi is Seretse. There will be more trouble if Tshekedi is allowed to return. If you had come with Seretse and referred this matter to him we could have told Seretse our views.

Akanyang Kgoslang of Maunatala: We do not mean to disrespect you. When the Rametsana people have their private discussions they will not meet us. We do not wish to argue with them.

Galatwe Moloi of Palapye: We did not chase Tshekedi nor did Seretse. He went on his own. He was afraid of what he said to Seretse. He said Seretse was married to a coloured. Before he could be questioned and tried by the Tribe he left. We cannot allow him to come. His master, Seretse, must call him. Seretse must come amongst us and gather with you and hear our views in his presence. This is being done by force. We shall not call Tshekedi in the absence of Seretse. If a shepherd allows a lion amongst his sheep his whole flock is exposed.

Ramapaiana Motswagae of Lecheng: The observers are siding with Tshekedi. (Mr. Lipson "We are for justice and fair play and side with no one.") If we do not hear Seretse's name we think that you are one sided. Tshekedi left of his own free will. Before any further disturbances occur let both Seretse and Tshekedi be brought to us.

Nwang Nwako a Sub-Headman of Palapye: Tshekedi has made disorder in the Reserve. We stayed with Tshekedi and respected and loved him. He acted as Regent for his brother's son. We expected Seretse to return and Tshekedi made an explosion. Tshekedi said he was leaving as he was afraid of a white woman. He said he was going to the Bakwena Reserve alone, and then we find a lot of trouble. Tshekedi cannot return except by oppression. If we are not forced Tshekedi cannot return. We say that there were previous banishments. Let Seretse return before Tshekedi as he is the rightful heir. Seretse will tell us of Tshekedi's apology and the Tribe will discuss it and decide that which is right. If the tribe then agrees to his return Tshekedi will return without further trouble. If Tshekedi returns without Seretse, this will be force.

Dotse Chakaloba of Palapye: I am surprised that these Rametsana people were present when it was agreed that they should not attend this meeting. We do not wish to speak of Tshekedi in [the] absence of Seretse.

Appendix L

Mr. Bullock: Closed the meeting by saying that the three observers had listened carefully to all that had been said.

Meeting of Women Held at Central School in the Afternoon of 17th August, 1951

(Botswana National Archives S 529/4)

Present. The District Commissioner Mr. Germond, Mr. Atkins, Sub Inspector B.R. Sands, Mr. Keaboka Kgamane, Manyaphiri Ikitseng Sekgoma & Petlo Sekgoma.

Keaboka Kgamane: I introduce to you women the three guests who have come from England. They are Mr. Bullock, Professor MacMillan and Mr. Lipson. They have come to hear your feelings whether Tshekedi Khama could return as a private individual or not then they will tell you their feelings.

Mr. Bullock: Mr. Chairman, Ladies, I am very glad to see so many of you here. It is so long since I last saw such a scene as this and I would like to say how beautiful you look in your beautiful attire. It seems to me your husbands have more money than I have for you look champion. If I was a member of the Bamangwato Tribe I would feel scared to be in the midst of you women for if you can attempt a march nothing would stop you. I shall go back to England thinking extremely highly of the women of this reserve. It is time your husbands do more work and give your women a rest. We have come six thousand miles to see you people and after listening to some of your husbands it will be quite a refreshing change to hear you. We shall be going back home within a week's time and thinking of this scene of women.

As you know there is a trouble in your tribe and Government have sent us out to you as people who can be relied upon to take no sides in order to find out clearly whether Tshekedi should come back as a private citizen or not. My colleagues and I will be very pleased to hear what you have to say.

Professor MacMillan: Women of Serowe, this is unusual to see so many of you here to-day. We have come a long way to hear the opinion of the women. In one school not very far off from here I once found that there were sixty-six girls to one boy. That should be a very hopeful sign for the future, and I can tell you also that only the other day in the Gold Coast the proportion were the other way round. There were forty-eight boys to one girl. You in any case carry a great deal of the burden in your country and it would be a great privilege to hear what you have to say.

Mr. Lipson: Women of Serowe it is a great pleasure to me as it is to my colleagues to see this very large meeting of the Serowe women and I believe that we can say that to-day you are making history and that not only amongst the Bamangwato but for the whole of Africa and long after this unfortunate quarrel has been forgotten this history will exist.

As you probably know in Britain the women take a very prominent part in Public Affairs and it has been a very good thing that it should be so. When I was a member of Parliament, I was able to listen to many speeches by women of Parliament and they have for the most part done this with merit. They did not make long speeches but made good ones and I believe that it is far more difficult to make a good short speech than it is to make a long one. To-day, this meeting is concerned with the question whether Tshekedi Khama was to return to the Bamangwato Country or not. You women have begun to take part in public affairs and in future you will have to deal with matters greater and more important than in this particular quarrel.

You will see, I am sure, that every thing possible is done to see that your children are given a proper start in life that they may grow up to be worthy citizens and lead them into a future greater than the past. I do not think that any of us can at this particular moment realise the significance of this gathering but I am sure that it is a conference which will greatly affect the future of the tribe. I want to most heartily congratulate you for asking for this meeting and I can assure you that we three observers will give careful consideration to all you have to say. We know that

Appendix L

you women want peace and not war and that [in] all you have to say [you] will bear in mind the great need to heal the wound that now causes this dispute in the tribe. We are looking forward with great interest to what you have to say to us.

Mrs. Rantsabo, Basimaneng Village: I want to ask one question. When you say Tshekedi Khama wants to come back to this country, where is Ruth and where is Tebogo? Tshekedi Khama stated in 1948 that Seretse will never come back to this village and one of his followers spoke and also said that Seretse will not come back. Now we do not see them and our hearts are very sore as women of Bamangwato tribe. There is disturbance in the country and the tribe is not at ease. There is no cure for all this; Seretse is the only cure. In 1948 the Police came and used tear gas on us. Other police were from Rhodesia. We see that if Tshekedi were to return we would be living in great distress. For our child to be brought up in England is not our custom.

Mr. Bullock: The question is one we are not competent to answer. We know as well as you do that Seretse was banished for five years. We just know that that is a fact but we are not able to say any thing about that because we have been sent to find the answer about Tshekedi Khama, and not about Seretse.

Otlotlen Lewakwa: We do not want Tshekedi Khama to come here, whether he comes as chief or not we do not like him to return to this place because Tshekedi Khama left us on his own. He was not ordered out by the tribe. He told us he was going to live in Kweneng. Why does he now want to return. If he returns to whom does he report. It was only right according to we women of Serowe that when Tshekedi returns he should come and ask for an apology and at the time when Seretse returns. During the absence of Seretse, we do not like to receive Tshekedi. He was not banished from the country so let him live at Kweneng.

Sepono O. Makwati: We do not want Tshekedi Khama to return to this country. The bitterness is known by the person who has

Public meetings with the "Observers" on the return of Tshekedi

the sore. It is not because we do not like him. He did not like us and we are afraid of his habits. How can he come as a private individual since he is the son of a king and can change the stone in a sword. He will come back and find representatives of the tribe, namely Keaboka and Petlo and he will not be pleased to be ruled by them. Tshekedi Khama has a hard heart; his weakest judgment even to widowers [widows]. If a widower [widow] can make a fault cattle are taken from her parents and she is thrashed being a woman and at time[s] banished from the country.

Naanie Wapula: We widowers [widows] remember Tshekedi Khama with bitterness and do not want to see his face. He has left us in bitterness. We are not able to carry on our duties because he has left amongst us his followers. All people speak in the same manner in which our chief has been sent away. We are living like people in banishment. We do not want Tshekedi. (At this stage women broke out weeping for some five or ten minutes).

Tshogan Sebona: We do not want Tshekedi Khama. Before I go away I should be glad if the three observers should note our faces of all the women here. We are very sad. When I look at the observer I become more sad because of what has been done by Tshekedi Khama. We do not want Tshekedi altogether. We do not know how we can live with Tshekedi as our child has been banished and Tshekedi Khama is responsible for this action. We are now without our chief because of Tshekedi. We are not free. Once we try to do anything we fail. You should not allow Tshekedi to come back to our country. Do not force Tshekedi on us. We have always worked side by side with Government. We women of Bamangwato, take Government as our protector. Tshekedi said he did not like Seretse's wife. We do not know of any reasons why he does not like Seretse. He said he will go and leave Seretse with his wife. We now notice that [the] Govt. of to-day are different to the Government of old. We request that Rametsana people should be removed from the Government huts. Our Children are like us and think that Government stands for Tshekedi Khama. Government knows that trouble has been for

Appendix L

some time now. We Seretse's followers have done nothing wrong and [what] we say is let the Rametsana people go away.

Senwetsi Molotane: We do not want Tshekedi. We are very sad at heart and we are very much hurt at what Tshekedi has done. He cannot say he will come back as a private individual he being the uncle to Seretse and he knows Native Law and Custom and the direct line of succession. Government knows that our chief is not at fault. Tshekedi told the tribe the chief was going to school and all the time he was misleading the tribe. When the tribe thought that the child was still at school[, Tshekedi] was planning without the knowledge of the tribe to spoil the chieftainship. It would appear that Tshekedi had pre-arranged with Government his father all this for a long time. We are surprised that Government supports Tshekedi. Our Request is that Rametsana people should be taken out of our midst.

Wapula Mabole: We do not want Tshekedi Khama. When Tshekedi left according to his plans he stated that he would divide the village. We now become sad when we hear that Tshekedi will return to this district. He has partly divided the village as he stated. We do not know what it is he wants to do amongst us. Let him remain at Rametsana.

Dikeledi Chaa: I have not much to say. All we say is that we do not want Tshekedi because he left of his free accord and said that he did not like Seretse. According to our law when a chief has left he has left for good. Now that he states that he wants to return as a private person we realise that once he comes he would not agree to bow down to his juniors. We say we do not want him. All women here do not like him. We say this to the observers who have come to find out our feelings. That is all we have to say in this village.

Kolobe Sekwai: We do not want Tshekedi. We as Bamangwato women, if we see him we will manhandle him. We will kill him.

Public meetings with the "Observers" on the return of Tshekedi

Mrs. Shashane: As Bamangwato women we do not want Tshekedi. Tshekedi should not come here. We are very sore at heart. We do not want him. We feel we will kill him.

Mrs. Kgagodi: We do not want Tshekedi. We as Bamangwato women, how can we like Tshekedi when he insulted us. Tshekedi is a hard hearted man and treated us cruelly. He burnt Mmabessie's grave that is why we do not want him. As he stated he had sent our child to school [and] when his Mothers asked when child will come back he [Tshekedi] arrested them and took my father's cattle because he knew that he was one of Sekgoma's children. Secondly, he arrested Kesibonyi because he knew that Kesibonyi was Sekgoma's child and Kesibonyi died in prison. We do not like him from the bottom of our hearts. If we can see him we will kill him and it would not be our faults. He burnt many houses of Sekgoma's children.

Inyatseng Motsamai: I have not much to say. I talk about Tshekedi Khama. I want Seretse and my mother and want to see the child of Seretse.

Ditsinyo Keseanye: It would appear that we have been found fault. We would like somebody else to rule us, whether he will make us sad or happy. We know all about Tshekedi's works which are bad. He sometimes called on the regiment to do his work and the regiment will do his work using our wagons and oxen. In 1947 men were used to go and without food.

Keaitse Molosi: We do not want Tshekedi. Tshekedi stated he looks after widowers [widows]. My cattle have been taken by Tshekedi and I am very sad and I am very sad as to what is said of him that he wants to come back as a private person. We do not want him. If Government brings him by force he may do so but we do not want him. He also thrashes women. Does Government agree to the whipping of women. Is it a good thing? Please do not bring Tshekedi here; we do not like him.

Appendix L

Lebonetse Mooketse: We do not want Tshekedi to return to this place. Even if he comes here once we would be very sad if Government brings him here. We as Bamangwato women never call such big meetings. It is the first time we have such a meeting because of Tshekedi's deeds. We have come so that you may satisfy yourselves that we are not happy. From our history you will see that our forefathers did not know of such big meetings it is only to-day because of this great sadness. He should be made to go away from us and all this crying is caused of sadness in our hearts. Since Seretse left we have not been happy. We request respectfully that we should be forgiven and that Seretse be returned to us. There is poverty and thirst since Seretse left. We are like cattle and I believe that cattle cannot live without a bull because they will never have calves.

Obeditse   ?: We do not want Tshekedi. As we are here our feelings are very much hurt. To-day there is famine in the land and if Seretse were [here] he would help us. If I should meet him being alone I would do some fault. Government does not understand and all rests with Government.

Baraang Seteko: We do not want Tshekedi. We do not want to see his face at all. I shall say to the observers, that according to Seretse's custom when a person has left his home and village and wishes to return he first comes to the Kgotla and asks for an apology. I do not know as Seretse is not present to whom will Tshekedi ask for an apology, because I know he will not go to Keaboka as Keaboka is junior to him. There are many instances of Tshekedi's badness. Tshekedi does not like to see his subject getting rich. As women if you have a lot of corn and you sell your corn, he will say I will buy it from you and give you little money for your corn. He would sell the same corn he bought from you for a higher price. We his subjects obeyed him. He is a cruel chief. To-day he has sent his elder brother's son away because he does not want Seretse to become rich.

Public meetings with the "Observers" on the return of Tshekedi

Lesoo Bathoen: I am going to say this to the observers from England. Now that we have come here as women of the Bamangwato we are very sad. We want Seretse and as you see us here we had hoped that Seretse will be brought from your pockets. We thought you would say here is your chief. We do not want Tshekedi. Tshekedi is no good. He is hard hearted man. How can we speak without a chief because if we try to drive the Rametsana away we are arrested. If you bring our chief we will be free. Through him we can speak against the Rametsana people. If Tshekedi should come we feel we can kill him.

Setefatso Morolong, Mahalapye: We do not want Tshekedi. He did not like us from the beginning. We as Mahalapye women sustained injuries through Tshekedi's followers. Police came to us armed. We do not want him. If we see Tshekedi we will [not] do our work.

Alleta Yona, Mahalapye: We do not want Tshekedi. Since I was born I have not seen a person being forced not to take a woman he loves. The woman is not his but Seretse's. I do not know if any of the observers know of a case where a man leaves his own country just because somebody has married the woman he loves.

Mr. Lipson: I do not know of any such case.

Alleta Yona: This has surprised me more for Tshekedi to go away and leave his country because of a woman he does not like. The truth is, he did not like Seretse. Now that he intends to come back to whom is he coming to. We are determined to die for Seretse. We have taken a strong decision and we are not afraid of death. Even our dogs do not like him; even our fowls do [not] like him, not even our stock like him.

Keaboka Kgamane: I hope your words have been heard by the observers. They are leaving and expect to arrive at Mahalapye before Sun-set. This is your Memorandum which you have asked me to give to them. I shall hand it over to them now.

Appendix L

Mr. Bullock: We thank you and every one of those who have spoken. We have taken careful note of what you have said, and what you have said will, with all the speeches we have here taken inside the Reserve take a very big part in our report which we feel very proud to tell the Prime Minister. We shall also tell them of the splendid women we have met. As you have expressed your sadness to us, you indeed have made us feel very sad. We hope that these difficulties will fade away and peace will once again be with you. As we shall be leaving we bid you good-by and may God bless you.

Appendix M

REPORTS OF "OBSERVERS" ON THE ATTITUDE
OF THE BAMANGWATO TRIBE TO THE RETURN
OF TSHEKEDI KHAMA TO THE
BAMANGWATO RESERVE (1951)

Joint Report* by
Mr. H.L. Bullock and Professor W.M. Macmillan

BACKGROUND

In July last we were asked by the Secretary of State for Commonwealth Relations to undertake a mission in the Bamangwato Reserve of the Bechuanaland Protectorate. The object of our mission is best set out in the following extract from a letter addressed to us by Mr. Gordon Walker on July 20th.

> As I have explained in the House of Commons the purpose of your visit is to report on the single question of the attitude of the tribe to Tshekedi Khama's return to the Bamangwato Reserve as a private individual.
> As I also told the House I intend to invite the Bamangwato tribe to hold a special kgotla under the presidency of an impartial person in order to establish

---

*This paper was presented by the Secretary of State for Commonwealth Relations to Parliament by Command of His Majesty, December 1951. It was published in *Botswana Notes and Records* (Gaborone: The Botswana Society), Volume 10, pp. 137-48 with the kind permission of Mrs. Macmillan.

Appendix M

their view on this question. I will cause my invitation to the tribe to hold this kgotla to be presented to them at a meeting with tribal representatives in your presence. I have made it clear to the House that in my view this kgotla should be attended by Tshekedi Khama and his followers.

I hope you will use your best endeavours and all the weight of your influence to persuade the tribe to agree to hold such a kgotla and to re-emphasize to them that Tshekedi Khama has renounced all claims to the chieftainship. I would be grateful for your views and advice on details of arrangements for the holding of this kgotla. Any decisions that have to be taken must of course be mine but I shall much value your advice and recommendations. Please do not hesitate to consult and advise me on any matters you wish at any stage of your visit.

I of course leave to your judgement any steps besides the holding of the kgotla that you may decide to take to ascertain for yourselves the views of the tribe on the question at issue and to consult with neighbouring chiefs and any other people you may wish to see. You may count on the full co-operation of my officers in any such steps that you may see fit to take and in all other ways.

The circumstances in which the issue of Tshekedi Khama's return to the Bamangwato Reserve came before Parliament are well known and need be recorded here only very briefly.[1] For 26 years 1923-49 Tshekedi Khama had ruled the Bamangwato people

---

[1] Further information may be found in Mary Benson, *Tshekedi Khama* (London: Faber and Faber, 1960); in Botswana National Archives File S. 529/1/1-4; S.535/12/1-3; S.599/1-13; and in S.M. Gabatshwane, *Tshekedi Khama of Bechuanaland: Great Statesman and Politician* (London: Oxford University Press, 1961).

as regent for his nephew Seretse Khama, the heir to the chieftainship. During all these years Tshekedi had been in the position of father and mentor to Seretse and had cared for his affairs within the Reserve. Differences arose between them over Seretse's marriage in 1948. The tribe also was divided on this matter and at the instance of Tshekedi, a series of kgotlas was held to discuss his position.

Later a judicial commission was appointed to inquire into the circumstances that had arisen. In consequence of that commission, it was decided by the Secretary of State that the chieftainship should be held in abeyance for five years and that Seretse Khama should for that period be required to live outside the Bechuanaland Protectorate. At the same time Tshekedi Khama was required to live outside the Bamangwato Reserve. These decisions, and the reasons for them, are recorded at length in the White Paper (Cmd. 7913) published in March 1950.

During the years of his regency, Tshekedi had cared for the cattle and other property that appertained to the chieftainship, to himself and to Seretse. In 1950 an effective distribution of this property was made. It is understood that, in fact, this distribution has given rise to disputes between the tribe, representing the chief, and Tshekedi, but such disputes will be a matter for the courts and do not concern this mission.

Since his departure, Seretse Khama has apparently experienced no difficulty in leaving his property within the Reserve to be managed by one Keaboka, fourth senior member of the chiefly family, who has since been nominated by the tribe as its leading representative and its 'messenger' for the purpose of dealing with Government. Tshekedi, on the contrary, has not found it possible to leave his property to the care of a representative and in 1950 sought and obtained the permission of the High Commissioner for a series of visits to the Reserve for the purpose of managing his affairs. These visits were made the subject of representations to the High Commissioner by representatives of the tribe, it being alleged that his presence in the Reserve was repugnant to the tribe, which was disturbed as to the intentions of both Tshekedi and Government. It is understood that the Secretary of State

Appendix M

entered into prolonged negotiations with the intention of arriving at an accommodation with Tshekedi Khama that would secure to him adequate control of his property and yet be acceptable to the tribe. Those negotiations failed and the Secretary of State thereafter decided that the interest of peace and good order within the tribe demanded the re-enforcement of the exclusion order against Tshekedi Khama. Thereafter Tshekedi, having publicly renounced all claim to chieftainship, demanded the right of free access to the Reserve as a private individual. The issue found its way to Parliament, in order to satisfy which the Secretary of State offered to send observers to the Protectorate to report on the true state of feeling within the Reserve.

The Bamangwato Reserve has an area of 40,000 square miles and a population roughly estimated to be 100,000 people. Of these only rather less than 20,000 belong to the Ngwato tribe proper, the remainder having from time to time broken away from their original tribes and affiliated themselves with the Ngwato tribe and acknowledged its supremacy. The Reserve is divided into nine districts, the chief of which is that surrounding Serowe, which is also the capital of the Reserve. The Serowe district is the stronghold of the Ngwato tribe proper, but a number of its members reside in the several districts and are normally amongst the most influential persons in them. The dominance of the Ngwato is ultimately due to the genius of Khama (1875-1923) who made his kingdom a rallying point for tribes scattered over a huge area in times when security was threatened from the North by raiding Matabele and from the south East by the encroachment of European farmers. Khama's protection of the lesser tribes was made more effective by the backing he himself enjoyed from the Government of his great patron, Queen Victoria. Yet at that time and even later, the protecting Government was in no position to assume what has come to be known as 'direct' rule over this vast territory, so that from the beginning the Protectorate administration came to rely even for the maintenance of law and order almost entirely on the discipline enforced, until 1923 by Khama, and latterly by the Regent Tshekedi. In consequence of this, native custom has been distorted and the power of the Chief raised considerably above any checks traditionally exercised by the people of the tribe on the chief's autocracy.

It was the great achievement of Khama's system that the rule he imposed through Bamangwato Representatives with the backing of the 'regiments' from Serowe and ultimately of His Majesty's Government was loyally accepted and still is by the out-lying dependents. More than once some of us were corrected and told not to speak or think, e.g., of Bakalaka or Bakalanga, since all claim to be Bamangwato. Even if they have made little material progress these people were wisely allowed to retain their own tribal headmen and they continue to speak four or five distinct languages.

The Reserve, and all its people, are normally ruled by the chief, who occupies his position by right of birth. To each district he nominates a person known as the chief's representative who rules on his behalf. The system is Khama's, and the agents of the system, though they may constitute something like a civil service, were and still are drawn largely, though not now exclusively, from the members of Khama's family, being thus undoubtedly also a privileged aristocracy. Their office clearly brings some profit as well as social prestige and they are intensely conscious and jealous of their order of precedence. In spite of the great almost untracked distances this ruling class maintains close links with each other and with Serowe, where they frequently gather for meetings, and where as a result, tribal politics often have the intensity and ferocity of a village dispute. The unity of the tribe is nevertheless something very real and jealously guarded even if the system is thus aristocratic and, although not exclusively, autocratic. Certainly it admits of no organized opposition: to stand out against the ruling power on any major issue is to be guilty almost of treason.

Yet there are certain checks upon the use of power by the chief. The first of these is the kgotla, a meeting at which, in theory, every male adult member of the tribe has the right to attend and to be heard. (We return to the point that the recent exclusion of Tshekedi's supporters is based on the ground that they have transferred their allegiance to another tribe, the

Appendix M

Bakwena.) Such kgotla meetings may take place at the village or district level, but it is accepted that all the great affairs of the tribe are discussed and determined in the presence of chief's representatives and tribal headmen in formal kgotla at Serowe. No vote is normally taken at such meetings. When all who wish have spoken, the chief, or person presiding on his behalf, assesses the feeling of the meeting and announces his decision. In theory, as Tshekedi Khama himself had lately claimed, that decision may be his own and need not accord with the feeling of the meeting; in practice a strong chief can possibly go contrary to the views of the majority. The meeting in kgotla, is, however, an essential part of the system of native rule and is accorded much respect by the Bamangwato, as by other tribes of the Protectorate.

The second check upon the absolute rule of the chief is the devotion to tradition and to precedent embodied in the complex and unrecorded system of native law and custom. Tshekedi himself told us it is 'case law'. Arguments may and do arise as to the particular application of native law and custom (e.g. as to the present claims of Tshekedi Khama), but custom is certainly a restraining force of some potency.

The Chieftainship of the Bamangwato has remained with the house of Khama, to which both Tshekedi and Seretse belong and which has included among its members some very remarkable Africans. Of these last Tshekedi Khama is acknowledged to be one, but all members of the very large royal family, whatever their personal merits, are to be reckoned with as people of influence.

The foregoing represents, in brief outline, the organisation of the tribe as it has existed for many years. It should be recorded that in recent months the Administration has been engaged, we understand with success, upon a series of reforms designed to establish more firmly the democratic principle. The intention is to establish councils on a more democratic model comprising representatives nominated by the village kgotlas in each district of the Reserve, these councils being advisory to the chief's representatives, who would themselves be nominated by the district kgotlas and confirmed by the full, i.e., tribal, kgotla at Serowe. The district councils would in turn send representatives to a central council at Serowe which would in due course become the constituted Native Authority, and in effect the executive, or working, committee of the tribal kgotla. In these reforms members of the subsidiary or 'allied' tribes were to have equal standing with members of the Ngwato and, in fact, a number of them had been nominated both as chief's representatives and council members. All progress on these reforms ceased when the future of Tshedeki Khama came before Parliament. Then, as is well known, disturbances occurred within the Reserve.

Moves Towards a Joint Kgotla

We arrived in the Reserve on July 27th and were met by the High Commissioner and officials of the Administration who most willingly placed themselves at our disposal and helped us in every way without in any way interfering with our judgement concerning the things we desired to find out. Indeed, we had made our minds up from the time of the appointment that nothing should prevent us from coming to our own conclusions; we made this quite clear to everyone concerned and it was appreciated by them.

We immediately addressed ourselves to the task of securing agreement to a special meeting of the tribe in kgotla with Tshekedi Khama and his supporters present. It had been hoped that the invitation to convene such a kgotla would be extended, and the arrangements for it discussed, at a meeting attended by representatives of both the tribe and Tshekedi (the latter had not himself yet returned to Africa). We were informed that the tribal representatives had resolutely refused to attend such a meeting and we perforce agreed to see the parties separately. We saw representatives of the tribe on July 29th and the supporters of Tshekedi, headed by Rasebolai, on July 30th. On each occasion the invitation to take part in the joint kgotla was extended on behalf of the Secretary of State by the High Commissioner (on July 29th by Sir Evelyn Baring, and after his departure, on the 30th by Mr. R.E. Turnbull). On the morning of the 29th the tribal representatives merely welcomed us as their guests and said that they were empowered to listen but not to answer. They

Appendix M

agreed to meet us again, for informal discussion, in the afternoon, but, in the event, maintained the same attitude. They would not give us a precise date for their reply but, upon our representations of urgency, promised that it would be soon. On July 30th the supporters of Tshekedi welcomed the proposal for a joint kgotla and promised their full co-operation. It can be stated that on that occasion and at every subsequent one of our meetings, the supporters of Tshekedi gave every evidence of desiring to face their opponents at a joint meeting. It was clear that our difficulties in arranging it would lie only with the established representatives of the tribe.

We also had informal talks with the lawyers representing both sides of the dispute stressing all the time the need for a large tribal kgotla with both sides present and taking part in the discussions so that we could obtain a free, fair and independent expression of opinion on the issue before us.

Meanwhile, on July 30th, a meeting stated to be representative of the tribe had been convened in kgotla at Serowe and a reply on behalf of the tribe to the Secretary of State's invitation reached us through the District Commissioenr on July 31st. The reply was to the effect that the tribe regretted that only under the presidency of Seretse, Tshekedi's one senior in the tribe, would it be possible under Bamangwato law and custom to permit Tshekedi's presence. It went on to suggest that the interest of all would be best served if we agreed to travel throughout the Reserve and make direct contact with the people in the villages and towns.

At our invitations a small deputation, led by Keaboka, visited us informally on the morning of the 1st August. They enlarged to some extent upon the reasons for the refusal (these reasons will be discussed later in this report) but were clearly unwilling to amend their attitude.

The refusal was firm, but we were not then disposed to accept it as final. It was nevertheless obvious that any process of persuasion would be prolonged and might even then be unsuccessful. It therefore appeared to us the wiser course to adopt, as an interim measure, the suggestions of the tribal representatives for a series of district meetings, in arranging which they were prepared to co-operate. It seemed, indeed, that quite apart from the knowledge we would gain of the Reserve and its people a programme of such meetings might be the best means of establishing confidence in our mission and thereby persuading the representatives of the tribe of the wisdom of holding a joint kgotla.

In the ensuing nine days we travelled an aggregate of 1,500 miles and were present, either together or separately, at 8 meetings attended by perhaps 4,000 members of the tribe. Before our departure the tribal representatives, though they could not agree to a joint kgotla with Tshekedi present, said they would not offer objection to the presence at such local meetings of any of Tshekedi's supporters who lived in, or happened to be present in, the several localities. In fact, supporters of Tshekedi appeared at only four of these earlier meetings. At Mahalapye some 30 of them appeared before our arrival, but the reaction of the gathering was so antagonistic that they had no choice but to leave under police protection. At Madinare nine of Tshekedi's supporters and at Bobonong one appeared; in both cases the people refused to proceed with the meeting until after they had departed. At Sefhare (claimed by Tshekedi to be a center where support for him is strongest) 30 Tshekedi men, some of them from Rametsana, sought to attend the meeting at which 300 persons were present. Mr. Lipson intervened in their behalf and in this instance the headman allowed them to remain. It is significant of the weight of influence attaching to rank that Tshekedi himself presently claimed that his Sefhare supporters owed this immunity to the seniority enjoyed by their foremost leader.

The meetings were most successful in the interest they attracted. At all times the tribesmen were most polite and courteous, making us welcome, but they also made overwhelmingly clear their attitude to Tshekedi. This they did not by vote so much, although in one or two instances votes were taken, but by methods reminiscent of a Quaker meeting, i.e., after many speeches from the tribe the headman expressed the spirit of the meeting. Often it was pointed out to us that the question we were putting had been answered by the tribe more than once or

Appendix M

twice before and they had given clear and definite answers which left no room for doubt.

On Friday, 10th August, we all three reassembled at Mahalapye and resumed our efforts to persuade the tribal representatives to agree to the holding of a joint kgotla. In those efforts we were supported by the Administration. On the morning of 11th August the High Commissioner met some 60 of the representatives and in the afternoon we saw the same people. Both meetings were unsuccessful and at the second the tribal representatives went so far as to suggest that if they were pressed further on the point they would be unable to continue their co-operation with us, even limited as it was to district meetings.

Time had begun to press and it was necessary for us to consider the recommendations we could make to the Secretary of State as to the proposed joint kgotla and our further programme. In the event, we advised the Secretary of State, strongly and unanimously, that the effort to secure a joint kgotla should be abandoned. In doing so we further expressed our unanimous and unqualified opinion that the alternative programme of investigation upon which we were engaged would give us all the opportunity we needed to arrive at a true valuation of the views of the people of the Reserve on the one question that was before us. Our reasons for making these recommendations may be summarized as follows:

1) The smaller informal district meetings which we had attended and which, as stated above number in the aggregate some 4,000 persons, had been a success in that we had been able to make intimate contact with the rank and file of the tribe, many of whom freely expressed their opinions in open debate.

2) The freshness of discussion at these meetings and the variety of speakers had been such as to rule out the possibility of wholesale previous direction. It is true that the failure to arrange for a joint kgotla meant that Tshekedi Khama had had no opportunity to state his case in person to the people of the Reserve and that, consequently, we had had no opportunity to observe their reactions to such a personal statement. It is not for us to hazard conjecture as to the effect upon the tribe of a statement of his case by so compelling a personality as Tshekedi Khama, but we

have no hesitation in recording our conviction that in their present mood the people of the Reserve would not, in fact, give him a hearing.

3) To force the joint kgotla against the wishes of the tribal representatives would almost certainly be answered with a boycott by their supporters. The ability of the tribe to boycott a meeting had been effectively demonstrated in 1950, and we decided that a kgotla summoned in such circumstances, attended as would be likely only by Tshekedi and his supporters, would in no way advance the primary purpose of our mission. More was likely to be gained from the meeting, already arranged, with Tshekedi and his people on his own ground, where there would be no opposition and no difficulty for him in securing the attendance of his supporters.

4) Again, we had already received evidence of such strong feeling within the tribe that we could not ignore the possibility that, even if a joint kgotla could be arranged, emotions might gain the upper hand and the kgotla end in disorder.

5) Finally, although we had faithfully undertaken the task imposed upon us by the Secretary of State of seeking to secure a joint kgotla, it was the case that native law and custom would make a full tribal kgotla essential only if a decision were required from the tribe. Our mission was only to assess the state of feeling within the tribe and our ability to do this in one large formal kgotla might actually be restricted.

In making these recommendations we received the full support of the High Commissioner and the Administration. On Tuesday, 14th August, we learnt that the Secretary of State had accepted our recommendations and had decided that the intention to hold a joint kgotla could be abandoned in favour of our alternative programme of investigation.

Alternatives to the Joint Kgotla

On Monday, 13th August, we met Tshekedi Khama at Rametsana, the locality within the Bakwena Reserve just south of the Bamangwato border, to which he had retired in 1949 and to

Appendix M

which Seretse's father had been exiled by his own father many years before. We held three private meetings with Tshekedi and attended a public meeting of fully 200 of his supporters at which Chief Kgari of the Bakwena was also present. Tshekedi repeated the arguments which have become so familiar in interested circles in London. He expressed the belief that if he were allowed into the Bamangwato Reserve he could ensure a joint kgotla. As we state elsewhere in this report, remembering how the High Commissioner's meeting was boycotted in 1950, we did not share his confidence.

On 15th August we were present at yet another district meeting at Palapye. A number of Tshekedi's supporters sought to attend, but their presence was resented by the mass of the people and the headman asked us to arrange for them to leave before the meeting could proceed. Appeals failed to move the people, and after some discussion between ourselves we agreed that since it was their own meeting the Headman himself must take responsibility for asking them to go.

On Thursday, 16th August, we held our final meeting in the Reserve, at the capital, Serowe. This was a most impressive gathering of between 5,000 and 6,000 people, presided over by Keaboka as leading tribal representative, who had also invited a small European population of Serowe to be present as witnesses. Keaboka did not himself address the meeting except as Chairman to introduce us and state our object. If there were nominated speakers among those taking part there were certainly more who spoke extempore and took their chance among the many who wished to speak. The refusal to agree to a joint kgotla was forcefully explained and on two occasions, by loud and spontaneous acclamation, the meeting left no doubt as to the general feeling on the subject of Tshekedi's return. No recognized followers of Tshekedi were present and none sought to attend.

In the afternoon of the same day we met and talked with more than 1,000 women of the tribe, a succession of whom passionately and even threateningly elaborated the theme "we do not want Tshekedi back". (Women, too, were the ringleaders in the disturbance at Mahalapye that made it impossible for

Tshekedi's small band of supporters to state their case at our meeting). This we note as a novel departure in local custom, since it is not the women's habit to engage in political discussion. That they should have done so on this occasion is evidence of the strong emotion they feel on the subject of the present dispute.

On the 17th August at Gaberones, we met, in the morning, some of the leading Europeans in the Protectorate, members of the European Advisory Council. In general they confirmed our interpretations of views expressed at the tribal meetings. They were helpful especially about the economic background, an important aid to understanding, but outside the scope of this report.

In the afternoon we met chiefs of other tribes in the Protectorate, with their leading advisers, in all some 26 members of the Protectorate African Advisory Council. It is of interest that this Council were strongly of [the] opinion that full discussion demanded the presence of both parties to the dispute, expressing regret that the Bamangwato representatives failed to accept the invitation to attend. Tshekedi was present, and the fact that those who spoke did so in his favour is perhaps a tribute to his great personal magnetism, but it also reflected the preoccupied concern of the speakers for the rights and privileges of chiefs and chiefly families.

There was also made available to us for questioning a panel of respected Africans versed in native law and custom. It is evidence of the difficulty of interpreting custom that Tshekedi objected to all three members of this panel (one of whom is an expert constantly used in the Courts) but by this we were not greatly moved since there was now little that we had need to refer to them.

We then left the Bechuanaland Protectorate for Swaziland, where on Monday, August 21st we had the pleasure of meeting Sobhuza, Paramount Chief of the Swazi Nation, and his Council. The Paramount Chief, a very distinguished African, strongly urged that the Bamangwato dispute in all its aspects be submitted to a conference of leading Africans. On a major issue, however, he

Appendix M

was skeptical about the very possibility of Tshekedi returning to the Reserve as 'a private citizen.'

Conclusion

In pursuing our task many matters came to our attention but only upon one, the views of the people of the Reserve on this question of the return of Tshekedi Khama as a private individual, are we called to judge. On this one question we have no hesitation in declaring that the return of Tshekedi Khama in any capacity whatsoever at the present time and in the present circumstances would be contrary to the wishes of the majority of the tribe and bitterly resented by a substantial number. On this issue emotions now run dangerously high throughout the tribe.

Only on one condition, that Seretse Khama were present to preside, would the people agree to hear Tshekedi. That possibility is outside our terms of reference.

The main reason advanced to us, at our many hearings, for the refusal to hold a joint kgotla in the presence of Tshekedi was this: that Tshekedi, having left the Reserve and declared his allegiance to the Bakwena tribe, had thereby surrendered his right to take part in Bamangwato tribal discussions, and that by departing from native law and custom so far as to permit his return to attend a tribal kgotla, they would open the way to a resumption by him, by the mere force of tradition, of all the authority that previously pertained to him as the senior member of the tribe second only to Seretse. This argument rests upon the claim that by native law and custom Tshekedi's presence in a tribal kgotla would make him again a member of the tribe, and the rest would inevitably follow. We do not regard it as incumbent upon ourselves to pronounce upon this question of native law and custom. It is sufficient to state that it is the view clearly and strongly held by the tribe. To them 'private citizenship' is impossible to a man of royal rank.

In fact, the mass of the tribe reject Tshekedi Khama's declaration of his renunciation of all claim to the chieftainship. In their view, whatever the intentions of Tshekedi, once he was again

Report of the "Observers" on the return of Tshekedi Khama

received as a member of the tribe, his claim to seniority within the tribe would be inalienable, even by himself. It is their contention that in making his renunciation, Tshekedi Khama was appealing to a British way of thought, and one that he knew to be foreign to the Bamangwato.

It must be recalled that the present division in the tribe arose not from Tshekedi's going but from Seretse Khama's defiance of tribal opinion by marrying as he did in September 1948 without the tribal sanction that custom demanded. The division only became palpable after June 1949 when, in the kgotla meeting called by himself, Tshekedi suffered political defeat. In this connection, we were impressed by the evidence that Tshekedi's action in leaving the Reserve was indeed "strictly in accordance with tribal law and custom." He then appeared to accept and act on the tradition that there is no place for an opposition party within the tribe and at the tribal kgotla and that a defeated leader can only "retire to his cattle post" or, preferably, banish himself altogether.

If Western phraseology is at all applicable Tshekedi's Government suffered a parliamentary defeat on a vote of confidence. It appears to the tribe, therefore, that Tshekedi's demand for re-admission to the Reserve goes back on his former decision and is an attempt to climb back to power, with his ministers, with the backing of the Bechuanaland Protectorate Administration and His Majesty's Government. It has even been suggested that the true analogy is to be found in Charles the First's dealing with his Parliament.

At this point the conventions of the tribal aristocracy and hierarchy, and especially their general acceptance by the people, gravely complicate the issue. At every meeting we attended it was obvious how every man knows his own station, from the lowest to the highest, and it is particularly at the highest levels that this matters. Genealogical tables are readily available making clear (what every tribesman knows) the present rank in the hierarchy of the almost innumerable individuals of the Royal family—Seretse is No. 1, Tshekedi No.2, Rasebolai (Tshekedi's right hand) No. 3— having been 'ordered' out of Serowe by the tribal representatives

Appendix M

was eventually bowed out with salutations of *'Nkosi'* (Chief). At every point we were met by the argument that these Royal rights are an inalienable birth-right.

The chief fear is that if Tshekedi returns in the absence of a superior he will and must step as of right into the position of Chief and bring about a counter-revolution–and this in spite of what amounted to his constitutional displacement by the kgotla in 1949. It is in fact impossible to conceive of Tshekedi "as a private citizen" so long at least as the Serowe kgotla is the dominant factor in Bamangwato politics. If he is at liberty to attend he automatically becomes its chairman and ruler and he has himself gone so far as to claim that, by custom the decision of the kgotla is the decision of the president alone.

In the course of our investigations we were faced with a series of personal grievances, some of them dating from many years past, against Tshekedi. After 26 years of personal rule personal grudges were perhaps to be expected. There can be no doubt of the great administrative ability shown by Tshekedi Khama in the past, nor that he has great ambitions for the Bamangwato tribe. We received an impression, nonetheless, that if only for want of effective administrative machinery, Tshekedi's personal exercise of power paid little regard to the individual and his rights. It is significant that the spokesmen of the allied tribes in the 'back blocks' were solid with those elsewhere in their expressed opposition to the return of Tshekedi. In their eyes even his laudable work for the Bamangwato Secondary School at Moeng involved them chiefly in the payment of a heavy cattle levy which left so much less revenue for the establishment or development of schools needed in their own localities. Clearly wishing to continue to enjoy greater freedom to manage their own affairs the people now fear the return of this powerful personality.

We would record also that we have received ample evidence that this hostile feeling extends in lesser but still large part, to the leading supporters of Tshekedi, the so-called Rametsanas. It is our view that this feeling is one of such strength that the Administration may have to give this minority positive protection. Although the emotional storm makes it hard to judge the number of those who would in different circumstances be prepared to follow Tshekedi, there is no doubt that his active supporters include a high proportion of the ablest and administratively most experienced members of the Bamangwato and that their permanent exclusion from the Reserve would represent an impoverishment of the tribe.

Perhaps our overriding impression is this: that the greatest need of the people of the Bamangwato Reserve is a period of peace to go about their everyday affairs freed from the distraction of continuing disturbances resulting from consideration of the affairs of members of the chiefly house.

Report by D. L. Lipson

The purpose of the visit of the three observers to the Bamangwato Reserve was to find out and report on one question only: whether the tribe was in favour of the return of Tshekedi to the Reserve as a private individual or not, he having renounced all claims to the chieftainship.

It was originally hoped to obtain this information by the summoning of a special kgotla to be held at the capital, Serowe, which Tshekedi and his supporters would attend. We were to convey to the tribe who were opposed to Tshekedi and urged them to accept the Secretary of State's invitation. They answered that before giving their reply they must consult those whom they represented in the various districts from which they had come. Subsequently they declined the invitation. The reason they gave was that it would be contrary to 'native law and custom'; to hold such a meeting. Tshekedi, they said, had left the Bamangwato and gone to the Bakwena tribe to whom he now owed allegiance and paid taxes; he could not, therefore, take part in a kgotla of the Bamangwato. They declared that they were at war with the supporters of Tshekedi and could not agree to sit down at a meeting with them.

Our approach to the representatives of the supports of Tshekedi, whom we next met, resulted in an immediate acceptance

Appendix M

of the Secretary of State's invitation. They welcomed, and to the end continued to ask for, a joint kgotla.

The representatives of the tribe, in refusing the Secretary of State's invitation, said that they were willing for us to move freely throughout the Reserve and to attend kgotlas in the districts. These would enable us to ascertain the views of the tribe on the questions of Tshekedi's return.

We decided that it would be unwise at this stage to press our request for a special joint kgotla lest it might lead to the tribal representatives being unwilling to co-operate with us in the holding of the district kgotlas. They had already told us that if a special joint kgotla was summoned by the District Commissioner, who was the legal Native Authority, they would boycott it, as they had done on a previous occasion. We should then be faced with the presence of only Tshekedi and his supporters and that would not serve the purpose of our mission. We hoped, however, that if the district kgotlas were a success and we were able to convince the tribal representatives, as a result of better acquaintance with us, that we were what we claimed to be—independent observers, not concerned with taking sides as to whether Tshekedi should return or not, but only anxious to obtain the true view of the tribe as a whole on this matter—that they might later be willing to reconsider their decision against a joint kgotla.

We then decided that in order to cover the whole Reserve it would not be possible for the three observers to attend all the district kgotlas, so agreed to go separately on tour and each one of us take his share of the meetings.

Before doing this we held a tribal meeting at Mahalapye at which all three of us were present and spoke and heard the views of those present.

At only one of the district kgotlas, that at Sefhare, were supporters of Tshekedi allowed to be present, and there it was in consequence of a special appeal made to the headman. At this meeting the 300 present included 40 supporters of Tshekedi, some of whom spoke and were heard without interruption by the rest.

These district kgotlas had this advantage: many of the speakers described themselves as private individuals. In this way we were enabled to obtain the view of the rank and file. At a special kgotla the speeches would have been made by the leaders only.

All the same the district kgotlas were only a second best. Nothing could help us so much to form a true opinion of the views of the tribe as a joint kgotla at which both parties to the dispute were present and were able freely to express their views.

On our return from tour we made a further attempt to secure a joint kgotla. An appeal was made to 60 representatives of the tribe but they persisted in their refusal.

We three observers then went to Rametsana to meet Tshekedi and 200 of his supporters who were there with him. We had three meetings with Tshekedi personally and one with his supporters. He and other speakers declared that he renounced all claims to the chieftainship, had committed no crime, all that he asked for was permission to return to the Reserve as a private individual and look after his own personal affairs. (He is the owner of a large number of cattle, the majority of which are in the Reserve, and maintained that their proper care required his personal visits to the cattle posts in the Bamangwato territory.) He asserted that he had been banished without trial not by the tribe but by the British Government.

The Rametsana meeting was followed by two others, one at Palapye and the other at Serowe. At the former, attended by about 400, the headman insisted on the exclusion of five Tshekedi supporters who had come there. A strong protest was made against their exclusion, but efforts to secure their attendance did not succeed, and the meeting proceeded without them.

The exclusion here and at other meetings of supporters of Tshekedi was proof of intimidation. It is true that the number excluded was small but it is reasonable to suppose that there were many other supporters of Tshekedi who were afraid to attempt to attend meetings because they feared violent treatment from their opponents.

The Serowe meeting was the largest we had attended. There were over 5,000 present. A final appeal was made there for a joint kgotla. It was pointed out to those present that large and

Appendix M

important as the meeting was, it was not the kgotla which the Secretary of State had hoped would take place because it was representative of only one side. The appeal fell on deaf ears. There can be little doubt that the representatives of the tribe had made up their minds before we entered the Reserve not to accept the Secretary of State's invitation to a joint kgotla. They paid no heed to the arguments used in favour of acceptance. In my opinion one reason for their refusal was their fear of the influence the presence of Tshekedi and his supporters at a joint kgotla might have in winning over some of their supporters to his side. The experience of the meeting at Sefhare showed that it was possible for supporters of Tshekedi to be present at a kgotla and speak without fear of violence, if the leaders gave their consent to their being present. The blame, therefore, for the refusal to hold a joint kgotla rests entirely on the representatives of the tribe. I believe that if they had agreed to a joint kgotla, their followers would have accepted their decision.

In the afternoon we attended a meeting of the women of Serowe at their special request. This was a unique event since the kgotlas were attended only by the male population; women had never before held such a meeting. Between 1,200 and 1,500 women came to the meeting and many of them spoke. They pursued the same anti-Tshekedi line which we had heard from the men speakers at their kgotlas. If anything they were more bitter in their denunciation of Tshekedi and indulged in more threats against his person, if he returned to the Reserve, than we had heard from the men. It is a matter of conjecture how they came to be so violently anti-Tshekedi.

In the course of these meetings we addressed, between us, from 11,000 to 12,000 of the adult population. It was quite clear that the overwhelming majority of them were strongly opposed to Tshekedi's return under existing circumstances. The principal reasons for this appear to be:

1) They held Tshekedi chiefly responsible for the banishment of Seretse. This, of course, is not true. They believed that his

opposition to Seretse's marriage was due to the desire to obtain the chieftainship for himself.

2) Tshekedi had been Regent during Seretse's minority for 22 years and had certainly many achievements to his credit, but it was alleged that his rule had become increasingly autocratic, harsh and cruel and that in the carrying out of schemes, excellent in themselves, he had shown no consideration for those who had to do the work they entailed.

3) They insisted that it was not possible for Tshekedi to return to the tribe as a private individual: he was by birth second in rank only to Seretse. If he returned while Seretse was absent, he would automatically have the right and influence which his royal birth demanded according to native law and custom. "He was a chief by birth," they said, "only God could take his right away." In practice, therefore, it is not possible for Tshekedi to live in the tribe as a private individual in the absence of Seretse.

4) They further declared that according to native law and custom Tshekedi, before he could return to the tribe, would have to come and ask for forgiveness from the chief of the tribe and obtain his consent to be re-admitted. In view of Seretse's banishment the tribe had no chief and, therefore, there was no one to whom Tshekedi could make his appeal.

During the course of our three weeks' stay in the Reserve we also discussed the question of Tshekedi's return to the tribe as a private individual with the lawyers representing both parties to the dispute, with representatives of the traders in the Reserve, with the European and African Advisory Councils, and other leading African chiefs. After leaving the Reserve we visited Swaziland and had a very interesting meeting with the Paramount Chief, Sobhuza, who discussed with us the reactions of the quarrel in the Bamangwato on the African race.

The meetings we had attended gave the impression that there was an overwhelming majority against the return of Tshekedi but, before coming to this conclusion, there are other factors to be taken into consideration. Tshekedi was banished from the Reserve. His opponents on the other hand were in control of the tribe and were free to organize opposition to his return. The

Appendix M

Secretary of State had undertaken that if a special joint kgotla took place, the banishment of Tshekedi would be suspended for the three weeks during which the arrangements for it were being made. He would then have been free to visit the Reserve, organize his supporters, deal with any attempts at intimidation of them and encourage them to come forward openly in his support. Further, at the joint kgotla he would have the opportunity of stating his case and attempting to remove what he considered to be unfair accusations against him. Tshekedi is undoubtedly a man of very great ability and, in view of this and of his right of precedence, his presence at such a kgotla might have influenced many to have changed over to his side. It would also have been possible to have put to the test the fears that were expressed in some quarters that his return to the Reserve would lead to serious violence and disorder.

It is not easy to assess what proportion of the tribe would have been won over to favour Tshekedi's return if he had been as free to make out his case for it as his opponents were to make out theirs against it. My own view is that in spite of all that Tshekedi could have done, there would still have been a substantial majority against his return, so long as Seretse remained in exile. The chief fear of very many of those who were opposed to Tshekedi's return would probably be removed had Seretse also been allowed to return. They would, for the most part, acquiesce in his return, if Seretse were back in the tribe as chief and agreed that Tshekedi might rejoin the Bamangwato. Meanwhile conditions in the tribe are deteriorating owing to the lack of strong leadership.

Appendix N

NOTES ON A MEETING BETWEEN THE RESIDENT COMMISSIONER AND THE CHIEFS AT LOBATSI ON THE 23RD OF JUNE 1962 DURING WHICH THE CHIEFS EXPRESSED THEIR CONCERNS ABOUT THE ROLE OF CHIEFTAINCY IN THE PROCESS OF CONSTITUTIONAL DEVELOPMENT

Report of a Meeting Between the Resident Commissioner and the Chiefs at Lobatsi on the 23rd June, 1962

(Botswana National Archives, Office of the President, H.145/GP)

Present: The Resident Commissioner
Chief Bathoen
Mr. Kenalekgosi
Mrs. Moremi
Mr. Kgamane
Chief Kgosi Gaberone
Chief Mokgosi
Chief Kebalepile Montsioa

Chief Mokgosi: said that changes were taking place in the Territory. He agreed with the Resident Commissioner that the Chiefs must adapt themselves and that they should not do it too slowly. At the same time they had to avoid going too fast, thereby bewildering the Tribes. A bad spirit had become noticeable in the African Council which was affecting the whole Territory. This spirit, which was also noticeable in the political parties, was to

Appendix N

some extent encouraged by Government and it seemed that the Territory might be heading for trouble. It was particularly distressing that, at the recent meeting of the African Council, proposals aimed at a reduction of the Chiefs' powers had been brought up and discussed in such a way that it appeared that the Chiefs were struggling against the tide. It was said that the Chiefs should not play a part in politics and should remain neutral but what would their position be if the parties took over? Indeed it appeared from the way that some members of the B.D.P. had spoken in the African Council that they were assuming that they had already taken over the government of the country. In his opinion the parties wanted to spoil the chieftainship and he did not think that they had been formed for the welfare of the country.

Continuing, Chief Mokgosi expressed the following views:—

(a) in the past Government had said that the Chiefs need have no fear as they would be retained; as he saw it however the Chiefs' day was ending quickly;

(b) the most important matters were now settled in the African Council and Tribal Councils and these things were not reaching the people themselves in the Tribal Territories;

(c) the political parties were permitted to go through the Territory, holding meetings and expressing their aims; the right thing would be for the Chiefs to go among their people too, to tell them what they could foresee as a result of these changes;

(d) the Resident Commissioner should consider what could be substituted for the rights taken away from the Chiefs:

(e) Chiefs' sons were not being trained in tribal law and customs and they would not be able to take up their duties as Chiefs;

(f) the political parties had all originated in the Bamangwato where the Chieftainship had already gone;

(g) the rapid tempo of change at the present time was due to the decline in the strength of the chieftainship and to the fact that it was coming to be despised;

(h) a possible solution to the problem might be to reconstitute the government of the country on a federal basis with

Meeting between resident commissioner and the chiefs, June 1962

regional governments for the Northern Protectorate and Southern Protectorate; such an arrangement would facilitate more rapid changes in the North where this was desired but permit the Southern Tribes to proceed at a more leisurely pace in accordance with the wishes of their people.

Mr. Kenalekgosi: said that rapid changes were taking place and Government should examine these very carefully. It was also essential that the consideration of these changes should not end in the Councils. The people must also be informed and changes should be explained to them very carefully.

He understood that rights over matimela cattle and rights to forced labour for personal services would have to go in the future. Matimela cattle would in any case fall away as soon as zonal branding was in operation.

Chief Kgosi Gaberone: said that he was not opposed to change but did not want too much of it. He agreed that careful preparation was necessary for all [the] changes which affected the lives of the people in the Tribal Territories.

Chief Kebalepile: made the following points:–

(a) he was not disturbed by the fact that the Chiefs' powers were being taken away; he was however worried about the sort of people who wanted to take over those powers;

(b) Government had never said that the Chiefs were retarding progress; that had been said by some of the people in the African Council but were those people speaking for the Tribes or just for themselves?

(c) the Bechuanaland Protectorate Chiefs were not in any way against progress; they had contributed much more to the progress of the Tribes than many of the people who were now making a noise;

(d) the British Government was proceeding to liberate the nations that they had ruled in Africa like Ghana and Nigeria; but there was a noticeable difference between these two countries, as in Ghana independence had come as a result of a struggle against

Appendix N

Britain and no thanks were given to the Colonial power after its departure; in Nigeria however independence had been achieved slowly and peacefully after the people had shown that they were ready to run the country themselves;

(e) the Government officials were not criticised like the Chiefs but it was painful to many Africans to be told that the British officials, including the Resident Commissioner, had only come to the Bechuanaland Protectorate to enrich themselves;

(f) the Chiefs and the Government were trying to serve the people but not for material reward and it was very painful to hear the things that were being said;

(g) if the Chiefs were themselves allowed to form parties they might do so but they were not certain if that would be the best thing for them to do;

(h) political parties were modern and necessary and he was not opposed to them in principle.

Chief Bathoen: said that ever since the day when he and another Chief had contested the African Administration and African Courts Proclamations he had watched every move made by Government to see whether he had been right or wrong to challenge those laws. Those laws took away some of the Chiefs' powers because the grant of rights to hunt and trade, etc. were entrusted to the discretion of the District Commissioners instead of being left with the Chiefs.

He said he had served on the African Advisory Council for 41 years. The old Council discussed everything affecting Tribal affairs but the new African Council had specific things to discuss and the first of these was the position of Chiefs and headmen. Nevertheless the African Administration Proclamation itself defined the powers, functions and position of the Chiefs. This Proclamation had been accepted at the time because it could be expected that the Tribe itself would be the first body to complain to Government about the misrule of a Chief and provision was even made in the law to allow a Chief to defend himself if this should happen. But in the African Council a Chief had no chance of defending himself properly. Whatever was the view of the majority would be carried. The Chiefs were forced to defend themselves all the time in that Council but their voice carried no weight. There were only eight of them and the vote must therefore go against them.

The elected members of the African Council were supposed to represent the views of the Tribes but there were a lot of new and young men on the Council who did not go round the Tribal Territories talking to their constituents. They had not emerged from the Kgotla and they wanted to do away with the Kgotla. They had emerged from behind the scenes. One could see the writing on the wall for the Chiefs but no specific complaints had been made against the Chiefs by the Tribes. The way the Chiefs had been treated in the Council had been most surprising and painful.

The African Council and the parties wanted to do away with the Chiefs and with the British Government. They talked in a very misleading way about independence in 1963, about a black Resident Commissioner and about the Abattoir paying £40 a beast after independence. He and those who shared his views wanted independence to come gradually so that senior posts could be filled by suitable Batswana as they came forward. The country was not ready for independence and it had only just discussed a localisation plan.

The British Government was preparing the people to take over and he was thankful but what preparations had been made to take over from the Chiefs and why was it necessary to take over so quickly and in such a rude manner? Any take over from the Chiefs should be done peacefully and quietly, after proper training.

Since 1939/1940 the salaries of the Chiefs had been increased by as little as £30 - £100. The Chiefs had made great sacrifices for little material reward and now they were being paid back in a most unpleasant way. Recently the African Council had voted unanimously that the Chief's salaries should be increased. This was just a bluff and the ultimate aim was to make the Chiefs paid servants of the African Council who, as paid servants could be

Appendix N

[re]moved at any time. The removal of the matimela rights was a further step in the same direction.

Turning to the Tribal Councils, Chief Bathoen said that he did not believe that they would function smoothly as had been anticipated. He was having difficulty with the members of his Council who were demanding allowances, although there were no funds to pay such allowances. This difficulty would increase with the loss of matimela cattle. The Tribal Council was tending to supersede the kgotla. In the Bangwaketse, the Tribal Council had 56 members, but the kgotla was formed by every male adult. It was not right that questions affecting the Tribes should be settled in the Council; they should go also to the kgotla where all types were represented, whether literate or illiterate.

Recently in the African Council questions affecting customary law had been discussed and these had been referred to the Standing Committee. But questions of customary law should be referred to every family. The husband would attend the kgotla and report back to his household. The wives would then air their views and these would be taken back to the kgotla to be fully considered. He was fully aware that Government did not want to do away with the kgotla but they should not attach too much importance to the Tribal Councils.

Chief Bathoen said that in his Tribal Territory he was not dealing very carefully with the kgotla and he felt that it would be unwise to press on with the appointment of an Executive Committee, because the Tribal Council and Executive Committee might try to usurp the function of the kgotla. Matters should only be referred to the Tribal Council when it was possible to report the full views of the Bangwaketse from the four corners of the Tribal Territory. Previously he had favoured Tribal Councils and Executive Committees as he thought that they would work peacefully. He had now found however that the members worked for their own ends and the evidence of this was the fact that many of the things they brought up for discussion had not been discussed in the kgotla.

The Resident Commissioner had helped to bring about good relations between black and white in the Territory but now there was a tendency to split hairs in the relations between the Chiefs and the Tribes. They were going hot and cold; the way was being paved for a black and white state but the other section (the eight Chiefs) were being held back. They did not want a Congo in the Bechuanaland Protectorate. They wanted to follow Nigeria, where the expatriate officials still took part in the government of the country and were happy to serve under African Ministers.

Chief Bathoen said that he fully supported Chief Mokgosi's suggestion in favour of the establishment of regional governments for the North and South. Recently a European had asked him whether he would be wise to sell up and leave the Territory because of boycotts and parties. He had laughed and said that these things were happening in the North which was the stronghold of the parties but there were only a few members of the parties in the South. The South was peaceful but there was trouble in the North.

At one time the Chiefs had met to try to achieve a Tribal Federation but before a final solution had been found the political motive had emerged. It was a serious matter when Chiefs were considering the possibility of becoming leaders of political parties themselves. This would be unheard of in Africa and a bad reflection on Government.

The Chiefs wanted to play a big part in the development of the country and they did not wish to be kept outside and viewed with suspicion on the grounds that they were ultra conservative.

The decline of the Chiefs was exemplified by the modern practice of referring to them as African Authorities or Tribal Authorities. The term "Chief" was rarely used in the laws and some departments were now addressing letters to them as African Authorities or Tribal Authorities.

Mr. Kgamane: said that next year the African Council might well say that the Chiefs should be abolished and the following year they would probably advocate doing away with Tribal Administration in the Tribal Territories. He could not remember any previous council in which the Chiefs had had to stand up and defend themselves and the Tribes as they had had to in the recent

Appendix N

meeting of the African Council. The meeting had turned itself into a fight against the Chiefs. Those same Chiefs could show by their record what they had done for the Tribes but what had their critics done? They had done nothing. They spoke for selfish ends, whereas the Chiefs spoke for their Tribes and all the Tribes.

He had allowed the parties in because he had been told that they were not dangerous. Recently however the parties had started boycotting the traders, thinking that they were punishing those same traders for their misdeeds. In fact they were punishing the African people with whose liberty they were interfering. He could not defend himself about parties because they had started in his area.

Mrs. Moremi: said that she was not opposed to the changes recommended by the African Council in respect of matimela cattle. In the Batawana this custom was rarely used and matimela cattle were treated with great care. They did not augment the Chief's salary.

She agreed with the opinion expressed at the meeting that most of the changes started in the North.

Appendix O

NOTES ON A MEETING BETWEEN THE RESIDENT
COMMISSIONER AND THE CHIEFS AT LOBATSI
ON THE 28TH AUGUST 1962 AT WHICH THE
RESIDENT COMMISSIONER ADDRESSED THE
CONCERNS OF THE CHIEFS ABOUT THEIR
ROLE IN CONSTITUTIONAL AND
POLITICAL PARTY DEVELOPMENT

*(Botswana National Archives, Office of the President,
H.145/GP)*

Present: The Resident Commissioner
           The Government Secretary
           Chief Bathoen
           Mr. Kenalakgosi
           Mr. Kgamane
           Chief Mmusi
           Mrs. Moremi
           Chief Kgosi Gaberone
           Chief Mogkosi
           Chief Kebalepile Montsioa
           Mr. Bogatsu Pilane

A. **Resident Commissioner's** remarks at the meeting of Chiefs, 28th August, 1962: I last met the Chiefs immediately after the meeting of [the] African Council in June at a time when they were feeling pained and worried over some of the things that had happened and been said in [the] African Council. They felt that they had been on the defensive against an organised attack on the Chieftainship. And it was not only the events of the African

Appendix O

Council that were worrying them; concern had also been caused by the behaviour and speeches of some of the members of the political parties, by the rapid changes that were occurring in the country and by the thought that there might be still further rapid changes leading possibly to a withdrawal of the Protecting Power before the country was ready to assume real control of its affairs either internally or externally. It was felt by some that the rapid tempo of change was due to the decline of the Chiefs and it was said that the emergence of political parties in the Bamangwato Tribal Territory was due to the fact that the Bamangwato no longer had a Chief at their head. All the Chiefs recognised that they must adapt themselves to the new conditions in the country and be prepared to share their power with representatives of their people. Nevertheless they felt that changes in the political structure should not occur too quickly or the people would be bewildered and a chaotic situation would ensue. They pointed out that the Chiefs had experience in administration and had proved their fitness for responsibility whereas the political parties were neither experienced nor responsible. They felt that it would be disastrous for the country if the Chiefs were swept away and replaced by political parties, some members of whom were trying to delude the people into thinking that they could be independent by 1963. Two or three of the Chiefs referred to Nigeria which had moved towards independence at an orderly pace with social and economic advance keeping pace with political developments and eventually leading to a smooth and apparently happy transition to independence.

I do not think I would be wrong in concluding that the general feeling of the Chiefs as expressed at the meeting was that the tempo of change away from the old order in the Protectorate is at present too quick and that it should be slowed down.

In the past, British Government officials and the Chiefs shared the responsibility for the administration of the Protectorate. They helped each other in discharging their responsibilities and generally I think that there was mutual co-operation and trust. Today the former position regarding responsibilities has changed with the new constitution as there are now new organs of

Meeting between resident commissioner and the chiefs, August 1962

government such as the Legislative Council and the Executive Council which have a definite role to play in the management of affairs. Inevitably the power and authority of these bodies will increase as the years go by. Nevertheless the Chiefs and the Government officials still play an important part and are likely to continue to do so during the next few years. We who are here today cannot prevent change but we can to some extent either stimulate it or inhibit it or endeavour to steer it in a certain direction. Because of our present responsibilities and our future tasks it is right that we should meet from time to time to discuss current events and problems. This has been done in the past and I am happy to meet again today at this rather difficult time in our affairs to consider how the Government and the Chiefs can best play their part in steering the Protectorate on its way forward in such a way as to give satisfaction to all its peoples. But I must make the point that we are meeting here today for an exchange of views and not with a view to making decisions on matters of policy, which is the function of the Executive Council.

Let me say at once that there is nothing that would give me greater pleasure than to see the Protectorate follow in the footsteps of Nigeria going steadily forward at a comfortable pace, leading eventually to independence when the time is ripe. I do not wish to go so fast that we get out of control and I made it clear in my address at the opening of the Second Session of the Legislative Council that in my opinion it was irresponsible to talk about independence in 1963. I should add that although I hope for constitutional advance in 1965 I do not believe that the country will be ready for independence or even for internal self government by that date. My views are therefore closer to those expressed by the Chiefs than to the views of the politicians who talk of independence in 1963.

But I must be frank and say that I think it will be much harder for the Protectorate to go comfortably forward like Nigeria did under the British Government over a period of 60 years or so, developing its resources, turning out more and more educated Nigerians and proceeding quietly from one constitution to another

Appendix O

with the people assuming new responsibilities steadily but without undue haste.

There are two main reasons why I believe that changes here must be fairly rapid and continuous, if they are to be orderly. The first is an internal reason and it is the fact that we have started much later than many other countries in Africa along the road of political emancipation. It was only last year that the Legislative Council and Executive Council were formed and that the first political parties appeared on the scene. There is no doubt that a big step forward was then taken but in spite of that our present constitution is regarded as quite a backward one as compared with those of countries in East Africa and Nyasaland let alone West Africa, even though the Africans there who form the vast majority of the population appear to be no better fitted to manage their own affairs than the Bechuana. Even the Basuto today are clamouring for internal self government immediately.

This brings me to the second reason why I think that we must move fairly quickly and it is an external one. Other countries in Africa are pressing on quickly to a state of independence or internal self government and African opinion and world opinion is becoming increasingly intolerant of the relics of colonialism. We should not allow all our actions to be dictated by the opinion of outsiders and we do not. But we cannot ignore African and world opinion and we will not be allowed to do so because efforts will be and are being directed from outside our borders to create internal pressures against the Colonial power. If we move sensibly forward at a controlled but reasonably rapid rate these pressures can be contained, but if we move too slowly they could build up quickly and end in internal frustration, racial animosity, [and] economic difficulties caused by loss of confidence and even in serious disorder.

Moreover the educated Africans in this country who are exercising increasing influence do not want to feel that their country is being left far behind other countries in Africa. I have spoken to many of the educated Batswana including Government officials, teachers and Members of the Legislative Council and Tribal Councils and I know that they want to keep moving

Meeting between resident commissioner and the chiefs, August 1962

forward. At present many of these people, some of whom are also members of political parties, are very responsible and recent visitors from the Colonial Office who know many countries and people in Africa have expressed admiration at their quality and at their responsible and realistic attitude to the problems of the Territory. And so I must say to you frankly that I do not agree with those who think that we should slow up the pace of change. If any hotheads try to take the law into their own hands we shall act against them as we have recently done at Francistown where I have approved a ban on all political meetings for a period of ten days. That sort of thing may be necessary again and I expect it will but I do not propose to turn this country into a police state and suppress freedom of speech and political activity for longer than is necessary. On the contrary I believe that it is only by continuing to move forward fairly rapidly in the future as we have in the last few years that Government and the Chiefs can remain in harmony and in sympathy not only with world and African opinion but–what is even more important–with the opinion of the increasing number of educated Batswana in this country.

With these introductory remarks I have tried to sketch the background as I see it to the problems which you placed before me at our last meeting concerning the relations between the Chiefs and the political parties and between the Chiefs and the African Council, the Tribal Councils and the Kgotlas. Turning to these specific problems I would like to say something first about the relations between the Chiefs and the parties.

I have advised the Chiefs not to get involved in political parties but when we last met one or two Chiefs queried the wisdom of this advice. They were not certain that it would be wise for them to join parties but equally they were not convinced that it was prudent to keep out. In the light of the views expressed by these Chiefs I have thought further about this question but I come back to the same opinion as I held before. The Chiefs are leaders but they are also public servants. They have exercised a great influence in the past and although their position is changing and will change further in future there is no doubt that they can still play an important part in Tribal affairs. But if they wish to retain

Appendix O

their influence as Chiefs it seems essential that they should remain aloof from politics and reasonably neutral. As Chiefs, they are required constantly to arbitrate and settle various sorts of disputes and problems and to do this effectively they must be seen to be fair and impartial. If they go into politics they will get into a position perhaps of violent dispute with some of their subjects and immediately the image of the Chief as an impartial arbiter will be obscured. I remain of the opinion therefore that the Chiefs should keep out of politics.

And what should their attitude be to the parties? I know and can understand that the Chiefs do not like the parties. They see their own people joining together in new national associations which can bring influences and pressure to bear on the Chiefs and on their people through the Legislative Council, through the African Council and indeed from below through their own Tribal Councils. This is a completely new situation and I am not surprised at all that the Chiefs are worried by it, particularly in view of some of the wild and irresponsible things being said by some party members.

But we must be realistic. We have started on the road of constitutional development and the Chiefs associated themselves with the decision to do so. Now we cannot stop and, as you know, the formation of parties always follows quickly after the first steps in constitutional development and indeed, it is only through parties that the later steps become possible. This is because parties are concerned with national, as opposed to tribal policies, and if the people of this country are to play an increasing part in the government of the country they must organise themselves on a national basis. All over Africa parties are playing a part in political development and if we suppress them we shall frustrate the continued constitutional development, which the country needs, for the reasons which I have already mentioned.

Although therefore I can understand and sympathise with your feelings that you cannot like the parties, the only advice I can give you is that you must come to terms with them and of course they must come to terms with you. As I see it there are two different duties which you have in your relations with the parties.

Meeting between resident commissioner and the chiefs, August 1962

As Chief of a Tribe you have the right to give approval for meetings to be held or to prohibit them. This power must be used carefully and not arbitrarily. If you are to preserve your reputation for impartiality and fair treatment you should not use the power to favour one party. But if one party behaves in a way that threatens a breach of the peace or other unlawful action then it would be reasonable after consulting the Government Secretary through the District Commissioner to withhold permission for meetings at any rate for a temporary period as Government has recently done at Francistown. If you act in this way you are carrying out your proper duties as a Chief and exercising some control over the behaviour of the parties in your Tribal Territories.

There is another duty that you and your people have in your relations with the parties and that is as voters. In a future election you and your people may well have to decide on the respective merits of the two parties—on the quality of their leaders and the value of their policies. Voting is an important duty and I feel that the Chiefs can play a useful part in advising and guiding their people about this matter. Not about the parties or the candidates that they should vote for but about their responsibilities to help to choose the men or the party who will help the country most. If the Chiefs merely take the line that all parties are equally bad the people will be confused about their responsibilities as citizens and voters. I think it is very important that the Chiefs should play an active part in making their people realize that they must choose their leaders in the Legislative Council and must therefore take note of what the different parties are saying.

If the Chiefs will act in this way I think that they will come to realize that the parties and the Chieftainship are not irreconcilable. It is not a question of the decline of the Chiefs following naturally from the rise of the parties because both Chiefs and parties can play a useful part in the Bechuanaland of the future. And so I must urge you not to adopt a defeatist attitude in this connection. You can get your backs to the wall and try to frustrate the activities of the parties and slow up constitutional development. But nothing that you could do would be more

Appendix O

certain to convince the ordinary man and in particular the reasonable responsible educated Motswana that there was no more value in the Chiefs. Rather than do this it would be better to abandon the struggle and give up the Chieftainship or alternatively to retain the ceremonial position of the Chief but abandon active participation in the administration of the Tribe.

But I do not believe that the choice before the Chiefs is either a last ditch battle against the new political forces or abandonment of their position as leaders. The other course which I believe to be the right one is for the Chiefs to recognise that the same sort of changes are now taking place in the Bechuanaland Protectorate as have taken place elsewhere in the world and that their future will not depend on the maintenance of all their old rights and privileges, some of which are out of place in the modern world, but on how they perform their duties; on their individual abilities and on the quality of their service. In the United Kingdom the aristocracy still plays a big part in public life, but they have no greater right to do so than anyone else. If they serve usefully their wealth and their birth are a help to them. If they do not, their birth does not contribute to their public importance. It seems inevitable that the same thing should happen here. If a Chief is able, energetic, modern in his approach and in good health he will be able to play an effective part in the future as in the past and his experience and background will be a great help to him. If he does not have those qualities of leadership he can remain a man of dignified position and perform ceremonial functions but he should not aspire to being an absolute ruler.

I have expressed the view that the country as a whole, at this stage of its history, needs to develop fairly rapidly, politically, socially and economically. I have no doubt that there are elements of the Tribal system which form a barrier to such progress and that these must be modified and this is what I believe the African Council was saying at its last meeting. If the Chiefs wish to be effective, useful rulers in the modern world they must play a part—indeed a leading part—in these modifications and changes.

This brings me to the question of the Chiefs' relations with their Tribal Councils and Executive Committees and with the

Meeting between resident commissioner and the chiefs, August 1962

Kgotla because it is with these bodies in future that they will make their main contribution to Tribal Affairs.

When the Local Councils Proclamation was being discussed in the old African Advisory Council and Standing Committee it was agreed that the creation of the Councils did not mean that the Kgotla should be replaced or abolished as it was felt that this would not be acceptable to the people. Thus today the two institutions of the Kgotla and the Tribal Council continue to exist side by side but I think that the extent to which one or other is used depends largely on the Chief.

At our last meeting some of the Chiefs showed a tendency to react against their Councils on the grounds that the members tended to speak for themselves and not for the Tribes and they suggested that in future it might be better to work more with the Kgotla.

My views on this are clear. I do not think it would be right to abolish the Kgotla but I think that it should be recognised that it is a traditional institution whereas the Council is a modern one. A Tribal Kgotla involves far more people than the Council and two things follow from this. The first is that it cannot be called so easily and frequently as the Council; the second is that it is more suited for the expression of a Tribal opinion on one or two big issues rather than for regular discussions on a vast number of complicated inter-related issues such as those which confront the Tribes in this modern world.

The Chiefs will not solve their problems by abandoning their Councils and going back to the Kgotla. Let them call their Kgotla by all means for consideration of big issues and to keep the people informed of developments but if the Chiefs want to be useful public servants they must come to terms with their Tribal Councils and Executive Committees. They must arrange regular meetings of these bodies; they must sit and work with them and they must give them a real opportunity to serve and play a part in the administration of the Tribe. It is no use paying lip service to the Councils. There is a real need for them now and they must be allowed to operate and develop.

Appendix O

I remember when I first came to the Bechuanaland Protectorate in 1954 attending some meetings of the African Advisory Council which were very frustrating and unpleasant from the point of view of the Government officers. The Council was very critical; it tended to react almost automatically against any proposals that Government made and its main theme was that the African Advisory Council was useless and should be replaced as soon as possible by a Legislative Council or a Federated Tribal Council. On one occasion they virtually refused to discuss the agenda.

After that meeting the matter was discussed with the Resident Commissioner at the time who decided that the blame for the bad relations between Government and the Council did not lie entirely with the Council. He felt that Government was also to blame for not consulting the Council sufficiently and for not paying sufficient heed to what they said and he decided therefore to try to work more frequently with the Council in future. A Standing Committee was set up and regular meetings were held at which Government's aim was to thrash out agreed solutions to the problems of the time. The Resident Commissioner did not go to those meetings without ideas of his own but he did not go to them feeling that his own ideas were necessarily right. He went to them with the idea of arriving at agreed conclusions as a result of discussions and negotiations and it was in that way that the new African Administration Proclamation was prepared and the Local Councils Proclamation settled and many other similar questions disposed of. My advice to the Chiefs who wish to go on playing a real part in local government is to do the same. Hold regular meetings with your Tribal Councils and Executive Committees. Do not condemn the members of these bodies as being purely selfish and self-seeking. Do not expect them to agree with everything the Chief says or wants. Do not expect them to be "yes" men. Go and work out solutions with them to the problems of the Tribes, by a mixture of firmness, readiness to compromise and patient negotiation. In future the Chiefs' right to rule will not depend on any divine rights. It will depend on the extent to which each one of them plays a part with their Councils and Executive Committees

Meeting between resident commissioner and the chiefs, August 1962

in fostering sound development and in resolving the conflict between the conservative forces and the radical ones which was so evident at the last meeting of the African Council. Before that meeting of the Council I felt certain that there was going to be a conflict and I therefore visited most of the Chiefs individually and advised them to take a lead in the way I think they should go and not to allow themselves to appear to be pushed by some of the younger members of the Tribes. It is worth mentioning now that the Chiefs' rights to compulsory personal services and to personal handling of matimela cattle were abolished in most other African countries years ago. In Basutoland I remember the discussion in the National Council about 1949/1950 when Chief Lerohioli Mojela, the father of the Paramount Chief's bride, took the lead in moving that compulsory personal services for the Chiefs on their lands should be abolished. I hoped that one of the Chiefs here would do the same thing in the African Council this year and thereby show that the Chiefs in the Bechuanaland Protectorate were looking to the future and not to the past. Although none of them did that I have not lost confidence in the Chiefs and I still believe that they will make a great contribution to the future of this country.

Finally, I end as I started, by saying that I do not believe that any of us can frustrate the forces of nationalism. I believe that we should move with them and only if we do so can we help the Bechuanaland Protectorate to stand on its own feet when the time comes. None of us know when the time will come but I think it would be prudent to prepare for it to come sooner than one would have thought five years ago. The country remains backward in many ways but we can all of us see the Batswana pioneers who are striving for an independent, self reliant state; they include the Members of the Executive Council and the Legislative Council; they include the leading Government officials who are qualifying for senior posts like Miss Chiepe; they include the members of the Tribal Councils and their Executive Committees and, of course, they include the master farmers and the progressive African ranchers who are helping to build up the economy of the Territory. The best advice that I can give to the Chiefs is that they should

Appendix O

not only encourage these pioneers of the new Bechuanaland State but that they should become pioneers themselves.

B. **Discussion:** In the discussion which followed his Honour's observations, the following points were made.

2. **Chief Bathoen** sought clarification of the functions of African Council in regard to the designation, recognition, removal and powers of Chiefs, and in relation to the African Administration Proclamation. *His Honour* explained (in terms of Section 57(2) of the Order in Council) that the Resident Commissioner was empowered to seek the advice of Council on the general policy to be followed in such matters. The Council however had no executive power and moreover it would not be consulted on individual appointments, etc. of Chiefs, Sub Chiefs and Headmen; such matters would be dealt with under the relevant provisions of the African Administration Proclamation. Thus Chief Bathoen's fears that there might be conflict between the powers of the African Council and the provisions of the African Administration proclamation were groundless. It would be legitimate of course for the Resident Commissioner to consult the Council on e.g. the question whether the African Administration proclamation should be amended–this being a matter of policy which "especially concerns the interests or well being of the African inhabitants." But the designation, recognition, removal and powers of individual Chiefs, must as the law now stood be a matter for each tribal territory and the Resident Commissioner, and would not be one on which the Resident Commissioner would consult the Council.

3. **Chief Bathoen** enquired what would happen if the African Council were to resolve that Chiefs should not sit in the African Council. *His Honour* pointed out that this could not be implemented without amending the Constitution which is in any case a matter for separate consideration on which the African Council would not be consulted. The Chiefs would be consulted when the Constitution is reviewed.

Meeting between resident commissioner and the chiefs, August 1962

CHIEFS AND POLITICS

4. **Chief Bathoen** and **Chief Kebalepile** re-iterated their view that unless Chiefs took part in politics they might find themselves without influence. In Basutoland and Northern Nigeria Chiefs took an active part in politics. Seretse Khama owed his political influence largely to his being of chiefly status. Chief Bathoen felt that the Chiefs had a right and a duty to play a leading role in building up one nation by uniting the tribes and their treasuries.

5. **The Resident Commissioner** said that as politics developed it was inevitable that the majority of Legislative Council members in future would belong to parties, although there was still a useful place for independents. Experience elsewhere showed that it was unlikely that Chiefs could become politicians and at the same time continue to be effective and respected Chiefs. Seretse Khama had made a deliberate choice between Chieftainship and politics, and had put aside the Chieftainship. Replying to a question by **Chief Kebalepile, His Honour** said that it would be possible for a Chief to retire in old age and in principle it would be right that he should receive some form of allowance in compensation for giving up his office.

NATIONAL AND LOCAL ADMINISTRATION

6. **The Resident Commissioner** referring to Chief Bathoen's views on the unification of the tribes agreed that this would have some advantage, but this was to some extent achieved through the medium of African Council. It was even more necessary to build up local government. The Government Secretary pointed out that as the Central Administration moved towards self-government it became vitally important that power at the center should be devolved to organs of local government as far as practicable. The central government could not itself provide efficient local services, and in the Bechuanaland Protectorate the Chiefs had had particularly valuable experience in this field.

Appendix O

CONCLUSION

7. It was agreed on Mrs. Moremi's suggestion that a note of the remarks made by His Honour should be circulated to the Chiefs; and if they wished to express further views they would do so in writing or alternatively His Honour would be pleased to meet them again if they wished. **Chief Bathoen** said the Chiefs still looked to Government as a friend and guide. The Chieftainship and the Government should pool their resources to help the Bechuanaland Protectorate. It was important gradually but steadily to equip Africans for responsibility; at the same time the status, privileges and rights of Chiefs should be safeguarded.

8. His Honour concluded the meeting by recalling that the Chiefs had always been foremost in loyalty and as a force for stability. It was within their power to continue to make a big contribution to the welfare and development of the Territory. He would at all times be ready to hold further discussions with them.

Appendix P

NOTES ON A MEETING BETWEEN HER MAJESTY'S HIGH COMMISSIONER AND THE CHIEFS AT LOBATSI ON THE 14TH APRIL 1964 TO DISCUSS CONSTITUTIONAL AND POLITICAL DEVELOPMENTS RELATED TO THE ROLE OF CHIEFS

(Botswana National Archives, I/6/2986, H.145 II)

Present: Her Majesty's Commissioner
Acting Chief Secretary
Attorney-General
Acting Administration Secretary
Kgosi Bathoen II, C.B.E.
Kgosi Mokgosi III
Kgosi Linchwe Kgafela
Kgosi Kgosi
Acting Chief Mack Sechele
Mr. Leapeetswe Khama

Her Majesty's Commissioner opened the meeting by welcoming the Chiefs. He said that the present meeting had been called to consider the position of the Chiefs in the light of the conclusions of the constitutional conference and the local government committee.

2. Full agreement had been reached in the constitutional talks and it appeared that the majority of people in the country accepted the conclusions, which had been published as a White Paper. It was possible at the present time to consider the future

Appendix P

of Bechuanaland in positive terms as the transfer issue which had for so long bedeviled the High Commission Territories was no longer a live one. The views of the Members of the Legislative Council on the transfer issue had been unequivocally stated at the last Legislative Council and even Dr. Verwoerd appeared to have abandoned hope of getting the High Commission Territories. It was now clear that the only acceptable future for Bechuanaland lay in the development of the Territory towards independence and economic viability.

3. Recent rapid developments had affected the position of the Chiefs and during the last two years it had been difficult to see exactly what part the Chiefs would play in central government and in local government in the new Bechuanaland that was emerging.

4. Until recently the Tribal Territories had virtually been separate political entities and the central government had exercised only a loose co-ordinating authority over them. In these circumstances it had often appeared as though the Chiefs and Tribal Administrations were something more than mere local government authorities.

5. The time had now come however when tribalism had to be considered in relation to Bechuanaland as a whole. The great task facing the Chiefs and all the people was to build a nation which would be strong and united and it was only in that way that the tribes and all the people of Bechuanaland could maintain their freedom and identity in the years to come.

6. In theory it might be considered that there were two ways of achieving a sovereign state. First by some sort of federation of the existing Tribal Territories and freehold areas. This idea had in the past had some support and even now some Europeans in the Tati Concession were found to be in favour of it. It was however, impracticable in the present situation. The country was grant-aided and the federal structure would be much too expensive for Bechuanaland's weak economy to bear. It would also be weak and cumbersome. Africa was a troubled continent and it seemed

clear that, to survive and prosper, Bechuanaland would need a strong constitution. A unitary state was therefore essential. This was what the country needed and there was every indication that this was what the people wanted. Moreover developments in recent years, first in the Joint Advisory Council and later in the Executive and Legislative Councils had all led in this direction. A larger political unit than the Tribes, the Bechuanaland nation state was emerging and it followed from this that the Chiefs and Tribal Administrations would in future be recognised more as local government authorities than in the past. Because of their special position it had been accepted at the constitutional conference that the Chiefs should continue to play a part in Central affairs through the House of Chiefs but it would be wrong to regard this body as in any sense a rival government and it would be inappropriate and misleading to consider the Tribal Territories as homelands in the South West African context, and the Chiefs as heads of state.

7. He was not suggesting that tribal loyalties should be destroyed. They were of great value and could contribute to effective local government. They should not compete however with the loyalties of the people and tribes to the service of the Bechuana nation.

8. There were two great questions now under consideration. First how to build a non-racial self-governing state which should be as strong as possible, and secondly how, inside that central government framework, to develop efficient non-racial local government bodies.

9. The first question had been answered by the recommendations of the Constitutional Conference. A responsible ministry would be drawn from the majority party after elections in which all adults would participate. The second question had now been answered by the report of the Local Government Committee which had recommended that new local government bodies should be non-racial, representative and responsible.

Appendix P

10. In the formulation of these principles all the leaders of the Territory including representatives of the Chiefs had participated.

11. The purpose of the present meeting was to examine the impact of these recommendations on the Chiefs. It was no secret that the Chiefs were extremely worried about the establishment of the House of Chiefs and Kgosi Bathoen had announced that they wished to abandon the idea and wished to be allowed to stand for election to the Legislative Assembly, at the same time retaining their positions as Chiefs. This was a vital matter and must be closely examined.

12. **His Excellency** asked the Chiefs to consider what the result would be if they stood for election. Even if all were elected they would only have eight Members in an Assembly of about thirty-two. They could not therefore form a government and their position would be dangerous, because they could frustrate the majority party. If they did so, the majority party would be determined to destroy the chieftainship as it had done in Nyasaland. The resultant friction between Chiefs and political leaders would do great damage to the country.

13. Alternatively there was some risk that one or two Chiefs might not be elected. What would be the position of such a Chief? He would surely be unable to maintain his position amongst his tribe.

14. He stressed that the Chiefs were not just ordinary individuals and the time had come when they must choose between retaining their chiefly status or entering politics on the national level. Even if only a few of them were to stand for elections they would be drawn into the political arena and this would damage their image as senior judicial authorities in the Tribal Territories and as respected and impartial administrative authorities.

15. He did not subscribe to the view that the House of Chiefs would be an ineffectual body. In fact it would be one of the many agents through which influence could legitimately be brought to

bear on the Central Government. All the Chiefs, not just a few of them would be represented on this body, they would be able to discuss certain Bills of particular importance to the tribal way of life and to send to the Legislative Assembly a point of view which was theirs and theirs alone. In this way they would be able to exercise a combined influence on the government.

16. **His Excellency** said that he would not pretend that he was not gravely disappointed and worried by the change of opinion indicated by one or two of the Chiefs. This was a late stage at which to go back on a decision which had been made with representatives of the political parties in the Constitutional Conference and published in the White Paper. The House of Chiefs was a major feature of the constitutional proposals. There was no doubt that this provision, which gave the Chiefs a special position in the new Constitution, would create confidence in the country and if suggestions were now to be made that it would be useless and should be thrown away there would be much unease and uncertainty, particularly among the more unsophisticated members of the Tribes.

17. **His Excellency** continued by discussing the relationship of the Chiefs to the proposed new district councils. He said that the fact that the district councils were executive certainly did not mean that the Chiefs no longer had any influence. Many of the recommendations made took account of the Chiefs' special position and these were set out in paragraph 19 of the Committee's report. In addition Chiefs would notice that, where possible, the boundaries of the new district councils would follow the old boundaries of the Tribal Territories. The Chief's position as senior judicial authority in the Tribe would be unaffected. Indeed the Law Reform Committee had recently recommended that the judicial powers of the Senior Chiefs courts should be expanded to give them jurisdiction over all races. There would also remain with the Chiefs certain very important administrative functions such as the allocation of Tribal land. Through this power the Chiefs could exercise an important influence over land tenure developments

Appendix P

which could contribute materially to the economic and social development of the Batswana. It had been noted that Kgosi Bathoen was already turning his attention to this matter.

18. Continuing, **His Excellency** said that the leaders of emergent African nations faced three great potential divisions among their people; that between the different races, that between the traditional tribal leaders and the national political leaders and that between the "haves" and "have-nots." In Bechuanaland the first of these had been virtually overcome. The agreements eventually reached between the Chiefs and political leaders at the recent constitutional and local government talks would go far to overcome the second one and if the traditional leaders and political leaders in Bechuanaland could co-operate and respect each other's sphere of influence—and not fight each other—together, they would help the country to progress economically and overcome the third of these potential divisions. The Chief's powers could not continue on the same basis as in the past. Nevertheless the proposals of the Constitutional Conference and Local Government Committee left them with a special position in which they could exercise a very important influence both in the Central Government and more particularly in local affairs. It was now for the Chiefs to decide whether to participate fully in all these developments and endeavour to ensure their success, whether to remain indifferent and watch them proceed from the touch line or whether to oppose them. The future welfare of the country depended on their decision.

19. In conclusion **His Excellency** said that throughout the constitutional talks he had maintained that it was for him to try to reconcile differences but not to settle the terms of the new constitution as this was mainly for the unofficial leaders. He had thought that full agreement had been reached at the end of the talks when in their final speeches, representatives of all the groups had deliberately associated themselves with the conclusions. If any group were now to have second thoughts, others might wish to do the same and wide-spread dissension and confusion might result.

Nevertheless it would be for the Chiefs to decide at the end of the present meeting whether they wished to re-open the question of the House of Chiefs as had been suggested by some. If they did **His Excellency** said that he would convene a further meeting of the conference so that the matter could be raised and discussed with all groups.

20. **Kgosi Linchwe** said that when the constitutional discussions had started certain political groups had been represented by their leaders. However the Chiefs present were not leaders of other Chiefs and it was therefore necessary for them to refer matters to the other Chiefs to keep them in the picture. This they had been unable to do during the talks and the talks were confidential. When they had eventually done so they had found that the other Chiefs were opposed to the House of Chiefs. It should also be remembered that at the start of the Constitutional Conference Kgosi Bathoen was wholly opposed to the House of Chiefs. He had eventually been convinced but when the local government talks indicated the full extent of the deprivation of the Chiefs' powers, he had had second thoughts. He, Linchwe, reaffirmed his belief that a democratic form of government was desirable, as the ultimate power in Bechuanaland should rest with the people. Nevertheless he was certain that people had confidence in the ability of the Chiefs to lead them and might wish them to play a part in national affairs. He therefore resented being shot off into a House of Chiefs and thought that the electorate should be allowed to decide whether or not a Chief should represent them in the Legislative Assembly.

21. **Kgosi Bathoen** said that it had not been possible previously to discuss the position with the other Chiefs and this was the first opportunity of doing so. He said he must still continue to express his fears about the future position of the Chiefs. Many politicians wished to destroy the institution of the chieftainship, although many pretended for their own advantage to be in favour of the chieftainship at present. The Chiefs were in a better position than

Appendix P

Government officials to assess the value of the politicians' protestations.

22. He agreed that it was very difficult for him to go back on a point already agreed upon. However the discussions on local government had revealed to what extent the Chiefs were being deprived of their powers and this had made him wish to re-open the matter.

23. He said that in his opinion the powers given to the Chiefs in the new proposed local government arrangements were not of great value. No special genius was required to enable them to carry out the functions which were set out in the proposed Chieftaincy Bill.

24. He was worried because the House of Chiefs seemed to have no direct link with the Legislative Assembly and could only directly contact the Prime Minister or the Cabinet. He said he thought that for the Chief to be chairman of the district councils and certain town councils was not an important job. He also thought that whatever the officials of to-day might say, the House of Chiefs would be of little value when the Ministers of a political party came to power.

25. He said that if the Chiefs really had a part to play in the Territory's future, surely they should play that part at the center and not on the outskirts. He said that many Chiefs would in fact prefer to live private lives and they only remained Chiefs because of traditional respect of the people for them and their own love of their people and their sense of duty. If they were to resign, they themselves would not suffer but their people would.

26. Many people said that the tribesmen were not in fact supporters of their Chiefs. He would welcomed Chiefs being allowed to stand in national elections as he felt certain that the results would prove these people wrong.

Meeting between the high commissioner and the chiefs, April 1964

27. He said he felt that Chiefs must be elected. Nomination was worse than useless. If Chiefs were nominated to the Legislative Assembly people would merely say that they had been put there by the Government.

28. Independence was often considered to mean independence from the rule of Chiefs and the Chiefs were not seeking the protection of Government. They wanted this protection embodied in the constitution.

29. The **Attorney-General** said that it was advisable for everybody to be realistic about what the future form of government would be. The Government of the country would be a cabinet of Ministers who would be drawn from the majority party in the Legislative Assembly. The only way of getting into the Cabinet would be by being a member of the party in power. Nobody else could share in the actual running of the central government. The function of other groups, including minority groups of the Legislative Assembly, would be to influence the Government. The question was how best could this be done by the Chiefs. Kgosi Linchwe had pointed out that the Chiefs had no leaders, and it did not seem that a few Chiefs in a minority position on the Legislative Assembly would have much influence or adequately represent the Chiefs' point of view. He suggested that the Chiefs when established in such a House of Chiefs would exert considerably more influence than they could as individual Members of the Legislative Assembly.

30. In answer to a question from **Kgosi Bathoen** the **Attorney-General** said that the House of Chiefs would have three main functions. First the Legislative Assembly would not be allowed to proceed with certain Bills affecting tribal affairs without referring them to the House of Chiefs. The House of Chiefs would receive the draft Bill at least thirty days before its introduction into the Legislative Assembly and the comments of the House would have to be laid on the table of the Legislative Assembly. Secondly they would be allowed to discuss any matter they wished to discuss and

Appendix P

would be able to make their own rules of procedure. Any member would be entitled to put down any motion within the executive and legislative authority of Bechuanaland for discussion. They would be able to make representations to the Prime Minister or to the Cabinet. Thirdly any Minister might ask the House of Chiefs for an opinion on any subject on which he required such an opinion.

31. **Kgosi Bathoen** supported by the other Chiefs then said that there appeared to be a gulf between the House of Chiefs and the Legislative Assembly and that this was wrong. The House of Chiefs should have direct access to the Legislative Assembly by some method.

32. The **Acting Chief Secretary** said that the power of the House of Chiefs should be very considerable as long as tribal loyalties were strong in the country. Supporters of the majority party would have loyalties both to their party and to their Chiefs, and if the advice of Chiefs was ignored on important matters they might well follow the Chiefs rather than their own party.

33. **Kgosi Linchwe** asked whether the House of Chiefs had any right to require a Minister to answer a question about his department.

34. The **Attorney-General** replied that this was not provided for in the constitution but neither was a similar procedure in respect of the Legislative Assembly so provided for. This was a convention and not a law. He said it was envisaged that the Minister would visit the House of Chiefs and make himself available to answer questions.

35. **Kgosi Linchwe** said that he thought that this should be made quite clear.

36. He continued by saying that the arrangements for a House of Chiefs were obviously only temporary as political leaders might wish to abolish it at the first opportunity. The Bechuana were

departing from their traditional ways and adopting political theories which had been evolved by white men. As had often been seen in other parts of Africa, these British traditions were often hard to transplant. He therefore felt that the House of Chiefs would soon die, either naturally or by legislation.

37. **Her Majesty's Commissioner** said that there appeared to be two main points of detail at issue. The first one was the link between the House of Chiefs and the Legislative Assembly which was a constitutional point. The second one was the desirability of ensuring, as far as possible, that Ministers were available to answer questions in the House of Chiefs; this was a procedural point. Nevertheless the fundamental question as to whether there should be a House of Chiefs or not had still not been settled. He stressed that in his opinion the House of Chiefs met two needs. First it gave the Chiefs a special influence in central government affairs and secondly it did this without drawing the Chiefs into politics. The proposal to establish a House of Chiefs had been published and was well known throughout the Territory, and he thought it was generally acceptable. Confidence in the Territory rested to a great extent on the fact that all the proposals in the White Paper had been accepted. To throw this away would, he was certain, reduce confidence in the Territory. He suggested that as the main comments had related to the way in which the House of Chiefs would work rather than to its existence, the proposals for this institution should be further examined to see whether they could be improved and thereby made acceptable.

38. **Kgosi Bathoen** said that he had suggested the abolition of the House of Chiefs mainly because he was worried about the connecting links between the House and the Legislative Assembly, and also because the functions of the House of Chiefs had not been to him at all clear. He had also felt that the responsibilities were very circumscribed. After the explanations given during the present discussions many of his fears had been overcome. If a draft amendment could be prepared setting out alterations which would give the House of Chiefs a direct link with the Legislative

Appendix P

Assembly and would ensure that as far as possible Ministers were available to the House to answer questions, he felt he could then accept the White Paper, as amended.

39. **Mr. L. Khama** said he was still afraid that people would go with their troubles to their elected Members rather than to the Chiefs. The **Attorney-General** replied that this should be expected in respect of affairs which were the concern of the new government. However the Chiefs would doubtless be the men to whom tribesmen referred their main local problems.

40. In answer to a suggestion by **Kgosi Linchwe** that if Chiefs had no male heirs the number of Chiefs in the House would gradually become fewer, the **Attorney-General** pointed out that if the previous Chief had no male heir the tribe would choose his successor from among his relatives. This man, once chosen as Chief, would automatically be a member of the House of Chiefs.

41. On the question of the Chieftaincy Law **Her Majesty's Commissioner** gave an assurance that Government would consult all the Chiefs before the Chieftaincy Bill was presented to the legislature.

42. **Kgosi Mokgosi** said that as long as the place of the House of Chiefs was clearly described in the constitution many of the doubts of the Chiefs would be stilled.

43. **Kgosi Kgosi** said that now that the position of the House of Chiefs was fully understood the Chiefs saw the light and agreed to it.

44. **Acting Chief Mack Sechele** said that he was glad to have had this explanation from Her Majesty's Commissioner and to learn that not all power was being taken away from the Chiefs. The Chiefs would only want to abolish the House of Chiefs if, when it was in operation, it was found to be of no value.

45. **Chief Linchwe** said he would like to ask three more questions. First he asked whether a Chief's son would be able to stand for election to the Legislative Assembly. The reply was that he would be able to do so. Secondly he asked whether there was any safeguard against a Minister ignoring the House of Chiefs and not sending bills to it which he should. The reply was that such behaviour would be in breach of the constitution and the Chiefs would be able to seek redress in the High Court. Thirdly he asked whether the House of Chiefs would be able to debate Bills other than those referred to it by the Legislative Assembly, and the reply was that they would be able to do so and would be able to submit any representations they wished on such a Bill.

46. **Kgosi Linchwe** said that he personally was not able to see that the House of Chiefs would be of real value. He remained opposed to the idea but he was nevertheless prepared to do his duty and serve in the House as a temporary measure while the electorate of the country was still immature. He thought that the Chiefs were the pillars which held the tribes together and that if he relinquished the chieftainship in order to enter politics it would be a dereliction of his duty. If it were not for the political immaturity of the electorate however, he would resign as a Chief and stand for the Legislative Assembly rather than be classed with the traditionalists. **His Excellency** said that he personally did not believe that the House of Chiefs would become a depository for outworn traditionalists and was certain that a number of the people who would serve in the House would not consider themselves traditionalists and in fact would be progressives rather than traditionalists. When one looked at the persons likely to be members of the House one could see a fine balance of experience and youth. It was this fact which encouraged him and led him to believe that the House could serve a valuable purpose, at any rate for some years to come. Admittedly much would depend on the attitude of the political leaders to the House of Chiefs, but even more would depend on the attitude that the Chiefs themselves adopted towards it. If they tried to exercise their responsibilities in the House and brought their important influence to bear on the

Appendix P

Government of the day without seeking to behave as a rival government, it would surely succeed.

47. **Kgosi Bathoen** said that the Chiefs no longer had the absolute power which their fathers had had and they did not in fact wish to oppose change as long as the change was reasonable. He thought that all the Chiefs felt as Kgosi Linchwe did but all were prepared to serve under the correct conditions. He himself was not a traditionalist. His aim was the same as that of Government and the politicians. He only differed from them in one respect in that he felt genuinely that the chieftainship was important to the future of the country. He also would resign as a Chief, did he not feel that the sufferers would be both the Government and the people themselves.

48. After an adjournment the meeting discussed amendments to section 55 and agreed that the following amendment should meet their wishes:-

> After the words "or through the Prime Minister to the Cabinet" the following words to be added "or to send messages thereon to the Legislative Assembly. It would be expected that the Standing Orders to be made by the House of Chiefs in terms of paragraph 52 would include provision under which the House of Chiefs could invite a Minister or his representative to attend the proceedings of the House for the purpose of taking part in any discussions held in terms of this paragraph but without a vote or for the purpose of answering questions."

49. This amendment was only finally accepted after considerable debate as to whether the words "for consideration" should be added after the words "the Legislative Assembly." This proposal was eventually rejected on the grounds that this might appear to indicate that a particular procedure would have to be followed by

the Legislative Assembly on the receipt of a message from the House of Chiefs.

50. In conclusion Her Majesty's Commissioner thanked the Chiefs for their constructive attitude during the discussions and said that he would now have to consult the other groups who had been present at the Constitutional Conference. If the proposed amendments were generally accepted then the amended report would be referred back to the Secretary of State. He stressed that the rules of procedure for the House of Chiefs would be discussed at a later date with the Chiefs.

MONOGRAPHS IN INTERNATIONAL STUDIES

ISBN Prefix 0-89680-

Africa Series

36. Fadiman, Jeffrey A. THE MOMENT OF CONQUEST: Meru, Kenya, 1907. 1979. 70pp.
    081-4 $ 5.50*

37. Wright, Donald R. ORAL TRADITIONS FROM THE GAMBIA: Volume I, Mandinka Griots. 1979. 176pp.
    083-0 $12.00*

38. Wright, Donald R. ORAL TRADITIONS FROM THE GAMBIA: Volume II, Family Elders. 1980. 200pp.
    084-9 $15.00*

41. Lindfors, Bernth. MAZUNGUMZO: Interviews with East African Writers, Publishers, Editors, and Scholars. 1981. 179pp.
    108-X $13.00*

43. Harik, Elsa M. and Donald G. Schilling. THE POLITICS OF EDUCATION IN COLONIAL ALGERIA AND KENYA. 1984. 102pp.
    117-9 $11.50*

44. Smith, Daniel R. THE INFLUENCE OF THE FABIAN COLONIAL BUREAU ON THE INDEPENDENCE MOVEMENT IN TANGANYIKA. 1985. x, 98pp.
    125-X $ 9.00*

45. Keto, C. Tsehloane. AMERICAN-SOUTH AFRICAN RELATIONS 1784-1980: Review and Select Bibliography. 1985. 159pp.
128-4 $11.00*

46. Burness, Don, and Mary-Lou Burness, ed. WANASEMA: Conversations with African Writers. 1985. 95pp.
129-2 $ 9.00*

47. Switzer, Les. MEDIA AND DEPENDENCY IN SOUTH AFRICA: A Case Study of the Press and the Ciskei "Homeland". 1985. 80pp.
130-6 9.00*

48. Heggoy, Alf Andrew. THE FRENCH CONQUEST OF ALGIERS, 1830: An Algerian Oral Tradition. 1986. 101pp.
131-4 $ 9.00*

49. Hart, Ursula Kingsmill. TWO LADIES OF COLONIAL ALGERIA: The Lives and Times of Aurelie Picard and Isabelle Eberhardt. 1987. 156pp.
143-8 $9.00*

50. Voeltz, Richard A. GERMAN COLONIALISM AND THE SOUTH WEST AFRICA COMPANY, 1894-1914. 1988. 143pp.
146-2 $10.00*

51. Clayton, Anthony, and David Killingray. KHAKI AND BLUE: Military and Police in British Colonial Africa. 1989. 235pp.
147-0 $16.00*

52. Northrup, David. BEYOND THE BEND IN THE RIVER: African Labor in Eastern Zaire, 1865-1940. 1988. 195pp.
151-9 $12.00*

53. Makinde, M. Akin. AFRICAN PHILOSOPHY, CULTURE, AND TRADITIONAL MEDICINE. 1988. 175pp.
152-7 $11.00*

54. Parson, Jack, ed. SUCCESSION TO HIGH OFFICE IN BOTSWANA. Three Case Studies. 1990. 443pp.
 157-8 $20.00*

55. Burness, Don. A HORSE OF WHITE CLOUDS. 1989. 193pp.
 158-6 $10.00*

56. Staudinger, Paul. IN THE HEART OF THE HAUSA STATES. Tr. by Johanna Moody. 1990. 2 vols. 625pp.
 160-8 $30.00*

Latin America Series

5. Wiarda, Howard J. CRITICAL ELECTIONS AND CRITICAL COUPS: State, Society, and the Military in the Processes of Latin American Development. 1979. 83pp.
 082-2 $ 7.00*

6. Dietz, Henry A., and Richard Moore. POLITICAL PARTICIPATION IN A NON-ELECTORAL SETTING: The Urban Poor in Lima, Peru. 1979. viii, 102pp.
 085-7 $ 9.00*

8. Clayton, Lawrence A. CAULKERS AND CARPENTERS IN A NEW WORLD: The Shipyards of Colonial Guayaquil. 1980. 189pp., illus.
 103-9 $15.00*

9. Tata, Robert J. STRUCTURAL CHANGES IN PUERTO RICO'S ECONOMY: 1947-1976. 1981. xiv, 104pp.
 107-1 $11.75*

11. O'Shaughnessy, Laura N., and Louis H. Serra. CHURCH AND REVOLUTION IN NICARAGUA. 1986. 118pp.
 126-8 $11.00*

12. Wallace, Brian. OWNERSHIP AND DEVELOPMENT: A Comparison of Domestic and Foreign Investment in Columbian Manufacturing. 1987. 186pp.
145-4 $12.00*

13. Henderson, James D. CONSERVATIVE THOUGHT IN LATIN AMERICA: The Ideas of Laureano Gomez. 1988. 150pp.
148-9 $11.00*

14. Summ, G. Harvey, and Tom Kelly. THE GOOD NEIGHBORS: America, Panama, and the 1977 Canal Treaties. 1988. 135pp.
149-7 $11.00*

Southeast Asia Series

31. Nash, Manning. PEASANT CITIZENS: Politics, Religion, and Modernization in Kelantan, Malaysia. 1974. 181pp.
018-0 $12.00*

38. Bailey, Conner. BROKER, MEDIATOR, PATRON, AND KINSMAN: An Historical Analysis of Key Leadership Roles in a Rural Malaysian District. 1976. 79pp.
024-5 $7.00*

44. Collier, William L., et al. INCOME, EMPLOYMENT AND FOOD SYSTEMS IN JAVANESE COASTAL VILLAGES. 1977. 160pp.
031-8 $10.00*

45. Chew, Sock Foon and MacDougall, John A. FOREVER PLURAL: The Perception and Practice of Inter-Communal Marriage in Singapore. 1977. 61pp.
030-X $6.00*

47. Wessing, Robert. COSMOLOGY AND SOCIAL BEHAVIOR IN A WEST JAVANESE SETTLEMENT. 1978. 200pp.
072-5 $12.00*

48. Willer, Thomas F., ed. SOUTHEAST ASIAN REFERENCES IN THE BRITISH PARLIAMENTARY PAPERS, 1801-1972/73: An Index. 1978. 110pp.
033-4 $ 8.50*

49. Durrenberger, E. Paul. AGRICULTURAL PRODUCTION AND HOUSEHOLD BUDGETS IN A SHAN PEASANT VILLAGE IN NORTHWESTERN THAILAND: A Quantitative Description. 1978. 142pp.
071-7 $9.50*

50. Echauz, Robustiano. SKETCHES OF THE ISLAND OF NEGROS. 1978. 174pp.
070-9 $10.00*

51. Krannich, Ronald L. MAYORS AND MANAGERS IN THAILAND: The Struggle for Political Life in Administrative Settings. 1978. 139pp.
073-3 $ 9.00*

56A. Duiker, William J. VIETNAM SINCE THE FALL OF SAIGON. Updated edition. 1989. 383pp.
162-4 $14.00*

59. Foster, Brian L. COMMERCE AND ETHNIC DIFFERENCES: The Case of the Mons in Thailand. 1982. x, 93pp.
112-8 $10.00*

60. Frederick, William H., and John H. McGlynn. REFLECTIONS ON REBELLION: Stories from the Indonesian Upheavals of 1948 and 1965. 1983. vi, 168pp.
111-X $ 9.00*

61. Cady, John F. CONTACTS WITH BURMA, 1935-1949: A Personal Account. 1983. x, 117pp.
114-4 $ 9.00*

63. Carstens, Sharon, ed. CULTURAL IDENTITY IN NORTHERN PENINSULAR MALAYSIA. 1986. 91pp.
116-0 $ 9.00*

64. Dardjowidjojo, Soenjono. VOCABULARY BUILDING IN INDONESIAN: An Advanced Reader. 1984. xviii, 256pp.
118-7 $26.00*

65. Errington, J. Joseph. LANGUAGE AND SOCIAL CHANGE IN JAVA: Linguistic Reflexes of Modernization in a Traditional Royal Polity. 1985. xiv, 198pp.
120-9 $12.00*

66. Binh, Tran Tu. THE RED EARTH: A Vietnamese Memoir of Life on a Colonial Rubber Plantation. Tr. by John Spragens. Ed. by David Marr. 1985. xii, 98pp.
119-5 $ 9.00*

68. Syukri, Ibrahim. HISTORY OF THE MALAY KINGDOM OF PATANI. Tr. by Conner Bailey and John N. Miksic. 1985. xix, 113pp.
123-3 $12.50*

69. Keeler, Ward. JAVANESE: A Cultural Approach. 1984. xxxvi, 523pp.
121-7 $18.00*

70. Wilson, Constance M., and Lucien M. Hanks. BURMA-THAILAND FRONTIER OVER SIXTEEN DECADES: Three Descriptive Documents. 1985. x, 128pp.
124-1 $10.50*

71. Thomas, Lynn L., and Franz von Benda-Beckmann, eds. CHANGE AND CONTINUITY IN MINANGKABAU: Local, Regional, and Historical Perspectives on West Sumatra. 1986. 363pp.
127-6 $14.00*

72. Reid, Anthony, and Oki Akira, eds. THE JAPANESE EXPERIENCE IN INDONESIA: Selected Memoirs of 1942-1945. 1986. 411pp., 20 illus.
132-2 $18.00*

73. Smirenskaia, Zhanna D. PEASANTS IN ASIA: Social Consciousness and Social Struggle. Tr. by Michael J. Buckley. 1987. 248pp.
134-9 $12.50

74. McArthur, M.S.H. REPORT ON BRUNEI IN 1904. Ed. by A.V.M. Horton. 1987. 304pp.
135-7 $13.50

75. Lockard, Craig Alan. FROM KAMPUNG TO CITY. A Social History of Kuching Malaysia 1820-1970. 1987. 311pp.
136-5 $14.00*

76. McGinn, Richard. STUDIES IN AUSTRONESIAN LINGUISTICS. 1988. 492pp.
137-3 $18.50*

77. Muego, Benjamin N. SPECTATOR SOCIETY: The Philippines Under Martial Rule. 1988. 232pp.
138-1 $12.50*

78. Chew, Sock Foon. ETHNICITY AND NATIONALITY IN SINGAPORE. 1987. 229pp.
139-X $12.50*

79. Walton, Susan Pratt. MODE IN JAVANESE MUSIC. 1987. 279pp.
144-6 $12.00*

80. Nguyen Anh Tuan. SOUTH VIETNAM TRIAL AND EXPERIENCE: A Challenge for Development. 1987. 482pp.
141-1 $15.00*

81. Van der Veur, Paul W., ed. TOWARD A GLORIOUS INDONESIA: Reminiscences and Observations of Dr. Soetomo. 1987. 367pp.
142-X $13.50*

82. Spores, John C. RUNNING AMOK: An Historical Inquiry. 1988. 190pp.
140-3 $13.00*

83. Tan Malaka. FROM JAIL TO JAIL. Tr. and ed. by Helen Jarvis. 1990. 3 vols. 1200pp.
150-0 $45.00*

84. Devas, Nick. FINANCING LOCAL GOVERNMENT IN INDONESIA. 1989. 344pp.
153-5 $14.00*

85. Suryadinata, Leo. MILITARY ASCENDANCY AND POLITICAL CULTURE: A Study of Indonesia's Golkar. 1989. 222pp.
179-9 $11.50*

86. Williams, Michael. COMMUNISM, RELIGION, AND REVOLT IN BANTEN. 1990. 356pp.
155-1 $14.00*

87. Hudak, Thomas John. THE INDIGENIZATION OF PALI METERS IN THAI POETRY. 1990. 237pp.
159-4 $15.00*

ORDERING INFORMATION

Orders for titles in the Monographs in International Studies series should be placed through the Ohio University Press/Scott Quadrangle/Athens, Ohio 45701-2979. Individuals must remit pre-payment via check, VISA, MasterCard, CHOICE, or American Express. Individuals ordering from the United Kingdom, Continental Europe, Middle East, and Africa should order through Academic and University Publishers Group, 1 Gower Street, London WC1E 6HA, England. Other individuals ordering from outside of the U.S., please remit in U.S. funds by either International Money Order or check drawn on a U.S. bank. Postage and handling is $2.00 for the first book and $.50 for each additional book. Prices and availability are subject to change without notice.

Ohio University

CENTER FOR INTERNATIONAL STUDIES

The Ohio University Center for International Studies was established to help create within the university and local communities a greater awareness of the world beyond the United States. Comprising programs in African, Latin American, Southeast Asian, Development and Administrative studies, the Center supports scholarly research, sponsors lectures and colloquia, encourages course development within the university curriculum, and publishes the Monographs in International Studies series with the Ohio University Press. The Center and its programs also offer an interdisciplinary Master of Arts degree in which students may focus on one of the regional or topical concentrations, and may also combine academics with training in career fields such as journalism, business, and language teaching. For undergraduates, major and certificate programs are also available.

For more information, contact the Associate Provost for International Studies, Burson House, Ohio University, Athens, Ohio 45701.

SUCCESSION TO HIGH OFFICE IN BOTSWANA

*Edited by Jack Parson*s

This book examines the process through which the mantle of leadership passed from one leader to another in Botswana. It concerns the succession to high office in Botswana over the course of more than half a century from the colonial time to the present. Three case studies explore the relationship between the British colonial authorities and the tribal leaders in affirming the legitimacy of the tribal chiefs of the Bangwato tribe in the former Bechuanaland protectorate. The studies examine the succession crises of the Bangwato first in 1925 and again between 1948 to 1953 and the political changes in Botswana up to the last few years. Extensive excerpts from the Botswana National Archives contained in the appendices fully support the text.

Jack Parson is Associate Professor of Political Science at the College of Charleston, Charleston, South Carolina, 29424. Neil Parsons may contacted through the School of Oriental and African Studies, London University, London, England. Michael Crowder at the time of his death in 1988 was affiliated with the Institute of Commonwealth Studies, London University, London, England. Previously he had been Professor and Head of the Department of History at the University of Botswana.

ISBN 0-89680-157-8